Women and Words in Saudi Arabia

Women and Words in Saudi Arabia:

The Politics of Literary Discourse

Saddeka Arebi

Columbia University Press
New York

Columbia University Press
New York   Chichester, West Sussex
Copyright © 1994 Columbia University Press
All rights reserved

Library of Congress Cataloging-in-Publication Data

Arebi, Saddeka.
    Women and words in Saudi Arabia : the politics of literary
discourse / Saddeka Arebi.
        p.   cm.
    Includes bibliographical references and index.
    ISBN 0-231-08420-X
    ISBN 0-231-08421-8 (pbk.)
    1. Arabic literature—Saudi Arabia—History and criticism.
    2. Women authors, Arab—Saudi Arabia—Political and social views.
    3. Arabic literature—20th century—History and criticism.
    4. Feminism and literature—Saudi Arabia.   5. Women—Saudi Arabia—
Social conditions.   I. Title.
    PJ8005.A87   1994
    892'.76099287—dc20   94–9898
                                                                             CIP

Casebound editions of Columbia University Press books are printed on permanent and durable acid-free paper.

Printed in the United States of America

c 10 9 8 7 6 5 4 3 2 1
p 10 9 8 7 6 5 4 3 2 1

To the memory of my beloved father,

Mohamed Al-Soghayyer Arebi,

a human rarity in time and place

Contents

6.

Conclusions and Implications:
Contexts of Resistance and the Dialectics
of Protest and Affirmation   268

Acknowledgments

During the preparation of this work, which I began as a Ph.D. dissertation entitled "Waging War, Waging Peace: The Poetics and Politics of Women and Words in Contemporary Arabia," I enjoyed the support of many good people both in the United States and abroad. My deepest thanks go to Professor Laura Nader for her mentorship, friendship, and continuous support during and after my studies at the University of California at Berkeley. She inspired my intellectual development, and it was from our discussions that I learned how cultural worlds are embedded in discourses of power. She also helped me understand the transformation in the use of power from its innate forms to the subtle and calculated ways of domination used in the modern world. The question of this transformation of power was to impose itself on me both in my relationship to the Arab society from which I came and the American society that I entered to receive my formal education—as well as in my attempts to understand the specific historical relationship between these two worlds. Later, questions of power were to become fundamental aspects of my research.

I owe special thanks to Professor Herbert Phillips for his continuous enthusiasm and unflagging support for my project, which was never dampened by the difficulties that surrounded the initial stages of my fieldwork. It was through his teachings on the use of indigenous literature in anthropology, and later the publication of his book on Thai literature, that revived my old passion for literature, having previously been a writer in Arabic. Our discussions have provided me with a way of dealing with what seemed at the time almost an unsolvable methodological dilemma with which anthropologists are faced when they attempt to integrate cultural meaning and social action in the making of ethnography. I shall also not forget the kind and encouraging words of his wife Barbara.

Special thanks are also due to Professor Susan Ervin-Tripp for her encouragement and her belief in the value of my research. As a sociolinguist with special interest in the question of power in various speech situations, her comments were most valuable in clarifying many areas of this work. I have also enjoyed the guidance and support given me by Professors Nancy Scheper-Hughes and James Anderson, and especially that from Professor Elizabeth Colson, at U.C. Berkeley.

My friends Dr. Dorothea Theodoratus, Dr. Donna Halstead at California State University at Sacramento, and Mildred Kolander have shown me their true friendship by giving me support and confidence at times when I most needed them. In addition, they have performed various editing and other critical tasks with endless enthusiasm. My debt to them is indeed great.

I also thank Moneera Al-Ghadeer, Susan Berry, Sarah Murray, Oyeronke Oyewumi, Nancy Abelmann, Jeanne Bergman, and Paula Cruz Takash, fellow students at U.C. Berkeley. I will remember with gratitude Jennifer Beer, who introduced me to the wonders of the computer at U.C. Berkeley's Quantitative Anthropological Lab, and also those who assisted me with the computer, especially Madeline Anderson.

This study would not have been possible without the help of many friends and friends of friends, both in the United States and Saudi Arabia. They are too numerous to list here, but I am particularly indebted to former Senator James Abu Rizq, Wafa Nasr, and the 'Aṭṭar family, especially the late Aḥmad 'abdul Ghafour 'Aṭṭar, his dedicated wife Muzayyan Ḥaqqi, and his daughter Dr. Iqbal 'Aṭṭar for their various forms of assistance in facilitating my field research. I owe the most thanks to the Saudi writer Dr. Hanan 'Atallah, who was there when the project was first conceived, and whose continuous support has kept me inspired for many years. My thanks also go to Dr. Faṭma Nasr, Professor of English at King Saud University in Riyadh, for making me feel at home in Riyadh, to the writer Thurayya Al-'Arayyedh for welcoming me in Dhahran, and most of all to the many Saudi women writers who opened their homes and hearts to me. Without their cooperation this project would not have been possible.

I am greatly indebted to my family for their encouragement. My family assured me through various ways that I am the "World's Best

Mom," and even inscribed the phrase on a coffee mug they gave me as a gift. My daughters Maha and Marwa took on various household tasks that made the process easier for me. My son Mohamed the pragmatist made sure I had accomplished my daily writing "assignments" before I returned home. At the young age of sixteen, my son Muad took up the task of typing the early drafts of the manuscript, putting up with my demands on his time.

The field research was made possible by grants from the Wenner-Gren Foundation for Anthropological Research and the preparation of the manuscript by a University of California at Berkeley Fellowship. In addition, the Doreen Townsend Center for the Humanities Fellowship at U.C. Berkeley not only provided me with the financial support while writing but also with a year-long, biweekly seminar that included fine scholars from various fields in the humanities. Without their input, this project would have been severely lacking in its interdisciplinary depth and scope. The book took its final shape while I was a visiting scholar at U.C. Berkeley. I am especially indebted to Professor Larry Michalak of the Center for Middle Eastern Studies for his encouragement and support.

I would also like to thank the reviewers and editors at Columbia University Press, who provided me with much help in revising and reorganizing my initial manuscript. Their constructive comments were indispensable to this work.

I dedicate this work to my parents whose firm belief in Allah ingrained in us that it is through fairness, hard work, moderation, and tolerance that one can reach other truths and hence achieve a fuller humanity. I have learned from them an important Islamic concept that "middleness" (*Wasaṭ*), being in the middle, even as a child, does not have to mean "between-ness," being torn or on shaky ground, but can be a firm and advantageous position from which one can see both sides more clearly. That positive image of being in the middle extends to my scholarly position between two discourses and two civilization. It was to dominate this work even in more subtle ways as the motion of two types of texts—one Arabic, the other English; one moving from right to left, the other from left to right—symbolizes my aim to bring two worlds to a mutual understanding, and perhaps signifies the inevitability of their meeting.

A Note on Transliteration

In the spelling of place and common names, I used the spelling adopted by the *American Journal of Islamic Social Sciences,* such as Makkah, instead of Mecca; Muslim, instead of Moslem. The system of transliteration I have followed is the one used by the *International Journal of Middle Eastern Studies,* the main features of which follow:

Vowels

Short: *i* as in *fit* or *feet; a* as in *fat; u* as in *foot*
Long: *ī; ā; ū*
Semivowels: *y* corresponds to the ya sound in Arabic; *w* corresponds to the waw sound in Arabic

Consonants

b	ب	z	ز	f	ف
t	ت	s	س	q	ق
th	ث	sh	ش	k	ك
j	ج	ṣ	ص	l	ل
ḥ	ح	dh	ض	m	م
kh	خ	ṭ	ط	n	ن
d	د	ẓ	ظ	h	ه
dh	ذ	ʿ	ع	w	و
r	ر	gh	غ		

Women and Words in Saudi Arabia

Introduction: On Women and Words in Arabia—Discourses of Power

The Problematics of the Study

In the early 1980s, when I started reading Saudi newspapers and magazines regularly, I became aware of an unmistakable preoccupation in this Arabian society with the subject of women—their education, their work, their mobility. Women apparently were a matter of great concern to the various forces in society to warrant this dramatic collective theorizing in which they were a key image—almost an obsession—of the entire society. Participating in this traffic of words about women were the religious *'ulama* (religious scholars),[1] the state-sponsored publications, as well as individual men. This army of male speakers, with unmatched fervor and intensity, has taken up the task of writing, and conceptualizing, women as private beings who must be hidden and concealed.

But in this Arabian society, in which the construction of images and concepts has historically been a means of institutionalizing consciousness and hence exercising power, women emerge not only as a subject of discourse but also as generators of discourse, producing their own texts and forming their own concepts for comprehending the universe. Since the late 1970s and despite the overwhelming power of the discourse about them, women's words were unrelenting and daring in their challenge:

> I will emphasize ahead of time and in great pride that I am a woman though I am not of those who believe that politics is a man's preserve.

. . . I do not like to wait for "the man" to talk and then nod my head back and forth in agreement or repeat in a strangled voice what he says in the manner that many expensive parrots would repeat after their masters in many of our luxurious homes. And I refuse to surrender my mind to the man allowing him to think for me only because I am a woman.[2]

Other women writers seemed to be interested in more than winning the right to participate in the game of power on both the personal and national levels. They were determined to traffic in words, provide revisions of major values and institutions by insisting on forming their own readings of culture and religion despite the risks involved in such a "trespassing" on this exclusive male right especially when they are as challenging as this piece: "Men believe that woman is another creature. They claim that she is 'lacking in both mind and religion'; they believe that they (men) are the guardians (*qawwamoun*) of women."[3]

The inclemency by which Shaikh Abdul-Aziz Ben Baz, then (1978) the Director General of Religious Research (now the mufti, the highest religious authority in the country) issued his response to this challenge in the form of a *fatwa* (religious legal opinion)[4] is indicative of the gravity of tampering with the well-established modes of religious interpretations:

Attacking men's guardianship of women is an objection to God and an attack on His Book and on His prudent law. This is great infidelity (*Kufr akbar*) by the consensus of Islam's *'ulama.* . . . It is absolutely necessary that the newspaper be publically punished by stopping its publication. The woman who wrote the article and the editor-in-chief must be tried and disciplined in a deterring manner.[5]

By rendering what the woman writer said as an "objection to God and an attack on His Book" and of "Kufr akbar," the *'ulama* have used the ultimate weapon that would ensure pushing women away from their territories for a long time to come. Some women may have been deterred from venturing into the territories of religious interpretation but not others. The attack on this woman, instead of intimidating other women and forcing them to abandon the enterprise of writing, or at least writing on such sensitive issues, seemed only to encourage them to change their strategy to combat this language of power. For women continued to insist on making the distinction between "man" and "God," between the "social" and the "religious," and ultimately on their right to go to the texts themselves, to explore their own history, in order to understand its relevance to their personal lives.

It is precisely at this time in the early 1980s that we witness a striking presence of women writers in the various literary activities as scores of college-educated women began to emerge. This presence of women in the institution of literature assumes a special significance because literature, in the broader sense, has historically and continues today to define reality. This inquiry is driven by several important questions: What happens when women, who are defined in the most private of terms [*owra,* which literally means private parts] emerge not only as speakers but also hold, if not seize, control over publication both in the sense of publishing and of making public? What forces in society are in charge of defining the scope of institutional constraints on the woman writer as a woman first and a writer second? In what manner do women writers in their various theoretical and ideological leanings disturb the whole verbal machinery in charge of theorization about women? How do women themselves use words as a means to counter the language of power, and aesthetics as a political strategy for revisions of concepts, ideas, and institutions that are used to control them?

I hope to answer these questions in the chapters that follow, in which I present and analyze the writings of nine of the most influential contemporary Saudi Arabian women writers, representing a variety of genres, themes, styles, and ideological orientations. Through their works, which I have translated myself, I hope the reader will also see their enterprise in terms of its implications on the society as a whole since they live in a time of critical social transformation and ideological rupture. By virtue of participating in the literary institution and by their sheer numbers, women are destined to play an essential role in the process of the ideological formation in their society. This study's objective, then, is to understand the extent to which these women contribute to the production of various forms of thought in their society by providing their own visions and revisions as they venture into interpretation and reinterpretation of religion, tradition, and history, as well as other major cultural institutions, values, ideas, and meanings formed in society.

Why Saudi Arabian Literary Women

Saudi Arabia seems to be suited to an anthropological study of both indigenous literature and gender relations. It provides an excellent opportunity for examining the effects of literature on a rapidly changing society, given its history which has reflected a powerful attachment to words (although admittedly it may not be the best place to study "the best" contemporary Arabic literature). In relation to women, however, Saudi Arabia has developed a reputation for being more restrictive of women's mobility and public activity than other Arab societies. Yet many women in this society participate in the creation of culture by acquiring a powerful device, such as literature, while remaining physically invisible.

My training in anthropology, in addition to my being a native speaker and writer in Arabic who also is equipped with the technical and historical knowledge of the literary tradition, has proved to be most valuable in conducting this research. This background was especially helpful in preparing me, before I left to do field research, to better understand the nature of historical transformations within the Saudi Arabian society, and in tracing cultural influences on style, imagery, and subject matter, as well as those bearing on the psychology of literary creation.

While the material I have collected extends back to the mid-1970s, the time frame for this research is mainly the decade of the 1980s. Although major transformations in Saudi Arabia have often been traced to the oil boom of the early 1970s, in which extensive changes in society occurred, including the emergence of scores of women writers, my systematic knowledge of the literary scene in Saudi Arabia has developed only during the 1980s. This period seemed an ideal one on which to focus mainly because the material written at this time was easily available to me[6] and the writers themselves were accessible. Most of the writers selected for this study began writing a decade or two before the 1980s, and are still present in the field. The period covered is lengthy enough to permit the identification of serious writers, as well as patterns in issues and themes. While Arabian women writers have existed for the past three decades, the 1980s is the decade in which they began to participate in large numbers, thus constituting a recognizable phenomenon. A number of these women were among the first university graduates to pass through the public education system instituted for girls in the early 1960s. It was in the 1980s, moreover, with the emergence of ideological revivalism, that the need for these women to fill ideological roles expanded. The demands for mobilizing public support for different ideological positions paved the way for a large number of women to gain access to the literary domain. Together these events seem to confer a kind of historical unity on the decade of the 1980s. To be sure, this historical unity is enhanced even further with what developed *after* that time. The political, social, and historical implications of the 1991 war with Iraq are too recent to assess. But in a society in which cultural discourses are formed around the challenge of Western civilization, the placing of the faith of the Arabian people almost entirely in the hands of Western powers and global protection will certainly make of the 1990s an era totally distinguishable from what preceded it. My hope is that this study, by documenting the social and intellectual history of the period of the 1980s, will furnish a basis for future comparative research.

Conceptual Framework and Theoretical Orientation

This study of the literature of Saudi women is based on an anthropological approach to literature in which literature is treated as a form of "intellectual activity . . . by which consciousness is institutionalized into specific culturally defined themes, forms, and goals, *regardless* of the 'objective' events affecting the culture" (Phillips 1975:328 [emphasis mine]). The literary texts are treated as social documents and the writers as key informants. The texts are viewed as "social," not in the sense of "reflecting" society but rather in two key respects. The language, subject matter, and symbolism used in a text are inherently social. The information the writers provide is not a result of the ethnographer's techniques but rather a product of the position writers occupy which makes them "socially situated to talk about things that in their culture are judged to be 'important' " (Phillips 1987:4). Second, these women, by participating in a literary institution that is by definition social, are contributing to the literary tradition and performing important ideological functions for their society. Although literature has always performed expressive functions everywhere, in contemporary Arabia, in the absence of other forms of political participation, literature is transformed into a political forum in which expression—however limited and constrained—gives the illusion of political participation. Because of this ideological function of literature in the society, the sense of the "social," as it is used here, departs from the Marxist view of the text as a depiction of the society. The women's writings show that they express, idealize, represent, indicate, codify, advocate, compensate, legitimate, and perform other conceivable functions.

This means that we go beyond the "reliability" of the text as an index of society, to explore, to use Maurice Bloch's phrase, "the systems by which they [in this case the writers] know the world and the systems by which they hide it" (Bloch 1977:278–92). For while the subject of women writers is no doubt literary in nature, as well as gender-related, the ethnographic aims of this book can best be met by not treating it merely as literary or as a question of gender.[7] As a study of a cultural phenomenon, the focus is on the women writers' forms of thought as manifested in their intellectual activities and the way in which these women experience their status and comprehend their universe as Arab Muslim women. The concern will be with relating text, context, and writer in such a way as to establish the connection between the meaning of the text and its function in relation to the more general discourse.[8] Reaching beyond these women's literary abilities and their gender to the larger contexts of power enables us to understand the rules that govern women as women and control their access to means of communication as writers.[9]

I utilize discursive as well as textual analyses to discern these functions. I draw on a number of notions, such as discourse, power, and resistance, developed mainly by Foucault whose subject of analysis has been the structure of human knowledge and thought and the relationship between words and things. I use these concepts with a caveat in order to avoid the risk of blurring historical, political, and cultural specificities in which they were originated. For Foucault's "analytics" of power take as its focus not gender relations but human sexuality; not Islamic but European societies. The concept of discourse that Foucault employs to mediate culture and ideology will be used in its broadest sense as the verbal machinery in charge of producing concepts for comprehending the universe.[10]

Used in this general sense, the concept of discourse is given prominence in the context of this Arabian society precisely because discourse acquires centrality in a literate civilization characterized by great tradition, such as the Islamic societies.[11] In these societies people continually intellectualize about their existence; they forever debate, hold dialogues, interpret, and reinterpret their cultural rules, constantly conscious of their place in time and space.[12] Anthropology has a great need for further study of the effect of literacy on the scope of human interaction with time and space. Literacy, as Giddens points out, provides a new dimension of time as a vehicle of "freezing" tradition through the existence of indestructible documents, and of space by providing a universal rather than a locally determined scope of its interpretation (Giddens 1979:200).

In literate societies the existence of texts as "indestructible documents" transforms the process of cultural production in a fundamental way for "a literate tradition is never a pure tradition, since the authority of written words is not dependent on usage and presumption only. As durable material objects they [written words] cut across processes of transmission and create new patterns of social time; they speak directly to remote generations."[13]

Texts "speak" to "remote generations" but, more important, they speak to the contemporary ones who speak back to them and from them. They become an authority in support of statements made by the generators of discourse to legitimate certain political ends. The production of "regularities" of such statements is what Foucault refers to as "discursive formations" or "epistemes."[14] The concept of discursive formation allows us to identify the speakers; the position of power from which they speak; what is said; and the basis of their legitimacy. The concept is especially merited with its tendency to highlight a high degree of creativity in the creation of culture, something to which anthropologists only recently paid explicit attention.[15] The analytic value of the concept of discursive formation lies not only in exposing power relations but, more important, in mapping out the role that language plays as a means of manufacturing consciousness and hence of acquiring power.

Ironically, indigenous literature has been neglected by anthropologists, whose discipline centers on the concept of "culture," which originates in "thought," and focuses on understanding the "native's" point of view. This negligence is partially related to anthropology's battle to win the status of a "science" based on the long-honored opposition between fact and fiction in Western thought.[16] But the predominating theories in anthropology, whether functional structuralism, Marxism, or even interpretive anthropology, have little or no place for the native's point of view. [17] This may have something to do with anthropologists' tendency to remain in the field for one or two years, which makes it difficult to attain a level of competency in the language necessary for conducting such research. But anthropologists' neglect of indigenous literature may also have been an extension of the Orientalists' tendency to maintain a monopoly over the representation of the East. Edward Said reasons that "since [any Oriental] poet or novelist . . . writes of his experiences, of his values, of his humanity, . . . he effectively disrupts the various patterns (images, cliches, abstractions) by which the Orient is represented." [18]

For whatever reason, anthropologists have traditionally focused on cultural institutions as they exist rather than the discursive formations by which they are produced. But we know that in Saudi Arabia, as in other complex societies, not only cultural institutions but also discoursing groups of men and women constantly reflect on their existence, questioning, modifying, and reshaping their thinking. This reflection usually has an ideological dimension that serves to legitimate or order social relations. In rapidly changing societies with "great traditions," such as the Arab societies, ideologies "become crucial as sources of sociopolitical meanings and attitudes" (Geertz 1973:219). The concept of ideology is used here to refer to the systematic use of ideas to serve certain interests, rather than to the ideas themselves.

In women's reflection on religion and history, for example, the tendency is to treat religion and history not as ideologies themselves but rather as symbolic orders that are put to ideological uses to sustain forms of domination by favoring certain interests. [19] This distinction is consequential in understanding why, even in constructing a discourse of their own, Saudi women writers do not present a form of negation to the religious and historical ideals by which they are presumably dominated, but rather tend to affirm these ideals while putting them to their own ideological uses. [20] These women reflect an understanding of what Foucault had dubbed the "regime of power/knowledge" and "instances of discursive production," of power that is based on silence, prohibition, and the circulation of systematic misconceptions (Foucault 1978:12).

In what follows I shall shed some light on the historical centrality of the institution of literature itself and the role it has played in forging a connection between the poetic and the political in Arabic-Islamic civilization. In addition to these institutional and historical contexts, I shall sketch the contemporary discursive contexts in an effort to make intelligible the enterprise of women writers.

The Poetic Is Political: Words, Power, and Ideology in Arabic-Islamic Civilization

The history of the Arabian peninsula reflects a unique interconnection between the poetic and the political in which the symbolic organization of society is based on coordinating cultural affairs in words. The construction of images and concepts becomes a means of institutionalizing social forms through which to exercise power.[21] Geertz observes that on the level of interpersonal communication, not only a remarkable emphasis is put on verbal fluency but also rhetoric is given "a directly coercive force; 'andu Klam, 'he has words, speech, maxims, eloquence,' means also, and not just metaphorically, 'he has power, influence, weight, authority' " (Geertz 1983:114). Speaking of the ideological role the poet plays within a contemporary Arab society, he also points out:

> Poetry, rivaled only by architecture, became the cardinal fine art in Islamic civilization, and especially the Arabic-speaking part of it. . . . Everything from metaphysics to morphology, scripture to calligraphy, the patterns of public recitation to the style of informal conversation conspires to make of speech and speaking a matter charged with an import if not unique in human history certainly extraordinary.[22]

Historically, the type of leadership in the tribal societies of Arabia has depended on the effective use of rhetoric in debate. Decisions have had to be made by agreement reached through persuasion and debate (Cole 1975; Meeker 1979; Nelson 1974). The political power of the poets, however, has sprung from their abilities to legitimate interests through disseminating personal as well as tribal reputation. A tribe's reputation and recounting of its history among other tribes has depended, to a great extent, on the excellence of its poets (men as well as women) (Al-Tayob 1988; Cunnison 1966).[23]

But the most important factor of all is that an element of sacredness is connected to Arabic that to this day makes it a religious symbol. That Arabic is as much a symbol as a medium has made "the status of

those who seek to create in words, and especially for secular purposes,
. . . highly ambiguous" (Geertz 1983:111). For poetry "is not sacred
enough to justify the power it actually has and not secular enough for
that power to be equated to ordinary eloquence" (ibid., 117).

Women and Words in Arabia: Cultural Dilemmas

This ambiguity that surrounds "those who create in words" is generally
even more intensified when we speak of women as creators of words. The
relationship between women and words becomes doubly problematic. In
a society that is historically characterized by the primacy of genealogy
and language, women and words share the function of being a bond
that unites people and as such become the mediums and most important
symbols of identity. As symbols, both women and words become
wrapped in the ambiguities and double-edged nature of the binary
opposition of strong/weak, good/bad, sacred/profane.[24] The outcry for
the protection of the Arabic language and the protection of women has
always been at the heart of the response to both internal cultural crisis
and civilization's challenges. Women and words, being at the heart of
ideological formations in society, not only emerge as objects of control
but also as idiom and instrument by and through which the whole
society is controlled.

Women's participation in the institution of literature provides them
with the opportunity to be not only in control of themselves but also in
control of language. This presents more than a challenge to the claim
the center of power makes to protect women and words; it represents a
cultural dilemma. This dilemma is rooted in the problematic relationship of women as a private category and words as a public one. Their
sheer presence in this Arabian society as women who traffic in words at
the heart of a literary enterprise that is, by definition, public is culturally problematic.[25] For one thing, women are considered the most
"private" of the private (*owra*) to be governed by strict rules of concealment. Words, on the other hand, are considered not only "public" or a
means of "publication" (in the sense of publishing, as well as in the
sense of making public) but also operate as agents of revelation, both in
the sacred and secular senses. For another, while these women submit
to the cultural and religious rules of physical concealment, in their

"presence" as writers they are also "revealed" if only because they have a "voice," which according to the Wahhabis is in itself *owra*.

The Power of Historical Precedence

The contemporary Saudi women writers have in fact opted for more than having a "voice"; they are concerned about transforming or at least affecting the entire cultural discourse. But with these cultural dilemmas surrounding their enterprise, it is remarkable that the literary enterprise of these women writers can attain any degree of legitimacy at all. Although important legitimizing elements are related to contemporary needs, which will be discussed in chapter 1, the Saudi women writers are not oblivious to the fact that if the relationship of women and words is culturally problematic, it is neither historically nor religiously so. To be sure, even in the contemporary Arab world, their sisters have been publishing their literary works for at least the past hundred years. In fact, today some 95 percent of those who own, publish, edit, and write Arab women's magazines in the Arab world, which number more than three hundred, are females. [26]

Women writers are acutely aware of the power of such facts and of other historical precedents pertaining to the participation of Arab and Muslim women in developing the Islamic civilization by various means, one of which is the word. Evidence is abundant, both in history and literature, that nothing in the Arab social organization indicates that women were excluded from the production and transmission of ideas. To the contrary, the evidence points to Arab women possessing the means to both formulate an ideology of action and to actively participate in action (the distinction is Smith's [1975]). [27] Although the extent of this influence has always been subject to historical variation, the evidence reveals more specifically that women, through their various means of expression, have always held positions of influence and control over ideological structures, especially through their poetry which has enjoyed free-floating access to the stream of public life around them. Literary works written since the eighth and ninth centuries include endless accounts of women who were distinguished in different fields of expression. [28] A recent book compiles in five volumes the autobiographies of more than twenty-seven hundred Muslim and Arab women from different classes and epochs who have affected history in a variety of ways (Kah'hala 1984).

While women of power existed in pre-Islamic Arabia, such as the Queen of Sheba, women constituted a historical force mainly during the first century of Islam. The Qur'an inaugurated a revolution in the conception of women by emphasizing that men and women are created from one soul, and that while both Adam and Eve had fallen victims to seduction, it was clearly Adam who went astray (Qur'an 20:121).[29] Moreover, the Qur'anic narrative of various stories of women not only emphasized such qualities as leadership and independence of judgment but also presented women as speakers in their own right. Sanctioned by Qur'anic stipulations, as well as by the Prophet Muhammed's recommendations, what women said had in fact become a basis of knowledge. The Qur'anic Sura of Almujadala (in some versions Almujadila) or the Chapter of Woman Debater, tells the story of a woman who complained that she was denied her sexual rights by her husband because he declared in anger that "she would be to him like his mother." Her own understanding of the spirit of the new religion had led her to believe that such a custom could not possibly be Islamic because it was simply unjust. The Qur'an confirmed what she had surmised: "Allah has indeed heard (and accepted) the statement of the woman who pleads with thee concerning her husband and carries her complaint (in prayer) to Allah" (Qur'an 58:1).[30]

With this verse a tradition was born that gave women the right to speak as authorities in religious and political settings. Historical developments of Islam testify to the actual participation of women in the shaping of religion through their leadership of major political revolts, such as the one led by 'Aisha, the wife of the prophet in the year 656 A.C., which shaped Islam's political and spiritual future in the most fundamental ways. The prophet had so enforced values of debate and consultation in his family life that 'Aisha became a major religious authority, recommended as such by the prophet himself.[31] Historical accounts also exist of an army of women who were not only knowledgeable themselves but were also involved in teaching countless known male religious authorities in major cultural centers, such as Damascus, Cairo, and Baghdad, in various centuries (Sartain 1975; Shalaby 1954; Tritton 1962).

Although this tradition has waned in subsequent centuries, it has never died. At the time of the Wahhabi movement in central Arabia in the mid-eighteenth century, Burckhardt noted:

> The Begoum Arabs, of whom some are shepherds, and some cultivators, were headed by a widow named Ghalya, whose husband had been one of the chief men at Taraba. She herself possessed more wealth than any Arab family in the neighborhood. She distributed money and provisions among all the poor of her tribe, who were ready to fight the Turks. Her table was open to all faithful Wahabys, whose chiefs held their councils in her house, and as the old lady was celebrated for sound judgment, and an accurate knowledge of the interests of the surrounding tribes, her voice was not only heard in council, but generally prevailed; and she actually governed the Begoums, although they had a nominal chief, or sheik, called Ibn Khorshan.[32]

Women in Contemporary Arabia: Discourses of Power

Women's position in Saudi Arabia today has been affected by the historical transformations caused by the major shift from the primacy of tribe to the primacy of state by the establishment of the kingdom of Saudi Arabia in 1936.[33] The transformation in the society's power structure has meant that the political arena is dominated by three centers of power: the royal family, the tribal leaders, and the *'ulama*. In reality, however, the political order is predicated on the king's authority, which often embodies the roles of both tribal and religious leaders. Maintaining a balance of power between these forces is crucial to their survival. This is essential to keep in mind because contemporary discourses on women in Saudi Arabia are greatly affected by the imbalance of power between them. One of the main characteristics of the contemporary political situation is that women have been placed at the center of this power struggle, especially between the *'ulama* and the state.

The emergence of the nation-state, as a regional demarcation involving control of the social management of space and people, posed a challenge to the tribal social organization. However, the forced and voluntarily established settlement of the Bedouins and the creation of national identity embodied in the state have altered in significant ways the concept of tribe and the role of tribal leaders (Said 1979). But even within the state, the tribes have managed to remain important units whose loyalty and support for the state have to be maintained. The "idea" of the tribe had to be preserved and even enforced by the state, because its structure, being based on collective will, serves naturally as an effective mechanism of control. Despite the state's catering to the tribal concept and its keen interest in protecting the tribe, however, the double-edged nature of the tribal system remains a potent threat to the state. In order that the state may rely on the support of the tribes, the tribal shaikhs' basis of power has altered from one emanating from the people to one that is dependent on the state. It is this detachment of tribal leadership from the tribal members that makes the state vulnerable in terms of the reliability of tribal support (Lipsky 1959: 99; Helms 1981).

With political unification, the *'ulama*'s role has also drastically changed. The preservation of religious institutions, according to Islamic political theory, is a function of the state, and the *'ulama*'s role is determined by this function. This has created a mutual dependency in which the state is always in need of religious support for its development plans, while the *'ulama* depend on the state for their survival (Piscatori 1983). Within the newly founded structures of Saudi Arabia, the *'ulama* were transformed from being a relatively autonomous institutionalized center of power to being "paid civil servants" appointed by the state, which also regulates their income and general activities (Al-Yassini 1985:59–68).

Despite the virtual weakness of the *'ulama*, the appearance of a balance of power between religion and the state had to be preserved (Nibloc 1981). For example, the primary objectives of development plans have always been gauged in terms of the "preservation" of religious values and traditions. The state's dependence on religion for legitimacy seems to have decreased as development itself has emerged as a new source of legitimacy. Development has led to the extension of state control to such areas as protection, health, and education (Nehme 1983). In the past some of these areas, such as education and administration of *awqaf* (religious endowment), were traditionally dominated by the religious establishment, which historically secured a degree of independence, ideological as well as economical (Al-Yassini 1985:59–68).

Despite the incorporation of these traditional functions of the *'ulama* into the newly emergent structure, their loss of power vis-à-vis the state should not be exaggerated.[34] For the *'ulama*'s power throughout Islamic history has always been predicated on the decisive role religion plays in mobilizing popular support with or without that institutional support. The state has no illusion about this; not only has religious rationalization always been sought to legitimize political measures but the state also has to make public the *'ulama*'s consent on many major issues.[35]

However, the state's monopoly of force and resources has occasionally been challenged by religious rebellions. The seizure by religious elements of the Grand Mosque in 1979 was the most serious such attempt in the state's recent history. For one thing, this action showed the regime its weak basis of legitimacy; for another, it brought the *'ulama* to the center stage and served as a reminder to them of their "real" role. The scorn and contempt for those *'ulama* who are, in the words of the leader of the rebellious group, "bought up by a corrupt regime with money and promises of promotion," finds resonance among many unsatisfied groups, even those with secular tendencies (Al-Yassini 1985:127). These groups, while they are often at variance with both *'ulama* and state, have always constituted a potential support for one or the other of these power centers. In the period that followed the insurrection at the Grand Mosque, the state tended to satisfy secular groups by promising—for the third time in the past thirty years— the establishment of a consultative assembly, something that has never materialized. But the threat of insurrection also forced the state to take a stance, if not to demonstrate more commitment to the enforcement of the *shari'a* (Islamic law) then to reconsider its relationship to the *'ulama*. The state's first initiatives after this rebellion were geared toward making symbolic gestures to confirm its commitment to Islam, especially through measures that restrict women, raising the *'ulama*'s salaries and allocating money to build more mosques and religious institutions at home and abroad.

The Creation of the Collage Culture

Whatever level of balance was maintained between the *'ulama* and the state, one fact remains: the relationship of religion and state in Arabia presents a rather peculiar situation in which a number of contradictory elements operate. Among these are development, which implements the Western capitalist model of change in a semitribal society; the austere principles of the Wahhabi ideology in an extremely affluent society; and an increase in secular education which has resulted in the formation of groups that demand political participation in an autocratic system that lacks representative institutions (Al-Yassini 1985:59–68).

These contradictory elements have had deep and lasting effects on society, if only because they have led to a type of "collage culture" that manifested itself in both the material as well as the symbolic. The collage can be observed in all aspects of life—in architecture, in marriage and weddings, in leisure, and even in the media's coverage of international sports events.[36] To begin with, Jeddah's physical appearance establishes continuity more with Sacramento or Stockton, California, than with old Jeddah, with its magnificent houses and narrow streets. Its fast-food restaurants, such as Burger King and Kentucky Fried Chicken, along with Toyland and Drexel Heritage, serves no reminder that one is in the land of religion, tradition, and history.

The clean and well-ironed white *thobes* (a traditional long robe) of male pedestrians and their headdress become one reminder of being in Saudi Arabia. The absence of women drivers or even at times of female pedestrians is perhaps another reminder. To make the collage more striking, women are seen being driven in their fancy American cars by foreign drivers, which is most remarkable in an ideology that deems being with a strange man an absolute breach of a woman's morality.

Cars, houses, wedding ceremonies, social hospitality, and vacations all become status symbols of personal piety and honor. Families spend part of *Ramadhan* in Makkah (Mecca) to perform *'umrah* (the short hajj), or even the complete hajj later. Their vacations may be spent in Thailand—especially those of unmarried men. Family vacations may be spent in London, Cairo, or North Africa. Women wear *'abayas* over the products of famous Italian and Parisian fashion designers, worn more often than not with exquisite taste according to the highest fashion standards. A woman may be allowed to choose the finest of hotels in which to hold her wedding, and to conduct it in a mix of traditional and latest Western fashion. But she may not be allowed to choose her husband or to see him before marriage.[37] These are only glimpses of material or symbolic elements of collage, which is deeply felt by many but especially the intellectuals, both men and women.[38] But for women writers especially, these contradictions in the society form the center of gravity for their enterprise. For it is precisely those contradictions that feed discourses which provoke the belief that women need to be controlled.

Defining Women

During the 1950s, debates have raged about women's education, and in the mid-1970s about their role in development and work outside the home. The notions of women's education and work were, from the very beginning, perceived by the *'ulama* to be Western ideas, the danger of which lay in their leading to a high degree of mobility accorded women in the West.[39] The *'ulama* were eventually to abandon their objection to women's education outside the home partly because the moderate elements in the state were encouraging it, and partly because the newly emerged middle-class men campaigned for women's education. In order to challenge the old tradition and authority, this group of men proclaimed that they would marry only those women who were educated (Al-Baadi 1982). Women gained the right to attend schools by a royal decree in 1959, a move that was justified in religious terms (see chapter 1).

In the 1970s and early 1980s women university graduates had grown in number, and state development strategists called for their integration into the labor force. The religious leaders, on the other hand, objected to any measures that would allow women a higher degree of mobility outside the home or lead to the relaxing of rules of sex segregation. A compromise between these two centers of power were reached in which the state made it legal to employ women provided that sex segregation was strictly observed. But by the start of the 1980s, and in the wake of a religious revivalism, the question of women has taken a new turn.[40] The state was required to appease the *'ulama*'s alarm at modernization programs that opened the door for Western influence; so, while keeping the field of work open for women outside the home, the state imposed more restrictions on them. For example, in the early 1980s measures were taken prohibiting women from traveling abroad without a chaperon for study, business, or tourism, and banning them from conducting their own businesses without a male representative who was a family member. This measure was to end over a fifteen-centuries-old traditional right for the Arab woman to be an independent entrepreneur.

But despite such "calming" measures that the state took to placate the *'ulama*, the increasing powerlessness of the *'ulama*, vis-à-vis the state, has become evident in their lack of influence on the state's policies regarding modernization in general and women in particular. The *'ulama* have increased their interest in "women's issues" as their awareness of the challenge of modernization to the religious establishment grew stronger and their power to change this trend grew weaker. By the mid-1970s the *'ulama* began conducting an intense campaign of theorizing about "the woman" as mind, body, and soul, advancing a conceptualization of women as weak and lacking (*naqisat*). Turning into the subjects of public speeches seemed to have become the means through which the religious *'ulama* would assert their power. "The Woman as a Nature and a Function" appeared frequently in titles of lectures given by religious leaders, as well as in articles and books. For example, an ardent traditionalist, who speaks of the "nature" of femininity, consistently suggests in his books, articles, and lectures that the "woman's nature" is based on weakness, lack (*nuqs*), and immobility.[41] Shaikh Ben Baz, the mufti, as the highest religious authority in the country, has himself set the tone for the ideology of lack. In his response to the woman who ridiculed the notion of woman's lack, Ben Baz said, "What is meant is the betterment of one sex over the other, and to show that the one is more complete (*akmal*) than the other."[42] Despite the fact that in the Qur'an the physical designations of "male" and "female" (*thakar/untha*) are actually distinct from the social "men" and "women" (*rajul/mar'aa*), "men" and "women" were transformed in Ben Baz's interpretation from being social elements in the Qur'an to mere biological beings. But in this discourse "the woman" is transformed in many religious interpretations into a physical being, who must constantly be reminded of her "lack," "incompleteness," "fragility," and "natural" propensity for perversion; in a word, of being an *owra,* a source of shame who has to be concealed. The power and effectiveness of this "political anatomy," to borrow Foucault's terminology, is manifested in invoking, as well as evoking, men's constant apprehension about honor seen to be invested in their womenfolk. The ultimate effect of this discourse on women was in mobilizing the efforts of both individuals and institutions to protect this honor. By controlling women, the man is led to believe not only that he protects his own honor but is also made to believe that in so doing he is also accomplishing the mission of protecting the honor of the Islamic civilization against the dangers of Western civilization.

This tendency to utilize women in the game of power has been geared toward enhancing the view of women as "a gate of Westernization," and has thus intensified apprehension about them.[43] It is this very apprehension that makes the power of this cultural discourse so overwhelming. It goes beyond controlling women to using them as a means of control for the whole society. As a result, measures promulgated against women, while used by the state for their symbolic legitimizing value, find support from all centers of power. This symbolic value of women constitutes a great discovery for both the clergy and the state. Converging with a crisis of identity and purpose in individual men's psyches, this discovery has invoked a collective interest in guarding women. The irony of converting women (a private category) to an object of public scrutiny was only to be further enhanced by another irony. As greater concealment of women was demanded and practiced on the institutional level, especially in terms of restrictions on their mobility, greater exposure and theorizing about them has become increasingly necessary to meet the various ideological demands. But this exposure is structured in such a way that, while women are still maintained as a legitimate object for public discourse, their diversity is suppressed and their experience is relegated to the status of the private that must be concealed. As will be seen, women writers respond in most powerful ways to these ironies.

Defining Historical Significance

Defining women forms only a part of the discursive context in contemporary Arabia within which women writers of the 1980s are placed and that they attempt to transform. Defining history is another battlefield on which the state and the *'ulama* assert their power and compete to effect cultural transformations. The discourse on defining historical significance is an age-old battle that was fought on literary, political, and religious grounds.[44] Culturally speaking, women, history, and language are intimately linked. People of the Arabian peninsula, by the primacy they accord genealogy as a basic organizational principle of their social structure, have by definition always been conscious of gender, as well as history. Also, in pre-Islamic times, kin affiliation among tribal members, especially those who affected the history of the tribe, was always recounted and kept alive in the public memory through poetry and storytelling. In contemporary Saudi Arabia, history is a point of contention among different groups in society, each advancing its own interpretation of history and competing for support. Among the existing representations of the past, two versions are the most powerful and pervasive: one advanced by the political apparatus, the other by religious institutions. The Saudi state has an ambiguous relationship to the past. It breaks with the past in its form (monarchy), as well as in its content and orientation (the Western model of modernization). It adopts neither the Islamic system of *shoura* (consultation of the knowledgeable and the trusted) nor a form of democratic representation with which Western systems identify. What is of interest here is that the state, in its representation of history, utilizes an amnesia in which "heritage" extends mainly to the establishment of the Saudi state less than seventy years ago. This period in history is carved out by the state and crystallized through the concept of "national heritage," around which people are mobilized (Arebi 1994).

The religious leaders, on the other hand, carve out the first half-century of Islam as *the* locus of historical significance. Ironically, the state was established with the aid of the Wahhabi religious ideology, which originated in Najd in 1745. This ideology is based on puritanical principles, believed to be of the early half-century of Islam commonly referred to as *Salafiyya*. Theoretically at least, religious and state definitions should not be inconsistent. But the state has on many occasions not only denied the status of the doctrine of Wahhabism but has also attempted rather passionately to dissociate itself from these beliefs.[45]

In the discourse on defining historical significance, women's history has been dominated—perhaps this is no different than occurs elsewhere—by an elitist and gender-biased definition of history that views what men and men of power do as its legitimate subject matter.[46] What is interesting in the Saudi case is that defining women is linked to defining history if only because they are both linked to modernization and the challenge of Western civilization to Islamic values which exacerbate an identity crisis. But even more serious is that defining history follows the contours of defining women in that women are also rendered "lacking," this time in history. The stripping of women of the ability to draw confidence and support from great women in history is what prompts women writers to weave their own. Women writers in full force participate in the battle of defining historical significance in a manner that would no longer render women as people without a history. Chapter 2 deals with the repertoire of symbols and other aesthetic devices by which the writers manipulate female historical symbols as a political strategy for establishing historical continuity.

It is against this background that the whole enterprise of women's writings can best be understood. The writings of nine women writers, presented in my English translations, will form the basis for analysis, supplemented with data collected through interviews conducted in the field in 1989 with more than twenty contemporary women writers.

Chapter 1 explores the social organization of writing and the basis of women writers' legitimacy and the structure of their opportunity to engage in literary activity, with consideration of the limitations on creativity and imagination that are placed on them as a result of cultural, religious, historical, and social values.

Chapters 2, 3, and 4 present translated selections from the works of nine women writers grouped in threes. Each selection is accompanied by a biographical sketch of the writer and a reflection on my own personal encounter with each one. In each of these chapters I provide textual analysis through which one can see the manner in which women writers have responded to larger discourses of power, to the contradictions that impinge on their lives as women and as writers, as well as the extent to which they engage in processes of cultural reconstruction, not only in matters that relate to gender relations but also to religion, tradition, and the definition of history. The analysis focuses on the relationship between the creative process and social considerations. By examining their chosen themes and messages, I hope to explore how decisions relating to what is artistically possible are made in relation to what is socially permissible.

Chapter 5 deals with the response of critics to their writing in which a shift has occurred from "the woman as private" yet a subject of public discourse to a situation in which the products of women's minds that are made public are privatized.

In the concluding chapter I draw the implications of the women writers' role within their culture, and the cultural apparatus that drives their discourse. I attempt to answer the question of whether we are justified in seeing their endeavor as a form of resistance, considering that they establish a dialectical relationship between opposition and affirmation of major cultural values and institutions.

Selection of the Women Writers

The inclusion of the nine writers was dictated by their historical significance, rather than by the literary value of their work. On the basis of my own reading and knowledge of the literary scene, I initially formed a list of more than thirty women writers whom I identified as regular participants in the field for at least the past ten years. I incorporated this list into a one-page questionnaire designed to measure the popularity of these women writers. The questionnaire was distributed in Jeddah, Makkah, Ar-Riyadh, and Jaizan among those who identified themselves as regular readers of major local newspapers and magazines, and who had a general interest in literary activities. The respondents, who were mostly university students, were asked to rank the list and identify the reasons for their preferences (that is, in terms of style, ideas, or the writer's approach). The response of the readers was one of the most difficult areas to explore because of strict university rules that prohibited the distribution of written material other than that which was curriculum-related. The questionnaire, which was mostly administered individually by women friends and acquaintances, was valuable in gaining a perspective on the readers sense of who is "important."

A list of a dozen women emerged who had been readily identified by these readers as the most distinguishable as well as the most important in the field by virtue of their contributions over a period of time. The list corresponded to my own impressions of "who's who" in the field. Other people, including writers and critics, also agreed with the selections, either on the basis of the exceptional quality of the writers' works or because of their persistence in the field for the past ten to twenty years or in many instances for both these reasons. For manageability I chose nine women who were not selected basically as "representative" of women writers but rather because they were considered the most consequential.

While the literary stature of these women determined their selection, the sample was surprisingly "representative" of the variety of participants in the field. Although no writer was selected basically because she represented a particular genre or region, the sample reflected a balanced distribution in terms of genre, regional affiliation, spectrum of ideological orientation, and even of age. That the group included more short-story writers than poets, for example, is only a reflection of their higher number in reality.

Aiming at generic representativeness would have been problematic if only because neither is that distinction salient nor is the distinction between the poetic and the journalistic sharply defined. Writers tend to practice both modes even within one form. The mode of narrative within a weekly newspaper column usually involves the use of poetic forms. In fact, many articles by these writers derive their force not so much from the message they attempt to communicate as from their imagistic function facilitated by the use of symbols, metaphors, and allusions. By the same token, the fictional forms tend to be full of ideological commentaries and make extensive use of rhetoric to facilitate persuasion. The response these articles invoke is on both the aesthetic and the ideological level. As the selection of women will be seen to illustrate, women writers seem to utilize three functions: the communicational, the symbolic, and the rhetorical, either situationally or as a matter of personal style and preference.

While all of these writers, regardless of their preferred genre, are columnists and ultimately essay writers, the three women chosen as essay writers, Juhayer Al-Musa'ed, Fatna Shaker, and Sohaila Zain Al-Abedin, have up to the present practiced only this form (at the time of the interview Fatna and Juhayer were each embarking on a novel). The decision to identify a particular writer by a particular form was made on the basis of her own literary priorities or the form by which she was known and wanted to be known. This was the case with the choice of Sharifa Ash-Shamlan, Khayriyya As-Saggaf, Ruqayya Ash-Shabib, and Najwa Hashim as short-story writers; Rajaa 'Alim as a playwright; and Fowziyya Abu-Khalid as a poet. The sample lacks diversity in terms of class affiliation. Almost all of these women belong to middle-class or upper-middle-class merchant families. Although it is said that some women members of the royal family were known to have been writers or poets (especially within the folk form of Nabti poetry), these women are difficult to identify because they either published under pseudonyms or did not publish at all. However, women members of the royal family are known to perform the role of providing a kind of sponsorship to women's literary events through their positions as heads of women's organizations in the various areas of the country. That writing is dominated by middle-class women should not be surprising. For writing, during the past three decades, has been undertaken mostly by the middle-class as a new source of prestige, although more so by men than by women. It provides mobility for those who are willing to take it on as a second job which, though it may not be very lucrative, incurs a degree of prestige.

In the Field: Interviews and Data Collection

After three years of attempts to obtain a visa to conduct the field research in Saudi Arabia, I was granted one for three months.[47] During these three years, in addition to carrying my teaching responsibilities, I immersed myself in the written texts that my Saudi female friends sent to me, thus bringing the field to me. Before leaving for the field, and even after I left, Saudi local publications kept me up-to-date on major as well as not-so-major cultural events.[48] I was also educating myself on issues of translation from a first language (Arabic) to a second (English). Given the demanding task, which I took upon myself, of translating a huge amount of literary material from Arabic to English, it seemed that no amount of time would have been sufficient to conduct such an ambitious project with the thoroughness needed or to which I aspired. But by the time I had to leave for the field, I had arrived at a good position to know who's who in the literary scene, having read and identified most, if not all, women writers of consequence.

Once in the field in early March of 1989, I had to deal with the realities of space but, most important, with the realities of time constraints. My decision was to use the time in the field mainly for interviewing the writers as efficiently as possible. Because these women constituted a center of attention in their society, both as women and as writers, I benefited a great deal from the general exposition their writings enjoyed in the newspapers, as well as from the many interviews their fellow women journalists conducted with them over a period of time. These were valuable sources of information and extremely helpful in identifying the gaps in my data.

Most of the data were generated through personal interviews with current writers, as well as with a number of women who either had written occasionally or had discontinued their literary activities. Interviews were also conducted with a number of men by phone. These men were either key literary figures, critics, publishers, editors of major newspapers and magazines, or supervisors of literary sections and supplements. Visits were also made to Umm Al-Qura University (the women's section) in Makkah, as well as to a number of bookstores and libraries in Jeddah, Makkah, and Madinah. That my host was one of the leading literary figures in the country, and that his wife was the manager of his extensive library, helped a great deal not only in my getting acquainted with the less accessible literary works but also in my establishing a communication network with some of the writers I was researching, as well as with women readers who came to borrow books from his library.

Specific details of the interviews with the writers are included in the chapters that follow. I should mention here that the degree of cooperation on the part of women writers was overwhelming. No woman writer declined to be interviewed. Three were hesitant at first, but after I explained my purpose in an initial phone call, they were generally receptive if not altogether enthusiastic. Many of the writers made an effort to provide me with their books, and some put together extensive collections of their writings, dating back many years (the largest of all was Juhayer's and Sohaila's collections of articles).[49] Others sent even more material by mail during and after the fieldwork.

Being aware of the problems of mobility for a woman as well as for a guest in Saudi Arabia, some of the women, at the outset, offered their drivers and their homes as sites for the interviews. Most of the interviews took place in the evening or during the night (especially during the fasting month of Ramadhan). Their generosity extended to sweets, nuts, and drinks (e.g., coffee, tea, juices). The shortest interview lasted three hours, the longest ten hours straight! Whenever possible, the interviews were supplemented by phone conversations or by other visits.

The interviews with the writers were minimally structured. A lack of rigidity was intended to allow them to talk about matters that they themselves perceived as important. A considerable part of the interview was geared toward questions concerning the writer's relationship to her readers, to the critics, and to other writers; her conception of whom she writes for; clarification of biographical facts, literary affiliations, and influences; extraliterary activities; events that affect her role as a writer; writing and publishing processes; and periods of silence.

I used a notebook to jot down main points of discussion, having ruled out the use of a tape recorder because of my experience at Jeddah's airport upon my arrival. I had been detained there for six hours. This made me feel vulnerable and virtually powerless as a woman traveling alone. I was in no position to provide or to promise protection of confidentiality to these women should I tape their conversations. The women, however, were ambivalent about the use of the tape recorder. On the one hand, as writers with a natural tendency to love their own words, they were not sure that these "words" would survive the tricks of memory (mine), and some eagerly suggested taping. On the other hand, in a highly censored society, my decision not to tape was a source of relief for some and encouraged them to speak more openly on various issues. This openness was more important to me than the ability to provide additional quotations of their words, since I had already accumulated much material through their own works.

The interviews were more adventurous than the anthropological conventions ruling the relationship between interviewer and interviewee would normally allow. In fact, in anthropological research, interviews in which the relationship between the researcher and the researched was not hierarchic or reciprocal were rare. Far from being passive interviewees, these women were as interested in my views as I was in theirs. Most of them were as good at speaking as they were at writing. As many of the writers are also educators, they are trained to respond to questions and to question in return. Far from being a passive interviewer myself, whose role was supposedly to record and extract opinions rather than to give them, I vehemently engaged in the discussions, debating, questioning, and at times even disagreeing. It was by all means an equal exchange.

The writers asked about my research, its goals, and its scope. How did I know about them and their work, and "why them?" Most seemed flattered, both by my interest in their work and my knowledge of it, as well as the possibility of the universality that would follow its publication in the West. They seemed anxious to be sure that I knew the literary scene well enough to be able to "evaluate" their status. They were acutely conscious of definitions of who was important, of choosing the "best" for my study, and concerned about my interviewing people they did not consider important writers. Some frowned on the idea of lumping together writers who were "less important" with those who were "more important" on my interviewing list. Of course everyone— besides the writers themselves—who had written, read, or critiqued was for me important. They were generally curious about my impressions of other writers whom I had interviewed but whom they had never met themselves. Eventually, however, the consensus centered mostly on eleven or twelve writers, the first nine of whom are included here.

These writers were also curious about me personally. Although their perceptions of me are difficult to assess, I think they saw me as not far removed from themselves, which paralleled my own thinking. I also felt they were not far removed from me. We had many points of identity in common—my being a woman, a writer, an Arab and a Muslim, all equally important. But most important, we identified with one another as people who were placed in the middle, between two worlds, whose effects have forever become part of our existence. The question that no writer neglected to ask me was this: How do I deal with Western civilization, and what kinds of challenges does living in the American culture—without "selling out" to it—pose to my sense of self and to my own identity? The question reflects their preoccupation, almost an obsession for some, with the search for a way in which the West and the East can meet on grounds other than threat, fear, hostility, or domination. Their plea for the right of difference to prevail—both within and between these worlds—was simple but profound. Haunted by the prospect of being crushed by time and space, an idea that dominates their writings, they probably saw in me an embodiment of their vision and hope for the power of difference and perhaps the power of indifference as well.

Selection of Works and the Process of Translation

In the organization of this book, the vexing difficulty was how to present a scholarly work that was ethnographic in aim, in which as much attention was given to the patterned as to the unique and the particular. The women's works naturally inform us about the different ways in which each writer apprehends her universe and conceives of social problems, as well as providing insights into her style and outlook. The collections I have accumulated through the years, along with the new material that I collected during my fieldwork, have mounted to thousands of essays and hundreds of short stories and poems. Within this large body of material one can see patterns in the types of issues and themes the women have addressed. However, within the limited material selected for translation, delineating these patterns was a complex process involving a series of complex decisions.

While the large body of material available was an invaluable source of data on these writers, as well as on their society, it made it difficult for any one selection to do justice to the diversity of their interests. At least three factors were considered in the process of selection. First, in the context of the author's work, I wanted to ensure that the selection illustrated her choice of themes, style, and nature of thought. The selection of three or four, and in some instances only one or two, pieces for each writer may even have constituted a misrepresentation of her craft—but the priorities were set so as to ensure a degree of representativeness within the work of each writer. Second, I placed the individual women writers within the context of all women writers in order to ensure that the overall diversity of women's writings, in terms of styles, concerns, preoccupations, and ideological orientations, was demonstrated. Third, given the purposes of this study, and being analytical rather than ontological, the works were chosen to provide "data" on these writers as well as on their society. The challenge was how to choose a piece that would tell us something about the wider context of the political and literary discourses without compromising the distinctive identity of the writer herself.

Reconciling all these requirements took tremendous time and effort, especially since a great deal of overlap existed in themes and issues. But once a selection was made, the major concern shifted to the process of translation itself. My idea of a "good" translation is one that ensures that it is the author's voice—in terms of both style and meaning—that is conveyed, rather than one in which only the meaning is communicated. I searched for ways to provide maximum faithfulness to the texts, as well as to the writers' own styles. The result was not so much a "literary translation" as "translated literature."[50]

In the process of translation I became acutely aware that the texts were written by Arab writers for Arab-speaking audiences with certain expectations. Moreover, an intertextuality was already inherent in the translation, in that these texts were written within a certain discourse and in relation to certain speakers. In this introduction I lay out the discursive context within which certain issues are addressed or defined to ensure that the reader knows more about the culture than may be addressed in the texts themselves. In the later chapters (3, 4, and 5) I provide an exegesis of the translated texts in a way that will give the reader a grasp of what makes a text meaningful to its original audience, especially in relation to aesthetics that drive the use or the choice of certain narrative structures, such as the use of symbols, allusions, or the manipulation of a certain logic of argument.

This exercise of providing the discursive context within which a text can be placed is most fruitful, but it is also risky. As in any ethnographic endeavor, one is never sure of how much context is sufficient. Context, like beauty, is in the eye of the beholder. Footnotes are used in the translated sections to establish a better understanding of the text, even though by so doing one runs the risk of obstructing the text or, in one's zeal to explain, to obviate the text itself. This exercise varied from one writer to another. Some writings yielded more to coherent translation than others. Articles were less challenging than short stories, plays, and poetry. Some styles were more difficult than others, especially when the writer had a tendency to describe psychological experiences and emotions. Some translations may reflect a degree of incoherence, but that is because the original was incoherent or because the piece derives its power from the emotions it invokes in the native reader. These instances, however, reflect the novelty of the enterprise of describing women's experiences, and are indicative of how certain psychological experiences women face are yet to be "named."

The resort to abridgement was minimal overall. It was used in cases where the text was too lengthy, such as in Rajaa's case, or when the text was both lengthy and seemingly repetitive. Juhayer and Sohaila had a tendency in their writings to speak of the same matters, albeit in different ways, in a single piece and across pieces. Juhayer's articles would usually run to more than five thousand words, but for a foreign reader who might be more concerned with content than style this could be shortened to five hundred words without betraying the meaning and purpose of the original text. For example, Juhayer may have said the same thing in at least ten different ways—but this should not be considered repetitive, because it was written within a literary tradition in which subtle levels of response are evoked by different ways of saying what may be perceived by the Western reader in translation as the "same thing," depending, of course, on how good the translation is. Saying things in different ways must be seen as an important indication of the writer's awareness of the diversity of her readers' levels of sophistication.

In this study I indicate abridgment of the original texts by the use of more than three "periods." The Arabic originals of the translated manuscripts also contain many series of periods, usually three, either to indicate a change of tone or the writer's desire for more freedom to use loosely structured language, in which case sentences may be disjointed but grammatically sound. Overall, I believe that the abridgments have resulted in reasonably coherent texts.

1

Women's Opportunities and the Social Organization of Writing

Beginnings

Since the early 1950s female names have frequently appeared in the readers' mail sections commenting and debating the issues, and at times appeared as "supervisors" of women's sections in the major newspapers. But the actual participation of women as writers in Saudi Arabia in fact dates back to 1956, when the first article by a woman was published in the Jeddah-based newspaper, *Al-Manhil*. The earlier articles that had appeared that had been signed with female names were later proven to have been authored by male writers who wrote for women's sections but found it inappropriate to sign with male names. However, it was not until the beginning of the 1960s that regular contributions by "real" women appeared. As soon as women entered the field of writing they were put in charge of the women's sections of newspapers and magazines. These sections carried various designations, such as "The Other Sex," "The World of Women," "Eve's Corner," or other names that referred to women, and were either supervised or often written in their entirety by the same woman. The first generation of these women who left their mark on women's literary history was mostly from the region of Hijaz: Fatna Shāker, Thurayya Gābel, Ruqayya Nadher, 'Ābdiya Khayyat, Latifa Al-Khateeb, and Huda Dabbagh. Women from the region of Najd soon followed suit, and names of women such as Hessa Al-Fadhl, Sultana Al-Sidairy, and others began to appear in the province's newspapers.[1] Some of these women have discontinued their writing careers; others, however, are still writing, more or less regularly.

In addition to writing in newspapers, women also made attempts early on at writing in other literary forms, such as short stories, poetry, and novels. Although novels enjoy little currency among women today, novels written by women appeared as early as 1958 with the work of Samira Khashog'gi, and later Amal Shaṭa, Huda Al-Rashid, and Hind Baghaffar. The short story is currently the most popular genre for women writers, and the consensus is that Najat Ḳhayyat was the first woman to publish a collection of short stories.[2] In the field of poetry, although some scattered poems appeared that were written by women, the first collection of poems to be published as a book was for Thuraya Gābel in Beirut in 1963.[3]

The idea of women writers in Saudi Arabia has gained greater legitimacy during the last twenty-five years or so, more than half a century later than in other Arab countries.[4] But any attempt to write the history of the idea is hampered by the general neglect in the local literary history books of women's literary contributions. Many of these studies either completely ignore the works of women writers, mention them in passing, or at best treat them marginally in very few pages.[5] This lack of recognition may be explained by many factors, one of which stems from the difficulty of determining "who's who" in the field. Many names appeared but few persisted long enough to be identified as serious writers. Even though new women writers emerged in the decade of the 1970s, some would disappear or lapse into long periods of silence.

To gain an appreciation of the number of women who have participated, more or less regularly, in the literary field at one time or another, one can cite the anthology of short articles written by Saudi women writers that appeared in 1983. The anthology does not specify the dates that individual articles were written or indicate whether the women were regular or one-time contributors. It includes the work of 103 women, and promises a further collection of short stories and poetry by an additional 220 women.[6]

Fewer than 10 percent of the names mentioned in this anthology still appear or are remembered, but other new names have emerged. In today's newspapers and magazines one can easily identify more than fifty women, at least thirty of whom appear regularly, mostly as essayists, as well as poets and short-story writers. Consensus on matters of evaluation is hard to achieve, but normally writers are identified as being the most important by virtue of their persistence in the field and the high quality of their work, which often is acknowledged even by nonlocal critics.

Today these women writers can no longer be ignored by the serious observer or researcher. One can identify names such as Fowziyya Abu-Khalid, Khadija Al-'Umary, Thurayya Gābel, and Thurayya Al-'Arayyedh, in modern poetry; in *nabti* (or folk poetry), Sultana Al-Sidairy and Reem Al-Sahra (a nom de plume); in drama, Rajaa 'Alim; and in short stories, Khayriyya As-Saggaf, Najwa Hāshim, Ruqayya As-Shabib, Sharifa Ash-Shamlan, Latifa As-Sālem, Fowziyya Al-Bakr, 'Uhoud Ash-Shibl, Qumasha As-Saif, Moneera Al-Ghadir, Lolwa Bugshan, Hessa Al-Towayjeri, Fowziyya Al-Jarallah, Wafa Attayyeb, and Laila Al-Ahaidab, among others. Although all usually engage in essay writing at one time or another, some are known for this particular genre, such as Fatna Shāker, Juhayer Al-Musa'ed, Suhaila Zain Al-Abedin, Noura Khalid As-Sa'd, Amjad Mahmoud Ridha, and, less frequently, Hanan Atalla and others.

The sheer numbers of these women may indicate recognition and social acceptance, but the structure of their opportunity—as women—to engage in literary activities is related to two major points. First, while mechanisms of recruitment, such as familial, personal, economic, and class affiliations, are important, the basis of the legitimacy of their enterprise has been founded on educational, religious, and sociocultural elements. Second, the full integration of these women writers in the social organization of literary production can only be understood by examining the cultural status of the institution of literature itself, in terms of the needs it serves and the functions it has come to perform in modern times. In fact, the social organization of writing has been affected by the adoption of journalism as a vehicle for literary expression, and has led to subsequent changes in the patterns of book production and consumption. It is to these interrelated factors that the remainder of this chapter is devoted.

Women's Education

The edifice of women's legitimization as writers is built, first of all, on their education. Writing has traditionally been based on assumptions of knowledge that in recent times came to be equated with acquisition of formal education. Before 1960 girls received their education from private female tutors or immediate male family members. A few private elementary schools were established in larger cities, such as Āl-Nassif and Āl-Jamjoom in Jeddah and others in Makkah, Madinah, and to a lesser extent in Ar-Riyadh. By the early 1950s some elite families entrusted their girls to boarding schools in Egypt and Lebanon.[7] Although the first girls' school was built in 1956, formal education for females in Saudi Arabia was introduced in 1960 after a long period of opposition in which it was viewed as compromising to female morality and a vehicle of Westernization.[8] However, when the royal decree institutionalizing female education was finally issued at the end of 1959, it had to be rationalized in religious terms giving assurances that "presently or at a later date," education would not "introduce change in our beliefs."[9] It is estimated that of 2.65 million students enrolled in the 1988–89 academic year, 1.16 million were female.

The expansion of female education ultimately led to the creation of college and university facilities for women. Female undergraduates were also allowed to study at home and obtain degrees from some of these colleges. While in 1960–61 only four women were enrolled in evening classes at Ar-Riyadh University, by 1990 thousands graduated and tens of thousands were students. To be sure, enrollment of women in the seven Saudi universities exceeds that of men. Figures for 1988–89 show that 19 percent of female students who graduate high school enter college as opposed to only 7.1 percent of male high school graduates (*Saudi Arabia* 1990:11). Whether in the fields of the humanities or sciences, women's educational institutions are all segregated from those for men. Often the women's facilities do not enjoy comparable funding, and administratively they are auxiliary to the male institutions. The lack of female instructors for women is usually compensated for by transmitting lectures given by male professors in the male sections through closed-circuit television. Women students may interact with their instructors but only through the media.

Educational Patterns and Professional Options among Women Writers

The available data, those published as well as extracted from personal interviews with more than twenty women writers, seem to reflect a changing educational pattern. The first generation of women writers (those born in the 1940s) was educated in private schools, and some continued their education in Bierut or Cairo. Few pursued higher education in the United States. Those who were born in the 1950s and 1960s, who by far constitute the majority, tend to be educated locally and to more advanced levels. Most of this group hold college degrees, many have M.A. degrees, and a few have Ph.D.'s. Their majors are either in the field of education or cluster around the social sciences and humanities (i.e., sociology, history, and Arabic and English literature). Only two obtained their degrees in journalism, one from Cairo, the other from Baghdad.

These educational patterns have affected women's professional options. The types of jobs they hold are mainly in the field of girls' education as lecturers, teachers, teacher's supervisors, deans of departments, or administrators at various levels. However, there are some exceptions. A number of business women conduct independent or family businesses, and at least one woman writer in the country is also known to be a physician. But it seems that whatever their vocational choices, all women writers are involved in jobs that require a high degree of proficiency in reading and writing.

One may speculate that an adequate education and fewer professional options may have in fact played a role in channeling many capable women into writing. But it is difficult to ascertain the extent to which women's participation in writing can be explained in terms of exclusion or restriction from other domains of work. For one thing, one has to take into consideration that what women lack in the number of fields available to them is compensated for by their opportunity to be recruited to the highest levels of the professional ladder within the fields that are open to them.[10] It seems that because of the very nature of segregated work places for women, these women are not put to major disadvantage by having to compete with men to fill certain positions.[11]

Cultural Basis of Legitimacy

In addition to education, one of the factors that helped legitimize writing for women and allow it to be seen as a proper occupation was its compatibility with the country's cultural norms of women's physical segregation and restrictions on their mobility. Women could write from their homes: they did not need to be seen by or to interact with publishers or newspaper editors. The necessity of leaving home and violating traditional norms was the basis of the debate regarding women's participation in other fields of work. Also, women's participation in writing predated their participation in other domains and the whole debate about women's work that followed. Discussion of whether women should be engaged in writing never arose, as it did in regard to their participation in other fields of work. Thus women writers were spared the negative implications of the debate, and established a greater legitimacy for their literary activities.

However, this combination of circumstances also led to a lack of professionalism for these writers, since, as women, they were partially isolated from the literary institution itself and deprived of the advantages of training, experience, and often financial gain. But ensuring that the basic religious and cultural tenets that govern woman are in operation is more crucial than professionalization for the continuity of their enterprise. The significance of this can be seen in a number of examples that reveal social opposition to any type of professionalization and the zeal for maintaining physical segregation.

In 1981 a semirevolutionary step toward establishing a form of professionalization for women writers by integrating them as hired journalists was taken, rather cautiously, by *Ar-Riyadh* newspaper. Several women with demonstrated writing abilities were hired to work as journalists. They were to provide daily commentary on societal issues and cover women's events. Their office was treated as one of the major departments of the newspaper, and the title of chief editor was conferred for the first time on a woman. However, the "women's office," as it was called, was established in a building that was physically separated from the main offices of the newspaper and, following the cultural norms, men were prohibited from entering this building.

The cultural norms regarding segregation and mobility also affect women in other aspects of their work as "journalists." For example, should the need arise to interview a male doctor on a health issue, the style of reporting must reveal that a distance has been maintained between the woman reporter and the interviewee. The usual procedure would be to send written questions, but should the interview be conducted by phone or—under special circumstances—in person, the report must deliberately blur the circumstances under which the interview was conducted. Statements such as "Doctor X says to *'Ukaz*" or to "*Ar-Riyadh,*" and other such passive forms, have to be carefully designed to prevent suggestions of a meeting or direct interaction between a woman and a strange man.

Probably no better indicator exists of the sensitivity of issues of segregation and of women's mobility, and of the drive of religious elements to maintain cultural norms, than an incident that occurred in the Jeddah Literary Club in 1989—only two months before my arrival in the field. At a poetry recitation meeting in which women poets were invited to participate, the female audience, as well as the women poets participating in the event, were, as usual, physically segregated from the men and placed in a separate hall. The women could hear and watch the men through closed-circuit television. However, the men could only hear the women but were not allowed to see them. According to eyewitnesses, a number of religious elements in the men's section, after hearing the women's reading, seized the microphone and attacked them verbally in rather harsh and insulting language. These men argued that women's recitation of poetry is in fact a form of flirtation with men, against which the Qur'an warns women. The incident, which was reported in the newspapers and discussed as a breach of segregation norms, proved to be a major setback to the idea of women attending literary events, even when physical segregation was observed.

Modern Journalistic Needs and Political Factors

Although women's opportunity is related to such legitimizing elements as their accessibility to educational training, their participation is also linked to the ideological functions literature has come to serve, as well as to the processes of modernization. Modernization processes in Saudi Arabia have required the mobilization of all social resources to fill the newly developed roles in different fields. As a pool of educated women, women writers provided a reserve army of workers able to occupy the newly created roles in the literary field.

The presence of women in the field of journalism has an additional advantage for the publishers of newspapers and magazines. It responds not only to modernizing needs but also to the journalistic necessities of publishing, since local newspapers rely heavily on advertisements for funding, and most advertised products are geared toward women and the household environment. These advertisements often are promoting the latest in Western consumer products, such as fashions, perfumes, watches, home appliances, and fast-food and take-home food items. The importance of women as consumers and as targets of Western as well as local business has had an impact on both the content and format of Arabian newspapers. Women's sections, usually seen by women readers as a sign of recognition for women, have become instrumental in attracting women readers to serve commercial purposes.

This marketing function that newspapers serve is stronger today than ever. But it is no longer served through women's sections alone but also through the general readership that individual women writers attract. It is difficult to assert with any degree of certainty whether women writers are read more by women or by men. But editors acknowledge that the readership many women writers attract, among men as well as women, establishes more loyalty to these writers than to the newspapers themselves. Because of difficulties in distribution, people tend to buy the most easily available local newspapers, and newspaper owners usually capitalize on the readers' loyalty to certain writers to guarantee the survival of their newspapers.

Although most women writers acknowledge more response from men than from women in the form of readers' mail, many indications point to the emergence of women as consumers of literature. One major indication is the growing literacy among women, but of no less importance are the pervasive changes related to life in the home. With the rising standard of living the tendency is to build more spacious homes. While this may require outside help in the home, often available from Southeast Asian female housekeepers, it also allows women more privacy for reading and writing. Not only are many women relieved from doing housekeeping chores but food is also increasingly prepared either outside the home or by domestic servants. Because new homes are dispersed in the suburbs, many women have less access to their kinswomen, and thus less time for socializing. In addition, because of persisting and sometimes increased restrictions on female mobility, including the restriction from driving cars, and severe limitations on forms of entertainment outside the home, reading has become a favored form of leisure activity for increasing numbers of middle- and upper-class women.[12]

Despite the increasing reliance of most major newspapers and magazines on their daily or weekly columns, women writers have also developed the reputation of discontinuity in their writing. Although men may exhibit as much discontinuity if not more, men often quip about women's constant need for periods of withdrawal to attend to family matters, such as marriage and childbirth. In addition to their work outside the home, family responsibilities have been acknowledged by many women writers to pose constraints on their production, both quantitatively and qualitatively.[13]

Women writers enjoy a higher visibility than men writers. Consequently, when male writers withdraw, their withdrawal is not subject to generalizations about their disappearance, as is the case for women writers. Men may withdraw for any period of time for what is viewed as "legitimate" reasons, such as their jobs or families, explaining that they have less time to attend to writing in comparison with women who spend more time at home. Men also point to the unfavorable economic compensation for writing, which is by no means sufficient to meet a male's traditional financial responsibilities for his family and kin. Within a financial structure in which the writer is often paid by the piece, it would seem that only those who are relieved from economic responsibilities, and presumably have more time, would be likely to engage in the profession (i.e., women, the wealthy, or both would be the best candidates). One is justified in surmising that without these two categories, writing in Saudi Arabia is almost bound to be a profession lacking practitioners, despite the number of middle-class men who are eager to accumulate the "capital" of prestige.

Historically at least, the first women who attempted to take up writing were those from upper-class families. Owning books has always been a status symbol in Arabia, and upper-class women enjoyed their family libraries. These women have also enjoyed a higher degree of mobility in terms of travel abroad, whether for family vacations, education, or fathers' business trips This meant that their access to book production centers in Beirut and Cairo was greater than for women from lower classes. Today most women writers belong to the middle-class but now, since the oil boom, they share these advantages formerly enjoyed only by the upper class. Many of these middle-class women writers also reveal that, early in their lives, they took advantage of traveling with their families or had a male family member bring home books from abroad (mostly from Egypt and Lebanon). Many writers state that it was through these books that they became acquainted with universal thinkers who wrote in Arabic or in foreign languages (whether in translation or in the original language), and that they owe the development of their interest in certain topics and issues to such books, whether written by men or women.

Family Influences

Despite the fact that the early training of women writers took place mainly in schools, family has exerted an important influence on their craft in the early as well as later stages of their lives. For the majority of the writers interviewed, both parents were Saudis. These women spoke with a sense of awe and pride of their families' encouragement and support of their writing. For some, the intellectual history of their families revealed that a father, uncle, grandfather, or mother had demonstrated religious knowledge or had experimented with oral poetry. Others, who were not able to trace intellectual elements, stated that books were, more or less, part of the environment in which they grew up.

Family support, or at least the lack of family opposition, was instrumental to these women. Since almost without exception they began their writing careers in the readers' mail sections, their work could not possibly have made it to the pages of a newspaper or magazine without the consent of at least one male in the family. Sending the material by mail, at least until recently when sending a fax from their homes or workplaces is an alternative, required a male who was willing to buy stationery and process the mailing. This alliance of women with their male family members, such as fathers, but to a greater extent brothers, has historically been an important part of Arab women's lives.

However, the continuity of family support cannot be taken for granted by the woman writer. As a woman, she has to abide by social rules. For example, the writers in this study who were not yet married all lived with their families, followed a socially acceptable life-style, and lived in accordance with social norms of veiling and sex segregation. Also, as public figures, they have had to maintain family support by recognizing certain constraints on their writings. Although some have used pseudonyms at the beginning (always female names), women writers normally use their real names in which their father's and family names appear in full (which remains the same even after marriage). As a result, they have a responsibility to that name. Although their writing may accord their families higher status, women writers are concerned about their family reputation and this may affect their writing style, choice of themes, or point of view.

Impropriety committed by a woman may raise suspicion or provoke an attack on her morality, the consequences of which the entire family would suffer. As a result, the earlier generations of women writers opted for safe topics, which meant if not an affirmation of the existing cultural values then an effort to avoid negating them. By the mid-1970s women's writings carried unsurpassed challenges to the existing institutions and centers of power. The responses to these challenges are more often than not rather harsh. The women who at one time or another were the subjects of attacks because of their dissenting views have all acknowledged with gratitude the great support they received from their families.

Literary Institution and Social Organization of Writing

While the structure of opportunity for women writers is governed by the special circumstances of being a woman in Arabian society, the amount of recognition a woman receives as a writer is very much related to the status and function of the literary institution itself. This means that these women, in addition to the factors previously discussed, share other general conditions with male writers.

The conditions shared are generally related to the political and ideological functions of contemporary literature. The written word has become an important means by which power centers in Arabian society disseminate their ideology and maintain their hegemony over historical reconstructions and orientation of change. The spread of literacy has naturally broken the monopoly of the elite over discourse, and created new demands by the literate for participation. The process of modernization itself has also created a climate of expectation regarding political participation by the excluded groups, whether men or women. Integrating these groups as "participants" has the function of maintaining an appearance of tolerance for views. Regardless of or because of their different ideological content, these views could be politically useful to those in control, if only by generating an atmosphere of debate and "free" expression and creating an illusion of collective will.

In fact, this political/ideological function is one of the hidden, yet instrumental functions of literature in Arabia. Literature plays a major role not only because it is perceived as a form of political expression but also as a forum for political participation. Although literary expression becomes a form of political participation only insofar as it affects decision making, because of a debating atmosphere, confusion of expression with political participation is so ingrained that it is seen by many as a form of democracy.

Problems of Contemporary Literature in Arabia

Women's status as writers and the literary value of their work is affected by factors that go beyond the political and ideological needs for their writings. Literary production is itself a matter of great complexity, in that it has social, cultural, religious, and political aspects. These are intimately linked to the historical development of literary priorities and taste, as well as the contemporary realities of readership, creativity, and censorship. These require some exploration because they constitute the institutional context within which literary production in general and literary enterprise of women writers in contemporary Arabia take place.

To begin with, contemporary literature in Arabia lacks recognition as an independent phenomenon and its cultural status is precarious, if only because it is situated between two powerful literary traditions, the oral or folk and the classical.[14] It is written not only in a distinct language that is neither colloquial nor sophisticated[15] but the folk and classical traditions are endowed with a special symbolic depth. Folk literature is highly valued for its simplicity, and the effectiveness of its maxims often stir nostalgic sentiments of a poor but pure "yesterday." Because of its tendency to transmit stories of the past through lyric poetry, folk literature formed a kind of popular history recorded by those who were not writing or producing books. Because it is considered to represent the real consciousness of the people and to be an indisputable "authentic" form of expression, folk poetry enjoys a growing recognition, increasingly manipulated by state apparatus to keep alive in popular memory a certain conception of cultural heritage. Whether by virtue of its being practiced by princes and prominent tribal personages, or by its growing tendency to be devoted to praising the royal family, it appears in print more regularly,[16] and the space allocated to it, in most newspapers and magazines, has been expanding.

Cultural and Religious Status of Classical Literature

Both the Arabic language and what is regarded as the "classic literature," especially in its poetic forms, originated in pre-Islamic Arabia. Pre-Islamic Arabia embodied a tradition of poetry that was highly developed linguistically, metrically, and artistically. This poetry, with its powerful language, vivid imagery, sophisticated meters, and perfect rhyme schemes, has set the standards of excellence for more than fifteen centuries. Literary prose used in the form of oratory was distinguished by a tendency toward brevity, which the Arabs valued as "the soul of eloquence." Aside from the Qur'an it was not until the eighth century that prose emerged as a distinctive literary genre.

The Qur'an, written in classical Arabic, is by far the most highly valued of all prose for Muslims. The Qur'an is not only seen to embody the ultimate literary elegance and grace but is also admired for its symbolic values.[17] The Qur'an is considered by Muslims to be miraculous, both in form and content. Its form is seen as a model of literary perfection. As a form of storytelling, the Qur'an contains magnificent narratives such as those of Joseph, Jesus, Mary, Moses, Solomon, and others. While rich in imagery, the Qur'an stands as the source of the highest authority for Arabic grammarians and lexicographers. The Qur'an presents the ideal and the ultimate in prosaic construction, and in addition becomes not only a religious testament but also "the finest achievement of the Arabic language, expressed in a distinctive genre of prose all its own."[18]

In addition to the fact that the study of the Qur'an has itself given rise to more vigorous attention being paid to the literary, lexical, and linguistic disciplines throughout the history of Islam, the Qur'an is also seen as equally miraculous in relation to its messages. Whether related to the physical and cultural nature of the human being or of the universe, Muslims believe that these messages are constantly affirmed by the findings of modern sciences.[19] Both form and content endow the Qur'an with an enduring emotional and intellectual power and explain its hold on the hearts and minds of Muslims even when Arabic is not their language.

Institutional Support for Classical Literature

Despite its high poetic quality, the Qur'an is by no means a form of poetry. To be sure the relationship of poetry to Islam was strained in the early days of Islam because its subject matter, which celebrated war, women, and wine, was unacceptable to the new religion. Moreover, Arabs have traditionally referred to poetic inspiration as satanic, which may make reciting poetry an inherently antireligious acitivity. However, the main source of Islam's strained attitude toward poetry is to be found in the age-old misinterpretation of one of the verses in the Qur'an. In the chapter entitled "The Poets," the Qur'an responds to the pagans who perceived the Qur'an as poetry. It makes a distinction between the Qur'an as "fact" and poetry as "fiction"; the fictional work of poetry is presented as work originating in the imagination of individuals, while the Qur'an assures its believers that it speaks of things that have happened or will happen, not necessarily as a prophecy of events but rather as a system of action/consequence from which patterns in historical development can be drawn and from which lessons, or *'ibra,* can be learned.

The Qur'an says, "And the poets, it is those straying in Evil, Who follow them: Seest thou not that they Wander distracted in every Valley? And that they say What they practise not?" (Qur'an 26:224). While this verse seems to be clearly scolding those who follow the poets and treat what they say as reality, religious interpreters tend to analyze the verse as a condemnation of poets themselves, if not of poetry itself. But the verse is clear on three points: first, that it is imperative for the works of the imagination not to be confused with reality; second, that these works exist autonomously and separately from existential experience; and third, that an individual's failure to distinguish between imagination and reality has serious consequences on the quality of the individual's faith in that it leads to enticement and disillusion. With these points in mind, it becomes clear that the verse, rather than condemning the creative process, in fact establishes its legitimacy and gives it emphasis.

The Qur'an's special status has had continuous impact on contemporary culture. It is taught in the mosques and by institutions in charge of teaching, such as government and private schools. The appreciation of classical literature is a skill that is learned in connection with religious teaching. Neither folk poetry nor the use of dialects in writing are permitted or recognized in school curricula (although for in-class instruction, local dialects are at times used orally). The classical Arabic language, literature, and religious studies form an important part of the curricula in all levels of education.[20] The students are trained in or at least made familiar with the classical sources, both Islamic and pre-Islamic.

It is through this training that the relevance of classical literature to contemporary writing is both kept alive and also made problematic. Classical literature, by virtue of its actual qualities and standards of excellence, as well as by being a symbol of identity, is used as a yardstick to evaluate contemporary literature. Classical literature is *the* tradition to which the students in all phases are exposed. It provides the intellectual and critical apparatus by which the student (whether a reader or a potential writer) is shaped. In the classic tradition, aesthetic perception is invoked by means of metaphors, allusions, and similies that form the backbone of that tradition.

Despite the existent hierarchy in which the classic form is considered a "higher" art in people's consciousness, historically the classic and folk forms of literature have remarkably coexisted. The two do not simply correspond to "good" versus "bad" art, but rather they seem to coexist as representing different levels of artistic excellence, intellectually as well as aesthetically.

Recently, ardent religious leaders who at times see folk literature as being "overemphasized" in the media now find this emphasis to be undermining or threatening to classical literature. These leaders argue that they are not so much against folk poetry as they are against the recognition it acquired through the studies of some literary scholars. In the debates on modernism, for example, the revival of folk poetry was considered to be part of a modernist conspiracy to undermine, if not destroy, the Arabic language as an important symbol of identity, and with it the means by which the Qur'an can be understood.[21]

Contemporary Literature: Journalism and the Question of Creativity

After World War II new literary forms and styles found their way to Arabia through the early groups of Arabian students in Egypt and Lebanon. Writers have experimented with these new models, which have been most adventurous in poetry. The new types of poetry, free in style and different in content, has modified the traditional structure of the old Arab ode or *qasidah*. Poets employed new poetic forms, different in rhythmical patterns, and created new images and symbols. This was deemed a violation of the conventional definition of poetry as "rhymed and metered speech," and a divergence from the aesthetic ideals of classic literature. Even more serious is the fact that the new forms, considered as Western influences, served as a constant reminder of the threat and thrust of the West on the Islamic and Arabic tradition. This has resulted in rendering everything "new" as Western, and everything "unfamiliar" as illegitimate innovation, or *bid'a*.[22] The ideal expectations in matters of taste and evaluation are not only formed in relation to the classical tradition but also the status of contemporary literature is further complicated by the institutionalization of journalism for disseminating ideas. Journalism, with its attendance to the tastes of wide audiences, caters to the newspapers' need for survival, both economically and politically. Writers are required not only to "communicate" certain ideas but also to "represent" them in a "literary" manner. This has given rise to what is often called "literary journalism" in which the writer can accommodate the requirements of journalism, with its tendency to immediacy and communicational priorities, within a creative literary work.[23] It is this blurring of the distinction between journalism and creative writing that constitutes one of the obstacles in according status to contemporary literature. Contemporary literature, because it clearly diverges in aesthetic matters at least from classic literature, is relegated to a marginal status or ignored as required reading in schools, and the few courses that are taught at one or two universities have yet to come to terms with a clear conception and definition of the field.[24]

Changing of Literary Priorities: Creativity and Realities of Censorship

The adoption of the press as a vehicle for disseminating ideas has probably been the primary contributor to the limitation of contemporary literature as an independent phenomenon. The push and pull created by the necessities of communication and the imperatives of representation lies at the heart of the dilemma of contemporary Arabian literature. The use of newspapers and magazines as vehicles of literary production may have led to increasing "de-literalization" and less utility for creative images, symbols, and metaphors in contemporary writings. Its reading public demands a "journalistic," straightforward, simple language. Although some writers enjoy the puzzlement their works may create, many others accommodate these demands and find that this not only strengthens their ties to their readers but also lessens the possibility of critics and readers misinterpreting their work. With journalistic demands, literary priorities have also changed. For example, for many centuries Arabic literature has functioned as a means of entertainment, which was reflected in language games such as maxims, ironies, satire, and allegory. While a good literary piece can still be judged ideally in terms of its originality and capacity to evoke aesthetic response by how skillfully the piece has been constructed, the reality of journalism places more value on approved subject matter, the appropriateness of the message, and the ideological purpose.

But one should also consider how censorship, whether as a reality or a threat, may in fact stimulate a higher degree of creativity. Within a context of a highly censored, highly ideological society, writers, whether men or women, are constantly conscious of the need to balance what is politically and culturally acceptable with what is intellectually possible. In reading Saudi writers, one must bear in mind that the creativity of most Saudi writers—males as well as females—lies in mastering the art of articulation. This is made possible only by inventing images and metaphors as communicative codes to combat both the reality and the threat of censorship.

On the other hand, this also carries the danger of hampering the originality of their craft. Under censorship from whatever source, literary creation becomes a highly conscious process that may lead to a serious deformity of their creative endeavors if only by depriving them of spontaneity. Surely topics have to be purposefully contemplated, and symbols and metaphors must be craftily designed to overcome constraints from different sources. In a word, creativity becomes translated into dexterity. The women writers who spoke of their creative processes, emphasized two phases of literary creation—one in which they attend only to literary and inspirational requirements, and another in which revisions take place. While revisions are a normal part of almost any literary process, in the case of these writers constraints seem to be so internalized that it is difficult to trace where and when the revision process starts or ends. But it remains true that whatever the nature of the unconscious revisions, those that are consciously made, more often than not, are made in response to sociocultural and political constraints rather than to aesthetic necessities (see chapter 5).

Changing Patterns of Production and Consumption of Literary Books

Despite its negative impact on the literary value of their works, the practice of publishing in daily newspapers or their literary supplements, and in the weekly, monthly, or seasonal magazines or periodicals, certainly gives writers greater access to readership. Saudi Arabian newspapers average a circulation of seventy-five thousand copies, with little competition from newspapers of other Arab countries. It is a common practice for writers, both men and women, to publish their works, whether in the form of poetry, short story, or commentary, first in newspapers and much later as collections in a book. Given the difficulties of book publication and distribution, especially for unknown writers, publishing in newspapers seems to be a practical solution, if not the only one available to reach as wide an audience as possible.

The problem of reaching a wide audience while at the same time maintaining the quality of their work involves a difficult compromise that most writers have to face. Although the general readership has increased, the reading public has become more diverse in terms of age, education, and background. This diversity makes it increasingly difficult for writers to cater to the tastes of different social categories (e.g., elite, students, women, traditionalists, modernists). One consequence is that writers have increasingly tended to write for a smaller but more devoted segment of readership in order to survive as serious writers.

But while one may write with a certain reader in mind, publishing in newspapers and magazines minimizes control over the type of readership, and this could have serious consequences. For example, the debate over modernism in literature, which was intensified by the mid-1980s, has started as a dialogue among literary men and women in which modern schools of thought were discussed and critiqued. Within the ensuing five years the newspapers were filled with editorials, commentaries (both literary and political), interviews, and reader's mail, in which the original dialogue was turned into a hot political and religious issue that was discussed on every level and by nonliterary institutions such as the mosques. During this time, antimodernism groups were formed that appealed to the sentiments of Islam and Arabism in ordinary people who came to the mosques to pray. The participants defined the issue for the public in their own terms, giving modernism and its derivatives strong pejorative connotations.

Of course the literary critics who introduced the concept of modernism in literature had in mind an audience more sophisticated than the average newspaper reader. The literary critics wrote articles about structuralism and deconstructionism in which the names of Barthes, Levi-Strauss, Derrida, and others, appeared along with their specific use of foreign terminology. The level of their arguments, as well as their use of foreign terms, probably contributed to the alienation of the average reader from those who came to be designated as modernists. The use of strange terminology by modernists was perceived by antimodernists as symbolic of a modernist Western orientation. The style of their arguments presented them as elitist groups who speak in codes. The traditionalists needed no more evidence than this to weave a theory of "the modernist conspiracy" and their "real" alliances to "foreign" forces.

The Writer: Conceptions and Models

These local debates over "modernism" are revealing of the nature of the constraints placed on writers, both men and women. But they also underlie a specific conception of the role that writers should play in their society. While writers are always disseminators of a culture if not its creators, in the Saudi society they are expected to be gatekeepers, advocates, protectors of the canons, and interpreters all at the same time. The purpose of writing, as defined by the centers of power, is to produce a perception of reality congruent with and guided by the ideas of these power centers.[25]

Saudi Arabian newspapers depend heavily on writers who hold other jobs rather than professional journalists who practice writing on a full-time basis. Generally, journalism itself is not highly professionalized. Despite the fact that newspapers and magazines are staffed with a number of routine writers who are usually recruited from communication departments in the universities, they have no professional journalists' association to represent them or to gain recognition for them. These recruited journalists have minimal input in establishing proper working conditions for themselves. As writers, they affiliate themselves with literary clubs. Ironically, because no ministry of cultural affairs exists, Arabian literary clubs are affiliated not with the ministry of information but rather—as clubs—with the Presidency of Youth, an administration in charge of sports.

Readership

Patterns of book production and readership are determined by these and other factors as well. According to the latest (1989) government figures, literacy rates are said to be 80 percent for males and 65 percent for females (13 percent of the total was accomplished through illiteracy reduction programs).[26] The criteria of literacy usually refer to the general ability to read and write. But the proportion of the literate population who actually read literary works, other than those works required in schools and universities, is contingent on the extent to which reading constitutes a social value. Historically, intellectual sophistication and knowledge have been culturally institutionalized as indicators of high social status in Arabia. In contemporary Arabia, this value manifests itself in the tendency of the middle-class to use reading and the acquisition of books as a means of acquiring social prestige.

But evidence also points to contrary trends in the contemporary society. Many writers, both male and female, have voiced extreme alarm at the negative effects of the spread of videotapes and sports on reading. Video stores are widespread, but whether videotapes are luring potential readers away from literature or whether it has created its own separate clientele is not clear. Writers have described these phenomena with great concern as the activities most competitive with book reading, and the general assumption is that viewers, in the absence of these attractions, would turn to reading. The hold that sports have on people— overwhelmingly on men and male children—is phenomenal. To appreciate the extent of its hold and the concern it generates among writers, it suffices to mention that literary activities, as a male writer once pointed out, have to be scheduled carefully so as not to conflict with the time of an actual soccer game or a game aired on television! Moreover, since literary clubs that organize literary activities are structurally auxiliary to the Youth Presidency, they receive far less support than sports—financial or otherwise.

But despite these effects on readership, one is justified in assuming that rising standards of education and rising rates of literacy have led to a general growth in the reading public. This growth is in addition to the emergence of women as consumers of literature. The indicators of growth in readership can be seen in the latest (1989) government figures regarding the increase in the number of institutions connected with book production. Printing houses reached a total of 716 institutions, and those in charge of publishing and distribution total 351. The number of periodicals totals ninety, ten of which are newspapers that are published daily (seven of these ten are in Arabic and three in English). Newspapers distribute between 50,000 and 150,000 copies daily in a population of more than fifteen million. Other newspapers publish weekly, monthly, or seasonally. The number of books published in 1988 reached 430. No data are available on whether all of these were published locally or on what percentage of these were written by women. This vast country has 2,006 bookstores and more than 5,000 booths (it is not clear if these figures include book sections in major supermarkets). Book selling appears to be a profitable business, as the sellers earn up to 40 percent of the book's price.

However, certain factors pose limitations on book consumption. These include the limited role of lending libraries; the high cost of publication and the difficulties of distribution due to the low density of the population in certain areas of the country; and the high price of books (paperbacks cost roughly between 10 and 25 SR; hardcover books between 35 and 100 SR [U.S. \$1 = 3.75 SR]). The actual number of people who read a book or periodical may of course exceed or be less than the number of copies sold. This readership can only be determined by examining patterns of borrowing, whether among people themselves or from libraries. Data that could aid in this enterprise or in the evaluation of the role of libraries in enhancing or restricting sales are hard to obtain. From my own observations of the types of books carried in the libraries, these do not seem to pose any threat to booksellers who sell recently published books, whereas lending libraries offer hard-to-find or out-of-print books.

General Libraries and Libraries for Women

Saudi Arabia has more than two hundred libraries, most of which are affiliated with schools, universities, and other state and religious

institutions. Women were not allowed to use the seventy public libraries except through the liaison of a male relative. College women students complained that not only do women have no public library but
their college libraries are extremely small and poorly equipped. With
such complaints one can understand why women—especially college
women—were jubilant to receive the news in March 1989 that women
had been granted permission to use King Abdul-Aziz's general library
in Riyadh two days a week. During these two days the library is staffed
by women who studied library science, and men are not allowed into
the facility. After the measure had taken effect, women interviewed by
the local newspapers expressed their gratitude to the heir to the throne
who had granted the permission. Calling it a "great gift," they reflected
on the difficulties they have faced in the past where they had either to
borrow from these libraries through their brothers, buy the books if they
were still in print, or borrow from the libraries of private individuals.[27]

That such a decision has to be made by the second-highest political
authority in the country is indicative of the revolutionary nature of the
measure. The idea of institutionalizing women's interests outside the
home naturally grants them greater mobility, and as a result has consistently been resisted by Arabian religious leaders. Education, work, and
lately women's "clubs" have faced great opposition. Political decisions,
especially in the form of royal decrees, have always been the decisive
factor, especially in matters related to women.

Forms of Support for Writers

Despite the growth of the reading public, which should naturally bring
to writing a degree of professionalization, writing in Saudi Arabia is
economically unrewarding. The structure of support for writers does not
provide the necessary monetary rewards that would enable them to
devote all their time to literary activities, which means that writers,
whether male or female, have other careers. Historically, writing has
been an avocation of, or under the patronage of, the independently
wealthy. Literary organizations provide some support but are limited to
rewards given for past contributions, such as the State's Appreciative
Reward for local writers or the King Faisal Universal Reward for which
local as well as foreign figures may qualify. These rewards have yet to
be won by a woman.

Writers not only lack financial support but also face other difficulties.

According to one writer, local printing costs are 150 percent higher than similar costs outside the country. As a result, the price of a Saudi book is too high to compete with imported books in the local market, not to mention abroad. The Ministry of Information, in an attempt to encourage local printing houses, has made it difficult for writers to publish abroad. And despite their large number, local printing houses seldom compete, for they are usually kept busy or overloaded by government publications and commercial orders. Moreover, the government has canceled all subsidies to books that come through subscriptions.[28]

Publishing Houses

Publishing houses also complain of the unprofitability of publishing separately from distribution. Selling books by mail is not a developed business idea for a variety of reasons, one of which is the high cost. Also, there are no book clubs to facilitate advance subscriptions. Publishers more often than not follow the contours of the market. In their assessment, Islamic books are the ones in most demand, followed by literature and history.[29] Universities constitute a part of this market, but they themselves have turned to publishing graduate dissertations and books of an academic nature.

These factors constrain the relationship between publishers and authors and make it less than a natural alliance. Writers may be given a percentage from each copy sold, usually about 20 percent, or the publisher may offer to buy the rights of publication from the writer for a few thousand SR. The number of copies printed rarely exceeds ten thousand.[30] Before 1980 publication centers were concentrated in Makkah, Jeddah, and Al-Madina. A shift has occurred in the last ten years toward Al-Riyadh where over 50 percent of all books are now published.[31] Writers must be in close proximity to publishers, booksellers, and printing houses in order for their books to be published and properly distributed.

Reviews

Reviews do not seem to be a major influence on the marketing of books. Despite the relatively large number of books published, no recognizable institutions exist to establish standards for evaluation. The concept of "best-selling books" is foreign to the culture, but a list of "latest publications" has recently appeared in some major newspapers and magazines. Also, *The World of Books* is a periodical devoted to reviews as well as to bibliographic tasks.

In general, reviewing is subordinate to social and ideological factors. Unless a publication is ideologically provocative, critics will tend to refrain from harsh criticism because of the complex and dense social networks in which writers and critics are involved. Social and ideological considerations form circles of control over the substance of reviewing, which may include regional or literary, religious, and political affiliations.

Realities and the Threat of State Censorship

Above all there is the haunting question of censorship. The growing rates of literacy and the breaking up of the elite's monopoly on reading are a challenge to the state's control over the spread of ideas among the masses. In fact, it is not a farfetched notion for writers to claim that the difficulty in getting books published is in itself a form of censorship. The high cost of printing, high prices of books, their unavailability, and the restrictive statutes or procedures by which permission to print or distribute a book is granted may all be considered forms of censorship.

But formal censorship includes religious and political stipulations. The former covers any perceived attacks on Islam or violation of Wahhabi moral standards. The latter pertains to any criticism, direct or implicit, on Saudi Arabia or on the House of Saud. In practice, the state's censorship of publications is made no less real by being more effective on the level of threat than reality. Means of control are not concentrated in an official censor from whom approval must be sought. Rather, the state holds the power of licensing all publishing institutions, including those of production, marketing, and selling. The Ministry of Information reserves the right to revoke licenses at any perceived violation of the guidelines.

As a result of the state's control over licensing, publishers as well as editors of newspapers and magazines become the real agents of censorship. What can and cannot be printed is left to their judgment. The perceived degree of their loyalty to the royal family, whether negative or positive, affects the extent to which they experiment with limitation. That publishers and editors carry the state's stick has relieved the state from being the subject of attacks, often voiced especially by women who blame "timid" editors for "strangling their words" (as writer Juhayer Al-Musa'ed once commented). Publishers thus serve as buffers for writers, both male and female, with the result that official proclamations for censorship are rarely enforced. Because writers and editors share responsibility for the survival of the publication, self-censorship has become the most widely practiced form of censorship. This latter form requires a high degree of awareness, not only of political consequences but also of religious and sociocultural constraints.

Censorship, both religious and political, casts a wide net of apprehension among writers. Once a book is declared "censored," for whatever reason, the writer is fortunate if persecution does not follow. It is unheard of for the writer to file a lawsuit against the state. Some writers choose, for economic or other reasons, to publish abroad; in these cases, obtaining permission for marketing the publication locally may prove to be the real challenge.

Women writers share all these difficulties of publication with men, in addition to those difficulties specific to them as women. Because the process of publication depends on the writer's initiative and ability to closely follow up and monitor the processes of printing and marketing, women by definition are at a major disadvantage. Because of the restrictions on their mobility and on dealing with men outside the family, their contribution to the publication process of their books is severely limited. Women not only have no input in the design or advertisement of their books but their books also suffer from chronic typographical errors, irrelevant drawings, and other major deformities (such as book size and illustration design). As a result, some women writers have resorted to publishing either at their own expense or abroad in Beirut, Kuwait, or Cairo in order to secure effective participation. Locally, however, because of increasing awareness of the production process, women writers attempt to exert more control over cover design and drawings. (In one case a writer's sister who was an artist designed the book cover, and in another the writers communicated their ideas directly to the artist chosen by the publishing house.)

Women writers acknowledge that they cannot possibly monitor the distribution of their books. Judging from my observation of the local scene, their books are embarrassingly inaccessible in Saudi Arabian bookstores. If carried in a bookstore or a booth, women's books are usually not displayed properly or are hidden in a remote corner of the store (unless the store is owned by the publisher of the book). In one of the major supermarkets in Jeddah, for example, an impressively large section attractively displayed hundreds of books and magazines on a variety of subjects and from all over the world. While there were more than fifteen titles for Agatha Christie alone, there was not a single book by a Saudi woman writer in that particular store.

History of the Present and the Presence of History: Traffic in Symbols, Knowledge, and Experience

What a happy (and lucky) nation that
allows for women to write its history.
—Hamad Al-Jasser, Arabian historian of the peninsula

This chapter will focus on representing and analyzing the writings of three women writers: Fowziyya Abu-Khalid, who is known mainly as a poet; Ruqayya Ash-Shabib, known as a short-story writer; and Rajaa 'Alim, who wrote short stories but pioneered in play writing. In reading the works of these three women writers, one must keep in mind that—regardless of the form in which they specialize—they are all involved in other forms of writing, especially the essay. In fact, often their literary products mix, in the same piece, the argument of an essay, the figurative language of poetry, and at times the plot of a story. The mixing of these modes is seen not as a confusion of forms but rather as culturally valued forms of literary creation. While the writers sometimes choose to express their thoughts symbolically, this is mainly because it is an effective way of dealing with the interplay of the said and unsaid and as a response to cultural, political, and literary realities of concealment and revelation.

Despite the diversity of their adopted genre, these three writers are grouped together as a result of their shared use of modes of expression, which include historical allusions as well as symbolic and allegorical representations of women's experience both in the past and the present. Their frequent use of historical symbols becomes almost a shared code that brings these three writers into a special relationship with one another—a relationship in which they develop, more or less consciously, a vocabulary that defines women's experience—both currently and historically. While they attempt to establish women's experience as a reality, they also use it as a metaphor or an allegory of human suffering and the struggle for a dignified existence. In doing both, they demonstrate a convergence of the personal and the political as they universalize an experience that is not only "womanly" but also personal.

In the works of these three women writers, the deep consciousness of the hegemonic forces of time and space appear in the form of a constant appeal to the past and to its heroes and heroines. Their acute awareness of the ideological function of control that history performs in their society is reflected in their intense engagement not only in reinterpreting and redefining past history but also in writing the current history of women and society. In the material selected, I explore the nature of the reading these women provide of their cultural and civilizational history, and how they use a number of key symbols as a means of remembering, recounting, and learning from that history. In their writings, they advance a cultural critique in which to examine the dialectics of power and knowledge in which relationship both of governor and governed, and of men and women, are embedded. In their use of historical symbols, which are invested with either religious, cultural, or political meaning, and which suggest strategies for action for women, they carve out a discourse of empowerment for themselves as women, and as writers.

Fowziyya Abu-Khalid: Selections from Her Writings

A Heritage and a Heritage[1]

It is not possible for me, nor can I . . . . . place a wager on the participants in the Janadiriyya Heritage Festival. But the yearly stir that the event creates in the stagnation of the year does not reach half of us except through the complexities of the technology.[2] It throws a stone in the heart, these are some of its waverings between a timid bore and a restive desire for dare.

Heritage is not a hearth made of mud, its fire turned to ashes in a gas burner. Heritage is not *dalla* or *mat'ouba* or *es'hala* or *mehmass* or a *zinbeel* with broken handles.[3] Heritage is not a Nabti poem or a Nejdi dance or some other southern dance. Heritage is not houses made of hay and mud or *okt* [cheese snacks] made of the racing camels' milk.

Heritage is the traces the trembling girls leave on the chunks of okt; it is the travail of lads who mix hay and mud with sweat and *sad danas* [melodies]. It is the darkly painted eyes (with *kuhl*) that weave. It is the roughness of the hand that creates . . . It is the relation of the spine to the ploughing of land.

Turath (heritage) is the people in their joy and sorrow, defeat and victory, in their dreams that take refuge in the future. Simplifying heritage by converting it to its elementary substance, in which life manifests itself in the daily struggle for continuity and growth, is one of the means of communicating with our heritage. This is the means by which we create a movement of social change that is not alienated from the present discourse of social history. The grieving tones about heritage, or tones of denial or superiority toward it, are products of periods of protrusion in which the general orientation of the society is not related to its heritage, and this heritage is not integrated into the present so as to constitute an element that may inspire the future. But integrating heritage into the present and being inspired by it, as all things we seek, seem easy but are not attainable. They cannot be reached by wishing or speaking . . . They have to be taken forcibly.

To revive the heritage and to establish continuity with it, there must be definite and clear conditions that bring this demand closer to realization on the levels of the general conduct of people. Without this, no revival of heritage can be accomplished. Public participation is the core of the social process in its two dimensions, the past and the future. Among those conditions, in my humble judgment:

- We have to locate where heritage stands in our present and future, in an objective way that is not subordinated to the long, taxing periods of defeat or to the joy of short-lived victories—whether vis-à-vis "the other" or vis-à-vis "the self." Here I would like to point to a rich heritage with which we have to be in touch. It is our relationship with "us" and with "the other," as revealed in our Arab-Islamic tradition.

- We have to examine and define the meaning of the revival of heritage, which can by no means refer to having the past occupy the present.

This cannot be accomplished by resorting to a lazy consumer-like attitude or closed-mindedness toward what our grandfathers produced.

• The circle of heritage has to be extended horizontally and vertically; that is, it has to be widened on the level of history as well as on the level of geography.

The heritage of human civilizations in general, and the Arab-Islamic civilization in particular, would not have enjoyed such appeal and richness if they had not originated in the depths of the societies' historic roots. They would not have survived if they had included only a short period of more recent history or if they had not extended far beyond an encompassing identity and rebelled against limited provincialism.

Emerging from a Childbirth Fever[4]

Tonight Shabbat[5]
brings you all to me
one . . . by one
brings you to me
dream . . . by dream
brings you to me . . . camp by camp
brings you to me
a flame in a contraction a contraction in a flame
it brings you to me
praise be to God, who has deposited all these
people in prisons!

Tonight . . . tonight my beloved
is the night of labor
tonight . . . tonight my beloved
you come together in sweat
you follow one another in a perilous fear
tonight my beloved
from the childbirth fever
you emerge
tonight . . . tonight my beloved
is the night of labor
tonight my beloved

is the mother of beginning
and the mother of the end
let this beat hasten

Tonight,
tonight, the Maḍloum neighborhood[6]
in the face of darkness rises
tonight,
the masses toward the Gulf are thrusting
tonight, Oh mother . . . do not cry
you need not braid my hair
you need not cook stones
these stones are now well cooked
tonight . . .
one neighbor calls her other neighbor
tonight . . . the impossible dream
begins only with stones
only when one nieghborhood
is thrust toward the other
the wild pain
is drumming in my flank
this is the night of labor
tonight . . . the labor of birth, in me, begins
and begins the birth of this land

Tonight,
I won't permit
the hunter
the swordsman
the treacherous
the sneaker between this house
and that house
I won't let him
abort my labor
or take one span of this land out of its borders
for his own debauchery
tonight,
who can stand in the face of the poor
as my labor has begun?
tonight, who can stand between the poor
and the bread?
this is Ṭofoul[7]

tonight,
casts the fruits of the passionate love

An Unannounced Trial of an Overt Act of Love[8]

My memory is hazy
like the lenses of your spectacles
in the investigation room
like the eyes of workers
in Dhahran or Ebgiag[9]
like a falcon
whose wings are clipped
and cannot fly
while it is free
forgive me for the wild digging

In your body
in my body
in our lovemaking I tasted
the many types of humiliation and torture that women of oppression in
    my country encounter
part of our civilization
part of our culture
part of our defeats
the Arab is born predisposed to suffering
the bottles of waves from the time of the flood
were clamoring in my breasts
this is part of the flirtations with thunder
with the bubbling of foam
who blames the dagger
when the space of walls
and scabbards
enclose it
when longing remembers
the taste of tear . . . squeeze . . . the taste of life
between womb and bone when it is threatened by siege

I remember how we met
we met in anger
we met in the conflagration of apples, anise, and grapes
as it burst into flame we met

in the year of Zahter [10]
we met
through your pride I knew the special subtlety
anger and defeated people as they change their destiny and defect
and the earth opens up

At the war zone
I was cast away
by volcano and earthquake
I came to you as a nomad
sharpening arrows
a slave I go
the color of your eyes is dark
like the face of my father on that June evening [11]
like the color of innocence in the face of a child when a veil struck it
    that same year
the edge of an axe bursting with desire for the distant land
I swore by the color of fire
by the distance of the way
and by all the carob and chestnut fields
I shall never be fecund
but from that
whose salt of longing
annihilates me on his lips
we entered the debate of love
as a grenade penetrates
the woods of jasmine
sulfur spread in a clay oven
Oh my friend, oh my country a toast to the sad happiness
you were like tenderness
and its antagonist
you were like childhood
and its antagonist
you were like love and its antagonist
and I was like sea
        time
        delirium
and I was like all their antagonists

You were the country
to become one front
against the plundering of crops
against the stopping of the struggle

and against hesitation
and I began to love in you
the resisting of Makkah
and the goodness of Yathrib [12]
and how the lips that
guided each other softened between the darkness of the womb
and a day; its sun
setting in the forenoon

At the beginning it was labor
we said, in the beginning labor comes and the last tasks
are platonic love
and legitimate marriage
and the couples' quarrel
about the seasons of harvest,
and making love
and months of pregnancy
we said, in the beginning to discern
the camel rider
and he who stole the load
and those who were contented with the feast
we said in the beginning
we vaccinate children for
dependency, indifference, and paralysis
we said and we said . . . and we said
and all that we said about the slaughtering of Arabs
    does not exceed eulogy
        and satire
        or love poetry

A dream never betrayed us
but the interpretation
a star never betrayed us
but physiognomy
I would draw your love
in every sword drawn in my face I came to draw your abandonment
in the face of June
that comes in my childhood
and returns in my daughter's childhood
where to my beloved
       my family
       my tattoo date
where do the years of exile

take us
how long 'til the oil's fire
seizes us
oh, my beloved nothing remains
from the children's good
and all components of capital
but a man and a woman
a woman and a man
and a simple choice
as the Palestinian choice
in the trap of the borders
either death
or love

With great . . . great brevity
as a moment of silence upon martyr
in a certain victory's dawn
Now I recall the act of love from the details of the map
a woman and two lovers
a woman and two bonds
a woman loves
a man
carries the history of Al-Hassan
and carries the wrinkles of Al-Hussain [13]
a woman they told her
you are from a curved rib
in the country's fence she saw
her pelvis
beloved, they said
mortal, they said
wanted
cursed
saint
devil
approachable
exiled
they said and said and said
they said in a night
she bears seven times
I am prepared
for stoning and splitting
I am a country in a woman
and an organized love haunts a country

Secret Diaries for Children[14]

These words are from the diaries
of Gamilah Buhayred and Laila Khalid
in the days of my country's children
now it is the role of woman to abolish the role of her breast . . .
the tiny lips starve . . .
the earth is breast, lactating blood
oil
into pledged bottles

A Personal Profile and Personal Encounter

Fowziyya Abu-Khalid is one of the most well-known Saudi Arabian women writers, both on the local and the international level. Her poetry is known not only in some of the other Arab countries, such as Lebanon and Kuwait, but also to Western readers. Fowziyya's poetry was selected for translation into English in at least two anthologies—Boullata's (1978) and Jayyusi's (1988). Fowziyya was born in Riyadh in 1955 and was raised there by Nejdi parents. She received most of her education in her native country before she left in 1974 to attend the American University in Bierut, where she obtained her B.A. in sociology in 1978. Later, Fowziyya pursued higher education in the United States, where she obtained an M.A. degree. After returning to her own country she held a teaching position at the Women's College of King Saud University in Riyadh.

Fowziyya's first collection of poems, *Until When They Will Abduct You on Your Wedding Night,* was published in 1973 when she was eighteen years old. Her second collection, *Secret Reading in the History of Arab Silence,* was published in 1985. In both these works she adopts a free meter structure, generally characteristic of modern Arab poetry. Both collections were published in Beirut, a significant indication of the challenging nature of her work (both in form as well as content), and a reminder of the constraints imposed on literary production in her homeland. Although Fowziyya's first collection dealt mainly with the theme of the relationship of men and women, it was not devoid of political implications. Her later work, however, published in the post-1967 war period, was dominated by political themes, as demonstrated by the poems translated here.

"The best of my poems were those I wrote between 1973 and 1981.

I have not published them all, but a day will come when they will see the light of day" (Saleh 1983). Fowziyya began publishing some of her writings in the late 1960s with articles that appeared in *'Ukaz* while she was still in preparatory school. By the early 1970s she had her own column—"Drops in the Neck of the Bottle." In addition to *'Ukaz,* she also wrote a weekly section for *Iqra* called "Drops in the River of My Country," and another column in *An-Nahdha* called "Small Love Letters." Because of its ultra-conservative bent during the early years, *Al-Yamama* magazine was not receptive to her work in the beginning but later opened its doors to modernist writers in general, who had gained more influence by the mid-1970s.

In Riyadh, through the concerted efforts of a wide network of friends and acquaintances, I was able to gain access to most of the women writers on my list except Fowziyya. My interview schedule was busy, as many of the writers I wished to interview were returning from their *Eid* vacation (the feast at the end of the fasting month of Ramadhān). During that time I made every effort to gain access to Fowziyya's phone number, even resorting to the Riyadh telephone book. There I was faced with pages and pages of last and middle names identical to hers. None of the writers I had met were acquainted with her; they only knew that she worked at the university section in Dar'iyya. Finally, after a complex process of inquiry, I made arrangements to meet with Fowziyya in her home in Riyadh.

Although most if not all other writers interviewed were generally curious about me and my work, Fowziyya took me by surprise by her insistence to "know" me before she could trust or talk to me. The situation was quite a contrast to the long-held image of the anthropologist dominating the field of inquiry by executing the role of the interviewer. But because I had already decided to accord all the other writers the right to ask me questions about myself and my work, and had found it to be an excellent opening for them to talk about themselves, she was no different in this respect.

I totally understood Fowziyya's reasons for precaution. At the time of the interview, she had already lost her teaching job at the Women's College and was placed under vigilance. She was especially concerned about an intellectual atmosphere that would allow an unknown writer to publish a book in which he mounted a personal attack not only against her but against other men and women writers whom he dubbed modernists. This writer and other traditionalists were accumulating evidence against her, taking statements or lines of poetry out of context, and freely casting moral judgments against her as a person and as a teacher. In such an atmosphere of persecution, guarding against misquotations and misrepresentation was only natural.

Fowziyya's concerns, which she spoke about and that resonate in her writings, include the meaning of national identity; the relationship between Saudi Arabia and other Arab countries; the relationship between men and women; dialectics of the past, the present, and the future; one's relationship to one's heritage; and the relationship of the Muslim world to the West. On the literary level, however, she is especially concerned about the issue of form and content, and the relationship of literature to religion. The pieces chosen here for translation faithfully portray these concerns and shed light on her style as well. Although she is mainly known as a poet, her contributions in prose, especially her articles, equal or even exceed in quantity her contributions to poetry. In this selection I felt it was appropriate to include samples of both. According to Fowziyya, while "the content has to be committed to our concerns, disturbances, and aspirations, the form, by the same token, also has to be committed. The writer has to feel no less of a commitment to create new language, and in fact should experiment with 'exploding' into new forms." Form and content, according to Fowziyya, should be brought into unity. The language, as a form of communication and as an expression of historical development, has to be simple, moving, and dialectical. It should be inseparable from people's awareness of daily issues and issues of their existence.

This emphasis on the unity of form and content, of simplifying form so it will bear on people, is related to Fowziyya's belief that the right of discussion and of participation in discourse should be accorded to everybody. Unlike Rajaa 'Alim, Fowziyya's bid for change does not depend on the intellectuals but rather on the masses. Her great faith in ordinary people's ability to understand and to take charge of a situation leads her to conceive of those intellectuals who are not committed to the masses, in action as well as in theory, to be implicit accomplices to the centers of power—if not by being silent then by alienating the masses. Unless the intellectuals prove this commitment, they do in fact form their own interest groups. Without this proof of commitment, their representation of the masses would remain just a claim.

Fowziyya's commitment to the masses and their history is obvious. Her poetry is filled with cultural, historical, and religious allusions and metaphors. She speaks of the martyrdom of Al Hussain, and recalls the history of Al-Hassan, of "a nomad" who is "sharpening arrows," of veil, of tribe, of sword, of war and defeat, and other motifs in the experience of the Arab people. But Fowziyya's use of language is also daring if only because she uses a vocabulary that many see as immodest, especially for a woman. She speaks of "lovemaking," of "woman's body," of "labor," of "breasts," and of "nipples," as well as other topics considered to be within the domain of the very private and very personal, and/or unacceptable for a woman to tackle. Turning these topics into a public issue shocked the sensibilities of many, even the more modernized elements in the society. It was probably such suggestive vocabulary that placed Fowziyya under constant attack, which amounted to moral judgments to her person, from the conservative elements: "If Fowziyya has taken off the clothes of modesty [referring to her uncovering her hair outside of Saudi Arabia], stood on podiums with men, sat among them with no protective veil, she should be in a hurry to take off her heritage too." This conservative voice incites action against her since "she is a lecturer to our daughters in one of the universities." [15]

This incitement to discipline Fowziyya has succeeded in creating an atmosphere of hostility toward her that led to her being deprived of her teaching job.

Textual Analysis

Remembering History and Recounting It

The question of history, as written, interpreted, and recalled, lies at the heart of Fowziyya's works in its poetic and prosaic forms. In the article "A Heritage and a Heritage," Fowziyya examines the notion and scope of heritage, and points to the silences and exclusions embedded in the formal representations of history in the annual spectacle of the Janadiriyya, held in a town by that name near her home town of Riyadh. Reading Janadiriyya as a text, she examines the manner in which this one institutionalized form of celebration of historical significance, interprets and defines the scope of history, of who and what is to be remembered. She observes that in Janadiriyya, objects of the material culture, such as hearths, coffee tools, okt snacks, baskets, and mud houses seem to constitute the pith and bone of the definition of history. To her astonishment, the human experiences of those men and women, young and old, who worked and made it possible, the personal history that lay behind the "trembling girls" who made okt, and the "travail of lads" who mixed clay with their sweat, was not only absent but was made irrelevant if not completely obliterated.

Heritage, according to Fowziyya, must be "converted to its elementary substances"—that is, converted to the people in their daily struggles and experiences of joys, sorrows, dreams, defeats, and victories. Any representation of history that neglects these elements alienates people from their own social history and its depths of experience. This alienation is compounded by the fact that the definition of history itself is restricted vertically in time and horizontally in space. This restriction demonstrates itself in the selection of certain periods that are confined to a limited region. The notion of heritage, Fowziyya maintains, should be extended to reflect the dimensions of the Arab-Islamic civilization, as well as those of human civilization. Heritage also must include the "history of the present" in the Arab world, which the current definers of historical significance tend to neglect or purposely overlook. Fowziyya rejects responses to the past, which so far have taken the form of grieving about it, denying it, or feeling superior to it. She speaks of how the past can and should inspire the present, and she expresses the necessity of establishing continuity with it. But this continuity does not mean that the past should "occupy" the present. Moreover, public participation in the defining of heritage should be secured. By establishing the right of the masses to participate in that definition, she challenges the view of history as the elite's prerogative. For her, self-identity—whether defined intraculturally or interculturally—will remain severely underdeveloped unless the masses seize the right to define their own history.

The full implications of Fowziyya's critique must be understood against a background of pervasive control over time and space exercised by larger discourses of power. Her article is a challenging response to the historical amnesia that characterizes the two types of representations of history advanced by state apparatus and the religious 'ulama. The state defines *heritage* as extending mainly to the establishment of the Saudi state less than seventy years ago. This period in history is carved out by the state and crystallized through the concept of "national heritage," around which people are mobilized. The religious leaders, on the other hand, carve out the first half-century of Islam as *the* locus of historical significance. These definitions are represented as authoritative and credible and are carried in the formal school curricula, such as in the history texts and in historical research institutions. They also include all the ways in which the past is constructed daily; that is, through archives, museums, brochures, guides, official histories, literature on royal personages, and such spectacles as the annual festivities of National Day and the Janadiriyya festival.

Mahrajan Al-Janadiriyya, an annual festival sponsored by the National Guard, places historical significance on the heritage of pre-oil Arabia, focusing on the spatial demarcation of the current state. This tendency is evident not only in the events promoted by the state, such as exhibitions inside the country and abroad, but is also reflected in the writings of state loyalists or functionaries. These speak of the difference—especially in material culture—between "today and yesterday" (e.g., affluence versus poverty; health facilities versus disease and lack of care; advanced technology versus "primitive" technology), providing examples of the contrasting themes of the past (pre-state, pre-oil Arabia) and the contemporary.[16] The religious leaders do not seem to have qualms about the state's definition of space, as related to the representation of the past, and even participate in it. However, their ways of recording history, of remembering it, and of using it are fundamentally different from those of the state. While the state idealizes the present condition of prosperity and emphasizes the notion of "progress" in comparison with "yesterday," the Salafiyya ideology of the Wahhabis advances a conception of the past that is based on a high degree of idealization of the first half century of Islam. The idealization of that period has led to a tendency to perceive everything and everyone in the past as sacred. The men—but especially the women who belonged to that "golden era"—are presented as if they were a different species— a species with whom contemporary women can find no affinity, having made important contributions in Islam's formative years. As a result they are presented not as models for action but rather as magnificent portraits that glorify the halls of the museum of the "golden past."

By invoking women of more recent history as living models of action, and women from Arab lands other than Arabia, Fowziyya lives up to her own definition of heritage. She alludes to the diaries and biographies of Gamilah Buhayred, the heroine of the Algerian resistance against French colonialism, and Laila Khalid, the Palestinian who was jailed for years in resistance to the Israeli occupation of her land. Both women were jailed and tortured for extended periods, and lived to tell their stories of resistance.

Fowziyya's endeavor is no doubt an attempt to fill gaps in the presentation of history that have been made by the exclusion of certain periods of history, of other Arab lands, and of women, but it is also a challenge to the centers of power in another respect. Her choice to use these women as symbols has further implications. In highlighting their personal histories while both are still living, she breaks the usual dependence on formal historical accounts as well as the monopoly on writing history. By registering these women's contributions to history, Fowziyya seizes control of the writing of history, which so far has been the province of the centers of power.

Affinity of the Personal and the Political: Woman in Country, Country in Woman

Fowziyya's poems also reflect concerns that are completely diverse from the formal state history and its narrow definition of consequential localities and historical events. The events and experiences of people that are "absent" in the prevalent representations of history are for her ever present. Women not only become historical personalities but women's experience becomes the means through which to forge the link between the personal and the political in a manner that obliterates any demarcation between the public and the private. In her poem *Emerging from a Childbirth Fever*, in the midst of the wild pain of labor she recalls the Palestinians "one by one" and "camp by camp." In this poem, along with *An Unnounced Trial*, she moves along a triangle comprised of a woman, a man, and a country (Palestine). The three sides identify with one another—in the pain of birth and labor, in their anger, and in their struggle for justice. The result is that the country's experience resembles the experience of women; what women experience is no different than what men experience.

Fowziyya speaks of the "labor" of men to redeem their history as she speaks of the labor of childbirth. She speaks of the nation's birth as of the birth of her child. In so doing, Fowziyya speaks of birth not only as a feminine experience but also as her own personal experience with the birth of her first child, Tofoul. Her child's actual birth gives her message insurmountable symbolic import. First, to those who cannot see the light at the end of the tunnel, her own child's birth heightens the reality of birth after the period of darkness in the womb. The joy of birth paints optimism for the oppressed. Once labor begins, no one can "stop the poor from seizing their bread." The birth of this child is not only the "fruit of passionate love" but also of legitimate love, of labor, sweat, fear, fever, and wild pain.

Meeting in Labor and Birth

Fowziyya's personal experience with birth enables her as a mother to understand the suffering of the Palestinian mothers. In her newly developed sense of motherhood, she sees them, the Palestinians, "one by one / dream by dream / camp by camp." The experience of childbirth in all its details stands in allegorical relationship to the birth of their nation. It takes labor to give birth to a child, as it takes labor to give birth to freedom. "In the beginning labor comes." The contractions, the burning pain, the fever, the darkness of the womb, and the darkness of the prisons are only some of the commonalities. The possibility of birth brings fear to forces that want to abort her labor. These are the "hunter," the "swordsman," the "treacherous," the "debaucherous."

The occurrence of a fever is always possible in birth. Fever usually brings mental confusion, a clouded consciousness that comes in the form of hallucination. The confusion is born out of the ambiguous nature of birth itself. For birth "is a beginning and an end." Birth, like love itself, brings a contradictory feeling of "sad happiness," it is a state of "delirium." But these "delirious" feelings become for Fowziyya not a form of hallucination but rather visions. In her "feverish" talk, she provides one of the most remarkably fulfilled prophecies. Her cry that "the impossible dream begins only with stones" was to be realized by the Intifada of the Palestinian children on December 8, 1988. The Palestinian children, who were spared imprisonment or indiscriminatory bullets, were to abandon their childhood and make an early leap into the world of adulthood. Fowziyya here recalls a folk tale about a poor woman who pacified her hungry children with stones boiling in a pot until the children fell asleep, thinking that their dinner would be ready at any moment. Although those stones kept their hope alive, it was only a matter of time before the children would realize that these were false hopes, that they were only a means of pacification. It was this realization that led the Palestinian children to discover that they were destined to extermination if they believed the lie. They, in fact, found in stones not only a symbolic device but also a real tool by which they could awaken a world that they believed had turned its back on their plight for half a century.

Fowziyya sees the Palestinian people's loss of their land and the assault on their history as the ultimate tragedy in all human history. But the Arab defeat of June 1967 seems to constitute a decisive point in Fowziyya's life, penetrating so deeply into her consciousness that it becomes a part of her personal experiences with love, birth, and labor. Love has been formed in its midst: "The color of your eyes is dark / like the face of my father on that June evening." June is not only an event but also a symbol of defeat that is doubly painful for Fowziyya because it could happen again: it "comes in my childhood / and returns in my daughter's childhood." The poet makes the point that the conditions that gave rise to June still exist and continue to incite similar events. For defeat is embedded in a situation of alienation from history, in "the years of exile," both from time and space. Thus an historical event, such as the June war of 1967, constitutes for Fowziyya only a phase in the continuous "slaughtering of the Arabs," which extended beyond 1967 and beyond Palestine where massacres in the Palestinian camps, especially in tel Zahtar, continue to the present.

Meeting in Anger

It is this "slaughtering of the Arabs" that makes Fowziyya angry. She is haunted by questions: Why is "the Arab born disposed to suffering"? Why is the Arab human being "exiled" even in his own land, not only deprived of his own wealth but also burned by it. The Arabs cook stones and fight by stones, but the world for some reason thinks of them not only as being rich but also connected with aggression and terror. Fowziyya finds in anger the least means by which a human being in the twentieth century can assert a degree of consciousness of shared humanity with the Palestinians. Anger at this unsurpassed human tragedy becomes the condition even of her personal relationship with a man: "We met in anger / we met in the conflagration of apples, anise, and grapes as they burst into flame."

It is in anger that all men and women can meet to "change their destiny." The boundaries and distinctions between men and women disappear once they unite in anger for their shared experience of humiliation, torture, oppression, and inequality. As the country, the man, and the woman meet in labor, they also meet in anger. For Fowziyya the didactic relationship between men and women may reflect this quality of life surrounding them, but it is only one facet, a symptom of a larger problem. What is at the root is a civilization that has been defeated and betrayed, not by its dream but by its interpreters. The "star" has always been there, has never given the wrong direction; it is the physiognomist's interpretation of what the star reveals that has misguided everyone. Fowziyya is angry at these star readers. These are the betrayers of a great dream and a great star. This great star is none but Islam.

These star readers, who are none other than the religious *'ulama* and other centers of power that use religion to further their interests, are one of the causes of that defeat. It was not the religion but rather they who told the woman that she was created from a curved rib, that she was not a complete human being. Because they reduced women to symbols that they could manipulate as the occasion demanded, they tore the woman between all contradictions: "beloved / mortal / wanted / cursed / saint / devil / approachable / exiled."

But the defeat did not result only from squeezing women into these symbolic categories that deprived them of their humanity but arose also from the centers of power treating men in an equally dehumanizing way. The Arab man is told by the same centers of power that he is not a total human being, that he deserves to be cursed, exiled, to be "stoned and split." He is evil, cursed, mortal, and deserves to die. In fact, while the woman is held in the ambiguity of love-hate sentiments, the Arab man is held in complete contempt and his humanity is totally dismissed. "The Arab is born predisposed to suffering," whether he is Palestinian, Iraqi, or Peninsular; whether a man, woman, or child. He is "like a falcon / whose wings are clipped / and cannot fly / while it is free." [17] The Arab is either tortured in the "investigation room" or as a worker in Ebgaig and Dhahran. Nothing is clear in the Arab present, not memory, nor spectacles; they are all "hazy" as are the eyes of the workers.

Meeting in the Struggle for Freedom

But the Arab man is also "a dagger in its scabbard" that will eventually emerge. Despite those who talk and promote the image of the Arab man as an oppressor of women, Fowziyya sees him as equally oppressed. She does not lose faith in him, and in fact is seduced by his pride and the resistant fighter in him. She is confident that they will meet in the struggle, because it is the only choice. For in the end, it is the woman and the man who remain and "a simple choice / as the Palestinian choice / in the trap of the borders / either death / or love."

That "simple choice" seems to require for the poet that women "abolish the role of their breasts." In her poem "Secret Diaries for Children," she describes her heroines Laila Khalid and Jamilah Abu-Hayred as women who "abolished the role of their breasts." This striking statement seems to be a conviction against motherhood. But Fowziyya, who holds birth in high esteem, is by no means advocating the abolishment of motherhood. Rather, it is by assuming the role of the fighter who is an equal participant in the struggle that the woman abolishes the idea that the only role she can play is through her breasts. This interpretation is more consistent not only with Fowziyya's general position but also with the real-life examples these women fighters provide. These two heroines are, as is Fowziyya, in fact mothers, and as such become a perfect example of how motherhood and struggle can by no means be contradictory or oppositional.

Neither is the relationship of men and women contradictory or oppositional. The woman's struggle, as Fowziyya views it, is not against the man but rather against "the years of exile," both from each other, from their country, and from real battles. Their real battles are against "the hunter / the swordsman / the treacherous." The battle against these forces will be brutal; it is a "flirtation with thunder." But the formula for victory is nothing less than an "organized love" between men and women. As a woman she is prepared for the challenge, prepared "for stoning and splitting." She has a history of anger that goes far into the past: "the bottles of waves from the time of the flood / were clamoring in my breasts." The man with as long a history of oppression as she has is no less prepared. For "who blames the dagger / when the space of walls / and scabbards / enclose it / . . . when it is threatened by siege."

Yes, "who blames the dagger" when the response to the "slaughtering of the Arabs" does not go beyond "elegy," "satire," or even at times "love poetry"? Who blames the Arab man when he is threatened by "siege"? The Arab is besieged by all forms of injustice, by inside as well as outside forces. For Fowziyya they are in the end one and the same. The Palestinian poor find their counterparts in the neighborhoods of Jeddah. But it is not in the nature of things for a situation that is built on injustice and severe contradiction to last. Soon "the masses toward the Gulf are thrusting." However, Fowziyya asks in a rather grim anticipation: "where do the years of exile / take us / how long 'til the oil's fire / seizes us?"

It was not to take long. Five years after the publication of her second poetry collection, *Secret Reading in the History of Arab Silence,* Fowziyya's image of the oil's fire seizing not only her land but also her dreams became another one of her visionary outlooks that was realized in the tragic events that took place in the Peninsula and the Fertile Crescent between August 1990 and February 1991, in what came to be called the Gulf War. In this inferno, both Arabs and Arab oil burned mercilessly. Fowziyya is haunted by the same question that has puzzled every Arab human being for more than five hundred years, especially during historical events such as these. Why, for all these centuries, is the Arab land, the Arab wealth, and the Arab fate in the hands of invaders? Why do the Arab people face exile from or in their own land? Why do the Arabs have oil but always get burned by it? Why do Arab people live in poverty and face every conceivable type of death, hunger, oppression, and torture, while others "feast" on their wealth?

The Camel and Its Riders

Fowziyya's answer may be found by a careful reading of the *Secret Reading in the History of Arab Silence.* In her diagnosis of the Arab's current situation, she uses the camel as a symbol of the Arab. In her skillful hands the camel becomes a loaded symbol, "we said, in the beginning to discern / the camel rider / and he who stole the load / and those who were contented with the feast." Once the Arab identified who rides the camel, who steals the load, and who feasts on it, the awakening would be inevitable. Through her use of the camel as a symbol, Fowziyya wants to reveal a political message as well as deeper truths about the Arab.

The camel stands as a symbol of patience and endurance. The camel is also known for neither forgetting nor forgiving. When the camel gets angry at his rider, he does not necessarily react immediately but usually awaits the right opportunity. Another unique correlation exists between the camel and the contemporary Arab at which Fowziyya seems only to hint. The camel is in fact "slaughtered" after this operation of piracy. For one of the misfortunes in being a camel is that, by virtue of its keeping water in its humps, the camel is "slaughtered" when the need for water arises—as it usually does in long travels in the desert. The contemporary "camel" has, instead of water, "oil" in his humps. Like his poor companion, the camel, the Arab occasionally has to be slaughtered should the need for oil arise—as it usually does in eras of militarism and materialistic greed. One cannot help but think that Fowziyya probably had this in mind when she spoke of the "slaughtering of the Arabs," as well as of "the earth" that "is breast, lactating blood / oil, into pledged bottles."

Publication of the Private: Allegorization of Women's Experience

In the poem in which Fowziyya describes the labor she experienced in the birth of her daughter Ṭofoul, the poet takes the pain of labor and the joys of birth to the wider realm of politics, "digging" for the causes that create hunger and oppression. While her writings say something about women, they also say something about the sad state of affairs in the culture as a whole. In so doing, not only does the publication of the private experience become possible but a new way of reading that experience is also engendered. What is important here is the orientation toward a mode of thought based on allegory. Through allegory, the literal meaning can be preserved and at the same time the figurative can be given prominence.[18]

It is precisely this process of allegorization that brings many male readers to associate and identify with the writings of Abu-Khalid. Along with 'Alim and Ash-Shabib, these women writers demonstrate a wealth of experience and the skill to use aesthetic devices in such a way that they are as much concealing as they are revealing of truths that can never be spoken of literally. Allegory is especially suitable because it is, in Fowziyya's words, a mode of "Secret Reading," of speaking in codes. Speaking in codes, by definition, conceals what is intended to be revealed. Paradoxically, it is exactly this concealment that makes conveying important messages possible.[19]

But in the *Secret Reading*, of the kind Fowziyya performs, when speaking of a country, a man, and a woman, she speaks in a code that the centers of power are able to decipher but often tend not to censor directly or publicly. Rather, they can only hinder its publication and its local distribution in the hope of minimizing its readership. But despite their efforts, centers of power are usually unsuccessful in presenting literary discourse as a free public forum. In this highly censored atmosphere, readers would naturally tend to interpret material allegorically; moreover, the lack of political participation among men and their general feeling of powerlessness has made it almost inevitable that women's experience of powerlessness would be presented allegorically.

Fowziyya had an important reason for relating her message in relation to the Arab's experience by speaking about it as a woman's experience of "humiliation, torture." Women often, and I suspect are encouraged by the centers of power, to protest against "their" own men's oppression (which will be discussed in chapter 4). As a result, a discourse on the oppression of women by men can easily be allowed to be generated because it performs for centers of power a double function of controlling both men and women. Men can never be spoken about as oppressed, not necessarily because it is antimasculine to do so but, most important, because to speak of men's oppression is to put centers of power on the defensive. To speak of men's oppression is to be political—to speak of women's, is personal.

Fowziyya's strategy is effective if only because she engenders a discourse on men's oppression with no less intensity than that which she makes on women's oppression. Perhaps this is what Fowziyya means when she speaks of "an organized love / that haunts a country." Fowziyya's ideas are "haunting" to the centers of power, because not only does she make women's oppression political but she transforms the entire political discourse. Fowziyya's skill is also evident in her ability to treat these three elements—man, woman, and country—as real subjects, with real experiences of oppression and humiliation, while at the same time using them symbolically to enhance and reveal deeper truths about the Arab existence. Treating a woman as the symbol of a country, for example, does not take away from the vivid and realistic expression of a woman's experience especially of motherhood. Similarly, using Palestine as a symbol of oppression does not take away from its actual tragic existence. The convergence of the woman and the country is consequential. Even if injustice in the experience of women is gauged in private terms, this cannot be applied to the experience of an entire country and people. Palestine becomes an allegory for woman, man, and other Arab countries, endowing private terms with political import.

Ruqayya Ash-Shabib: Selections from Her Writings

The Appeal[20]

In this spacious court it is the same to receive the death sentence now or to wait for it later.

The judges lined up . . . Three, and the bell was their fourth, or probably they were four, and the bell was their fifth, or somewhere in the middle.[21] I was taken by a sudden loud laugh made even louder by the echo, which caused the eyes of my judges to bulge out . . . Then I was overwhelmed by a strong outbreak of sobbing, which seemed to soften their hearts . . . A moment of strong dry coughs followed. I felt as if it was sweeping away or crushing my stomach or craw. I smiled when I remembered that the human being has no craw, and I am not, after all, a hen or a rooster.

Not even one eyewitness was in the court, nor was one there for the prosecution or the defense. It was as if the hall were the only suspect.

Although shackled in my cage, I was possessed by a burning urge to jump and embrace my judges. The odor of the first judge resembled my father's. The one in the middle wore a shirt with a ring of dirt around its collar. I thought to myself, "He may have quarreled with his wife last night, and she rewarded him with such an appearance." When I approached the third judge, however, he was dozing off and ready to fall asleep.

The bell rang, and the face of the gray-haired judge looked sullen. He seemed to be in a hurry . . . The court seemed empty . . . Being the only suspect, I thought, I too should level my own accusations at your honor, my master, the judge. I too should defend myself strongly . . . I lifted my forefinger, but I first had to practice the role of prompter on myself.

In a husky voice, I started in the name of Allah. Then I began to draw the judges' attention to the dimensions of my tragedy. How I entered this prison from one door, while Jacob's sons entered from twelve doors . . . That the birds which were torn asunder and thrown all over the mountains, unlike me, have come flying back . . . [22] The judge's cruel glance invaded me and seemed to arrest my words for a short moment, . . . I stammered, and he screamed . . . "Proceed."

A strong laugh came from under my armpit. . . . My own frustration sparks this roar . . . I have exhausted the largest amount of vanquishing last night, before I received the death sentence in this court, empty except for me and the judge. . . . The judge tapped his gavel . . . and took pleasure in sipping water. . . . It occurred to me that he was sipping from the breaths of a woman he loves . . . I held my laugh . . . as I saw traces of deep wounds between his eyes . . . I thought to myself, "The judge was probably a hero warrior" . . . but quickly remembered that judges are supposed to be only fair and impartial, not heroes . . . I gathered my breath and felt splinters piercing me all over, and acute pain suddenly invaded me.

I lifted my hand and let my finger comb through my dark hair. I felt as if the judge had been taken by a fever; he seemed to be struck by a hidden shiver. I jumped at the opportunity and sent some of my scent to drive him to acknowledge his infatuation through a gaze.

I decided quite suddenly to measure the distance between him and me, in feet. I started to get closer and his eyes began to bulge out . . . I got closer and his breaths came even faster . . . I got closer and his hair began to stick up higher . . . I got closer and he positioned his eyelashes like swords to stop my attack . . . He decided that the moment of deliberation must begin, and for the court's session to end soon . . . I laughed, and told his honor the judge and his counselors that the distance between me and him was four feet.

He hammered on the table rather strongly. He stood, tall and corpulent as a mountain, then he sat. He commanded me to "shut up"; I shut up and closed my mouth. Knowing that he was tracing the corners of my mouth, and measuring the roundness of my lips . . . I pursued him even further with my glances. The judge extended himself on his seat . . . He had to make a decision to end this unresolved case . . . His forehead was covered with perspiration as I resumed answering questions I was not even asked.

The bell rang again in the court, empty except for me. As he was pressing on the bell, his fingers seemed cruel but as weak as a spider's web. I protested and insisted on a long, complete, and detailed confession. I also insisted that he should listen with his ears and not with his eyes.

But I felt an urge to seek a truce or peace treaty in the presence of the judge . . . He stood up, hammered the table with his gavel, rang his bell, then sat . . . I leaned backward and rested my back on the seat, then told him that I had four conditions with which I could accept his decision. The first was that the judge would give me permission to free my glances and let them reach the furthest piece of hair on his head, and the deepest layer under his skin. Then to allow me to plow his skull and prepare it for implanting great numbers of solutions to all unresolved issues.

He also had to determine the size of the losses we had sustained in this ongoing war . . . I told him that "there should not be in the field of litigation anyone except you . . . You get rid of all the Arab caravans and all the ready armies inside you. You have to strip yourself of provincialism and warn the 'comrades' that modernity may mean to throw stones but not to build a home of glass." I told him that all fluid things will evaporate . . . that the human race will be exterminated by hunger, and water will vanish . . . I also told the judge, in addition to all this, that he had to sentence all broadcasting companies to be hanged to death. Only then could I accept his decision.

"My honorable judge, I appeal to justice in your cloak, to come unprepared . . . without ringing a bell and without sips from your scarce water, and without the grumbling of your counselors" . . .

"My honorable judge, I have already finished my defense, about which I have not yet uttered one word. But you certainly have understood it . . . You should remove your spectacles and examine my conditions with your naked eye. Forget ringing the bell . . . The world is in slumber except for a judge and an accused . . . and come close, my honorable judge, where the sun is round and beaming, where the moon is always a crescent, and when the Arabs will agree next year on one day for Eid, when we will never be invaded by starvation . . . and when the skies pour rain."

The judge suddenly laughed, so strongly, coughing at the same time. He spat in his white handkerchief . . . By that time I had finished my speech . . . "Disease will not invade us, but we the Arabs will unite and fight with one wooden cane."

"My honorable judge, how about if you set me free so I can fight with you by your side; what do you think?"

He sipped from his cup, and then turned to his counselors, as if he heard their snoring for the first time.

He leaned on the table, and resumed his sleep by their side . . . He warned that he should not be awakened until the light swept the court . . . I started laughing again . . . then I pointed to my handcuffs . . . but he was already in deep sleep.

But before he fell asleep, he pointed out that I had stated more than four conditions, that I had to remember that a man's testimony is worth the testimony of two women . . . "What about my handcuffs?" I asked.

There were three judges and the bell was their fourth . . . A mix of smells from their lazy breath penetrated my nose . . . I decided to break my chains . . . and sneak out, escaping to an aperture of light, before my judges woke up . . .

I should probably secure a life jacket around me . . . I thought to myself. There will be no more conditions . . . He would, most likely, be delivering the decision in my absence . . .

I slipped away . . . after I seized the judge's bell so he would not ring it again in the face of a woman, hoping to control her by it.

I also took his spectacles with me, so he would stop enlarging the letters and counting the pearls of the woman laughing at him.

Before I attempted my escape, a powerful sleepiness attacked me. Leaning toward the cage from outside I piled myself up like a bundle, then soared in dreams . . . I was flying and the space was extending . . . But I was maimed . . . I had wings, but they were clipped.

I said to myself: "How can I soar with clipped wings? Until now I have not awakened . . . my judges are floating in another world" . . .

The pages of the calendar fell one after the other, ending one year. The appeal has yet to be heard.

Signed,
a suspect

The Nights of Sheherazade: The Second Night[23]

Sheherazade tells the stories of the nights of heroism . . . Shahrayar appears bored . . . Oh Jerusalem, the era of heroism has ended . . . Oh Jerusalem . . . the land has swallowed Salah Addin's corpse . . . We are in the era of prattling, sleeping, and death by betrayal . . . Ibn Al-Walid,[24] we all know his wish . . . The most wonderful thing is when you belong to all . . . when the belief in Allah is great . . . when the human soul becomes free of all shakings . . . Oh Lebanon of Fakhr Addin,[25] Oh, the mother of all alphabets . . . The bells in your churches are ringing in grief . . . The era of heroism, has it ended? The chanted psalms in your churches are rising to embrace the *adhan*[26] in your mosques . . . Where is love . . . the land of love? Then what, Sheherazade? Her talk kills Shahrayar . . . He does not like speaking about blood . . . and he sheds it every night!

It is strange, Oh human being, the pauper of all eras, you rove in the curves of life, lower your tongue, and swallow your sticky saliva. You search for Sheherazade's stories, idly being told to you . . . You twist your mustache . . . exhibiting your powers . . . sweat is pouring from your forehead . . . filled with anxiety when you imagine her . . . You have a vivid imagination . . . she loves you . . . and nothing more.

The Fifth Night

Oh Balqees[27] . . . the crowned Queen . . . Spread the incense . . . gather all the priests . . . Oh Queen of the happy land[28] . . . All civilizations ruled by women have failed.

Eve does not perfect anything except love, blaming, nagging, tears, and stubbornness. Eve does not know neutrality, has no law. Her way is to give and give, but she takes many times as much . . . The night is raving with Sheherazade's stories . . . and distances produce but mirages.

The curves of time are no longer consolation . . . Oh Balqees, you were fascinated by his world[29] . . . your pride has disappeared . . . and hope . . . is it lost, or still hiding in some corner? The memory is aging . . . Oh the time of arrival . . . The spearheads are broken by other spearheads, the days hatch illusory dreams.

The crested bluebird returns, Balqees . . . carrying good news. Your queenly ornaments, you throw in at the first meeting . . . All your priests, army leaders, and your fortune do not fascinate you. You reject them as men, and rule them as subjects . . . Oh Balqees . . . you thought you had won . . . But you gave away everything . . . You left the throne and the crown and went to him.

You turned out to be a woman like all women . . . seduced by wisdom, protection, and other things that spin from the threads of the sunrise, a sash for a meeting that was never completed.

Oh time . . . the hook of hopes and sorrows . . . Where is Sheherazade?

Al-Yamama and the Betrayal of Time and Space[30]

Blue her eyes as the sky . . . No lover had cherished her or told her, "Oh my sunrise" . . . She had not been clothed with the best of attire. She had not walked with arrogance . . . She was *Nejdi* (woman) to the core, glaring, and with her piercing eyes she brings closer what is far away . . . Is it fog or is it dust that clouds her vision? She said, "The palm trees are moving" . . . The fat man laughed and told his companion . . . "Finish your story," they said . . . and said . . . Oh the tall and slender . . . Oh Zarqa, how were you? Have you warned your people out of fear? The Nejdi woman since Laila had to conceal secrets . . . The Nejdi woman since Laila was sobbing . . . licking her pain, she said, "The trees, gentlemen, are moving" . . .

Oh, the betrayed time and space . . . No one would capture these eyes . . . She dreamed once that the night got shorter . . . but she sees it long . . . They said, "Could Nejd breed a blue-eyed woman?" They searched the books and discovered that blueness came of your very dark eyes . . . Who are you and where did you come from? Who are your people . . . Where are you?

She said, "Oh my people" . . . but all ears were deaf. But Zarqa was not quiet . . . She breathed fear . . . You said, "Oh my people," then were swallowed by their silence . . . Their snores become louder . . . she says the trees appear as men . . . Necks are shorn around you . . . Would you be taken as a slave? As a barren land are your days. Sails of fear are drawn in the pupils of your eyes . . . The clot in the brain afflicts those who do not live middleness . . . "No" means not to accept being in-between as a temporary solution . . . She said: The trees are moving . . . Oh, tall and slender . . . men in your time twisted their mustaches . . . Oh Zarqa, the woman wants a savior . . . Have you seen how believing depends on being convinced that there is a source, and an echo . . .

Say it . . . so loudly, Oh betrayal of time and space . . . For what is feasible will remain feasible in every time and space . . . You said that trees are moving . . . as a clear pond seem your beautiful eyes . . . trees are moving . . . and behind the hills lies what no one knows . . . He said, "Oh Zarqa, do trees move?" A sincere tear jumped, then silence.

Oh, betrayal of time and space . . . Zarqa spreads love but her heart is empty . . . She sees them, the stems are necks of men, not of trees . . . Zarqa is captured . . . She is pulled, killed, and enslaved. There is no compatibility between what you want and what they want . . . You have to shut your upper lip, and firmly, on the lower . . . And let the time betray you, and is there anything else for it . . . Oh, the tall and slender . . . The days wrap you in a black sash.

To go with the heart, Zarqa, means defeat . . . The inner weakness paralyzes the eye and the heart . . . Oh Zarqa, look around you . . . Ravishment, even if it was permitted in your time by the logic of ends justifying means, is objectionable by the logic of the heart . . . that organ that comes in the size of a fist, but bears what is heavier than mountains.

Oh Zarqa . . . let all your standards drop . . . and may you be swallowed by Nejd's love. It is not important to know or not to know! There is a difference between knowing what you want and wanting what you know . . .

Oh, betrayal of time and space . . . say it, Zarqa, and tousle your hair . . . sob and let it be heard or keep it to yourself, either way, weep . . . swallow it, as bitter as colocynth.

History, Zarqa, did not acknowledge that you were suffering in vehemence . . . All it said was that you had seen something for three nights . . .

Do you see now that it is the betrayal? Especially when it comes from a time and a place you love . . . She asked . . . "Has the son of Adam planted betrayal or is he implanted by it?" Oh Zarqa, there are no miracles . . . You will be captured.

Say it in a shaky voice . . . Oh, betrayal of time and place . . . You were not heard [then] Zarqa . . . But, someone, someday, will probably hear you!

A Biographical Sketch and a Personal Encounter

Ruqayya, born in 1952, was the first child of her Nejdi parents in 'Ar'ar, near Ḥail, in the northern part of Saudi Arabia. This area, being closer to the centers of book production in Lebanon and Syria, was much more open in terms of book markets than were other parts of the Peninsula. Although no other family members were writers, her father played a leading role in encouraging and supporting her reading. Due to the family's frequent summer travels to Lebanon, Ruqayya had access to a variety of historical and fictional works of leading Arab writers from different parts of the Arab world. These works sparked the young girl's interest in reading history until she reached the university level where, in the mid-1970s, she obtained her B.A. in history from Imam Ibn Saud University in Riyadh. Married, with one child, Ruqayya currently works in the field of education as a supervisor of teachers.

Following the path of so many other women writers in her country, Ruqayya started writing when she was in elementary school with contributions to the readers' mail sections of local publications. But her real contributions, she maintains, began only in 1976 with the articles and short stories she had published in various local newspapers and magazines. She has contributed, more or less regularly, to such publications as *Al-Yamama, Iqra, Al-Jazeera, Al-Ḥaras Al-Waṭani,* and more recently to the London-based *Ash-Sharqul-Awsaṭ* and *Sayyedaty.* The latter, a women's magazine owned by Saudis and published in London, carries Ruqayya's weekly column, "Short Dreams," through which she reaches a wider audience of women in the Arab-speaking countries.

I met Ruqayya in Riyadh. She seemed a self-assured writer and a gracious host. The setting was quiet, and she spoke softly but with great enthusiasm about both her writing process and her cultural and literary concerns. She defines herself as a woman, a mother, a working woman, and a writer. These attributes may be shuffled, depending on the circumstances, but they are normally in the order stated. For Ruqayya, writing is certainly a mission. The issue of women occupies the center of her concerns, and drives her to continue writing. As she puts it, "My issue is the woman first. My own continuation as a writer represents the continuation of woman's insistance on finding a place for herself, and on establishing herself as a thinking human being."

However, she also admits that, like all writers, she also writes for "selfish" reasons, that is, to explore, identify, and realize her own philosophy and values in life:

> Through writing I can breath, revive, and feel moments of salvation. There is a passionate love between me and my pen. We eagerly meet and I always find in it a consolation for many things that are missing in the world. The sense of fulfillment writing gives has enabled me to leap over many hurdles in life. My writing process does not follow any pattern, when my pen calls upon me, I just submit.

She pointed out that she is constantly self-critical and that she seldom feels a sense of satisfaction with her work. If it should come, she added, it lasts only a few moments. Despite this self-criticism, Ruqayya has managed to produce two collections of short stories. In fact, as is the case with other women writers, she herself had to approach the publisher and propose that her work be published. The first collection, entitled *A Dream,* appeared in 1984 and contained fourteen stories. One of the stories, "A Dream," from which the title of the collection was derived, was translated into English and included in Jayyusi's anthology (1988). In addition to "A Dream," the collection includes "The Nights of Sheherazade" and "The Yamama and the Betrayal of Time and Space," both translated here; "A Reading in the Record of History"; "A Letter to Shajaratul-Addur"; "Horizontal Circles"; "The Gap"; "The Night of Rhymes"; "Asmā, You Inhabit Me"; "That Free Woman"; "Between What He Said and What She Said"; as well as others, all of which were written in a span of ten years. Ruqayya dedicated this collection to her brother and to Asmā, a seventh-century Muslim woman who epitomized to her the values of sacrifice, patience, and wisdom.[31] Her choices of dedication reflect her interest in reviving historical women models, and also emphasize her affiliative qualities as an Arab woman, symbolizing her commitment and loyalty not only to family but to the cultural values as a whole.

Her second collection, *The Gray Sadness,* was published in 1987. Both collections were published by the Association of Culture and Arts in Ar-Riyadh.[32] "The Appeal," translated here, is one of eight stories in this collection. Also included are "The Gray Sadness," "The Hidden Sore," "The Shadow," "Dialogue," "The Circle," "The Speaking Rays," and "The Woman and the Mirror." This collection carries no dedication, but in the introduction Ruqayya writes:

> These stories, as I see them, are not merely stories. They are sections from my days. . . . Small sections that are penetrated by rays coming from the inside of a woman who always dreams of something different than the normal things. These are sections of a woman who failed to be a section of one thing in this large world.

The two collections seem to correspond to the two threads of thought that permeate Ruqayya's writings in general. One is her interest in digging into historical records and excavating Arab and Muslim women personalities. The other is her exploration of the mental and psychological make-up of the contemporary woman and her relationship to the contemporary man. Ruqayya's interest in history carries no notion of nostalgia. The past is not recoverable, and one can only learn from it.

She presents historical personalities as "real," not "ideal," human be-ings, and refuses any interference in the way she calls these women to the stand, so to speak, to bear witness to the grievances and concerns of the contemporary woman.

It seems striking to Ruqayya how the connection of contemporary women to their predecessors is so severely blurred. As she expressed it:

[It is] as if women's history were a page that was eaten by historians. . . . It has almost been forgotten that the Arab woman has a history. People tend to forget that Islam was built on women's shoulders. They freely embraced Islam, they were the financiers of the movement, and they were its first believers and martyrs. They were courageous soldiers who fought for it. We do have a fund of models from our glorious history on which contemporary women can draw. They were strong women who took matters in their own hands, whether to determine their faith, finance, marriage, or ownership. These women wrote their history not by being passive. I would like my writing to serve as a reminder. (personal communication, 1989)

Ruqayya's knowledge of the history of the Arab/Islamic civilization, if only from her academic training, lends authority to her reading of history and legitimizes her claim on its interpretation. She manipulates history by exploring contemporary situations, either in terms of histori-cal precedent or by establishing analogous relationships to the present. She projects the qualities of these women onto contemporary women, forging a link between the past and the present. Women of the past were not "passive," and Ruqayya's reading of the present tells her that the problem is not male dominance but rather female submission. For her, the man is as responsible for changing the situation as is the woman. Her later stories are mostly about a man and a woman who "meet in a circle," separated from the world, in which they hold a dialogue to explore their inner feelings and "settle matters" without intermediaries.[33]

Ruqayya's style is unique. In her fictional mode, she blends historical facts with current historical realities, revealing the motifs of the time and space in which she lives. Her stories often lack the structure of a modern story, of plot, sounding more like a soliloquy. In her writing style, Ruqayya relies on the power of language, which she manipulates to reveal subtle messages. However, along with her constant reliance on allusions to historical events and personalities—to the extent that the only names in the stories are historical figures while the protagonists in her fiction usually go nameless—her style is difficult to understand by those who lack sufficient knowledge of either Islamic history or language or both. Ruqayya is often frustrated by the critics' tendency to designate her writings as poetic. Although this may seem high praise, Ruqayya's frustration springs from the fact that because her writings can never really be confused with poetry, this designation is used simply to justify ignoring the importance of her messages—political as well as philosophical.

Textual Analysis

Ruqayya and the Appeal to Justice

"The Appeal" is a story that depicts a woman suspect on trial. The story takes place in a courtroom. The choice of the court as a setting symbolizes and defines the issue as one of justice. Ironically, the court, while it conjures up an image of justice, does not conform to it—neither in form nor in content. The protagonist does not tell us—nor apparently is she told (although she knows)—why she is on trial or of what she is accused. We know at the end that she was accused of making an attempt to free herself, "trying to escape to an aperture of light." But it seems she is in the same prison from which she tried to escape.

The protagonist is without a name. In fact, at the end of her appeal she signs her name simply as "a suspect," apparently an allusion to the commonality of women being suspected. To give the woman a name would be to give her specificity, while Ruqayya's intent is to show that the experience is not hers alone; it is the experience of all women. Perhaps the woman is not named because the experience of the woman who is a prisoner and a suspect, though common, is itself not named.

In addition to not knowing her name, we also do not know her original crime. The court has no witnesses. The judges are not listening. They are in slumber, and seem to be assured that as long as the woman is in a cage—handcuffed and chained—they should not worry about her escaping again. The court delivers decisions in the absence of the accused. In addition to all these violations of the concept of justice, the judges use tools unusual in other courts—such as the bell—to maximize their control over the court audience.

The woman's attempt at escape failed because she herself "dozed off." Her attempt was not an ordinary escape, however, but rather a grave crime. For she had "slipped away after seizing the judges' bell and spectacles." The attempt was daring because she had control of two very important tools—the bell and the spectacles. The judges, as a result, were completely disarmed by this seizure. Not only did she try to escape but she also disarmed the guards and stole their weapons! No wonder, then, that the woman is not only handcuffed and chained but has also been placed in a cage.

Still, although the woman may have been physically immobilized by these measures, she is by no means powerless. She is not deprived of her ability to challenge her judges and speak. She has written and signed an appeal for justice. She is even in a position to dictate conditions. In fact, she constantly reminds her judges that she possesses knowledge. When she makes allusions to the Qur'anic story of Jacob, demonstrating her knowledge of the religion and her ability at analogy, the judge "arrests her words." She is trespassing on a domain over which only the judges have a monopoly.

The character seems to assert herself and her feminine powers in a rather theatrical manner. She laughs, weeps, sobs, coughs, and smiles as she sees fit. She can even be sarcastic. She reminds us that she is a human being, not a hen, and in fact a woman who has certain physical beauty (mouth, teeth, eyes, and dark hair). She is especially daring when she combs her hair with her fingers. Her hair is apparently uncovered. She shows the judges her hair, which they consider a private part of her body. She does not lower her gaze or cast down her eyes as she should. Instead, she sends one of them a scent and a gaze. She dares him to stand up to her feminine beauty, especially as she gets closer to him and "pursues" him with her glances. In a word, she is a flirt. But her flirtation is as much to measure his integrity as it is to assess and be assured of her powers. She tries to make him uncomfortable; to expose his weaknesses; to expose the contradictions embedded in the situation in which she is desired but at the same time sentenced to death. This contradiction, which seems to be so ingrained in the conception of woman as a symbol of honor, is also echoed by Fowziyya and other women writers.

The protagonist is also a keen observer and a shrewd analyst. Despite her confinement in a cage, she seems to have created an advantageous position for herself. She can identify these judges and "see" what is beyond their appearance. She can penetrate their minds. She observes one of the judge's hair, his perspiring forehead, his shirt with a ring around the collar, his figure, "corpulent as a mountain." Even his fingers, which seem "as weak as the threads of a spider's web," are not spared—nor is the wound between the judge's eyes. She sarcastically asks: "Is it a sign of heroism?" But the judges could not possibly be heroes. They are supposed to be fair and "impartial" but not heroes. At this moment she feels acute pain at the realization that they are neither heroes nor fair and impartial judges.

These judges are not only lacking in heroism but are also participants in a huge slumber party. The "sleeping" notion, to which Ruqayya repeatedly alludes, reflects her conception of the reality of the centers of power in particular and Arab men in general. Ruqayya's character uses the power of analogy, as well as religion, to make her point. She uses an effective allusion to the "People of the Cave," whose story was related in the Qur'an. Their number, which was not determined, and their sleeping for more than three hundred years provided a perfect parallel to the court judges. They were accompanied by a dog, for which Ruqayya substitutes a bell. Ruqayya's adoption of the Qur'anic language and style of narration reflects her knowledge of the religious text.

However, it is not only history and religion that are under this character's scrutiny but also the judges themselves. When she decides to pursue the judge with her glances, she reaches "the furthest hair" and "the deepest layer under his skin." The judges represent a variety of human types and social positions. One resembles her father; another is described as a husband who is at odds with his wife; the third was not identified except by his sleepiness. One is gray-haired with a sullen face. The suspect is not only able to identify the judges' situation but can also identify the tools by which they maintain control of the court. They have a "bell" to ring, a "gavel" to tap, "spectacles" to enlarge objects, and "water" they can sip and from which they can take pleasure and sustain their energy. These elements seem to symbolize what Ruqayya believes to be the agents of control (i.e., religious interpretations and traditions, as well as state regulations). When she tries to escape, she wants to seize the bell so they will not "control her by it," and she takes the spectacles, which symbolize the controlling agents' vigilance of women.

Soaring in Dreams as a Means of Redefining Reality

The protagonist, however, is capable of more than mere observations. She acquires the tools by which she can conceptualize and comprehend the reality that lies far and beyond, through metaphors as well as dreams. The protagonist, being a part of this slumber party, dozes off along with the rest. She dreams. Dreaming, while it may become a means of alienation from reality, becomes for the suspect a means of grasping reality as well as of resisting it. For in her attempt to soar in dreams, she remembers, "How can I soar with clipped wings?" The dream itself becomes an element in her realization of her reality. In fact, dreaming becomes the only way for the suspect to practice the impossible, to fly "with clipped wings." Only through dreams is she able to get a court to convene to view her case, to be allowed to state her grievances, to display her knowledge, and even to set her own conditions. She uses dreaming to make sense of reality. It is as if in order to make sense of reality one has to momentarily escape from it. Dreaming provides a means, not of permanent escape but rather to contemplate and work on escaping. Given the constraints on action, distance from reality becomes a necessary means to view it critically.[34]

In this sense the dream becomes a means of freedom, of knowledge, and of empowerment. But the dream, being one of the most dominant metaphors Ruqayya uses, may have other functions as well. The dream may exacerbate a sense of confusion over what constitutes reality and who defines it, bringing alive the notion of multiplicity of definitions. On the one hand, new definitions of "reality" presented forcibly in dreams enhance the possibility of change, endowing them, if not with power and legitimacy, then with pertinence. On the other hand, the dream may, instead of blurring the distinction from reality, work to polarize that distinction; that is, it may establish that what women write about in stories are just dreams—by no means realistic or attainable. They are to be seen as reveries, as musings. The depiction of women as dreamers honors the "reality" that exists, relegating any attempt toward change to the status of fantasy. It also honors the stereotypical view of women as idle dreamers (daydreaming).

But dreams can be threatening, even when the dreamer is "maimed" with "clipped wings." Regardless of whether it is seen as dreadful or pleasant (depending on the reader), to dream implies the possibility of *ro'ya,* or vision—something akin to foresight—a dream that may become true. By the same token, dream as a metaphor could also indicate awakening. Although those who dream are those who are asleep, to be asleep is not, after all, the same thing as to be dead or in a coma. Sleep is normally followed by awakening. Dreams, which signify the unconscious, point to the "existence" of something that is real, even if it is not seen or actualized. They may even invoke the danger of "sleep walking"!

Seeing Connections and Seeing Double

The woman in "The Appeal" is certainly an outrageous suspect. Not only does she dream and make leaps to other worlds but she also has stepped over her limits by dictating conditions in the first place. Moreover, these conditions have nothing to do with her freedom as a woman, for she is concerned with issues that go beyond. She deals with larger issues that span the globe, which she identifies as her issues. She makes no division in her mind between the political and the personal. She has allegiance to no region, and seems to think that the whole world is her business. She wants to take the universe in her hands, to abolish starvation, hunger, drought, propaganda, disease, militarism. The judges see these as impossible conditions. But she thinks that they can only be realized and understood if the judge removes his spectacles and stops ringing the bell. His spectacles seem only to enlarge for him her feminine beauties, but they do not enable him to see anything else. The judge can only have access to these realities by coming close to where "the sun looks round and beaming" and where "the skies pour rain."

The woman is incomprehensible to the judge. She "sees" connections where the judges see parallelism and separation. The world for her is not one line—it is a circle. If the universe is seen as a line, then everything simply ends up in parallel lines, indefinitely. The meeting that was "never completed," which Ruqayya speaks of in "Zarqa," came about because of this parallelism. In her introduction to the second collection, *The Gray Sadness,* she speaks of how "the one cannot be separated."

In fact, Ruqayya so often uses the circle as a metaphor that one of her stories is entitled "The Circle." It is by no means accidental for her to advance this critique of separation, whether between the personal and the political, between men and women, or between "we" and "the other." The circle reveals the notion of continuity in Ruqayya's conception of social issues and of the relationship between man and woman. It is only when they form a circle that they preclude both isolation, separatism, and conflict, ensuring the flow of their human energy. "The most wonderful thing is when you belong to all," says Sheherazade in her "Second Night."

Image of Contemporary Men: Era of Death by Betrayal

The protagonist's perception of the connections between men and women as a circle seems only to exist on the ideal level. The actual state of affairs reveals that men and women are in a state of war in which the woman is held captive. She pleads for peace, and she wants to be set free so she can fight at his side. She is not his enemy. In fact, she is willing to bestow the title of hero on him but only if he acts as a hero, only when he deserves it. Twisting of mustaches and snoring can no longer be acceptable qualifications.

The slumber party in "The Appeal" may be initiated by the judges (the symbol of centers of power), but it seems that the phenomenon is much wider. In the "Second Night" of "The Nights of Sheherazade," the protagonist makes generalizations about Arab men: "We are in the era of prattling, sleeping, and death by betrayal." The men of the present, especially when compared to the men of the past, are unaware of their place in the world or in history. "The woman wants a savior," Ruqayya relates in "The Nights." She longs for a hero, but "The era of heroism, has it ended?"

In almost every piece, Ruqayya amasses allusions to male historical personalities, invoking the heroes of Arab history, such as Ibn Alwalid, Salah Addin, Fakhr Addin, and others. She finds in these heroes an implicit critique of the modern Arab man, with the comparison they provide between the qualities of bravery, chivalry, and knighthood on the one hand and those of "prattling, sleeping, and death by betrayal" on the other. Ruqayya also refers to spatial entities, such as Jerusalem and Lebanon, to revive in modern Arabian men a sense of connection to their land, as well as a sense of direction and goal. The failure on the part of contemporary men to retrieve the Quds (Jerusalem) or to stop the bloodshed in Lebanon stands in sharp contrast to the accomplishments of Salah Addin and Fakher Addin. Ruqayya may or may not be successful in teasing men with her allusions without exacerbating their sense of insecurity and failure.

Balqees as a Model of Resistance: Doing It All for Love

On the fifth night Sheherazade tells the story of Balqees, the queen of Sheba. Sheherazade, a heroine herself, is inspired by another: she reads history and finds inspiration in a woman predecessor such as Balqees. But Ruqayya sees Balqees as a disappointing example because she gave away her throne for love (of Solomon). "She turned out to be a woman like all other women." Ruqayya sees her as a woman who failed to be a woman and a leader at the same time. Balqees had to sacrifice her throne to be a woman: "Love means defeat." Balqees, unlike Sheherazade, had no sense of mission; she stands as a model of a woman who was defeated by love. "O Balqees . . . and you thought you had won . . . But you gave away everything . . . You left the throne and the crown and went to him."

Balqees, whose love story with King Solomon is told in the Qur'an, is presented as a historical person. The historical records tell us that she came to power by helping her people in Yemen get rid of her cousin, who was a tyrannical king. Balqees was seen as a savior, and in gratitude and appreciation of her qualities of leadership, she was appointed Queen. The Qur'an commends her as a successful and capable queen. This capability was demonstrated in her following of the shoura system of governance, which Islam promotes, constantly consulting with her people in running the affairs of the kingdom.

One day a letter to Balqees arrived via a bird messenger. It was from Solomon, the King of Jerusalem, who was endowed with the power of controlling the jinn and the wind, and was able to understand animals. Solomon, in the letter, invited her to become a Muslim in the original sense of the word, to submit to Allah. Balqees gathered together her people, who worshipped the sun, and told them about the letter. Her people advised her to travel to Jerusalem and investigate this religion firsthand. In Palestine she was given a great reception by the king, who immediately gave her her own throne and built her a fascinating palace on top of water, with a floor made of glass, under which fish could be seen swimming. Balqees converted to Islam; some stories assert that she in fact married King Solomon, and after a few years returned to her people to invite them to convert to Islam as well.

The Qur'an commends Balqees for her qualities of wisdom and independence of intellect by which she was able to recognize the validity of Islam and act on that recognition, even to the extent of dissenting from her people's beliefs. Balqees, by virtue of these qualities, stands as by far the most revolutionary of any woman symbol. But for Ruqayya to emphasize the qualities of rebellion in a woman would certainly only cause a backlash. Ruqayya's primary concern is to ensure Balqees's presence as a powerful figure. It is only the "selling out" to Solomon's type of power that Ruqayya criticizes in Balqees. Ruqayya does not mean to undermine her as a model in the personal qualities she possesses. Through her critique, Ruqayya brings a new perspective to Balqees and creates an aura of excitement around the symbol, inspiring an overwhelming desire to know more about her. Balqees's name, which conjures up images of power based on fairness and justice, and reflects an appealing quality of independence that led her to the "right" path rather than to subversion, says it all. The ultimate reason for Balqees's presence in Ruqayya's story is to give prominence to these qualities that usually go unmentioned.

Sheherazade: Recalling the Nights of Heroism

Sheherazade, the fictional heroine of the epic *One Thousand and One Nights,* has been endowed with life as a symbol of strength, wisdom, and courage.[35] She stands by far as the most favored symbol, not only to the writers presented here but also to the many other women writers who commonly allude to her. But more than in the works of any other writers, Sheherazade dominates the works and vision of Ruqayya, Rajaa, and Najwa. Najwa (see chapter 3) has published a series of articles entitled "Nights of Sheherazade," in which she reflects on life. Rajaa has written on "Her Days," speculating on what Sheherazade might have done during the daytime hours.

Strikingly beautiful, Sheherazade was the daughter of the Wazir of King Shahrayar. She was knowledgeable in philosophy, medicine, history, and poetry. The story tells us that when Shahrayar discovered the infidelity of his first wife, he vowed to take revenge on all women. He ordered his Wazir to bring him a wife every night; then he would have her killed in the morning. The bloodshed of these women had long been going on when one day Sheherazade asked her father to give her in marriage to King Shahrayar. Her father, the Wazir, was shocked, for he never planned to include his own daughter in the massacre. The victims were usually poor women who were either cajoled or forced to serve their country and sacrifice themselves for their king. At first, the Wazir naturally refused to grant his daughter her fatal wish. But the strong-willed Sheherazade, with a sense of womanhood that was far above the class concerns of her father, was determined to save the other women. Under her relentless insistence the Wazir finally yielded to his daughter's will, and agreed.

Sheherazade embarked on her risky and dangerous mission with all the dedication of a savior. She constructed a plan based on female solidarity, in which she engaged her sister's assistance as well as the support of other women in the king's palace. Sheherazade's sister, with a keen sense of timing, was to interrupt at the decisive moment on the first night and ask her sister to finish a story that she had begun the night before. What Shahrayar heard of the story engaged his attention and sparked his interest to the point of making him forget his vow for revenge. These stories—told with Sheherazade's captivating narrative style and vivid depiction of a world of heroes and villains—soon became an indispensable part of the king's existence. On the night after a thousand nights had passed, King Shahrayar decided to marry Sheherazade and live happily ever after.

Sheherazade's power as a symbol lies not only in her representation of courage, wisdom, patience, and selflessness but also in the manner in which she is treated as a real, historical person. One reason for this treatment lies perhaps in the enigmatic nature of these stories themselves, in which fact and fiction are closely intertwined. The people, the sights, and the sounds of the time as well as the place were so vividly depicted that they seemed strikingly real. In fact, many characters in those stories were real personalities who had actually lived in those places and in those times—such as the Caliph Haroun Al-Rashid. Therefore, it is no wonder that Sheherazade is often celebrated in these women's writings as though she were a real person rather than a fictional character.

However, the fascination with which Sheherazade is held by these women writers makes the issue of her "factuality" or "fictionality" almost irrelevant to their purposes. Too many points of affiliation exist between her position and theirs, both as writers and as women. A victim turned heroine, it was Sheherazade's inexhaustible memory, her use of words to save herself and other women, that form the main points of attraction for these modern writers. The allusion to Sheherazade reveals many messages that are made more or less explicitly. Not only her wisdom, courage, sacrifice, wit, and imagination but, more important, her strategy for resistance endows her with special significance.

Sheherazade, through her persistent and systematic form of resistance, provides for these writers more than a symbol; she provides a scenario for action. By telling her fascinating stories, she chose a method of resistance through words—a peaceful and almost feminine weapon—used for the purpose of preserving blood, not shedding it. Unlike Balqees, Sheherazade was not willing to adopt Shahrayar's model of power but instead pursued her mission of resistance with her own qualities. As a woman with a will, she would never succumb to naked power and oppression, although in her case this was fatal, in a literal as well as a figurative sense. She worked through long nights to change her destiny. For Sheherazade, night was not the time to make love but rather to make history.

While, fundamentally, Sheherazade symbolizes women writers themselves, her story tells us many other things—not only about Sheherazade but also about Shahrayar. Significantly, the symbol provides a unique opportunity to make a statement about men through Sheherazade's encounter with Shahrayar. Her contrast with Shahrayar brings more sharply into focus the images he presents of brutality, injustice, wrath, and irrationality. Shahrayar is consumed by anger, which is appeased by Sheherazade's gracious style. His unjust wrath she tames with words. Shahrayar is presented as a weak, almost childish character. He generalizes about the nature of women to the extent that the infidelity of one woman, or two, becomes a reason to believe that all women are untrustworthy. Sheherazade's main task is to break down the category of "the woman, the infidel" in his mind. Sheherazade teaches Shahrayar to "know" the "woman," and by her sheer existence, she exacerbates in him a sense of loss when he realizes he had made a mistake in generalizing about all women.

For Ruqayya, Shahrayar is also a hypocrite. "He does not like speaking about blood . . . but he sheds it every night!" He is an idle man, whose main sign of power is in his mustache: "You search for

Sheherazade's stories, idly listening while they are told to you . . . You twist your mustache . . . exhibiting your powers . . . sweat is pouring from your forehead . . . filled with anxiety when you imagine her . . . You have a vivid imagination."

Reviving the symbol of Sheherazade in the writings of women serves women by providing them with a model for action. The story also presents a model of man that is not far removed from the realities of the world that contemporary women aspire to change. But Shahrayar is not treated as a model about which one can generalize. Ruqayya's presentation of such heroes as Ibn Alwalid, Salah Addin, and Fakhr-Addin on the one hand, and Shahrayar on the other, reveals her belief that men can choose to be either heroes like Salah Addin or cowards like Shahrayar. Men only have forgotten how to be heroes. To remind Arab men of Lebanon and of Jerusalem is to remind them that their real battles are not with women. In fact, women will always wait and watch for the appearance of the hero in men.

While this reminder may mitigate men's negative response, the story of Sheherazade may invoke a negative response among men for another reason. To revive the story of Sheherazade is also to revive notions of women's infidelity. Shahzaman, Shahrayar's brother, shared with him the same experience of marital infidelity. Some women are represented in the stories as disloyal; they betray their husbands' confidence. By showing men as sharing a common misfortune, the story seems to assert that infidelity is almost the unavoidable fate of all husbands; it thus exacerbates men's sense of anxiety about their honor.

Zarqa Al-Yamama in History: Tragedy of Betrayal by Time and Space

In a way, Balqees seems to be for Ruqayya a model by which to critique contemporary women. They know no neutrality because they love. "To go with the heart means defeat." Women are "seduced by wisdom, protection, and other things that spin from the threads of the sunrise, a sash for a meeting that was never completed." But while Balqees represents all other women, Sheherazade and Zarqa Al-Yamama present women writers themselves. Ruqayya's heroine Sheherazade has no time for love, for she is a woman with a mission.

If Sheherazade, with her remarkable memory, serves as a model of a woman with a great sense of womanhood and a mission to save other women, Zarqa, with her unmatched visionary powers, attempts to save her people.[36]

The symbol of Zarqa is used extensively by both Ruqayya and Rajaa Alim. As a symbol, she crystallizes women's consciousness of history, of models, and of time and space. Vision and foresight are what Zarqa is all about. She warns her people of invading forces, but they discount her "story." They do not listen because what they cannot see does not exist for them. Rajaa picks this aspect of the story to reflect on the knowledge/power relationship. But for Ruqayya, the story of Zarqa seems to reflect two notions: one, that Zarqa's qualities of vision and foresight are similar to the writer's own charted mission in life; and, two, that by virtue of her fate Zarqa is a haunting symbol that generates a sense of pessimism about the future. It seems that the cultural scenario of Zarqa's tragedy bears a striking resemblance to the cultural scenario in which contemporary women find themselves controlled. Ruqayya sees in the present an "era of sleeping, prattling, and death by betrayal," similar to Zarqa's people, whose "snore" became louder.

Zarqa was betrayed both by time and space. When she warned her people that she saw trees "appear as men," the people were silent except for the sound of their snoring. Zarqa saw what lay beyond the hills—something they could not see. They ridiculed her: "O Zarqa, do trees move?" But she saw it all coming, the "shorn" necks of men and the enslaved women, including herself. Their ridicule, their silence betrayed her, because she not only suffered ridicule but also capture and death. This fate that Zarqa faced haunts contemporary women. She was captured and killed. She "breathed fear," and even when they refused to listen she kept on warning and pleading, "O my people." She wanted heroism; they wanted silence. No compatibility existed between "what they wanted and what she wanted." Women who bring vision and foresight still suffer the same fate. Although it occurs in a different manner, they are "pulled, killed, and enslaved" and die by betrayal.

For Ruqayya, Zarqa was doomed. Even her great vision could not save her from that fate. "Oh Zarqa . . . there are no miracles . . . you will be captured . . . The days wrap you in a black sash." The invaders ever since have resembled trees moving, and visionary Arab women continue to issue warnings. The tragedy in Zarqa's story seems to be perpetuated. The women always pay a high price. They are captured and enslaved, if not by the invaders then by their own people. They become defined in terms of that encounter with the invader. They become alienated from their time and space. They are sentenced to "death by betrayal," the ruling that the protagonist in "The Appeal" appeals.

Women, in any type of cultural encounter with the other, are destined to "live middleness." They are in the middle, not only between spaces but also between times. To accept being "in-between" is to perpetuate contradictions. Ruqayya alludes here to the collage culture that exacerbates a sense of incoherence in human existence. The siege mentality, which places women between the definition they have been given by the invader and that of the invaded, was born out of this collage. Women do not know to what time or space they should belong. "Living middleness" means that siege is imminent—if not from the outsider then from the insider. The tragedy of contemporary women is that they are besieged by both.

Zarqa was betrayed not only by her own time but also by the author's time: "Who are you and where did you come from?" If Sheherazade told her own story, Zarqa's story was told by others. And they did not say much about her. As a human being who suffered and experienced pain, betrayal, and ridicule, she as a person was blurred. All that is known about her is that she was distinguished by her eyesight. The people speculated about Zarqa's name, which literally means "blue-eyed woman." But "Could Nejd breed a blue-eyed woman?" We deduce that, like most Nejdi women, she must have been tall and slender, with glaring eyes that pierce the horizon and "bring closer what is far away." Despite Zarqa's "suffering in vehemence," despite her sobbing and "licking her pain," history concealed all the suffering and pain she experienced. "The curves of time are no longer consolation." Whether in time or space, "distances produce but mirages." "The memory is aging," and the days "hatch illusory dreams."

Zarqa: Haunting Symbol or Model for Imitation?

Zarqa may have been doomed, but she may bring hope to other women. They can still resist her fate. Time might be on their side: that "someone, someday will probably hear" them. Contemporary men can learn from the experience of their predecessors, to believe in women's ability to bring foresight. But, most important, women have to "say no." They have to know the difference between "knowing what you want and wanting what you know." The woman has to continue to speak; this is the only chance she has of ever being heard. Even by sobbing and "tousling" her hair, she can "say it." She must express herself and never succumb to the conspiracy of silence, if only because she is its first victim. The victimization of women in time and space is not total as long as women refuse to be silenced or blinded. Through their vision and foresight, they can spark an awareness of the unseen.

These symbolic models are not difficult to imitate. Except for Balqees, the Queen of Sheba, whom Ruqayya criticizes for failing to be both a woman and a leader, these models were mostly ordinary women who held no positions of formal power but nevertheless changed history in a profound way. These women were not obsessed with men's models of power. Ruqayya establishes women's tradition of making history through their own vision, memory, nurturing, and sacrifice. These women's "lack" of the capacity or the desire to shed blood does not mean they were doomed to inconsequentiality. These models made their mark on history through what they possessed as women. Sheherazade in contrast to Shahrayar, or Zarqa in contrast to those men who ridiculed her, acquired their power by preserving blood, by attempting to save lives, not through the shedding of blood. The key to Ruqayya's choice of these two women as models for action lies in her perception of a type of continuity in which the personal and the political form a circle, not two parallel lines.

By conversing with these three women models, and bringing them to bear witness on the current state of affairs in their society, Ruqayya makes the connection between time and space. They were all situated in a contemporary context dominated by motifs of modernization, wealth, change, and "living middleness." Ruqayya leaves a pertinent question dangling: what would happen to these historical women, whose greatness is not questioned, if they were alive today? Ruqayya, by asserting that contemporary women of Arabia do possess the qualities that the literature tends to idealize in earlier Arab women, uncovers a severe contradiction embedded in the perception of the past as a model and an ideal. The qualities of strength, courage, sacrifice, wisdom, and independence, recognized as heroic qualities in historical Arab women, are now ironically considered to be signs of failure, deviation, and even of the creeping decadence of the West into their lives. The qualities that led to the realization of these women as great models are exactly the qualities for which women are condemned in the twentieth century. All heroic female personalities—and males as well—whom the Qur'an itself has commended, have deviated from conventional definitions of the proper and the typical.

Rajaa 'Alim: Selections from Her Play "The Final Death of the Actor"[37]

"To the Ad-Libbers I Dedicate *The Final Death of the Actor*"

CAST OF CHARACTERS

ACTOR WHO PLAYS SAMSON, main character, twenty-one years old
    (hereafter referred to as SAMSON'S ACTOR)
ZARQA AL-YAMAMA, a woman beyond the influence of time
ESCAPED CHARACTER, a changing character who fled from the
    author's control and chose his own time and character
VIEWER, a man in his thirties who never grows older
MASTER OF THE DOLLS, a short man in his forties who owns a factory
    that produces wooden dolls
SCENARIST, the factory owner's assistant, in his thirties
DELILAH, a wooden doll who belongs to the MASTER OF THE DOLLS
SALESWOMAN, mother of SAMSON'S ACTOR
OLD MAN, a phantom apparition who appears to SAMSON'S ACTOR
MAN
ADVERTISEMENT MAN
POLICEMAN
GROUP OF WORKERS, EXPLORERS, AND ACTORS

Time and Place of the Action:
Act 1: Theater stage.
Act 2: The same theater stage after twenty years.
Act 3: The cities of stone in the desert.
Act 4: Return to the theater stage.

Act 1, Scene 1

(*The theater stage is dimmed . . . A high balcony is on its left side, representing a part of a wooden doll factory . . . A long line of dolls appears, moving along an endless metal wire that penetrates the wall of the balcony and exits from the other side without a break. The dolls' features are obliterated. Their foreheads extend to the mouth, which occupies most of the face. Each doll carries a serial number.*

(*Huge pictures of a woman*—ZARQA AL-YAMAMA—*occupy all the walls. The pictures are deformed and full of holes. A wall separates part of the balcony. A small door in the dividing wall connects the two parts. The separated part opens toward the audience with a railing that extends and joins the balcony railing.*

(*A statue of* ZARQA AL-YAMAMA, *made of polished wood, occupies a large part of the separated corner. The statue is situated in the midst of a strong light that surrounds it and constantly falls on it . . . The light reveals thin pins piercing the area of the statue's eyes . . . A thin thread is wrapped many times around the neck and body. . . .*)

(*The light in the factory is strong . . . and the marching of the dolls, which are connected to the wire, continues endlessly. {The main characters are using the statue as an arrow-shooting target.}*)

MASTER OF THE DOLLS (*after a strong shot at the statue*):   Creating a rebellious doll can only be explained by stupidity.

SCENARIST: But Zarqa was not . . .

MASTER OF THE DOLLS (*interrupting impetuously*):   No one mentions her name in my presence . . . (*sending another arrow to the statue*) no one mentions her . . . (*in a commanding tone to the* SCENARIST) make sure that no one leaves the factory unless they carry their numbers . . . only numbers . . . and no more names.

SCENARIST (*repeating mindlessly*):   All will carry numbers . . . and no more names.

MASTER OF THE DOLLS (*putting out the lights around the statue . . . the room becomes dim . . . he speaks to the statue*):   It was a seeing name . . . that which I gave you . . . Zarqa Al-Yamama . . . Zarqa Al-Yamama . . . (*whispering the name repeatedly*) . . . Why did I choose this name out of all names?!

ZARQA'S VOICE (*coming from behind the theater*):   I will go out (*the word echoes*).

MASTER OF THE DOLLS (*with an evil expression on his face*):   Oh no . . . you are not going anywhere . . . (*he mumbles the name backward*) Amamayla . . . Amamayla . . . you will relinquish it [the name] and come back . . . No comment?! Fine . . . you will learn, we will see how you will come back more lively and obedient . . . No . . . but more helpless and humiliated . . . Your look at me, penetrates me, pierces me. You only want me to suffer . . . I know, through these pins I see your eyes ravish my face . . . and they fire . . . I did not ask you for a thing. (*Tenderly*) All I asked for was some warmth, some gratitude. . . . Is that too much to ask?

ESCAPED CHARACTER (*from behind*):   You wanted her to be a doll who carries a torch of gratitude, too!

MASTER OF THE DOLLS: At the time I thought the difference was only an eye . . .

ESCAPED CHARACTER: She was no more than a skeleton and a piece of white surface . . . It was not possible for something like that to come to life and give you warmth.

MASTER OF THE DOLLS (*in a mix of frustration and sarcasm*):   But I naively believed that the eye could send a spark to that cold heart . . .

ESCAPED CHARACTER: But it flared . . .

MASTER OF THE DOLLS (*interrupting*):   Yes, but with ingratitude, with rebellion . . . and you were the reason, . . . I was going to see for her . . . She only had to listen, then follow . . . That is what I wanted . . . But you interfered and . . . in my desperation, I followed your advice.

ESCAPED CHARACTER: And she defeated you.

MASTER OF THE DOLLS (*erupting in anger*):   And who do you think you are to discuss my doll?! I don't even allow you to stay here.

ESCAPED CHARACTER: And I don't need permission from anyone. . . . As you can see, I am a loose character . . . outside your control . . .

ZARQA'S VOICE (*echoing around the theater*):   I have grown bored with paper. If I only could go out to them?!

MASTER OF THE DOLLS: Go out? To whom?

ZARQA'S VOICE: To those who are dying, but live only on paper . . .

MASTER OF THE DOLLS: I did not dictate this to you, I did not teach you this, Zarqa!

ZARQA'S VOICE: I want to go out and to know why they are dying . . . why they are spilled on paper . . .

MASTER OF THE DOLLS (*angrily*):   Go out? Who inserted this word in your vocabulary? Go out, go out, you repeat this word as a doll. This word is created for them . . . Those, the burning wood, the wretched of the earth . . . your place is always here . . .

ZARQA'S VOICE: I will know when I go out . . .

MASTER OF THE DOLLS: I warn you against disobeying me and against repeating this word . . .

ZARQA'S VOICE (*coming calmly*):   Don't you see?! I am no longer the doll that you used to play with.

MASTER OF THE DOLLS (*his eyes bulging in anger*):   Repeat what you have just said!!

ZARQA'S VOICE: I am no longer good for playing . . . no longer good for playing . . .

(MASTER OF THE DOLLS *rises up on his toes, piercing the back of* ZARQA'S *neck with a giant pin.*)

MASTER OF THE DOLLS: I am your master, you have no life outside my authority (*the door squeaks, then, begging*) . . . please . . . wait . . . you have no need to go out . . . I . . . I did not mean to hurt you . . . your anger is beautiful . . . but I did not mean to . . . (*then, as if an idea sparked in his head*) . . . Listen, those whom you want to see . . . I can bring them here . . . I'll bring them to you . . . here . . .

ZARQA'S VOICE: Here?!

MASTER OF THE DOLLS: Look. . . . (ESCAPED CHARACTER *hands him piles of newspapers . . . the* MASTER *scatters them around the statue*) . . . They are here, they have always been here . . . can't you see?!

ZARQA'S VOICE: I will know then why they have always been here . . .

MASTER OF THE DOLLS (*sarcastically*):   You? know?! You?! What a joke!! (*The sound of the squeaky door closing echoes in the theater.*)

MASTER OF THE DOLLS (*screaming madly*):   Come back! . . . I command you to come back! . . . (*then tensely*) . . . All of you, do something . . . do not just stand there and watch . . . she wants to know . . . she is a dangerous doll, she seeks knowledge . . . (*sitting on the ladder, holding his head with his hands, he shivers*) . . . I am to blame . . . I am the one who set free that genie of ambition in her (*he laughs uproariously*).

ESCAPED CHARACTER: Aren't you tired of repeating this play every day?! She . . . nothing will bring her back!

MASTER OF THE DOLLS (*screaming defiantly*):   She will return . . . the Master of the Dolls knows how to make her come back humiliated! . . . (*He climbs up the ladder, pulls long hairs from the scalp of the statue . . . wraps them around a piece of wood the size of a finger . . . then descends . . . dips it in the fire . . . A yellow smoke rises and fills the room . . . then, muttering her name backward*) Amamayla . . . Amamayla . . . put off . . . put off, put off . . . you come back . . . put off . . .

(*His words echo all over the stage. He climbs the ladder and pricks two pins in the eyes of the statue, then wraps the thread around its neck three times . . . He descends, seemingly satisfied. Going out, he closes the door behind him . . . ESCAPED CHARACTER explodes into laughter . . .*)

Curtain

Act 1, Scene 2

SCENARIST (*angry at the* ESCAPED CHARACTER):   You don't believe in me!? . . . I set you free and you don't believe in me?!
ESCAPED CHARACTER (Carelessly):   In fact, it is not my responsibility to believe or not to believe in you . . . (*then, sarcastically*) . . . You didn't release me . . . you wanted to imprison me in a stupid role . . . But I chose to be anything I wanted . . . Every morning I choose a new role for myself. Every day I discover a beautiful face for myself . . . until (*beating his chest*), until I fill this emptiness here . . .

Act 2, Scene 1

ESCAPED CHARACTER: We are in a theater . . . We don't care if you don't understand . . . (*sarcastically*) Do you think you are coming to a classroom?!
VIEWER: I too agree, I know now what I want . . . I want a real text . . . a narrative . . . After thirty years of professional viewing, I can't bear sitting in my seat for hours so you can recite an old memorized school piece . . .

Act 2, Scene 1

VIEWER: While I was watching, I felt nothing real was going on . . . Even you . . . (*pushing his fist into* SAMSON'S ACTOR'*s chest*) . . . No truth . . . No life . . . Why am I feeling this emptiness? (*Again he beats his chest.*)

Act 2, Scene 1

SAMSON'S ACTOR: I shall not start an argument about the significance of my role. It is a carefully plotted text . . . Any simple man would have understood the meaning of my standing in the mouth of the cave . . . The author implies this . . .
VIEWER: I didn't understand . . . Tell me what standing in the mouth of the cave means?
SAMSON'S ACTOR: The role says everything . . . (*with confusion*) I have nothing to add . . .
VIEWER: But I saw you. . . . The role really threw you . . .
SAMSON'S ACTOR: Maybe in this text . . . But . . . it is a periodic text (*closes his eyes and continues*) . . . What am I except a phase?

Act 2, Scene 1

ZARQA AL-YAMAMA: And your real existence? Where did you want to be?

SAMSON'S ACTOR: On stage, of course . . .

ZARQA AL-YAMAMA: On stage you repeat what others have written for you . . . But what about what you yourself want to say?

SAMSON'S ACTOR: I'm not an author . . .

ZARQA AL-YAMAMA (*interrupting*):   You are disguised in acting . . . from role to role to . . .

SAMSON'S ACTOR (*sharply*):   And why shouldn't I . . . ?!

ZARQA AL-YAMAMA: You are an echo then . . . You are not the one who rebelled or the one who surrendered . . . or the one who sweated or the one who lived and died . . .

Act 2, Scene 1

ZARQA AL-YAMAMA: I came from there . . . from the dry broken skins and blackened faces. I saw them while they were living . . . Nothing reaches them except the calling of the roosters at dawn, the burning of the sun, the howling of the air and the smell of the rain . . . Your voice, the roles that you play have no meaning for them . . . They don't need this from you . . .

SAMSON'S ACTOR: You don't understand, you are ignorant of the role of theater . . .

ZARQA AL-YAMAMA: You want a role? Fine. . . . Set fire to the dolls or stop echoing their empty words . . . what do you know about sweat, rain, cold, and pain?

SAMSON'S ACTOR: I played all this . . . And you say, why don't I sweat?

ZARQA AL-YAMAMA: Nothing but the sweat of numbness . . . You are drugged . . . how can you speak about the real sweat of people?!

ZARQA AL-YAMAMA: A dream kept me awake since I heard of your village being brought to life by the arm of a man . . . I experienced dreaming . . . I used to climb the mountain of the village often, there the desert and cities of stone came to me . . . I would draw a circle in the sand and I would listen . . . I heard it as a well . . . that lost well . . . I closed my eyes and I hid my heart. The well was wasted . . . I wanted you to resurrect this inner conviction strongly . . . But what appeared was not only a well, it was eyes [or springs of water] and a city and burning men, and your place was among them . . .

Act 2, Scene 1

ESCAPED CHARACTER: There is no written text . . . except as a structure for studying, or exploring . . .
SAMSON'S ACTOR: Do you want me to improvise?
ESCAPED CHARACTER: Exactly . . . you will improvise everything.
SAMSON'S ACTOR (*objecting*):   Improvisation leads to chaos . . . Disaster sometimes . . . There is no escape from a written text. One dot changes the word and inverts the meaning.
ESCAPED CHARACTER: These are our rules here.
SAMSON'S ACTOR: I have heard of those theaters that call for the actor to write his own text . . . But . . . for which causes do you play?
ESCAPED CHARACTER: The life of the cities of stone is our cause . . .

Act 3, Scene 1

SAMSON'S ACTOR: We need a new text in which I can grow . . .

Act 4

VIEWER: You are entering an ambiguous text . . . It requires an effort to understand . . .

Act 4

VIEWER (*smiling*):   He doesn't resemble Samson's Actor, nor even a clown . . . I can see everything from my place . . .

Act 4

VIEWER: An idea occurred to me . . . an unusual idea . . . It is the result of ten years of viewing, I am ready . . . I in fact might agree to be the new hero for your play . . . with a condition . . .

Act 4

MASTER OF THE DOLLS (*in terror*):   Shut up . . .

A Personal Sketch of Rajaa 'Alim

Before I left for the field I noticed that of the personal data I had on the writers, I had the least amount on Rajaa 'Alim. Despite my efforts during the previous seven years to collect interviews with Saudi Arabian women writers conducted by newspapers and magazines, I was surprised to find that my collection included not a single interview with Rajaa. As I made contacts in Jeddah, I discovered that this lack of a personal profile was due mainly to Rajaa's shying away from interviews rather than my own failure to obtain them. When I expressed a desire to meet her, those who either knew her or knew about her would nod and say, "Forget it, she does not give interviews." I was troubled at the thought of leaving Jeddah without interviewing her. When I met in Jeddah with the writer Noora Khalid As-sa'ad, one of Saudi Arabia's most respected and talented essayists who was also a friend of Rajaa, she promised to speak with Rajaa and give her my host's telephone number. She was at the time attending a training program for preschool educators arranged by UNESCO. A few days later I called her at work and she returned my call at my host's home. We spoke for almost half an hour about my project, after which she seemed excited and invited me to visit with her in her home.

I met Rajaa a short time after the breaking of fast one Ramadhan night, where both she and her sister Shadya greeted me at the door. Shadya, who is a talented painter, has designed the covers of some of her sister's books. The two sisters seemed close. Shadya participated in the discussion from time to time, while ensuring that the etiquette of the well-known Arabian hospitality was not forgotten. Traditional Ramadhanian sweets, nuts, teas, and soft drinks were placed before me on the coffee table in rapid succession. During our discussion, I learned that Shadya was Rajaa's most enthusiastic reader and at the same time her most ardent critic. The interview lasted five hours, and it was one of my most memorable meetings—as enjoyable as it was intellectually stimulating.

At the beginning of the meeting, Rajaa laughingly remarked, "Did you expect me to look like an ugly old maid, deformed like my characters?" I did not, but I had to admit that her strikingly gentle appearance carries no resemblance to any of her "deformed" characters.

I probably imagined her to be a few years older, but she was barely approaching her thirties. The flash of Rajaa's eyes sparked in the softly lighted room, and told of a brilliant mind. The distinction between interviewer/interviewee was abandoned, to the point where looking at my note cards seemed an oddity, leaving our discussion to take a life of its own. The interview centered on her literary and cultural concerns, and on her conception of the role of intellectuals and literature in her society. But in the interview she also spoke about her childhood in Makkah, her close attachment to nature, and her fondness for its creatures. Her happiest childhood memories centered on the times her family spent in the cool orchards of Ṭaif, the famous summer retreat from Makkah's sizzling heat, Jeddah's unbearable humidity, and possibly Riyadh summer dust storms.

Before she moved to Jeddah with her parents, Rajaa spent her childhood in the holy city of Makkah, where she and her parents were born. Rajaa spoke of the atmosphere of tolerance and open-mindedness that her father had established in the family. He was a middle-class man who, although religious, was also an independent thinker. In the 1940s, amid the religious leaders' strong opposition to allowing radio into the country, her father was one of the first Makkans to bring a radio into his home and to listen to songs aired from Cairo. Also, he did not hesitate to ensure that his daughters were properly educated. Rajaa and Shadya both obtained their B.A. degrees in English literature from Riyadh University, and both currently work in the field of education.

From her early childhood years, Rajaa demonstrated a keen interest in reading whatever was available in Arabic translations of children's world literatures. She was especially fond of mythology and animal stories. These influences were to appear in her own writings, in which she extensively uses animals and other creatures of nature as symbols. Although she started writing at an early age, she appeared in the literary field in the mid-1970s. She has written articles, short stories, and plays, as well as novellas. She wrote for the *'Ukaz* literary supplement, contributed regularly to the *Riyadh*'s weekly column, "Letters and Thoughts," while also contributing other columns such as "The Sand Clock" and "The Mirror's Memory." These titles reflect her consciousness of the dimension of time in human existence, as well as her belief in the human being as the maker of reflection, not as a reflection—a belief that the metaphor of the mirror signifies.

Despite her contributions to the literary movement in her own country, Rajaa has received most of her recognition from abroad. Although active in the field of writing by the late 1970s, her name was not included in the 1984 *Guide to Saudi Writers*. Rajaa has participated in the activities of the Jeddah Literary Club by reading her stories, and has authored four books, three of which were published in Beirut by Dar Al-Adāb. These latter three include *The Final Death of the Actor,* parts of which are translated here (1987a); *Holes in the Back* (1987c); and *Dancing on the Edge of the Thorn* (n.d.). The fourth volume, entitled *Four/Zero,* won the Ibn Ṭofail Award in 1985 from the Spanish Arab Institute in Madrid. This was also the only one of Rajaa's books to be published by Annadi Ath-Thaqafi Al-Adabi in Jeddah (1987b).

This lack of recognition in her own country is partly due to Rajaa's ideological orientations, which make religious leaders uncomfortable with her messages. The genre she favors, play writing, is in itself the most marginalized form of literature, being nonindigenous. But it is also partly her style that puzzles (if not antagonizes) many segments of her audience: critics, fellow writers, as well as readers. Rajaa's previous remark about the nature of her characters reflects her awareness of the kind of image her writing style (or perhaps her critics' interpretation of it) has created in people's minds. Her use of symbols, for example, appears to be inconsistent in the manner in which they act as symbols. Fish, as she points out, might at one point symbolize life, at another might symbolize death.

Also in her characterizations and settings, Rajaa tends to highlight either pathological states or to portray situations that are most unfamiliar. Her characters are often deformed, with "holes in their backs." They often carry numbers rather than names (e.g., Four, Zero, The Millionth). They may be patients in a hospital, they may be in a coma, or they may even be dead, but their ghosts dominate the setting. Their sick, pathological, powerless bodies, as well as the tone of their dialogue, are all geared toward making symbolic statements and are made to yield to allegory. "The smell of death is strong in this room," says one of her characters in *Holes in the Back,* in an apparent reference to the political malaise in her world.

While these characteristics of style have identified Rajaa in the minds of many critics (some of whom are local but most are from other Arab countries) as one of Saudi Arabia's most original writers, with a genuine bent for symbolic thought, these same characteristics have also had a negative effect on the reception of her works on the local level. Some modernist critics judge her according to, as she says, "a naive conception of realism. They do not think that I portray reality. This is because even as thinkers we have no vision and are not equipped to see what is beyond." Her traditionalist critics believe this "lack" of realism to be a sign of her lack of attachment to her culture. But Rajaa insists, "All my images are related to this land. True, I dream of extending my existence beyond it, but never to abandon it. I cannot imagine myself living in another culture. It is the challenge that this culture poses to my intellect that feeds me with my ideas." Her female audience also accuses her of being overly philosophical, and of suppressing women's issues. Even college women feel frustrated at their inability to follow her train of thought. When I asked a female student in the University of Jeddah if she reads Rajaa's works, she replied, "I did once, but I hate to be made to feel stupid, which I know I am not."

In fact Rajaa has frequently been quoted as saying, "It does not matter if people cannot understand me," a statement that is often interpreted as a sign of condescension toward her readers and a lack of sensitivity to their need for clarity. But despite all these charges that restrict her readership to a small circle (consisting mostly of men), she voices no anxiety over her limited number of local readers. "When I portray deformed characters," Rajaa explains, "I in fact signify a deformed reality. I have come to realize that people do not want to see themselves as deformed. They are afraid that if they look harder they will recognize themselves in my characters." She may be right—but on the face of it, it seems that while Rajaa in her work asserts the right of everyone to participate in the formation of discourse, she ends up speaking in codes and being elitist in her choice of a target audience. Indeed, one can only understand Rajaa's work by understanding her conception of writing and the role of both reader and writer as intellectuals in the society.

Rajaa does not deny that, more by virtue of their content than by their form, most of her works have in fact been geared toward the intellectual. Her choice of intellectuals as her target audience has to do with the significance she accords their role as leaders if any movement for change were to occur. The subtlety of control of what she calls "the culture of the center" requires intellectuals to form a kind of counter-culture, which she calls "the culture of the periphery." The intellectual should not only register social protest but should also advance a theory of reality, of change, and of practice. As can be seen in the extracts of her play translated here, the intellectual (as represented by the Escaped Character in *The Final Death of the Actor*) has supposedly "escaped" the trap, and thus is able to provide a vision.

The primary function of literature, according to Rajaa, is the "liberation of the individual."[38] Intellectuals can make their mark by breaking the patterning of thought that the "culture of the center" imposes on individuals. Patterning of thought [or *tanmeet* in Arabic] is for Rajaa a powerful tool, utilized by the centers of power to ensure a high degree of consensus in their definition of "truth." Rajaa attempts in her use of symbols to engender a new way of looking at them. She chooses the manner in which they act as symbols, and creates for them a new context:

> I do not let the reader assume that I use a camel, for example, as a symbol of patience. I would use a camel in different contexts to break this pattern of symbolization. But even in my own writing I face a contradiction. I am basically against patterning, which means that I am also against naming. Once you name something, you create a pattern. But in order to give recognition to the new world I create in my stories, I have to give it a name. As a writer, I realize the power of naming and I have to use it, but at the same time I try not to subject my reader to new patterns or new forms of enslavement [of thought]. (personal communication, 1989)

Basically, the reader should be encouraged to generate his or her own interpretations. According to Rajaa, reading is not a passive activity; it should be as active and as creative as writing. She sees the multiplicity of readings as a measure of the writer's success at breaking old patterns. It is no wonder, then, that Rajaa dedicates her play to the "ad-lib-bers"—a role that can be performed by both writers as well as readers. Rajaa's favorite type of readers are those who improvise—who read "outside" the text. Only thus does the reader attain "liberation." While this conception burdens the reader with the role of critic, it also frustrates the traditionalists. Rajaa's superb use of language, with her extensive knowledge of its rules and her powerful and felicitous form-ulations, give her control over connotations, thus depriving the tradi-tionalists of their authority and the right to control meanings. It is probably this trespass on what the 'ulama see as their province [lan-guage] that endows Rajaa's undertaking with such seriousness (see chapter 5). The selections from Rajaa's play presented here were chosen because they are representative of her concerns and her style—both within the play itself and throughout her works. While admittedly other segments of other plays were as good as these, these selections yielded more to translation because of their clarity of ideas and their minimal use of allusions. These are important considerations when presenting literature to a foreign audience.

Rajaa's Settings and Patterns of Characterization: A Model of Reality?

The play opens with a scene from a doll factory. The dolls are feature-less. They have only foreheads and mouths. The mouth occupies most of the face. These dolls are attached to a string and carry no names, only numbers. The absence of names enables Rajaa to undermine the status of the real for these dolls, as well as to emphasize their lack of rooted-ness. Lack of names is consistent with Rajaa's conception of the uproot-ing of individuals and their alienation from the realities of the present as well as of history. Names, while by their very nature are a means of individualization, are paradoxically a means of connectedness through genealogy. Only three women are named in the play. Zarqa's name is a "seeing name." Her name can make things happen and, in fact, is treated by the Master of the Dolls as a magical formula. Numbers, on the other hand, are characteristic of depersonalization, alienation, and individuational tendencies.

The play's characters are mostly men, signifying their dominance of the stage in real life. Only three women characters are in the play— Zarqa, Delilah, and the Saleswoman, who is the mother of Samson's

Actor. Delilah's name, as Samson's, is derived from the Myth of Gilgamesh. Zarqa is portrayed as a statue, and identified as a woman who is beyond the influence of time. The other two women's ages are also unknown. The male characters belong to different generations, which seem to correspond to times of upheaval in Arab history. Samson's Actor was to be born in 1967, the year of the Arab-Israeli war, while the Viewer and the Scenarist were born in the 1950s, the major event of that time being the triple aggression of Britain, France, and Israel against Egypt in 1956. The Master of the Dolls was born in the 1940s, a decade that witnessed, in addition to other developments, the occupation of Palestine and the post-World War II partition of the Arab world into small "independent" states.

The scene is carefully designed so that every element conveys a symbolic statement. The huge pictures of Zarqa reflect her dominating presence in the scene. She is at times a doll, at other times, a statue. A statue is almost a doll, except that it signifies higher status and perhaps reverence. Two processes go hand in hand in the idea of Zarqa as statue and as doll. Women, while they are used as a symbol, idealized and venerated, are at the same time denigrated as "real" human beings, their individuality suppressed—mass-produced toys. The statue is of "polished wood," occupying a "separate" corner. The statue is situated in the midst of a strong light that surrounds it constantly, signifying the vigilance under which women are constantly placed. The statue's arms are tied. A thread surrounds the neck. The mouth occupies most of the face. Obviously, she is capable of speaking. In fact, Zarqa herself is present mostly as a "voice."

It is the "light" that reveals to us that "pins" pierce the area of the eyes. The eyes are obliterated because the statue seems to embody a "wishful thinking" conception of the woman—that she does not need eyes, that she is not able to see, or even possibly that she should be blinded. But that she is pierced in the area of the eyes in order to prevent her from seeing does not end the fear that even without eyes she might be able to see—for she has a "seeing name." The pins, as well her pictures that are full of holes, signify more than an attempt at blinding her—they signify vengeful acts against her. Even when the eyes are obliterated, the Master of the Dolls never ceases to feel he is under her scrutiny. She "penetrates" and "pierces" him with her glances. He retaliates by piercing her with huge pins.

The vengeful act seems to be in response to a feeling of frustration that dominates the relationship of the Master of the Dolls and his creation. The Master's frustration with the doll springs from his helplessness and lack of control over her. He thought he had created no more than a "skeleton and a piece of white surface" on which he could write any text. But she proved him wrong, and he seems unsure of her nature. When she speaks of "going out," he accuses her of repeating the word like a doll. He expected "warmth" and "gratitude" from her, but these cannot be obtained from a doll. The Escaped Character confronts him with the contradiction embedded in his expectations by asking: Was it a doll that he wanted or a woman? The Master thought the only difference was in an "eye." The Master's plan was to "see" for her; she was to listen and follow. He created an area for the eyes, hoping they would spark with the right amount of warmth. They not only sparked but flared with rebellion.

Genre as a Conception of Reality

Although she also writes articles and short stories, Rajaa's choice of play writing as a favorite literary form is not only a function of her personal talent but also of her conception of reality and her philosophical stand on the nature of society. Wherever she turns, Rajaa finds people who are deeply alienated from reality. Society for her is only a spectacle consisting of actors and actresses, of stages, and of parroted texts.

If Ruqayya uses the court to reflect her preoccupation with the question of justice, Rajaa uses the stage to convey her conception of society as a theater, to indicate the undermining of reality. In Rajaa's play, because it is written mainly to be read rather than performed, she is careful to attend to many details that facilitate the shifting of the reader's role to that of director. While these details give a determinant role to the reader, they also function symbolically to visually convey the nature of the spectacle. For example, she manipulates such elements as the structure of the stage, which is "closed," not only to signify the element of enclosure in reality but also because of the advantage of such a structure in controlling the lighting. Lighting plays an important symbolic role in making statements on the nature of the power centers' control of knowledge. In addition to her dialogue, with its images and symbolic import, the time, the plot, and the locations of the scenes all have important symbolic functions. Other details are also used symbolically, such as scene shifting, stage entrances, dividers, background, sound, and names (or lack thereof).

The stage is so important to Rajaa as a means of reflecting on reality (or lack of it) that it is transformed to a concept, to be manipulated symbolically within the text itself. She creates a play within the play— with its actors and actresses, director, scenarist, and viewers. Not only does Rajaa describe minute details of the structure of her own stage but also of the stage on which the story takes place. In fact, the actors themselves discuss these elements. Zarqa, for example, analyzes the stage on which she is standing: "Touch this ground . . . listen (knocks on the ground with her foot) . . . This ground is made of wood . . . Wood is easy to disintegrate . . . with all this humidity it won't last . . . As small an insect as a termite is enough to transform your ground to sawdust" ('Alim 1987b:72). In fact, the Escaped Character reminds everyone, "We are in a theater . . . We don't care if you don't understand." The Viewer also pops up from his seat from time to time to protest or comment.

The dialogue itself centers on the connection between stage, script, role, and reality. Especially through her dialogue with Samson's Actor, Zarqa highlights the notions of acting, and expresses concern with reality. Samson's Actor wants to be on stage, to act endlessly. Zarqa is repelled by the idea: "On stage you repeat what others have written for you . . . But what about what you, yourself, want to say?" Samson's Actor seems to be aware of the difference, stating: "I'm not an author." But Zarqa is not convinced that he has an existence outside of his "roles" as an actor: "You are an echo then . . . You are not the one who rebelled or the one who surrendered . . . or the one who sweated or the one who lived and died." For Zarqa, Samson's Actor has no real existence, he is "disguised in acting," he is an echo, a shadow.

Not only is the whole stage a representation of reality, with its structure, design, and doll factory, but the lighting also plays a decisive role. While lighting is normally a complementary element to a closed-stage type of setting, in Rajaa's play it functions as a statement on the nature of knowledge and the function of the knowledgeable. On the one hand, light could function as a means of vigilance. We are told that "the light in the factory is strong," that the statue of Zarqa is situated "in the midst of a strong light that surrounds it and constantly falls on it." On the other hand, light is a means of controlling knowledge which, according to Rajaa, has always been the power centers' favorite method. Light becomes a means of gaining access to a reality that is otherwise dimmed. It is the light, for example, that reveals to us the statue's condition: "thin pins piercing the area of the eyes . . . and a thin thread wraps around the neck and arms . . . " It is the function of the intellectuals, which the Escaped Character symbolizes, to throw light on aspects of our lives that have been kept in the dark, and that as a result have been denied existence.

To Know or Not to Know: The Nature of Spectacle and the Nature of Reality

In addition to the symbolic use Rajaa makes of the setting, the stage as well as the lighting), and of characters and names, Zarqa embodies another element that enables Rajaa to make a broader statement on the relationship of power and knowledge. In Rajaa's hands, the symbol of Zarqa acquires additional power through context. Zarqa's qualities of vision and foresight, for example, while making statements on the position of women in her society, become an important means by which to explore other broad issues—such as the relationship between power and knowledge. Zarqa's experience as a statue in the play, especially in terms of her relationship to the Master of the Dolls in the doll factory, symbolizes power relations in society at large.

The existent relations of men and women are important mainly in their epistemological implications; that is, they constitute a concern for Rajaa insofar as they serve as a model to critique the existing power/ knowledge relationship. Relations of men and women stand in almost an allegorical relationship to relations of the governing and the governed which, according to Rajaa, lies at the heart of all issues, including those of women. Women's oppression is only one manifestation of the relations of power in society. But these relations of power, if they are to be understood, have first and foremost to be deconstructed.

Because of her epistemological concern, the juxtaposition of reality/ spectacle permeates the whole play. Reality does indeed exist, but it only exists "outside" the theater. People "outside" experience "sweat, rain, cold, and pain." Zarqa had access to these people when she went "out." She found that they do not respond to acting:

> I came from there . . . from the dry broken skins and blackened faces. I saw them while they were living . . . Nothing reaches them except the calling of the roosters at dawn, the burning of the sun, the howling of the air, and the smell of the rain . . . Your voice, the roles that you play have no meaning for them . . . They don't need this from you.

But if Samson's Actor is so keen on "acting," Zarqa suggests to him that in reality there is room for "action." A theater is no substitute for reality, but the opposite is true: "You want a role? Fine. . . . Set fire to the dolls or stop echoing their empty words." His sweat in acting is "nothing but the sweat of numbness."

The reality for Zarqa, far from being a stage made of wood, lies in "the life of the cities of stone." Unlike a stage made of wood, these cities are a symbol of solid reality, as well as of rootedness and historical achievement. The motifs of reality include—in addition to the cities of stone—the desert, the sand, a well, the springs, and the burning men with "dry broken skins and blackened faces." Anything that happens on the stage has no bearing on them.

Reality may be betrayed through a lack of light, but a lack of access to light is also a function of a confined space. Light seems to reflect both the spatial and the temporal aspects of the problem of knowledge. One has to "get out" if one is to have access to the truth. This is a critique of the mentality that treats what is hidden and kept in the dark as nonexistent. To believe that what we see is what exists is to give the centers of power the weapon by which they can defeat the powerless. To promote the belief that what we see is what exists is an effort both to promote an illusion and to create a consensus in order to curb dissent.

The people who lived in Zarqa's time acted according to a theory of knowledge based on the "faulty" assumption that what they saw is what constituted reality and truth. The real Zarqa, with her qualities of vision and foresight, "knew" that reality lay beyond. Zarqa, the character in the play, is also able to see through that control and beyond it. It is noteworthy that her "seeing" or "awakening" is partly accomplished through dreaming: "A dream kept me awake." Paradoxically, dreaming for Zarqa does not occur while she is asleep, in fact it is by virtue of her dream that Zarqa is kept "awake," and thus able to have a grasp on reality as opposed to those who are eternally "sedated." When she climbs the mountain of the village to see what is beyond the hills, as the real Zarqa did, "there the desert and cities of stone came to me." She draws a circle in the sand, she listens, speaks, sees, feels, and even dreams. She is all aware, she uses all her senses without "numbness" or "sedation," for to know is to exhaust all senses and never fall out of consciousness.

"Going Out": The Need for Reinterpretation of Texts

Unlike Ruqayya's protagonist in "The Appeal," in which the character ventures "outside" the institutionalized reality only in dreams, Zarqa is able to realize and grasp the reality mainly by "going out." It is only by "going out" that she can see through the deception. But the word *out* is dangerous. For a woman—or for anyone, for that matter—to be "out" means subversion and being "out of control." When Zarqa "goes out" the door always squeaks, and the noise echoes throughout the theater. Her going out is an event that never goes unnoticed or unannounced or even unheard. Mainly a function of her being under vigilance, if her movement is not seen it is heard. Her going out is seen to be fatal by the Master of the Dolls, for she can never have a life "outside his authority." The Master has to do whatever it takes to keep her "in." He first tries to convince her that he is capable of bringing the "outside in," but he fails. In order to control her, the Master then resorts to magic. For him, her name contains the magical formula. If pronounced backward, the effect of the name will be reversed.

When he reminds her that her "place is always here," Zarqa becomes even more determined to finish her journey to knowledge. To his amazement, she replies: "I only will know when I go out." She wants to "go out" not only to know the "real" others but also to know her place. Zarqa wants to make sure of where she stands in relation to a larger context. She might end up preferring her "place," but that will only result from her own discovery—her personally established knowledge and choice—not from coercion or from being kept in the dark.

When the Master of the Dolls proposes to bring the outside reality "in," the solution is not acceptable to her, for he does not bring "the real" but rather brings "them" as texts—they are "spilled" on paper. Zarqa obviously "reads" about "them," they exist for her only on paper. The real people exist only as a subject of discourse; what is said about "them" is what constitutes her knowledge. But she rejects this type of knowledge that deprives her from access to them as real human beings who live with "dry broken skins" and "dark faces" burned by the sun. She discovers that the texts written on them not only are misleading but are also deceptive. For while they live in these texts, in reality they are dying. It is imperative, then, for Zarqa to "go out" of the text in order to have access to the truth, to reality.

When she faces the Master with her disillusionment with texts, he is astonished. How does she know all that when he did not teach her? This question, to which he finds no answer, haunts the Master. He seems to be puzzled and confused about her nature; he is not sure if she is a doll or a woman. He forgets the implication of her "seeing name," which enables her to see what is far and beyond. For him she becomes a dangerous doll who is seeking the forbidden fruit of knowledge. Not only does she now know but she also wants to act on her knowledge and rebel against what has always defined knowledge, that is, texts.

The concept of stepping "outside," then, entails the elimination of all types of confinement, primarily the confinement to a certain text or to a certain reading of a text. The texts, being unreliable sources of truth and a source of deception, are also alienating from reality. Other characters agree with Zarqa. The Viewer wants "a real text . . . a narrative." The texts at hand, the Viewer asserts, have "nothing real going on . . . No truth . . . No life." Zarqa advocates experiencing life, not reading it as a text. She redefines knowledge in total negation of what exists by advocating reading what is outside the texts. That alone makes her a dangerous doll. But her real danger lies in the fact that she advances a theory of knowledge that resonates. Even Samson's Actor, the assistant of the Master of the Dolls, wants a "new text" in which he "can grow." He discovers that "the" text is not a "carefully plotted text" after all. He looks for a solution: "I have heard of those theaters that call for the actor to write his own text." The Viewer himself (he is a man) complains of the ambiguity of meaning in the text; he does not, for example, understand what "standing in the mouth of the cave means." The Escaped Character suggests that he improvise.

But Samson's Actor resists that idea. Perhaps fearing to make explicit a sexual implication in the phrase, he announces that "Improvisation leads to chaos . . . even disaster sometimes . . . There is no escape from a written text. One dot changes the word and inverts the meaning."[39]

Improvisation breaks the mechanism of control, of consensus. To engender resistance to the prevalent patterns of thought is a form of empowerment to the powerless.[40] Rajaa maintains, not only in this play but also in her other writings, that the only guarantee against domination is to resist falling prey to the patterning of thought. Patterning is designed only to generate consensus—a consensus she sees as existing only to serve the power structures rather than as a means of transforming them. Oppressive power for Rajaa can only be defeated by engendering different readings and engaging in reinterpretation. Rajaa is against consensus but not consistency, and the dedication of the play to the ad-libbers is consistent with her flair for improvisation.

Victimization/Literature:
The Poetics of Justice and
the Politics of Representation

This chapter investigates another aspect of the relationship between the creative process and social considerations within the works of three short-story writers: Sharifa As-Shamlan, Khayriyya As-Saggaf, and Najwa Hashim. Selections from their works are presented, followed by a personal sketch of each writer. Instead of their works being analyzed individually, as in chapters 2 and 4, their works are analyzed in terms of themes and messages. The purpose of this is to explore how these writers' decisions regarding what is artistically possible are made in relation to what is socially permissible. Specifically, the patterns of characterization and vindication of action that emerge in their fiction are examined by addressing several questions: Who is the victim? Who are the victimizing agents? How and why is one agent blamed rather than another? Why are women characters often sentenced to madness, death, ostracism, or all three? How do solutions proposed bear on the experience of women and on notions of consciousness and resistance? Finally, how are settings and modes of interaction within the fiction used both to affirm and to challenge social demarcation of space and time?

These, as other women writers, seem to be in a constant state of decision making—and at times compromise—regarding certain elements of storytelling. Although these decisions are made more or less consciously, they reveal the nature and scope of limitations that are placed on the writers' craft—whether social, cultural, or political. The constant balancing of protest against requirements of social rules seem to point to the writers' profound understanding of the interplay between the spoken and the unspoken. While they ensure a safe passage for their messages, they maintain the balance between social constraints on their enterprise and their desire for their literature to be an element of resistance and protest—not only in relation to issues that pertain to women but also to other serious issues, such as those that pertain to social class.

Sharifa Ash-Shamlan: Selections from Her Writings

Sections from a Life[1]

First section: I am twenty now, I am sure. My mother died when I was ten. I was brought here when I was seventeen. Every year I would plant a palm tree. I have been here for three years now. I know that from the number of my father's visits. Every Ramadhan, he visits me three times.

Another section: Today is the Waqfa, tomorrow is the Eid of Sacrifice.[2] They are decorating the place, not for the Eid but because an official is said to be visiting. I asked for a pencil and paper. I told them I wanted to write a long, long letter to my mother and a greeting card to my father. They refused. They were afraid I would write a complaint to the official. I laughed at them secretly, and so hard. I don't even know how to write in the first place!

And another section: The official has arrived. I laughed so hard as I was watching the official. He was puffed up, so puffed up indeed. The nurses lined up on both sides, clean and shiny. As he came close to me, I heard the chief doctor whispering to him, "She's dangerous!" I tried to extend my hand and touch his *abaya,* he drew a smile on his face and said, "What do you wish for, young woman?" I said, "I want to touch your *abaya.*" "Why?" he said. I gestured to him to bend down and bring his ear closer. He did, and I whispered, "I want to see how much your *abaya* can be sold for, and if the price would be enough to buy candy for the children of my village . . ." He laughed, and then left. The eyes of the chief doctor bulged out in terror . . .

A rear section: The look of the chief doctor with maps on his face makes me laugh. I myself drew those maps with my own fingernails . . . One day he wanted to break my pride (. . . . !). I tried to break his nose, I could not . . . I only colored his face with his own blood.

A small section: A female worker brought my food . . . I asked no questions. She said she gave my slice of meat to the neighbor's dog because it was hungry. I said he probably deserves it.

Horizontal section: The nurse comes, as usual, with a needle in her hand. She does not plunge it into my arm; instead she pours its contents in another bottle that she hides in her bra. It doesn't matter anymore. It is true, the needle takes me to beautiful worlds, to spacious universes . . . but it also leaves me in a dark world and with horrible headaches. I said to the nurse: "I wish you would bring me some palm prickles . . . a lot . . . please . . ." "Why?" she asked mindlessly. I answered, "I would like to use them to make a rail around my bed . . ." I then pinched her belly, rather harshly . . . She whooped, wrapped her coat around her, and hurriedly disappeared.

A section of pain: One day my father bought me some bracelets. My stepmother brought them to me, along with the golden necklaces and anklets. I was so happy and showed them to my friends . . . I didn't care much for them. I was only happy because my father had become a rich man. I stood there looking at my bracelets; they were shining in the light of the sun. I heard a resonant sound . . . A huge tractor was sweeping away the orchard. It was coming close to my palms. I screamed and screamed, and then ran and sat in front of the vehicle. . . . My stepmother pulled me away, saying, "We have sold the orchard; it is going to be made into a paved street." I pulled her hair and scratched her face. She said, "Shouldn't you ask where the bracelets came from?" I threw the bracelets under the huge vehicle. . . . At this point I was brought here.

Last section: The woman worker came to me one day and said, "They wrote about you in the newspapers . . ." "Why?" I asked. She said,

"The official has sent candy to the children of your village." I asked, "Were the children happy?" She said, "Yes . . . they sent a telegram thanking the official."

Secret and Death [3]

On a rock at the edge of a stagnant pond she sat, pressing the washed clothes on another rock, then squeezing them. She repeated the process over and over again . . . rinsing them, then dropping them in the wash basin, piling them on top of each other. Around her exhausted head, filled with thousands of images, she wrapped a ragged piece of cloth. Wiping the sweat off her wrinkled forehead, she tried to stand up with the wash basin on her head. But a prickle with a long thorn pierced through her toe. She put her load down, bending to take it off and throwing it aside carelessly. Her foot, which had never known shoes before, had gotten used to thorns. She put the basin back on her head, wrapping her old apron around her skinny body, which was so in spite of the two bulges on her chest which signified her sex and nothing more.

She walked heavily, while mumbling a sad, folkloric melody. A group of children interrupted her singing, yelling "The crazy one is here . . . the crazy one is here . . ." They threw stones, some of which fell on the basin, producing a piercing sound. She screamed, "Sons of the ——! Am I the crazy one or your mothers who left you roaming the streets?" "It is you . . . you . . ." said the most ferocious of the boys. The veins in her neck bulged out as she continued: "The crazy one does not wash clothes . . . I wash your clothes, your filth." "That is because you are crazy," answered the same boy, sarcastically.

Enraged, she bit on the lower part of her dress as her apron and basin fell to the ground. Holding a big stone, she ran after the boy. He hid behind one of the houses. . . . At this moment, a young man emerged from the dusty alley. He seemed to be a company worker . . . When she saw him, her fingers relaxed and she let the stone drop to the floor. "What is it, Zahra?" inquired the young man, rather sympathetically. "They call me crazy . . . I am not crazy . . . the crazy one is your sister who labeled me . . . your sister, the criminal who made people believe her . . . I am not crazy . . . I say what I feel."

His sister was Zahra's stepmother. Fearing that her brother might one day marry Zahra, she spread the rumor that Zahra was crazy. People believed her because Zahra actually acted in a way that people normally view as crazy.

He patted her shoulder and said kindly, "No, Zahra, you are not crazy. You are a good-hearted person at a time when goodness is considered sheer madness." She felt as if the heavens opened up for her . . . the world was in celebration . . . The drums were beating and the singing became louder and louder . . . She ran and ran to reach that wedding celebration she perceived. Overjoyed, she danced and danced . . . The boys gathered and clapped . . . The mothers emerged from their houses . . . The one who gave the clothes for Zahra to wash yelled, "Oh, my children's clothes!" An old one-eyed woman responded, "Don't you know she's crazy?" The woman answered, "It's probably my bad luck . . . her madness shows only when it concerns me."

Zahra danced until she fell from exhaustion. One of the girls with dirty, dusty hair went to Zahra's brother's house and told him about her. The brother and his wife came. The man extended a warm kind hand, while his wife's hand, cold as nails, pierced Zahra's arm. When they entered their house, the wife said disgustedly, "Am I fated to live with crazy people?" Her husband gave her a look that prevented her from saying more.

Since that day, Zahra entered a new phase. She formed a shell within herself. Looking around, she found no one to lean on . . . They were all gone. She cried bitterly. But every day she would go to the stagnant pond to wash clothes, meet with the lover, then dance—which was followed by her total collapse . . . Soon the women of the village refused to give her clothes to wash anymore, because she would go and come back without them . . . She was also spared the children's stones and screams, because the school year had already started.

The dusty quarter was wrapped up in calmness when the lover whispered to her to meet him tomorrow, Thursday, in an isolated spot . . . An overwhelming joy tickled inside her tiny chest. She felt the beating drums turning to soft melodies . . . She did not dance or fall to the ground this time. She walked to her brother's house with the lightness of a fourteen-year-old girl . . . She washed her dirty old dress . . . She sneaked perfume, some *kuhl* for her eyes and blush from her brother's wife's room, and hid it under the old mattress.

Before anyone woke up, she sneaked outside to go to the meeting place. She spread the fragrance all over her body, and applied the makeup. Her face looked like a painting scribbled by a careless child who tried to apply the colors in the right places but whose hand went left and right. When she met with her lover, a bird sang within her heart. Thursday became a sacred day in her life . . . she became more quiet . . . more serious . . . she stopped roaming the streets and dancing . . . she also stopped sleeping two nights a week, Thursdays and Fridays.

Days passed, and two things became enlarged in Zahra's body . . . her belly and her foot. Nobody paid attention to the foot. The belly, however, attracted all the attention. It shook the mustaches and beards of the old men as well as the young men of the village . . . What had been a whisper turned into a loud protest . . . "The crazy Zahra is pregnant!" echoed along village walls and the prickles of the palm trees. Her brother tried to find out something from her, begged her, told her that he would do what he could to protect her, but she would not tell him anything . . . The authorities also tried to interrogate her and her brother, to no avail. She wept silently at first, then her cries turned to howling. She howled like a hungry, sick wolf.

On a misty, gloomy morning, a car stopped at the end of the alley . . . The wooden door squeaked when Zahra emerged and entered the car . . . The village children and women lined up around the scene. One woman held her child up to get a better view of what was happening. Meanwhile, the company's bus was picking up its workers . . . One of the workers looked down, quietly and sadly . . . A child who was standing by him turned to him and said, "Father, they took the crazy woman." His father looked at him with tears in his eyes. He wished he could have screamed, telling the world, "No, she is not crazy, she is the most sane of all the sane . . . she had protected his name, his reputation . . . she had protected him, the sane, while he let her down and left her to face the unknown."

Days passed . . . the memory of the crazy woman faded in people's minds. Men's mustaches calmed down . . . women resumed their normal talk. But two people had not forgotten Zahra—the young man and her brother. The first was left with a hole in his heart because of her silence. The brother searched the eyes of all men for the one who committed the crime against his mad sister.

The Eid of Sacrifice approached; the wealthy slaughtered sheep for their dead, and people were overjoyed with the occasion. The mayor of the village knocked on the door from which Zahra had left two months ago . . . Her brother invited him in, while a strange feeling crept into his heart . . . The mayor handed him an envelope. It was already opened, although it was addressed to him personally. He read it once, but could not understand its contents until he read it for the third time.

The brother let out a loud cry and dropped the letter. The last hope had vanished. His mad sister had left this life as a result of the poisoning in her foot . . . The baby had died with her, and so did a secret she would never reveal.

Nawal[4]

I felt the burning sun of July under my bare feet. The blaze of one o'clock in the afternoon penetrates my *abaya* and sets my brain on fire . . . Oh no . . . but my heart is also in flames. My daughter Nawal was on my shoulders. For the first time I took her out at this hour; we were burning together in the sun after I was thrown out of the house . . . I tried to shelter her from the sun's blaze anyway I could . . . but the blaze was my fate from which there was no escape. A white car reflecting even more of the sun's rays was following me and my little girl . . . I was in a state of mind that allowed me neither to think nor to remember.

What I have just described is all I can remember before I reached this place, I don't know what I have done . . . I don't know the fate of my Nawal! Nawal has a tanned complexion, black hair and dark eyes. She has a dimple in the right side of her face that goes even deeper when she laughs . . . I have a burning desire to see her . . . I don't know where she is now . . . All I remember is voices clamoring around me from the left and the right . . . Papers were held by a policeman who led me to the huge door . . . The door that would make me shiver just imagining my having to pass through . . . The policeman took me to a woman, dark and huge . . . her lips jutted out and dangled on her neck. Her nose was big enough for a mouse to enter quietly. She dragged me by my hair to a dark place. I imagined each wall as a black mountain sliding toward me to crush me to death, then sliding back, pressing me time and again. The woman pushed me into a room that had no door. I was received by the impudent laugh of one of the women in the room. It made my hair stand on end . . . Another yelled in an accent of one of the Arab countries, "Why is the moon embarrassed . . . we are all in the same trouble!" . . . Laughs came from all sides, hammering at my head . . . I asked Allah to protect me. I could not even move my lips . . . I felt I was losing control of my entire body . . . Again the dark woman pulled me to another place, I did not know what it was until I found myself falling on a foam mat with no cover. One of the women yelled . . . "Don't sit on my bed . . . you need to be sanitized . . . you still carry all the diseases of the outside world." I dragged my body as a bundle to the cool floor. Its coolness gave me comfort. I don't know how much time passed . . . I probably came in the afternoon and woke up the next day, or the opposite . . . I don't know . . .

I looked around me . . . Three women wearing only their slips were cracking sunflower seeds . . . four other women lay flat on their stomachs, whispering, and seemed totally absorbed in chatting . . . Two of the women on the right side had striking make-up and tattoos—one with a big tattoo on her chin, the other with a small one between her eyebrows. I was still in my *abaya* when one of those in their slips screamed at me, "Take off your *abaya!*" And then she added bitterly, "It is safe here, there are no men." Two of them suddenly pulled off my *abaya* . . . I felt exposed . . . fearful, I resumed a fetal position . . . I don't know how but I was able to utter something to the effect that I take off my *abaya* only at home . . . Their impudent laughs rose again, and one of them said, "This is your home until you go back to the other one . . . " A woman with a stern face, but who was clean and well groomed, came in and turned off the radio that was hidden under the mats. She headed toward me, and I felt my heart shuddering: "Are you Maryam?" In humility, I nodded yes. "Follow me." I dragged myself, following her to her room . . . In front of her gray desk, she sat, and I sat down on the floor in front of her . . . She introduced herself to me as "the social worker." She asked me my full name and address, and about my home and children. I answered, then I started to ask her about Nawal . . . "Nawal was on my right shoulder . . . Nawal, where is Nawal?" "Who is Nawal?" she asked. "My daughter, she was here with me."

I did not know what happened. I heard myself screaming and screaming . . . They led me to the inside, and I heard them whispering later about how I killed my daughter. Impossible . . . I could not have killed Nawal . . . I was embracing her, protecting her from the blazing sun . . . Who stole my Nawal? With her black hair and dark eyes . . . I did not, I could not have killed my dearest . . . Who would bring back my Nawal?

A Personal Sketch of Sharifa Ash-Shamlan

The biographical information on the book jacket of her only published collection of short stories identifies Sharifa as "the writer who is most attached to the land and the human being" (Ash-Shamlan 1989). Although she is uneasy about the superlative, Sharifa does not object to the description given.

I met with Sharifa in her home in Dammam. She was gracious to take the time to see me despite her responsibilities at home and at work. She also showed me some of her stories that had not been published. Our meeting lasted more than two hours, during which time we mostly discussed her writing process. Sharifa was easy to talk to although at times she felt uneasy about "complicating" a simple process such as her writing. However, despite the brevity of the interview compared to my interviews with the other writers, I was able to fill many gaps, thanks to Sharifa's expressive nature as well as her generosity in granting interviews with the local newspapers. These were of great assistance in providing me with an understanding of Sharifa's work and Sharifa as a writer.

She was born in 1946 in Azzubair, near the Saudi border with Iraq. In the mid-1960s, while her family lived in the southern part of Iraq, Sharifa left for Baghdad with the intention of studying medicine. At the University of Baghdad she decided instead to register for journalism, in which she obtained her B.A. in 1968. Married, with five children, she currently lives in Dammam near Dhahran, in the eastern province of Saudi Arabia. In addition to her writings and her family life, Sharifa is also committed to her work as the head administrator of the institution of social services for delinquent women in Dammam.

In her early years she mostly wrote articles for the local newspapers, especially *Al-Yowm,* where she had been supervisor of the woman's section since 1976, and which is still published in Ad-Dammam. She began writing short stories as a hobby, her first effort being "She and the Story of Dates." The short story is her favorite form because, as she explained, "it grants the writer more freedom to pass messages, and minimizes his or her responsibility for the points of view expressed."

Despite her long association with the short story, Sharifa's first collection was published only at the end of 1989. This was fortunate because I had been able to track down only three of her stories, even though all had been published in newspapers and magazines. The collection contained fifteen short stories, from which I selected "Nawal" and "Secret and Death" for translation. Surprisingly, "Sections from a Life" had not been included in the collection, although Sharifa had chosen this story for participation in one of the Jeddah Literary Club's evening activities, and it had been published in *'Ukaz* in 1987.

Entitled *Extremely Quiet,* the collection includes short stories that are not consistent in their literary value. Some seem too simple, and some would be lost in translation because their value is based on a subtle use of language that appeals to the local reader but they are otherwise lacking in plot and technique. My choice of the three stories presented here is based on how successfully they can be translated and still retain their original value. I think that "Sections" stands by far as the best of her work; not only does it yield to translation but it also is both simple and symbolic.

Sharifa draws most of her stories from the real lives of women with whom she comes in contact as a social worker, especially those in prison. In fact, she said that her work provides her with most of the events and human types portrayed in her stories. If she feels a story is worth telling, she waits for the right time to tell it. She literally "carries" the idea of the story until it is time to "give it birth." The right time is often at night, after her children are asleep. She usually finishes her story in one session, which is not surprising considering that she writes the shortest stories among her fellow short-story writers.

For Sharifa, the process of writing follows no daily pattern or previous planning and preparation. She writes the story as inspired at the moment. She said that when she writes she has nothing in mind except telling a good story, with no thought of technique or symbolic value. Sharifa surprised me when she told me that her stories rarely need revision after the first draft.

Despite her skill in developing the symbolic value of her work so naturally, with no sense of its being forced on the characters and events, Sharifa reflects less awareness of the creative process than do the other two short-story writers, Khayriyya As-Saggaf and Najwa Hashim. Khayriyya teaches Arabic literature, which probably results in her writing process being more influenced by schools and models, while Najwa seems to reflect on her awareness of the process of communication between the reader and the writer in the articles she writes for the newspapers. Sharifa, on the other hand, is equipped with an uncomplicated but keen sense of what makes a good and meaningful story.

Sharifa's writing process reflects a great deal of spontaneity. As a result she feels uneasy about critics who either make more or less of her work; that is, they either "polish or blur the work." First and foremost, as she points out, she writes to and for the ordinary person, and has never geared her writing toward satisfying the elite or the critics. Still, the critics are respectful of her work, and she usually receives more praise than criticism.

Sharifa's readers, regardless of their place on the continuum of ideological orientations, grant her a great deal of respect and support. This is due perhaps to the fact that she delivers her political messages (such as the ones in "Sections"), which are no less serious than those of Abu-Khalid or 'Alim, in casual language with little interest in being daring. When it comes to the use of words, Sharifa's basic style of language not only grants her message a safe passage but also appeals to all levels of readers. But her stories also may project an image of naivete that is rarely considered to be dangerous or to spark a sense of alarm among the centers of power.

Khayriyya As-Saggaf: Selections from Her Writings

The Reflection[5]

That hope . . . is filling her soul . . . If it became a reality, it would seem as if an angel's hand had touched her in a gleaming light, and had taken her away from this world. When she finally settled in the far away horizons, she opened her eyes on a fantastic scene!

I will find myself in the company of a handsome knight, riding a gray horse. He will take me exactly as Sinbad did with his Iraqi girl, when he took her on a flying wooden horse away from the claws of the beasts and the thieves . . . I am still living among the beasts who rob me of my freedom, strip me of my will—controlling my steps and actions, marring my laughs and cries, and probably weighing the bites of my food! "Ha . . . the knight you talk about has become a legend. This is not an era of horses and knights any more. The knights have died under their horses when they tried to escape out of the boundaries, out of the possible and out of your comprehension." But she did not pay attention to the dialogue in her mind . . . She said, "It does not matter . . . even the dream, they want to deprive me of enjoying . . . Ha . . . do you run away from your people . . . your mother . . . your father, brothers? There is no difference, no difference at all between all of them and any other thief . . . since they practice the same means to reach the same goals and ends."

She paced her room, moving back and forth nervously, then dropped her body on the floor in a sudden move. The rectangular room was omposed of a bed, a cupboard, and a small desk. In the middle was a fancy throw rug where some of her small things were scattered. The shoes had been placed quietly at the side of her bed . . . As for the only

window in her room, it was closed and veiled by a thick velvet curtain
. . . A lonely fly was roaming the room as if trying to escape the
boredom that prevailed all around her . . . There was no way out . . .
The fly took a position on her nose; she moved her hand quickly to send
it away. "Shame on you! . . . do you only enjoy bothering me at a
moment like this . . . !?"

She felt her dreams live for moments, then vanish. She did not know
the cause of her boredom . . . or her pain . . . "It is just a feeling . . .
Oh what mysterious feelings they are! . . . They fall as fate, control as
destiny . . . We submit to them without objection, completely helpless,
and astonishingly impotent . . . We can resist everything, except that
which is beyond will and choice . . . Oh God!" Then she sighed.

That day, in her family's house, there was unusual locomotion . . .
She heard feet moving near her room. There was a knock on the door,
then it opened before she could answer . . . A face appeared, it was the
dearly loved brother: "My father wants to talk with you . . . " She rose,
and with heavy steps directed herself to where he sat. He talked to her;
she did not know how she listened to what he said or how she spoke
with him or even how she said yes . . . yes . . . to what he said . . .

After that talk the quiet home turned into a bundle of light and
happiness, but all the gloom and silence was bundled in the depths of
her heart . . . She remembered all this as she sat. Nervously, she recalled
the events, while resisting the fly . . .

Mona was the oldest of three sisters and one brother . . . They all
lived together under one roof, along with their two parents who were
constantly fighting. Many times the neighbors would hear, and the
relatives would know and attend one of these battles at least once every
ten days . . . One day, my mother left our home . . . She was angry
. . . We followed her and clung to the edge of her *abaya,* but she would
say, "Get away from me, children of the dog[6] . . . I am going to the
burning red hell . . . " She departed . . . We were not even able to
catch up with her *abaya.* We all sobbed together . . . At that moment
we felt united by tears, although we were different, in dreams, in
handling the problem, and in our ability to take a stand . . .

That day, the red cheek of the sun was revealed . . . The face of the
earth turned into a yellow sheet, as if suddenly attacked by a disease . . .
There was a knock on the outside door of our home . . . We all ran to
open it, thinking it was our mother who might have found our hearts
scattered under her feet and had come back to put them together . . .
There stood my grandfather, my maternal and paternal uncles, the
neighbors' children, and behind them my maternal and paternal aunts
. . . My mother was not with them . . . The usual procession turned

into a funeral-like silence. In seconds, the clamorous voices were mixed and confused . . . They were searching for reasons, they wanted to know why.

The procession moved to the neighbors' house . . . and within less than an hour, all came back accompanied by my mother. She was bitterly sobbing . . . My father was involved in the clamoring . . . we could not understand anything . . . Two or more hours later, everyone had left except one of my maternal aunts who came closer to my mother and whispered in a rather commanding tone, "Don't ever give up on your demands . . . You have to wake up, you will be naked if you trust or count on a man . . . I will back you up."

After she said that, she left . . . My father called her "that hateful disgusting bug . . . that bitch!" . . . My mother wiped her tears, and drew anger on her forehead . . . Our home was never to know the taste of peace . . .

Oh . . . my siblings . . . they go and come and I hardly know anything about them except their names. All we did together was weep. That is what happens when my mother steps on our hearts and leaves! Other than that I talk to my brother Khalid when I want a notebook, a pen, or some other things from the store around the corner. He usually produces no sound, and no response . . . All I see are his eyebrows moving, his back is to us. If he ever talks, it is to give us commands, "Do not leave home, daughters of a dog."

As for the youngest sister, Hanan . . . Oh . . . One day she stole money from her classmates and bought a bouncing ball, a pen in the shape of animal, and some candy. My mother did not know anything about her . . . My father only saw her every few days! Oh mother . . . Oh father, she has stolen and bought . . . what is she going to steal or sell tomorrow?

As for you, my father, you are an obscure world. All I know of you and from you are those two reddened eyes. I kiss your hand in the morning and the evening . . . and if I don't, hell would be burning the whole day, and my fingers would have the taste of it.

Oh mother, you have always been distant from me . . . All I hear is "take these clothes and wash them" . . . Or "Good . . . good . . . every time I enter your room I find you reading, you have no shame . . ." Oh mother, the book in your hand turns to bits and pieces, and with the book you tear my soul and thoughts, and smash my nerves. You only call me to cook, clean, wear this or that, or to scold me; don't laugh, don't buy that, and . . . Oh death . . . Oh death . . . At night I screamed, but no one heard me. In the day I cried and no one saw me

. . . I searched for someone who could understand me, but no one was there for support . . .

Then an idea that restlessly moved inside my head came to me . . . School! Ah . . . in school I will find friends and teachers, I will find someone who can understand me . . . It will get better. The fly returned to her nose, and she impatiently screamed, "Shame on you, disgusting fly . . ."

His voice came from outside . . . Oh brutal times . . . that was his voice . . . The fat old husband . . . His gray mustache joined the hair on both sides of his face. His head had always been hidden under the red worn-out *ghotra*. He did not take it off even when he came to bed. Initially I thought he was bald or had a disease in his head. As days passed, I discovered that his hair was gray and frizzled. He also walked barefooted all the time.

She was awakened by his sharp acute voice: "Get up . . . prepare some food . . . I have guests." "Fine."

Do I have something else to say except yes? Oh . . . Time . . . Oh (then she bit her lower lip) . . . She rose, moving her feet slowly, after he disrupted her train of thought and memories . . . She looked for her shoe lying in a corner. She tried to pick it up and fell, bumping her head on the side of the bed. With fiery eyes, he watched her, and in a horrific angry voice he kicked her, screaming: "Hurry up!" He thinks I pretend . . . That I am lying . . . But lying is all I can do to spare myself his wrath. She faced him and loudly screamed: "Enough . . . enough . . . Why do you kick me . . . why all this cruelty . . . until when, when . . . " She continued to whoop. He attacked her with his hands, his ropelike *aqal* (headband), and his feet. Then angrily and in a fiery voice he screamed: "Divorced . . . Divorced . . . Divorced . . . "

She sighed and smiled from beneath her tears . . . She tried to carry herself with what energy she had left . . . She ran her hand through her tousled hair, picked up her *abaya,* not looking around her . . . Nothing she would leave behind was worth feeling sorry about . . . She felt as if she needed clean air . . . as if she were emerging from a dark stuffy hole. She quickly moved toward the street . . . Tears froze in her eyes . . . There was nothing worth crying about . . . oh, her heart, oh . . . her youth . . . how could she ever console herself for their loss . . . Absolutely nothing could bring youth back to her heart or treat its wounds.

Groping about awkwardly, she walked, not knowing where she was going . . . She wiped her nose on her sleeve, along with the tears . . . The string of thoughts, which the fly had interrupted a few minutes ago, are rejoined . . . I escaped to schoolmates . . . all they cared for was to tell stories of their adventures and tricks, true or imaginary . . .

Oh, I still remember Haifa's face . . . She was a spoiled child . . . her mother listened to her and her father understood her needs . . . She did not suffer my hunger. And Ghada, the flirt, she did not fear anything . . . I was afraid I would go in the same path . . . and many times I wanted to bury my problems in that dreamy world of hers . . . As for Su'ad . . . She was exemplary, and at the top of the class . . . and so were Fathiyya and Jowhara, because they lived in happy stable atmospheres.

I still remember that day when on my way out of school I heard a voice within me yelling, "Complicated . . . You're complicated . . . " Another voice urged me, "Come with me . . . we'll go somewhere else . . . let's enjoy our youth and rejoice in our beauty . . . let's laugh . . . let's dance . . . do anything . . . " These are some of the voices of those girls who left bad memories . . . those who kept saying to me, "We don't understand you . . . you're strange . . . do something about your problems before you come to us . . . " All of these people have contributed to this agonizing moment . . . yes . . . yes . . .

She sobbed as she walked the street aimlessly. "Oh . . . this world is a greedy thief, and confused . . . I do not know if I have strayed from the orbit or if the compass has pointed in another direction."

That day . . . I was completely stripped of my will. My father asked me if I wanted to marry this man. I insisted on marrying him, on accepting him . . . on destroying the distance between him and the knight of my dreams. That was the only day in which my mother's voice came out soft, kind, and loving: "Get up and wear the best clothes you have." Can anything I had be described as the best?

Walking the road, her tears fell for the first time . . . The street before me seems like his face when I met him for the first time under one roof. That day, just like today, I sobbed . . . that day everything in me was destroyed . . .

No birds were in that home, no garden, no fragrance of roses, no aroma of kadi.[7] No horse neighing or horseback . . . no snowy day in which lights reflect on roses . . . no rosy night in which voices, words, laughter, and incense are all in harmony . . . Everything was bleak . . . Oh . . . my father . . . my husband had a hand that extended further than yours . . . and a tongue that was even sharper . . .

The long street swallowed her. Entangled in her tears, she heard a voice interrupting, saying . . . stop . . . go back . . . you . . . woman . . .

And in the crowd she experienced dizziness, nausea . . . and collision
. . . She then disappeared beneath the feet.

Ḵhayriyya As-Saggaf: A Personal Sketch

Ḵhayriyya is one of the best-known women public figures in Saudi
Arabia. Born in Makkah in 1951, she spent her early childhood there.
Her family soon moved to Ar-Riyadh, where she attended private
schools before the institutionalization of women's education in 1960.
Despite her early move to Ar-Riyadh, Makkah seems to inspire and
provide most of her stories' settings.

She obtained her B.A from King Saud University in Riyadh. In 1976
she obtained an M.A. degree in the teaching methods of language and
literature from the University of Missouri at Columbia. While a lecturer
at the Women's University College in Ar-Riyadh, where she taught
modern Arabic poetry and prose, she completed her Ph.D. in the Arabic
language and literature from King Saud University in 1988.

Ḵhayriyya, who is married and the mother of four children, participates vigorously in activities that simultaneously relate to writing,
education, and women. In addition to her short-story writing, the genre
with which she is mostly identified, she writes articles, prepares material for a literary radio program, and delivers public lectures to women's
associations of which she is a member. In 1981 the Ar-Riyadh newspaper established the first office for women journalists, which Ḵhayriyya
was chosen to head. Thus she was the first woman in her country's history to achieve the status of chief section editor on a major newspaper.

Ḵhayriyya recalls that she began writing when still a child in elementary school. She wrote articles at home and sent them to the various
local newspapers and magazines, such as *Al-Yamama, Al-Riyadh,
Adda'awa, Al-Madinah,* and *Al-Bilad.* Thinking back on those early
days, she recalls how her tiny figure and young age almost prevented
her from receiving the first payment for her writings. Judging by her
appearance, the deliverer could not believe that she was "the writer" for
whom the check was intended but thought she was only a child who
was trying to play tricks on him.

Ḵhayriyya enjoys a good reputation and is respected by both modernists and traditionalists. Although the latter may at times classify her as
being a modernist, she may be mildly criticized but is rarely severely

attacked by the traditional elements (see chapter 5). Although she often severely criticizes social values and institutions, she practices the utmost caution to avoid shocking the sensibilities of the traditionalists or undermining loyalty to the culture.

This is a case in point. When her husband, Dr. Yahya As-saati, who is the chief editor of the only review periodical in the country, *'Alem Al-Kutob,* was asked in an interview in Al-Yamama (1990) if he ate what his housemaid cooked for him, he answered jokingly that he had to, because Khayriyya rarely found time for cooking. When she was interviewed for the same column a few weeks later, she was asked about cooking. The quick-witted Khayriyya responded: "I will find time for cooking when I find time for my afternoon nap." She was apparently quipping at the luxury men enjoy at home, where their time of rest, especially their afternoon nap, is considered sacred. Her answer also carries a sharp criticism of the traditional emphasis on women's role in the kitchen, even when, just like their husbands, they are working outside the home. Why does no one seem concerned about whether these working women find time to rest at home, and yet everyone wants to know if they find time to cook. And if they do not, it is seen as a breach of their mission in life? In her short and simple reply, Khayriyya pointed out the absurdity of this notion. In fact, in that interview not only did she make no secret of her resentment of assigning the kitchen as women's domain but she also rendered it a "historical" and "cultural" conspiracy against women. By no means are these conventional views. But the witty spirit in which they were related, and the form they took as an implicit, and probably joking, exchange between a public couple, gave the remarks an umbrella of legitimacy.

One of Khayriyya's strengths as a writer, and what may be a reason for her popularity, is her sensitivity to cultural values. First, she said: "Adab is Ta'addub," meaning, literally, "literature is politeness." If the writer wants to make a connection with the reader, then he or she can do so without compromising either cultural standards or the message. But she points out that this is, as in any effort to communicate, a two-way street. Just as the writer has a responsibility toward the reader, so too does the reader have a responsibility toward the writer. "I don't write for someone who is in a hurry, who reads in a car, or who reads while busy doing something else," the writer informs us, pointing to the fact that her writing style requires more than such a reading. At the same time she criticizes writers who turn their writing into symbolic puzzles that would take a lifetime to solve. Writers, she maintains, should reexamine their writing style if their readers contend that the writing is too ambiguous.

Khayriyya's own conception of the writer's mission, and the role of literature in society, provides her with the means by which to maintain the balance between art and readability. In her introduction to her only collection of short stories, *Sailing Toward the Dimensions,* published in 1982, she writes: "These portraits . . . are only a direct reflection of what is happening in reality . . . my words are a bridge between the soil and the paper." While reflecting reality, the writer has the responsibility of "sailing" with the reader toward discovering new "dimensions." The reader accompanies the writer on a journey to explore new meaning for existence. This meaning is not offered by the writer but rather comes as a gift of mutual discovery.

Her book *Sailing,* which contains eighteen stories written between 1978 and 1981, was widely hailed by critics. One of the stories in the collection has been translated into English and published in Jayyusi's anthology (1988). Her story, "The Reflection," which is selected here, best exemplifies Khayriyya's artistic technique and point of view. The theme of arranged marriage has been one of the most prevalent themes among women writers. Khayriyya deals with its cyclical nature, and its effect on men and women as they struggle with realities of change. As a result, her stories are as much devoted to exploring men's experience as they are to exploring the experiences of women.

I had corresponded with Khayriyya before my arrival in Ar-Riyadh, and she helped me to obtain phone numbers of other writers in the city. I met with her numerous times, mostly in her home, and sometimes in the presence of her family or other women, some of whom were writers themselves. Aside from being gracious hosts, and in addition to numerous offers of help in various areas, Khayriyya's husband, Dr. As-Saati, a distinguished bibliographer, offered me invaluable advice on where to locate material related to my topic. Because of their long experience and presence in the literary domain, my meetings with them not only made me feel at home but also proved to be of great value in rounding out my knowledge of "who's who" in the field. During my stay in Ar-

Riyadh, I bore witness to Khayriyya's extraordinary ability to juggle academic and administrative responsibilities with family obligations, as well as with social engagements.

Najwa Hashim: Selections from Her Writings

Fever in a Hot Night[8]*

"Dear Khalid:
  I write to you, so we can both write the history of the birth of the end."
  After a long attentive look at its characters . . . she folded the letter. Glancing at them, . . . every one seemed to have a special flavor, a different taste.
  The universe becomes restricted and limited. It gets narrower and narrower . . . The global circle shrinks to include her . . . Time stands in ecstasy . . . "What if these letters gushed water?" she imagined . . . All boundaries and distances are abolished in this dark moment in time. Her feelings abound with boredom and fretfulness. She feels a desire to sob. Everything around her seems to go through a moment of destructive explosion. Her inner self screams, burned and torn apart . . . She sobs, never feeling closer to madness . . . Depressing feelings attack her . . . She tries to escape . . . She faces herself . . . Her veins stand up and so does her hair. Her mind, embracing her heart, explodes in the idea of the letter: "What a wonderful idea, to write one single line . . . it sounds like an exceptional language between the two of us . . . It may settle in his depth and tear his arteries apart so they gush manhood and gallantry, so he can make a decision and put 'dots on letters.' "[9] Her sighs come long and deep. She hides in her pain . . . She leaves her room for the living quarters, where all the family members gather. In the long corridor between her room and the living area, a sudden feeling of intensive joy touches her . . . Double vision blasts her . . . She feels she has put a nail in the tomb of the end . . . She communes with herself:
  —No, not a nail but rather an ear of corn . . . a plant of hope to free a weak being.
  Before she crosses to the sitting area, she suddenly stops . . . she smiles . . .

---

*I should note here that the series of periods in the translations are not an indication that parts of the original text were eliminated; rather, they typify Najwa's writing style.

—No, I am not a vulnerable weak human being, but rather a giant . . . I cannot be weak! Weakness is a suicidal choice . . . Am I being weak?!

She suddenly retreats . . .

—But I possess a will. Within my madness, a wonderful mind inhabits me . . . I can feel that . . . She leans on the wall . . . In the corridor . . . she looks around:

—Is the eye asked what color it prefers? When human beings are born, are they asked to choose a name for themselves? When our homeland inhabits us, and as blood penetrates us . . . do we ask why? When love knocked down Qays and Laila, they did not ask why. [10]

She staggers . . . a horrific headache tears the right side of her head apart . . . She holds her head: "It is certainly caused by psychological troubles . . . If these causes were taken care of, the headache would disappear . . ." That is what the doctor told me when I consulted him about my eternal headache. "You have to overcome these troubles in order for the pain to be lessened."

What a wonderful prescription! Where do I find a refuge from all that I am going through!

She carries herself back to the living room. But before she steps in, she surreptitiously glances at the convened family. In this place all colors interweave. Everyone seems elated . . .

That is Sami laughing . . . Sara is dancing, following some musical tune . . . My father is sitting in a corner, not uttering a single word, seeming to be fixed on our faces, almost feeling exulted by the moment . . . My mother hastily walks to the kitchen, calling: "Afaf . . . Come here and help me prepare the dinner." The little Afrah likes to be neat and tidy, constantly trying to attract our attention to her elegance . . .

Only a third of the night has passed, and I am still standing in my place. The night whispers to me . . . Sadness extends within me . . . Sorrow crystallizes . . . The night spreads its phantoms for the sleepless and the dreamers . . . My dreams gradually retreat until they disappear:

To whom do I project my longing?! I long for myself . . . This strange feeling attacks me . . . the question melts my self-confidence into a sense of sarcasm . . . Again I stare at the faces . . . but hold a silent dialogue with myself:

—I do long for you.

—Me too, the painful distance is growing deeper between us . . . the blood gushing from the wounds is clotting, ever since freedom became a dream to seek, and life was spilled in the private pains . . .

—Since you extended your memory for others, so they can inject it with a moment of choice that was never yours . . .

—Ever since the labor to give birth began, through a cesarean section, to give you new life, thousands of knives have torn your feelings apart.

—That is, ever since you have sneaked your plundered will to your inside like a fugitive.

Moments of standing extend . . . She moves restlessly, then leaves the living area . . . Returning to her room, she embraces the letter, trying to paint a picture for the upcoming dreams . . . She tries to paint the coming joy . . . in her mind, she mumbles and dances, then extends her body on the bed to relax . . . Attentively, she looks around her but suddenly something jumps into her mind:

"Dear Samia:

I have received your letter . . . Sorry for all that has happened. I will come soon to witness the birth of the end, as you wish."

Her senses suddenly wail . . . her soul soars in the sky of freedom. Now she possesses will.

—Good-bye to alienation, good-bye to being torn apart . . . good-bye to being at a loss . . . good-bye to the pavements of sadness, to the sails of pain . . . She sits quietly:

—I have retrieved my plundered freedom . . . I am giving myself a return ticket to myself after I have lost it . . . My tears gush, sprinkling around, rejoicing at my freedom . . .

She smiles, leans on her arm, soars far away . . .

—Oh the era of pain, you robbed me of my will . . .

—The angry time has broken its flask, to mix with the wondering time . . . announcing my coming with them . . . to the moment of takeoff.

The birds came back to the skies singing, as they were given their freedom . . . She suddenly cries, after she was swept over by a flood of rosy dreams . . . Her eternal sadness returns . . . She leaves the room . . . carrying her wounded heart on her palm . . . Standing at the door . . . she looks at her youthful picture hanging on the wall . . . — Why did they want something you never wanted for yourself?

An echo of her words reverberates within her . . . As she takes off like an arrow, the phone rings:

—Hello . . .

She hangs up without saying a word . . . Before she lifts her body, the phone rings again. She ignores it this time . . . Leaning on a couch in the sitting room . . . she is inadvertent, . . . outside of herself . . . outside of her body . . . Everything around her seems to be in a dialogue . . . She fails to feel her suffering . . . the wandering eyes besiege her

. . . the death that spreads in her soul is so slow . . . the emotional devastation nests in all corners of her being . . . This time her sister runs to the phone:

—Hello.

—. . . .

—She's not here.

—. . . .

—I said she's not here.

—. . . .

—I said she does not want to talk to you . . .

Suddenly everyone jumped, the father, the sisters, the mother. All these watchers, even the roof, the walls, seem to be shaken up . . . What a terror . . . Everyone and everything is watching this repeated drama. The father asked who was on the phone. "Khalid . . ." the little one replied . . . All were silent . . . but turned their eyes suddenly to her . . . the phone issue was folded, but her files were now opened . . . The number of investigators is multiplied . . . The investigation this time is not in language . . .

Arrows shoot from their eyes . . . It is these moments of silence that precede the storm . . . The birthday party awaits me to put out the candles, and then sing . . . I am the star . . . the suspect . . . the judge . . . and the executioner. Looking at the faces: "Excuse me ladies and gentlemen . . . My sun will not rise . . . my flood tide will not extend beyond the shores . . . my sky's clouds will not gather . . . there will be neither lightning nor thunder . . . that is what I want . . . rather, that is what I wanted. I have to leave chance to will . . . now . . . even in unimportant matters . . . The will, the will, the will, where is the will?!"

Minutes passed in terror . . . as formal mourning rituals . . .

—My wounds extend from one vein to another. The eyes are increasingly widened . . . my father wants to say something . . . or probably wants me to say something . . . Between what he wants and what I want, the moment magnifies . . . the will . . . the will . . . I began to believe that they now accept the principle of my saying what I want to say . . .

She stops suddenly to regain her breath . . . as a knight just returned from a losing battle . . . Feeling more attached to herself, she senses a shattered being within her:

—I am not annoyed . . . nor am I angry . . . These phone calls do not cause me pain anymore . . . for one reason . . .

—What is it?

—I now possess will . . . no one will be able to dissuade me . . . no one will stand in my way or force me to go back to the hell he has created for me . . . Never again will I swallow the bitter defeat . . . His phone calls will not make me angry or provoke me anymore. Not after I have planted within me what I want and don't want.

Then, catching her breath:

—It is society that has stabbed me in the back with a poisonous dagger. It is society that has betrayed me . . . She walks hastily to her room, closes the door, and dwells within herself, trying to get rid of the provocations of the moment . . .

—Just as if it were tonight. The joy was the master of all colors . . . The mountains failed to carry my happiness . . . As if tonight . . . I laid down on the sad shores . . . As if tonight, it is exactly a year ago. The human waves were running in this corridor . . . I was kept in this room . . . surrounded by stares . . . As if it were tonight, when I felt the beginning of a new age . . . seeing it as the summer that would melt the past glacial age of my adolescence . . .

That night, I was eighteen years old, everyone was holding me, trying to help me be more beautiful . . . The protocol is for the bride to stay quiet and for everyone to be in her service . . . She tries to hide from the critical eyes, so they do not slaughter her on her wedding night. The attendance was huge, the atmosphere suffocating, and the dark night had a speedy tone . . . I must have looked so beautiful . . . because that is what has been said, a fact I had known all along . . . I have always felt a sense of pride in being beautiful, although I chose to bury it deep . . . That night, it did not matter much who I was . . . what was important was to pass to the unknown and go beyond myself.

Khalid was not the first man to ask for my hand . . . Without exaggeration he must have been the twentieth . . . But my father, may Allah forgive him . . . rejected all proposals . . . He wanted to paint a new and more suitable life for me . . . Khalid was the first of the dry seasons of my future life . . . Khalid was the hero who put an end to the play of proposing heroes . . . He lowered the curtain, grabbed the heroine onto his horse while galloping at full speed.

She leaves her place. Leaning on the vanity, she stares at herself in the mirror:

—How much my face has changed! . . . My eyes store a horrible exhaustion. Then sighing: How wonderful it is to fly like pigeons . . . how wonderful it is to penetrate the world with joy . . . how wonderful it is to establish a memorial for my pure soul . . . That feeling of pride and freedom . . . was an illusory freedom! . . . It is horrible for a human being to be separated from self . . . to be deprived of soliloquizing with self, from taking refuge in self . . . This is a burden beyond belief.

Wearily she adds:

—Soon all these boundaries will disappear and everything will be one. Her eyes fall again on the mirror:

—At the time of my wedding, I had passed my eighteenth year and finished high school. I was swept by a great desire to realize my academic dreams and to excel in school.

Sighing:

—None of these dreams should perish . . . This time the will has to prevail . . . I abandoned my will once and everything was destroyed . . . How terrible it is to destroy the life of a human being who has no choice . . . I am not the only woman who is crushed in such a manner . . . Thousands of others are, like me, corroded . . . The colors of pain and hurt undulate within me like a rainbow . . . blood is mixed with tragedies . . . resulting in a human being with no will . . . The family . . . the society . . . the tyrant man . . . They are the three parties of the tragedy . . .

The conflict inflames her . . . She opens one of the drawers and takes a tablet . . . pressing on the bottle and contemplating:

—Tranquilizers . . . tranquilizers . . . they are not of any use for my life . . . There must be extirpation . . . I know many women who chose to remain in the dark corners of life . . . and were satisfied by it. I know many who gave up, opened their arms to bewilderment. They, with no resistance, submitted to coercion and were forced into a life of dullness . . . How terrible it is for the human being to be penetrated with dullness . . . This is no doubt the end . . . Life would have no meaning for them anymore, for their will was killed.

She screams . . . banging on the vanity so forcefully that make-up and perfume bottles fall to the floor. The mirror vibrates with a tremulous motion, and so does her blood . . . Agitation shows on her face . . . Feeling exhausted . . . she quietly walks to the cupboard and opens it:

—Photo album . . . photo album . . . time is decisive, and it may cut as sharp as a knife. She sits on the couch facing the bed . . . quietly surveying the area, she remembers:

—Until my eighteenth year, and up to now . . . no one had inhabited me . . . I had not defined my emotional life . . . I was preoccupied by my future in school. That was all I thought about . . . I wanted to put forth all my effort and carry my success in school to the neighboring country and finish my studies . . . Alas, everything is gone now . . .

—Samia, the wedding is after the Eid . . . My father's tone was decisive. A year had passed since the engagement, but I did not think anything would happen so quickly . . . They told me the groom's name, but I did not know how he looked or who he was . . .

—The will . . . The will . . . No one else had inhabited me. I had no reason to give, to justify my rejection of the proposal . . . There was not enough understanding or faith in objection without a good reason . . . But I did object anyway . . .

—I don't want to get married now . . .

—The girl has no other alternative but marriage . . . The boy is good and we know his father . . .

As a thunderbolt came their answer, as an earthquake . . .

I asked:

—Whom am I marrying, the hero or his father? . . .

There was the wedding . . . and I tried to adjust and accept the fact, thinking that the old saying "this cub is from that lion" might be true . . . but . . . he was not the cub of the lion my father knew . . . He was a sly fox . . . In his Pandora's box were many surprises. He was full of jealousy . . . suspicion . . . and bad thoughts, all of which would wound a woman's dignity . . . His constant attempt to possess me almost destroyed me. . . . . His ill treatment was disastrous . . . How terrible it is for a woman to be faced with all this, by someone with whom she will spend her life . . . The stings of pain . . . ache, exhaustion . . . humiliation, were the forces of terror that possessed my body . . . contempt was spread all over the nest that brought us together . . . Patience was my virtue at the beginning.

—The shared language, which is what usually brings two people together, I have never known . . . All I have known is a life with a bitter taste . . . I tried to finish school, but couldn't . . . I did not try to seek help from anyone . . . I had to decide for myself . . . Only I could change the situation . . . To seek help from another person would prevent me from establishing my own identity . . . From now on, I will take refuge in myself . . . the greatest asylum in the history of humanity . . . I will take refuge in truth . . . it is the only virtue . . . I will take refuge in the remnants of hope that were left within me . . . To take refuge in the warmth of my words is fantastic. To choose silence as a defensive means is even more terrific!

This is the only chance to return to myself . . . My rejection of him was unthinkable, was seen as a disaster, a thunderbolt . . .

—Why do you refuse to stay with me?

—When fear flaps its wings, we have to clip it. When springs dry up

. . . we have to revive them! When a tooth aches endlessly . . . we extract it, despite the fact that it is an organ in our bodies . . .

—This is a view I fail to understand . . .

—No, these words are clear . . . your narcissism prevents you from understanding . . .

—You will stay with me . . . whether you want to or not . . .

My heart turned to stone . . . The roses of tenderness withered within me . . . Only one issue remained:

—I have to travel to myself . . . to my depths . . . they need me more than you do. I want my freedom.

—Your freedom became dependent on my will the moment we were united by a formal contract . . .

—After today I will not allow our freedoms to be mixed . . . I will not allow myself to be a necklace that adorns your neck, . . . that you move as you wish and when you wish . . . I will not be a Solomon's ring on your finger, fated to stay in place because a wall of flesh has piled up on it . . . I will destroy this frail wall . . .

This dialogue was the beginning of the end . . . It was the beginning of the setting off of the tragedy of our life . . . The dialogue turned to inhuman language . . .But I will not give up my freedom . . . Killing oneself is a crime . . . I committed suicide once when I abandoned my will and accepted him . . . Now, I will not do it again by continuing to live with him . . .

The burned time within me refuses to remain burned . . . Forests of joy . . . and flowers of a green life lurk more clearly now . . . telling me to rejoice in the future . . .

She throws the photo album as she glimpses into the past . . . Remembering the past brings an overwhelming astonishment . . . Tribal customs still insist that a woman should not be given her freedom . . . even when her innocence is established . . .

Ugliness is reigning . . . The closed society that does not appreciate the woman's freedom sharpens its spears . . . The family was still gathered . . . her brother's voice was loud as he called: dinner . . . dinner . . . She laughs secretly . . . Nothing happens without noise . . . That wonderful young girl who dresses herself elegantly has no idea of what the future is hiding for her.

She leaves the room after she folds the letter and hides it under her pillow . . . The dinner was ready . . . All sat around the table . . . she sat along with everyone and started eating . . . The moment of convergence with the television set diminishes the significance of the eating time . . . All meandered with an Arabic show . . . the hero of the show is arguing with his father about marrying someone he loves . . . The father seems to refuse to accept it. The son tells him:

— I have decided to marry . . .

— Marry whom?

— Afaf, she works with me . . .

— Who is Afaf . . . Who is her father . . . What does he do?

Eyes are tied to the television . . . All devouring food without feeling . . . The dialogue heats up:

— A person's worth is not with his or her father . . . Afaf works with me, and I know her very well . . .

— Fine . . . but can I meet with her?

— Why not? But there is one thing . . .

— What is that, boy!?

— Afaf is divorced.

The episode ends with the father screaming:

— My own son marrying a divorced woman!?

The discussion of the episode started among us . . . My aunt gave it a boost:

— A boy should not marry a divorced woman . . .

Another relative interferes:

— People will have no mercy on him.

The issue acquires a serious tone . . . Everyone has an opinion . . . The divorced woman has no existence in society . . . At that moment, they forgot about me and my problem . . . These surgeons did not take good care of their patients . . . They only stood with them at the time of the operation but left them to suffer the pain of waking up . . .

I left the dining table, torn apart . . . my face showed all the colors, red, yellow, black, white . . . My tongue failed to say a word . . . All the words I know melted, the spoon fell. I was the knight who fell from his horse because he was not able to saddle it very well. It was a terrible moment in which I roamed the province of loneliness and alienation . . . Without a sound, my eyes became motionless, my heart shivered . . . I withheld myself . . . and wished for a kind loving heart to contain me, to strangle the anguish and put out the fire inside me . . . My head almost fell . . . I touched my face . . . Sometimes beauty is so harmful that it has to be interdicted.

I remember the sadism of all those around me . . . They must have not known . . . Sadistically, they enjoyed my torment . . . No one felt what I have felt . . . All were busy with the episode . . .

— Should he marry her, or should he leave her?

All colors, words, and moments were mixed within me . . . I decided to leave the place . . .

My mother's voice came to me:

— Samia . . . you have not eaten your dinner.

— I had enough.

I then hurriedly went away. The killer does not feel his victim's pain when he plunges his knife into her. The clown does not care whether the audience laughs or not. All he cares about is to play his role correctly . . . When bitterness chooses to dwell in us, it does not pick sweet places.

All these thoughts went through my mind in the corridor, but no one felt anything. I felt as if I were left on the roadside and asked to walk alone, to overcome obstacles and jump over barriers . . . I must try, however . . . Taking risks is a must . . . A moment of madness is better than a long life of dull rationality . . . There must be change . . . To live with anger at an early age is an awful thing, but it is the only choice, the only alternative to a slow death . . . Flowing strongly, the lights in the room . . . gave me more determination . . .

—I must want, I must . . . Anguish has died inside me, as it was overwhelmed, and gave up . . .

She continues to sit . . . holds the letter and opens it.

"Dear Khalid: I write to you, so we can both write the history of the birth of the end."

Divorced . . . divorced. . . . I will not care . . . This unjust society lives around itself and puts up high walls in fear of rumors. Running on the roads of freedom is what is important . . . I have to run and run . . . I have to run away from the desert to the hills . . . I know, in advance, that they all will be asking me:

— Divorced? He has divorced you? Were you divorced?

Stupid questions asked without feeling.

— What a pity . . . divorced, but you're still young.

— Traveling on the edges of glass and under the sun's blaze is only felt by the traveler . . . The suitcases full of pain are mine alone . . . Experiencing anguish every day is painful.

— Society is incredibly cruel . . . The world is corroded . . . A great deal is diminishing in my small world . . . The lost and hungry world . . . I am the issue of the hour . . . I am the shadow, the colors, the nests, and biographies . . . What is happening is strange. I may find an excuse for my family, but I cannot excuse myself . . . I have to want . . . nothing else matters.

— When I traveled to what I did not want, it was my choice, my silence . . . Now I seek freedom, I can depart by my own will and choice. The time is one o'clock in the morning . . . The letter almost soaked in my hand . . . It was a humid night . . .

— This night, the seagulls have started their usual journey.

—The waters of memory, mixed with the will, are made calm.

— The burning inside and outside is put off . . . The mysterious gap between myself and me has vanished.

— Tomorrow, a new journey of awareness and humanity will begin through this letter . . . I stood . . . All doors to myself were wide open, to face all challenges . . . I will not hide in my eyelids . . . I will not submit myself to others to defend me . . . Believing in oneself is the existence and the will . . . When the will becomes the drink we taste, we live a better life.

She turns the lights off.. slips the letter under her pillow. She then closes her eyes, trying to save herself from a fever in a hot night . . .

Najwa Hashim: A Personal Sketch

Najwa is the youngest of the nine writers included in this study. She was born in 1960, the first child of Saudi parents from a middle-class family in Jaizan, in the province of 'Assir in the southwestern part of the Peninsula. Najwa began her schooling in Jaizan, and later attended King Abdul-Aziz University in Jeddah, from which she obtained her B.A. in sociology. She returned to Jaizan, where she currently lives and works in the field of education. Najwa also participates in numerous literary and extraliterary activities in the women's association of her province.

Najwa said that her family encourages education and has much appreciation for the word. Her grandfather was knowledgeable in religion and literature. Najwa was the first female writer in the family, but not the first to demonstrate literary capabilities. Her mother often recited folk poetry, although she never wrote it. Najwa owes much to her family's unfailing support. According to Najwa, her family "would express concern when I stopped writing, and would never interfere in what or how I write. In fact they gave me complete freedom to travel and to attend various literary activities in the different parts of the country. All members of my family take pride in my being a writer. They firmly stood by me against those who tried to block my way in the name of social rules." This is not easy to do and requires great sacrifice in a small, closed society like Jaizan's.

Like all her fellow women writers, she started writing for the readers' sections of local newspapers and magazines. Her first expressions in 1976, as she recalled them, were renditions of an adolescent girl in search of herself. Since then, Najwa's writings have witnessed increasing growth, but her objectives in writing have not changed much. Writing still performs important psychological functions; it is a therapeutic process and a vehicle of self-knowledge: "I write to lighten up moments of anxious dialogue within me . . . to keep in touch with reality. I write to heal deep wounds and prevent them from getting deeper." But she also writes "to all people around me, I want to let them hear my voice . . . I write to those who are, like me, frightened, so we could together besiege fear and lock it out . . . I write to the human beings in their long journey in search of self."

During the 1980s Najwa wrote scores of short stories and articles for the daily newspapers such as *Ar-Riyadh*. In 1986 her first collection, *Travel in the Night of Sadness,* was published by a reputable publishing house in Jeddah. The collection, which contained nine short stories, did not carry the customary preface by a well-established (usually male) writer, because Najwa wanted her work "to stand on its own feet" without crutches. It has, however, received a warm welcome by many of the local critics, as well as by others in Iraq, Sudan, Egypt, and Kuwait.

Najwa is often criticized for the sad tone that pervades all the stories of the collection (see chapter 5). But she defends herself by saying that sadness is a "trophy," a sign of being in touch with "reality" and with the ability to tell the "truth." In most of her stories, as in the one selected for translation, "Fever in a Hot Night," she reflects her desire to explore women's inner experiences and thoughts about love or deprivation of love; of searching for self and for new values that recognize women as thinking and feeling beings. Najwa's style is based on describing emotional states and inner feelings, especially of women who struggle with the discrepancy between the real and the ideal. Najwa seems to experience difficulty in expressing these emotions, and this has made her story the most difficult to translate. I should note here that the series of periods in the translations are not an indication that parts of the original text were eliminated; rather, they typify Najwa's writing style. The extensive use of these ellipses, however, is not peculiar to Najwa, who legitimately uses them as an indication of disjointed streams of thought. Other women writers, even within articles, resort to this usage either to relax some of the grammatical rules of Arabic composition or perhaps as a play on the notion of the unsaid, to indicate omitted words.

Najwa's appeal is mostly to well-educated women, but she also appeals to men. The importance of her contribution lies in the publication of women's experiences, and in legitimizing and engendering a new understanding of women. She has recently turned to writing about women's lives in Jaizan, using their regional dialect which she heavily footnotes. These women characters explore the meaning of their existence, not through internal monologue, as she does in her collection, but rather through holding a dialogue with other women. Moreover, unlike Najwa's other characters who are usually young and educated, these Jaizani women are ordinary and perhaps illiterate women of an older generation. In her experiment with portraying the local and personal experiences of small-town women, she has indicated that she was inspired by Najuib Mahfouz's winning of the Nobel Peace Prize in 1988. Mahfouz, in his portrayal of life among the poor inhabitants of Cairo's alleys in the 1930s, has demonstrated that particularity of experience, as well as provincialism, not only should no longer be considered a hindrance but should also be considered the legitimate ticket to excellence and universalism.

Najwa, who lives in Jaizan, was the only writer of my sample whom I did not meet personally, despite two arrangements made with the help of her friend and mentor Fatna Shāker (see chapter 4). My interviews with Najwa were conducted by telephone and through correspondence. Najwa made available to me most of the materials I requested, which included tapes of her participation in various literary activities, interviews in local newspapers, and critics' comments on her work both in the local as well as in the Arab newspapers and magazines. She has also assisted in the evaluations in local readership through questionnaires.

Textual Analysis

Men, Women, and Society: Who is the Victim and Who is to Blame?

The realities of social life that these women writers depict in their stories reveal a pattern of characterization in which characters appear as victims. The collections of the three women writers deal with a variety of topics, themes, and experiences, such as marriage, polygyny, divorce, modernization, change, and its human cost and consequences. Most of their female protagonists are portrayed as victims with whom the reader should sympathize. They are victimized by one or a combination of agents: by a man (i.e., cruel husband or father); by caretakers (i.e., family members, health agents, or officials); by society and its institutions (i.e., arranged marriage); by political institutions (i.e., poverty or development forces); and so on.

While the protagonists are mostly women who are victimized by men, the stories also include women who are victimized by other women (a mother, a friend, or a co-wife). Sharifa's female characters, for example, seem to be victimized as much by men as by other women. Zahra in "Secret" was victimized by her brother's wife, as well as by the women of the village; in "Sections," the female protagonist was victimized by the stepmother as well as by the female nurse who stole her food and medication. In "Nawal," the women in the prison all took part in intensifying the mother's agony. In Khayriyya's "The Reflection," the girl was, in a way, victimized by her mother. In Najwa's story, "Fever," it was the female relatives who made cruel comments about the divorced woman.

In their craft, these three women writers do not refrain from passing moral judgments. In approaching social issues, they are not so keen on detachment. Not only is this evident in the tonal variation and in their passionate dialogues, which serve to indicate an evaluation of attitudes toward characters, values, and issues but the clear juxtaposition of good and bad—of victim and villain—lends no notion of neutrality or impartiality in relation to these issues. The reader is ultimately coaxed into blaming a character or an agency, or in adopting a certain point of view. This is done more or less explicitly, depending on the writer's style.

The Man: Victim or Victimizing Agent?

Not only women are seen as being victimized. Almost half of Khayriyya's protagonists in her collection of eighteen short stories are men, and several of these men are presented as victims. They appear in a variety of roles—as fathers, brothers, and husbands—and are usually victimized by other men (a son by a father or a father-in-law). The reasons are usually related to conflicts and divisions of social class along tribal lines, degrees of affluence, or religious or regional affiliation. Considering the variation in the backgrounds of the victimized (men, women, the young, the old, the poor), these women writers seem to be saying that whether the victim happens to be a man or a woman is only circumstantial. Elements of victimization that deprive the individual of the right to choose a life partner, for example, are indeed shared by both men and women. Because these elements are inherent in the social system itself, almost every member of society—be it man or woman—stands almost the same chance of being a victim, depending on the circumstances. As a result, portraits of victimization usually depict men and women as inmates in the big prison called society.

It is in the light of this that one can understand the writer's portrayal of the man's double nature—as a victim and as victimizing. The stories display an ambiguous attitude toward defining man's responsibility. The characters are indecisive about man's role in the victimization of women. Women oscillate between blaming society and blaming the man, but more often than not, they end up vindicating the man and establishing society as the villain that oppresses both men and women.

In "Fever," Najwa's protagonist Samia focuses on three threads of the "tragedy": family, society, and the man. In moving along this triangle, she blames the man for two reasons. First, he is in a better position socially than the woman to resist an arranged marriage. It is man's lack of will that has compounded the situation for both men and women. Second, the man is blamed for his suspicions and ill treatment of his wife. This seems to be the specific role the man plays in the triangle Najwa traces.

But what happens when the man, even in an arranged marriage, turns out to be a kind and loving human being? Would that justify the arranged marriage? And if an arranged marriage is just as arranged for the man as for the woman, why does Najwa refuse to see her male character as victimized, rather than as victimizing? Najwa has chosen to portray an extreme example of an ill-matched couple—for some reason the exception rather than the rule within arranged marriages—to give legitimacy to her resistance of the institution. The same is true for Khayriyya's protagonist, Mona, whose misfortune brings her under three extremely oppressive males: the father, the brother, and the husband.

In both Najwa's and Khayriyya's stories the reader is left with the impression that the blame is intended to fall on the man as much if not more than on society. This is not because they believe the man to be the victimizing agent rather than the society but because the writer's main focus is the victimization of women. Both Najwa and Khayriyya must rely on devices that exacerbate the readers sense of their female characters' victimization. In order to elicit the readers' sympathy, the readers must be convinced that these women are in fact suffering. Arranged marriage or forced marriage is not sufficient grounds for gaining readers' sympathy. Perhaps this is because readers may not consider that a woman's unhappiness warrants sympathy unless they are convinced that it is a life-or-death matter. As a result the writers amass all elements of victimization to make their point. In Khayriyya's story, for example, not only are the father and the husband extremely undesirable characters but so is the brother and even the mother.

By portraying extreme types of men, the writers are able to highlight women's victimization while at the same time asserting that it is not men in general they are accusing but rather a particular man with a particular personality. Najwa does not generalize about men. To ensure a distinction, she presents two men. Khalid is characterized as an immature, suspicious, self-centered male chauvinist while the father, on the other hand, appears in the background and is simply "there." We are not told much about him. He is portrayed as distant but not violent. In fact, he seems to take pleasure in his family's well-being, at peace with them as well as with himself.

Najwa's message is not that we should be antagonistic toward men but that a woman should have the right to choose her lifetime partner. Khalid's unattractive personality serves only to exaggerate her point. By portraying the grave consequences of an arranged marriage, both Najwa and Khayriyya legitimize their message. Portraying a less extreme type of male personality would have undermined their point about women's victimization and shaken the ground under the message regarding arranged marriage. To be sure, other stories tend to portray the man as an indispensable part of a woman's life. In tone as well as in content, the man in Najwa's stories—whether father, lover, husband, or brother—is seen in more conciliatory terms, if only because he is portrayed as part of the solution to women's problems, including arranged marriage. In fact, he holds the key to its elimination.

This is understandable for Najwa's target is not the man but rather the institution of arranged marriage and the precarious position of divorced women. It is as if society entangles the woman in a web of interests, and locates decisions concerning her outside her own will. Najwa makes the point that when the wrong match is made, society devises ways for the marriage to continue, for society never acknowledges a mistake. Despite the failures of arranged marriage, society insists that the institution is right. Ironically, when the marriage fails, the woman herself is blamed, not the institution. By ostracizing not the man but the divorced woman, society forces the woman to enter a new marriage by the same method, ensuring the continuity of the institution of arranged marriage and perpetuating its ills.

These writers may have little choice but to portray these men as virtually impossible to live with. This would lead, however, to the vindication of society. The dominant portrayal of the man as victimizing agent may carry a message that is antithetical to the one the women writers intend to make, which is to blame society rather than the individual man. In Khariyya's and Najwa's stories, the failure of arranged marriages seems to be a function of the two husbands' personal ill behavior, rather than a result of the institution of the arranged marriage itself, which they purport to undermine. But women characters seem to persist in registering their protest against society. In the words of Najwa's protagonist: "It is society that has stabbed me in the back with a poisonous dagger. It is society that has betrayed me." Society is responsible insofar as it channels the choices of marriage partners and defines them, at best as familial rather than as a personal affair between a man and a woman. Moreover, it is society that punishes the woman whose marriage fails, and even ostracizes the woman who "chooses" to bail out, sentencing her to social death. "The family . . . the society . . . the tyrant man . . . They are the three parties of the tragedy." With a man like Khalid, and a family like the protagonist's in Najwa's story, the triangle of oppression becomes complete.

Poetics of Justice and the Vindication of Man

The man appears in Sharifa's stories as husband, brother, and father, as well as a nonfamily member. As a father, he is generally passive or even dead. In "Secret," the brother seems to be kind but helpless. In "Sections," the doctor is clearly the one agent of victimization that surpasses the stepmother's greed, the nurse's lack of ethics, and the official's sheer superficiality, if not stupidity. In "Nawal," Maryam is victimized by her husband who throws her out of the house on a mid-July day. In that story, we are to deduce the husband's cruelty by his act of throwing his wife and daughter out of the house into July's blazing sun.

That the husband is present and absent at the same time allows Sharifa to make use of the character symbolically. Through the image of the woman being "thrown" into the "blazing sun," she sends her readers a message regarding how society generally treats women. Here the man stands as a symbol of those forces that crush women. Women are "thrown" into the blaze, a "fate from which there was no escape." Women are also "divorced" from a way of life, placed in the "middle," then thrown into the "heat." Najwa uses the same image when her character describes her condition as "Traveling on the edges of glass and under the sun's blaze."

Sharifa's portrayal of the company worker in "Secret" is intriguing in a number of respects. While the doctor in "Sections" was clearly guilty of the rape attempt and deserving of no sympathy, the author's view of the company worker seems ambiguous even though his sexual encounter with Zahra has to be defined as rape, at least culturally. On the one hand, despite her insanity, Zahra's lover realizes her "goodness" and gives her love. His recognition that her "insanity" is only a function of other people's definition allowed him to treat her as a sane person. But this man in fact exacerbated Zahra's initial victimization by his sister— who is also her stepmother—by taking advantage of Zahra's lack of awareness of the social and physical consequences of their sexual encounter. The man, we are told in the story, leaves her puzzled and tormented to face the consequences of her pregnancy alone; a pregnancy which ends with her tragic death.

Although we are disdainful of his actions and even see them as cowardly, the author passes no direct moral judgment against him. Neither the character nor the author seem to view what he has done as a crime—or even as a cowardly act. He almost seems to make up for it by simply interpreting her silence as a sign of sanity. The badge of sanity he gives her is through a statement he tells only himself: "No, she is not crazy, she is the most sane of all the sane." When Zahra is taken away, he stands in the street watching the scene. He is left with "a hole in his heart," as if this "hole" is meant to compensate for the "bulge" in Zahra's stomach. Here, while Sharifa's poetic justice sentences Zahra not only to madness but also to death, the company worker is sentenced to a feeling of guilt and an empty recognition of Zahra's noble silence, which he cultivates to his advantage.

The writer clearly does not view the company worker as "the" victimizing agent. If Najwa and Khayriyya have portrayed extremely oppressive men to legitimize their messages about the victimization of women, Sharifa has chosen to ignore even more extreme actions on the part of men in order to focus on her primary target—society. Sharifa does not blame the company worker for Zahra's death because she reserves the blame for society. Zahra's death, as well as the death of the unborn child, from the author's point of view, was caused by the poisoned foot—not by the pregnancy, much less the rape. If society had paid more attention to the foot and less to the belly, Zahra would have lived.

"Two things became enlarged in Zahra's body . . . her belly and her foot. Nobody paid attention to the foot. The belly, however, attracted all the attention." This is a strong critique of society's fixation on the woman as a symbol of honor rather than as a human being who needs to be cared for in her suffering. The idea is not only challenging but is almost revolutionary. In her country such a message would never have been allowed to be voiced, even within a fictional mode. But Sharifa's choice of a mad character to relate the message, as well as her juxtaposition of the belly and the foot, are brilliant devices for getting the message across and even of making it convincing.

Other Forces of Victimization: Of Mothers, Mothering, and "S-mothering"

Whether for aesthetic or cultural reasons, agents of victimization are so far portrayed mainly as men, although in some cases these men are strangers, either caretakers (such as health agents) or more commonly members of the woman's family. Similarly, female characters other than the protagonist are usually family members, such as mothers, stepmothers, sisters, or relatives, although these characters may also include neighbors, strangers, and health agents. The part played by mothers and stepmothers, however, is by far the most important— either by virtue of their actual role in the events or the possible symbolic manipulation of their role.

The mother is presented in three different ways. Najwa portrays her as passive and mute. We hear the mother's voice coming from the kitchen, setting an image of the traditional wife. A distance and a lack of shared language seem to exist between the mother and her daughter. But compared to the mother in Khayriyya's story, she appears to be less controlling of her daughter. She does not tear her daughter's book apart, for example, nor does she place her under constant surveillance. She shows that she cares for her daughter by observing her eating habits. In fact, Najwa's protagonist Samia's familial atmosphere—the little girl's dressing and dancing, for example, and the lack of interference and pressure from her mother—does not support the constraints of society, but rather plays an important role in mitigating those constraints.

Khayriyya paints the mother, on the other hand, as domineering, although she is as helpless and as oppressed as her daughter. A victim of a vicious husband herself, the mother constitutes an element of victimization for her daughter. They do not appear to be close, and her constant vigilance of her daughter seems to cause friction. She tears her daughter's book apart, requiring that she cook and clean instead. The mother tries to make her daughter internalize the cultural rules, thinking apparently that only this will ensure her daughter's happiness. The mother tears the book apart because she sees it as a rival to this mission. The book is viewed as an alienating element for the daughter—not only from the culture but also from the mother who is illiterate. In the absence of any guarantees regarding marriage, the only form of protection available for her as a mother is to provide her daughter with the necessary tools for married life—the ability to cook, clean, and present a good appearance.

For Sharifa, the mother is present only in "Nawal." In the other two stories she is absent—either dead or divorced.[11] The stepmother, however, is usually present as a substitute. She is portrayed as an outsider, a materialist, and an element of victimization. In "Sections," she represents forces of destruction. It is as though only a stepmother, not a real mother, would consent to the selling of the land. The stepmother symbolizes "foreign" forces.

In Sharifa's story "Nawal," the tension between victimization and protection takes a more dramatic turn. In this story, the mother causes the death of her daughter, albeit unknowingly. The child apparently suffocated to death as a result of her mother's attempt to protect her from the heat. The mother covered her with her *'abaya* and held her tightly. The child's tragic death was caused both by being "thrown" into the blazing sun and by the mother's desire to "protect" her daughter by "covering" her, as well as by constantly "embracing" her.

Many elements in "Nawal" are symbolic: the *'abaya* is a symbol of darkness, of lack of air; the sun, the husband, the divorce, and even the prison are symbols of punishing elements in society. But the image of a mother trying to protect her daughter and instead suffocating her to death is by far the most powerful aesthetic device that Sharifa uses to reflect society's attitude toward women. The child herself becomes a symbol of woman. Along with her dimples, her "tanned complexion, dark eyes, and dark hair" represent the ideal beauty of the Arabian woman.

Society, just as any mother, has good intentions. With this same "maternalistic" attitude, and in the name of protection, the society "covers" and "embraces" women. Ironically, it is also society that "throws" them out into the "blazing sun," from which there is no protection. Moreover, because the mother is clearly not venerated, the reader is left with the suspicion that the child's death was probably an unconscious attempt, on the mother's part, to spare her female child the fate of growing up to be a woman in a culture that "covers" women to the point of "s-mothering" them. The child's death is akin to female infanticide (a metaphor used by other writers; see chapter 4).

Since this "female infanticide" is considered to be a crime for which the mother has to be imprisoned, Sharifa implies that society, too, is committing this crime against women. Women, too, are smothered in the name of protection. Why then is society not on trial? Sharifa pursues the question by advancing an implicit warning. The writer sentenced the child to a tragic death, threw the mother in prison, and put her on the road to madness. Neither of them deserves this fate, but in these portrayals the writer spreads her message, which can best be related allegorically if it can be related at all.

Society on Trial! Plot or Plotting?

While these women writers point their finger at society, indicating its responsibility for victimizing women, they seem to do so within a limited range. In their fiction, whether in their characterizations or in matters that relate to the demarcation of space and time, they have to recognize certain limitations. Whether in offering solutions or in designing plots, these writers reflect a keen awareness of the balance a writer needs to strike between intellectual adventures and cultural imperatives.

To be sure, while the series of events that lead to women's victimization center ultimately on society or on one of its social institutions as the cause, women writers do not attempt to present a kind of utopian thought in which a new structure is suggested. In fact, solutions to societal problems are usually sought elsewhere rather than in the institution itself. The solution in "Fever" is sought in the woman herself. By advocating her right to say no before and after marriage, the woman should be able to generate the will and the ability for resistance. In "Reflection," Khayriyya gave her protagonist a death sentence as a solution. The character seemed a hopeless case, because she had been deprived even of the means by which to resist the institution of arranged marriage, namely a stable family life. Her marriage was an attempt to escape the dire consequences of her parents' failing marriage. When hers failed, too, she had no place to go.

Najwa's and Khayriyya's stories about the consequences of a lack of choice in a marriage partner depict how women are placed between two swords: the sword of arranged marriage and the sword of divorce. The stories' plots suggest that this type of marriage is doomed. The reasons for the failure of marriage can be established on various levels. The marriages of the protagonists obviously failed because the men treated the women badly. The poor treatment is related either to incompatibility, inability to adjust, or because of other personal factors. In every case the writer always emphasizes the fact that the family has forced the girl into marriage. The stories portray how the ultimate friction between marriage partners is brought on by the partners not knowing each other to the point where they can develop affection for each other before marriage. The woman, after all, is forced on the man just as he is forced on her. Even when they both consent, they both lack choice.

In the writers' treatment of this problem, as in others, they try to dispel the contradictions embedded in social life; however, in their exposition they remain silent on the solution. Neither Najwa nor Khayriyya address or even hint at institutional changes in society. If these women refuse to be part of an arranged marriage, and cajole other women to resist it also, what are the alternatives? What other mechanisms are available in their society that enables a woman or a man to choose a lifetime partner? In fact, how can the possibility exist at all in a society where segregation of the sexes is the norm?

Women writers' silence on the question of concealment or segregation of the sexes does not go unnoticed. But it is one thing for them to address a problem, another to suggest or propose a solution. While the problem of incompatibility between the two partners can be addressed, it is too risky to recommend directly that the solution lies in some type of interaction between a man and a woman before marriage. The former may be seen as a *plot* for a story, but the latter would certainly be construed as a form of *plotting* against established norms. The writers have the added responsibility in designing the plot so as to preclude its confusion with plotting.

The writers could criticize the institution of arranged marriage by playing on the contradictions between religious and social interests. Najwa, for example, has referred to the arranged marriage between families as "tribal marriage," as a cultural residue from times past. This reference is meant to weaken the legitimacy of the institution because arranged marriage is not sanctioned by religion but rather is developed as a response to men's (fathers') various social interests. Religiously speaking, compatibility is an important element in marriage. The man and the woman are, in fact, permitted before marriage to see each other, under the family's supervision, to determine their compatibility. Moreover, religion requires the two parties' consent in order for the marriage to be legal. But women, because of social norms that deem their refusal of the father's desire a shameful act, choose to honor the father's choice.[12]

Najwa, as well as Khayriyya, seem to use their awareness of this fact to avoid dealing directly with the segregation issue. By leaving proposals of change lurking in the background, the reader is left wondering about this deliberate silence. It is a clever maneuver because the unsaid becomes as prominent and consequential as what is said, if not more so. To advocate—if only by hinting at—the mixing of sexes would be detrimental not only to the writer herself but also to her message. Allusion is more fruitful than evoking unnecessary apprehension and opposition.

Questioning Power and the Powerful

In her stories Sharifa is as keen on conveying messages that relate to injustice committed against women as she is on extending her messages to other types of injustice. Her stories often reveal serious messages about both. But in no other story is the critique of class more pronounced than in "Sections." Sharifa produces one of the most memorable critiques of class differences—of the uneven distribution of wealth, power, and prestige between the rich and the poor—not only among individuals but also between the village and the city in her homeland.

What is intriguing about Sharifa's stories is her tendency to pass these messages through women protagonists who are either mad or socially troubled individuals. Far from being meant as a form of punishment to women, "Sections" suggests that madness is in fact used as an effective tool in response to a variety of constraints, aesthetic as well as social. In addition to being used as a means of gaining sympathy, these characterizations provide a valuable technique in gaining legitimacy for certain points of view, and to pass serious messages that otherwise would be intercepted.

To be sure, in the observation that the mad protagonist Zahra in "Sections" makes about the official's *'abaya,* Sharifa points to the convergence, in the political structure, of money, power, and legitimacy in one person. In fact, she adds ignorance. For the official did not seem to lack a charitable attitude, but his ability to comprehend reality or to recognize the full implications of her remarks about his *'abaya* was certainly limited. The mad character spoke figuratively and sarcastically, but he took what she said literally. The children of the poor village received candy instead of a classroom, a factory, or a paved street. This is an almost implicit allusion to Marie Antoinette's famous charitable attitude.

The chief doctor was supposedly an agent of health, but he was corrupt. He wanted to "break her pride." Here the author indicates his attempt to rape the protagonist. The word *rape* is as taboo as *class.* The author cannot mention either nor can she name such matters as the hypocrisy and corruption of the system.[13] To reveal messages about such a suppressed issue as social class, Sharifa had to play on notions of sanity and insanity. Only through a mad character can the unjust distribution of wealth and power be addressed. As if to question class is a function of being crazy, and to be crazy is a function of questioning class. Sharifa had to establish that the character was, without a doubt, crazy. She was a patient in a mental clinic, and violent. She was the narrator of the story, but she remained nameless. (A name would probably establish her too firmly in reality.) On the other hand, Sharifa portrays her mad characters as having an unusual access to the truth— even more so than the sane. What they say always seems to make sense. In fact, their insanity is almost always seen as "the" means by which they establish their ability to see what is beyond and to speak the unspeakable. To protect herself from being held personally accountable, and to free her message from social and political consequences, Sharifa had to free her characters first from social norms. The only form of freedom that seemed possible at all was simply through madness.

Madness, Death, and Sympathy

Madness not only ensures a degree of freedom for passing serious messages, it also facilitates a higher degree of receptivity to the message by virtue of the sympathy the mad characters invoke, especially women such as Sharifa's characters. Generally, women writers, by approaching these various issues, purport to secure the readers' involvement in the stories by leading them into thinking about the fictional situations as moral dilemmas. Naturally, the reader is cajoled to identify with a character, but when this, for whatever reason, is not possible, then invoking sympathy, whether by madness or death, becomes an important means by which to secure the reader's involvement.

However, sympathy is not readily given to a mad or troubled character. The reader's sympathy can only be gained if he or she is convinced and made aware of why they should grant the character the "right" to happiness in the first place. Najwa may, for example, vividly and strongly portray her protagonist as an unhappy woman, and with the aid of imagery and symbols, she may invoke the reader's sympathetic response. But the character projects too strong an image for a woman to be, socially speaking, convincingly worthy of sympathy. Aware of this, Najwa, as well as Khayriyya, had to employ all possible devices to exacerbate the reader's sense of their characters' victimization. To be sure, in addition to sentencing their women protagonists to madness, death, or ostracism, they portray men as extremely undesirable characters to enhance the reader's sympathy for the victim.

By so doing, the writers have to be careful not to alienate the reader. Both male and female readers may find it difficult to identify or sympathize with a character such as the one in Najwa's story, for example. Najwa's character is less likely to invoke sympathy among male readers because she sounds like an angry woman. Anger is not only a culturally undesirable attribute but also projects an image of strength that is not particularly desirable in a woman. Women readers, on the other hand, may find it uncomfortable to identify with such a character precisely because her strength is not only difficult to acquire but also because it is costly. They may not be willing to pay such a high price for nonconformity or they may be repelled by the type of poetic justice that sentences women to madness and death, viewing it as an act of injustice against women on the part of these writers.

This fear of alienating the reader is probably why Khayriyya chose that her character Mona meet death by being run over by a car. The writer seems to be telling us that Mona is doomed anyway. The character's father, who is supposed to be her refuge, is no better than her husband. In addition, if she is not dead she will be divorced—and to be divorced is to be sentenced to social death. But Khayriyya's character is not made to walk to her death consciously. One is not sure whether the death is an accident or suicide, and Khayriyya is clever in giving no clear indication. Because suicide is religiously a sin, to indicate suicide would be to turn the victim into the accused, hence depriving her of the reader's sympathy. Khayriyya wants to solicit as much sympathy for her character as she can muster. Leaving the cause of her protagonist's death hanging is a brilliant solution. By sentencing her character to death, she in fact punishes society. The reader is suspended between feelings of sympathy on the one hand and, as a member of society, of guilt on the other.[14]

Publication of Women's Private Experiences: Speaking the Real Through Models

Women protagonists, when portrayed as mad, dead, or pathological, may be effective vehicles for passing serious messages, but their very abnormality may function to blur women's real experience, making identification with them difficult. This need not be the case, however. Mad characters, especially Sharifa's, in addition to their symbolic utility, also have a "real" function. The protagonist in "Sections," for example, may be uncommon as a character—but her experience of madness is real, and the forces that lead to her victimization are no less real.

Sharifa's tendency to choose pathological characters and unfamiliar settings is probably a function of her access, as a social worker, to these human types and places. Sharifa acknowledges that her stories are drawn mainly from the lives of real women whose personal experiences have touched her personally. In all fairness, she feels uncomfortable with those interpretations of her work that may bury its "realistic" value under a heavy blanket of symbolism. She wishes for the reader to appreciate them, first and foremost, as "real lives," and she aspires to achieve her desired effect through this very conception.

Sharifa is not alone in this aspiration. In fact, all writers—regardless of form or genre—equally insist that their stories and topics are, more often than not, derived from personal observations, readers' mail, and the private lives of people with whom they are in touch—either through their work with other women or through social relations. While they always attempt to shift the subjective experiences to the larger social context, these subjective experiences, they emphasize, exist in their own right and have value of their own.

In Khayriyya's story "The Reflection," for example, she holds up a mirror so that society can see itself. It is both a reflection *of* and a reflection *on* reality. In fact, in her introduction to her only collection, *Sailing Toward the Dimensions,* Khayriyya suggests that "These portraits . . . are only a direct reflection of what is happening in reality . . . my words are a bridge between the soil and the paper."

The writers' special sensitivity to the real reflects their commitment to their readers, but it has other consequences as well. In portraying real experiences of women and men, and in emphasizing them as reflections of actual conditions, they use the power of imitation. The mimicry of men's actions, for example, may appear as a harmless expressive tactic, but mimicry has serious consequences. On the one hand, by repeating men's assumptions, conceptions, and actions about women in their stories, the writers may be seen as ridiculing men. On the other hand, by holding a mirror by which men can see and hear themselves, it may lead men to a greater self-knowledge. Whatever role it plays, mimicry may become a source of empowerment to women if it effects a change in men.

In the five stories, women are depicted in a variety of experiences and with various personalities, degrees of victimization, and degrees of being aware of their condition. Women writers, while they emphasize the commonality of women's experiences of victimization, they equally emphasize the diversity of women's response to it. The protagonists in Najwa's and Khayriyya's stories respond to the experience of arranged marriage differently. Najwa's protagonist intellectualizes her experience of arranged marriage and finds salvation in the "will." She finds in words means of salvation, as well as meaning, by reflection, and by naming her new experience. Khayriyya's protagonist's personal experience has been compounded by the depth of her family's history. That failed arranged marriage was her mother's experience, as well as her own, also affects her. Those two failures in marriage were the decisive elements in the dramatic turn of events that culminated in her death.

Although Sharifa's women protagonists are mostly represented as victims—particularly as mad, dead, or both—they, by virtue of their resistance, are presented, if not as real heroines then as models. Even the mad, or especially the mad (such as Zahra), can reflect, remember, or at least possess a sense of time and history. Despite their madness, or because of it, they act as models for resistance. If Zahra was portrayed as mad, she was also depicted as angry, and one who responded to her own anger in a courageous act of resistance. The representation of women's experiences in most of these stories reflects three forms or levels of resistance: the level of reflection, the level of consciousness, and the level of providing models of action. It is to these themes that I shall devote the remainder of my analysis.

Power of Reflection: Stream or Scream of Consciousness?

Although the stories are at some level reflections of reality, what is more important is that they tend to portray characters who constantly reflect on reality. The existence of mirrors in their rooms symbolizes that reflection of self and on self. But their reflection is not a passive flashback but rather an exercise of the power of memory and a means of establishing continuity. Women protagonists practice this art not only through the technique of flashback and stream of consciousness but also by looking at photograph albums.

In the use of stream of consciousness as a narrative technique, the tendency is to reduce what is often called dramatic distance. Dramatic distance, which allows the reader to know more than the characters do about themselves, is an important part of the traditional Arabic *hikaya* (story). The stream of consciousness, with its built-in mechanism of revealing mental processes, is an especially useful and effective strategy in empowering women characters and in presenting them as being conscious of their condition, so that their situation can be transformed profoundly. Through that consciousness, the protagonists assert that they are not submissively accepting their victimization and that their defeat is only temporary.

Najwa's and Khayriyya's characters demonstrate no less awareness of their situation. Khayriyya's protagonist's reflection on the events in her life promotes a type of self-examination that leads her to be acutely aware of time and of the power of history (her family's). Najwa's protagonist, like Khayriyya's, reaches self-knowledge through a continuing dialogue with herself. She arrives at a level of consciousness that enables her to distinguish between her real or true self and the social self. "I do long for you," says the social self to the estranged true self. By knowing herself, she closes the gap and puts an end to her alienation. By closing the rift, she soon discovers that she possesses will. By virtue of her self-knowledge, she is no longer a vulnerable being.

Even when women are portrayed as mad, as with Sharifa's characters, they seem to be more conscious than any of those who are supposedly not so divorced from reality. The protagonist Zahra in "Secret" is deemed by the male character as "the most sane of all the sane." She knows the days of the week, and she can remember when and where her meetings with her lover take place. In "Sections," despite the discontinuity of the woman character's life and the general incoherence of her existence, she is, astonishingly, so aware of time that she misses no detail related to time or place. She remembers when and why she was institutionalized as a mental patient. She knows her age. In fact, she devises her own method of keeping track of all the important events in her life, either by the occurrence of religious occasions, such as the month of Ramadhan and the Eid, or by planting a palm tree every year.

Words as a Means of Engendering Consciousness

These women use words to reach a level of consciousness. They find salvation in words, in letters, and at times in centers of learning (schools). Najwa's protagonist takes "refuge in the warmth" of her words after she discovers their power, both the said and unsaid. "To take refuge in the warmth of my words is fantastic. To choose silence as a defensive means is even more terrific!" Discovering the power of silence in leading her to her present agony is to discover the power of words in changing her fate. Now it is the letter, even yet to be sent, that provides the means of escape from her existential chaos. The idea of the letter is born of the "embrace" between her mind and her heart or between her two selves. Moreover, as a part of the solution, Najwa's character makes the escape to school, which offers her not only an alternative but also a means of continuing her journey to self-knowledge and of regaining control over her life. It is through Samia's understanding of the dialectics of words and silence that words have become the core of her resistance. It is through words that she moves from a state of consciousness to a state of action. In her choice of talking about divorce over "suicidal" silence, she is committing a rebellious act.

Khayriyya's character tries at first to escape her tragic family life by going to school and later by reading at home. But the school, as well as the schoolmates, had failed her. Unlike Najwa's character Samia, whose family situation seems to enable her to have a "room of her own," both literally and figuratively, Mona's—Khayriyya's character—activities are monitored and constantly interrupted. When Mona tries to escape from her situation into the world of books, her mother tears up a book she is reading, seeing it as competition in the monopoly of her daughter's socialization, as well as a form of alienation both from the mother and from culture. These events in Mona's life are, literally, fatal. They diminish her choices and leave her trapped. In comparison with Najwa's character, who chooses life as a divorced woman over a "suicidal" silence, it is as if the lack of a means to develop consciousness that sentences Khayriyya's character to death.

Sharifa, on the other hand, does not even grant her characters the ability to read and write. This is probably a function of the poverty and deprivation of the village or of its conservatism in relation to the education of girls. However, as a symbol of the authenticity and purity of the land, the mad character in "Sections" is made to be illiterate perhaps because education may be seen as an alienating element if not altogether adulterating to its purity. But despite her illiteracy, the character threatens the hospital administrators with writing a letter.

Neither her illiteracy nor her madness prevents her from knowing the value of the word. The administrators' refusal of her request to write a letter, however, reflects how much the centers of power are fearful of the word.

Naming the New Experiences

As a result of their self-reflection, the characters experience new understanding of their situations and make new discoveries about themselves as well. They discover not only new relationships but also new selves. What does it mean to have a will, to make a choice, or simply to acquire the right to be angry and to resist? What are the means by which these characters express and name this new experience?

Naming the experience seems to be difficult. In Najwa's story the protagonist seems, in narrating her story, to vacillate between the use of the first and the third person. There is a constant shifting back and forth between the "I" and the "she." This cannot simply be attributed to inconsistency on the part of the author. The character experiencing the transformation within herself is not in fact sure that only one self is involved; as a result, the author treats the character as two separate selves. One is the "I," who has been socialized to be silent; the other is the "she," the newly discovered self, who discovers the power of words. The character becomes conscious of the rift, as well as of its consequences, and seeks unity. "It is horrible for a human being to be separated from self . . . to be deprived of soliloquizing with self, from taking refuge in self . . . This is a burden beyond belief." Taking refuge in herself is "the greatest asylum in the history of humanity . . . I will take refuge in truth . . . it is the only virtue . . . I will take refuge in the remnants of hope that were left within me."

The protagonist also seems unsure of how to express her resistance to this split. Samia, Najwa's protagonist, sobs, laughs, weeps, cries, screams, wails, and sighs. She at times reaches a state of discomfort where she, rather violently, bangs on the vanity table. She does not seem sure whether she is happy or sad or what she should feel. She uses images to help her clarify this emotional turmoil. She cries when "she was swept over by a flood of rosy dreams." When in shock, she uses "earthquake," "thunderbolt," or simply "how terrible" to voice her feelings. To express "that feeling of freedom," she speaks of flying "like pigeons." Her joy is never pure; it is always mixed with pain. Pain itself is sometimes as colorful as "a rainbow." Tears of pain and joy gush. She designates this experience of mixed feelings as madness. How else but as madness can one explain talking to oneself and having all these contradictory emotions at the same time?

This new experience is not only difficult to express but is also difficult to conceptualize. As a result she seeks the help of images to understand it, to make others understand it, and as a means by which to overcome her uncertainty. She speaks figuratively to her husband because she does not have the words to express her experience directly. "When fear flaps its wings, we have to clip it. When springs dry up . . . we have to revive them! When a tooth aches endlessly . . . we extract it." When she speaks of "springs that dry up," the "tooth" that has to be "extracted," the clipping of fear's wings, he fails to understand, despite the fact that, for her, these are "clear words." They are clear because they enable her to conceptualize the problem and devise a cure. Societal norms, like her headache, are not curable: "tranquilizers, tranquilizers," she exclaims. They don't cure anything. To uproot the pain "there must be extirpation." The only way for a woman to uproot the pain is to acquire a will. To choose will is to choose life over death. For "weakness is a suicidal choice." The protagonist not only seeks to express the experience or to name it but she also seeks to legitimize it. That experience is personal but it is not hers alone; it is shared by many women. "I am not the only woman who is crushed in such a manner . . . Thousands of others are, like me, corroded." She chooses to make it public only because others choose to remain silent or to give up in despair. "I know many women who choose to remain in the dark corners of life," she explains. The character seems to be well aware of the irony that, as common as her experience is among women, it has no name.

In fact Najwa, in her attempt to name that experience, at times calls it "madness": "A moment of madness is better than a lifetime of dullness." At other times, however, she renders it feverish talk, an "unconscious" hallucination in a hot humid night. But for the whole issue to be reduced to a form of madness or to a "fever in a hot night" does not only seriously undermine the reality of the experience but also defeats the seriousness of her message. But the protagonist labels it madness only in the absence of a language that can adequately describe the experience. She does not necessarily believe it to be so, but rather she uses it because it is the name that is given by the forces of conformity to dissenting views.

Poetics of Concealment and Revelation: Madness, Anger, and Resistance

While it is a function of the lack of proper language, designating these experiences of women as a form of madness is similar in consequence to portraying characters in other instances as mad. Ultimately, it is an attempt to legitimize women's resistance. For one thing, these women protagonists are angry. To legitimize their anger, these women are either said to be mad or to have had "a moment of madness." In order to legitimate her anger, does the woman have to be considered mad or her rebellious act considered a form of madness?

These women writers answer in the affirmative. But to sentence them to madness is not to render them invalids, powerless and helpless. To be sure, even though they are mad, Sharifa's protagonists, for example, are not deprived of their ability to resist. Whether this is done by stones as with Zahra in "Secret" or by scratching as in "Sections," these protagonists have succeeded in resisting the power exercised on them.

Zahra's madness is an act of resistance to the forces of discontinuity and destruction. The modernization forces, "the tractors, the paved street," are forces that represent how women have been uprooted. Zahra's madness gives her access to the truth. The truth is revealed to her through the juxtaposition of orchard and bracelets. It is through this juxtaposition that she is able to grasp the opposition between the nurturing elements, life-giving elements connected with the land on the one hand and bondage and destruction connected with bracelets and what they symbolize on the other. The bracelets are made of gold, symbolizing bondage that masquerades as prosperity.

Zahra's resistance to the violation of the land stands in allegorical relationship to her resistance to the more general forces of bondage that masquerade as protection and care in the mental hospital. Zahra and the land are both victimized in almost the exact same manner. The "rape" attempt victimizes both. But more important, both are not totally defeated. In Zahra's case, the rape is only an attempt by the doctor, because her resistance, although rudimentary (scratching), proved to be effective and actually succeeded in preventing the assault, not only the physical assault but the assault on her dignity.

Zahra also used scratching to stop the assault on the land, but she failed. She was angry when she tried to stop the violation of the land. It was when she tried to stop the tractors, scratching her stepmother's face and pulling her hair, that she was declared mad. She was designated as mad and subsequently institutionalized precisely at the moment when her anger brought her to an actual act of resistance.

It is the consciousness and the anger that lead to action that Sharifa presents as a scenario for resistance. This form of rebellion may be suggested only through a mad character. Madness bestows legitimacy, but it also draws sympathy for her cause. Najwa's character, on the other hand, is sane but angry. This projects more strength and deprives her of sympathy, not to mention legitimacy. In both Sharifa's and Najwa's cases, madness functions as a means both to reveal the truth and to conceal the negative connotations of an angry woman.

Resistance or Affirmation? Rebellion and Its Discontents

This interplay of elements of anger and madness, and of concealment and revelation within the victim, makes the portrayal of women characters ambiguous. On the one hand, by virtue of their resistance, whether on the level of reflection, consciousness, or action, they may serve as *models* for other women. On the other hand, their victimization may work to undermine or even to diminish the significance of their resistance, because they are turned into examples.

To be sure, in their plots some of the women writers (in sentencing women to death, for example) may have intended to punish society rather than the women. But this intention more often than not is blurred. The effectively rendered grave consequences of death, madness, and ostracism that these women are made to face become almost reminiscent of Eve's banishment from Paradise. As a result, this victimization may become a powerful means of engendering conformist tendencies among women. It may result in coaxing women into accepting their position, into preferring a disadvantaged or incoherent existence over death, madness, and ostracism. While written to challenge norms and to engender the notion of resistance, this literature of victimization becomes an element that emphasizes the safety of conforming to norms, perpetuating the status quo and glorifying conformity.

Paradoxically, the notion of resistance may also be challenged by the very portrayal of women as models from which to draw examples. Women have to be careful and provide examples that can be considered as viable models of behavior. In presenting a strong-willed, aware woman, other women may be alienated from such a figure, for as a model she may be difficult to imitate or even to identify with.

Although Najwa's character probably places too much burden on women by seeking solutions in no other element outside the woman herself, Najwa's character brings hope and possibility. Unlike Khayriyya's and Sharifa's characters who are condemned to death and madness, Najwa's character is the closest to setting patterns of imitation for other women. She believes the woman's will to be the shortest way, albeit the most painful. But it is also the most rewarding.

The skill in presenting a character as a viable model has special significance. In this period of ideological rupture, women as well as men are anxious for any meaningful scenario of how to cope with oppressive forces. That fiction in many ways is treated as fact (see chapter 5) may facilitate even more, for the female reader, the prospect of imitation. The perceived "factuality" of these characters, even when conveyed through fictional characters (especially since the stories are often viewed as autobiographical accounts [see chapter 5]) enhances even further their attractiveness as viable models of behavior and legitimizes new aspirations and emotions for women.

One of the attractive elements in Najwa's character is that the model she proposes is not based on adopting qualities that are too alien to the woman as a woman. The woman character does not voice a cry of envy to men or contemplate changing herself into a man. In fact, despite her victimization as a woman, she is portrayed as a model without giving up feminine qualities, including beauty. "I must have looked so beautiful . . . because that is what has been said, a fact I had known all along . . . I have always felt a sense of pride in being beautiful." Khayriyya emphasizes women's intuitive quality, expressed and referred to as "mysterious feelings" by her character.

Even within madness, Sharifa emphasizes the qualities of nurturing, and of being connected to a larger group. They all bring the Sheherazadian qualities of vision and memory, but Najwa's character brings even more of Sheherazade, namely self-sacrifice, persuasion, endurance, patience, self-worth, and mental strength, as well as the ability to use words. If her character succeeds in standing as a model for women, it would be by virtue of her search for and assertion of those female qualities rather than her undermining of them.

What is noteworthy is that, considering all the impossible situations in which women find themselves, the solution may be madness or death but it is never the switching of gender roles to acquire power. It seems that man may stand as a victim of society or as a victimizing agent to women but he does not stand as a *model* for women. Women's lack of desire to trade positions with men is either a function of a sense of shared victimization or of contempt for the qualities of oppression which may present themselves in some men.

Settings in Time and Space: Women Venturing into Public Places

Social norms regarding segregation and concealment seem to affect the setting of interaction between the characters in these stories. The effect of social norms on monitoring the setting of interaction is evident in the spatial and physical aspects women writers emphasize in the setting. Generally, the spatial aspect of setting defines the domain of interaction between men and women, and draws boundaries for their venturing outside concealed or private places. But these women writers use setting, spatial as well as temporal, in a way that, while conforming to the social institution of concealment and segregation, poses a challenge to the domination over space and time.

In almost all the short stories of these and other women writers, the indication of space is rarely omitted. The most commonly used locales are home (especially a room with a bed and a window), a prison cell, a hospital, or a street. But indications of space are also given in many other ways, such as customs of dress (*abaya*), lack of interaction between men and women, regional names, and in such physical characteristics as those of a desert, of village life, and so forth.

Normally, the writers' use of familiar settings is to lend realism to the story and credibility to the characters. Even when a character is portrayed as unfamiliar, in a sense "abnormal" (i.e., insane), her environment is not completely transformed. Normal or not, the female character is not at liberty to mingle freely with men, to discard the *abaya* or head cover, or to conduct a conversation with a strange man in a strange place, for example in a movie theater.

While the familiar setting conforms to and sustains the demarcation of space for women, women writers exercise control of space and define women's space in a way that challenges norms. In these five stories, women are portrayed as being primarily within the confines of a house, a room, or a hospital. But women characters are also portrayed as venturing outside the home—and this to a considerable degree.

Except for Najwa's story, in which the events take place primarily within the house, the room, and the corridor, female characters in all the other stories move within public places. Sharifa's stories take place mostly outside the house, and during the day rather than at night. The characters are either in a mental hospital (as in "Sections"); roaming the village streets or by the pond (as in "Secret"); or in a prison (as in "Nawal"). (In other stories, women characters even interact in an airplane and in a supermarket.) Sharifa's use of background is often intended for symbolic purposes (such as a village standing as a symbol of authenticity and being rooted). The motifs of rural life in Sharifa's selection extend to orchards, palm trees, thorns, and prickles, as well as to traditional ways of doing things (i.e., washing clothes at the stream). In Khayriyya's story the spatial setting includes the street and the neighborhood, in addition to the house and the room, while the temporal setting is left unclear. In Khayriyya's story a sense of time was perhaps irrelevant to the life of her character since heavy curtains are constantly drawn, making day and night virtually indistinguishable.

However, to set women venturing freely in the streets cannot be left to aesthetic necessity alone. Whether women are portrayed as functioning within open or concealed spaces, women writers have to conform to the social rules concerning concealment and segregation. The women may be "outside"—whether in symbolic or in actual terms—but it has to be only temporary. It has to be a justifiable presence. Being "outside" in the street poses a challenge on both the actual and symbolic levels. To be in the street constitutes an invasion of the public place, but the street is also a symbol of "outsideness," of lack of control.

In both Khayriyya's and Sharifa's stories, women venture outside normative space. But these are not "normal" women. Khayriyya's character is troubled, and in a way "in trouble"—both socially and psychologically. Sharifa's characters, as well as Khayriyya's, wander in the village streets only as a function of their troubled condition or as a function of being rural dwellers. Restrictions on women's mobility are more pronounced in the cities than in the rural areas, and codes of modesty constitute less of an obligation for the insane. The mad Zahra in "Secret" is not confined. She ventures into the streets freely, but by ending up being "raped," the implication is that the rape has taken place as much as a result of her wandering in the streets as of her being crazy. She is in the street rather than at home precisely because she is crazy. Ironically, the other mad woman, in "Sections," is confined to an institution, but that confinement does not protect her from an attempted rape either.

Space and Modes of Interaction between Men and Women

The accountability of action, for those who are accountable, the sane, is the same in fiction as in reality. The writers are obliged to establish some legitimacy in their stories for any interaction between men and women. This legitimacy can only be established through the existing rules of interaction (i.e., between kin: brothers, fathers, or cousins). Physical interaction between women and men outside the family is closely monitored in fiction and subordinated to the rules of conduct in real life. Najwa writes to a husband. To send a letter to a lover would be considered too suggestive, and even an attempt at legitimizing the illegitimate; that is, an attempt at "plotting." As such, not only is it culturally unacceptable but also subjects the writer to a great deal of criticism and censorship.

In order for the writer to introduce any unfamiliar mode of interaction between characters that is not socially sanctioned or to portray rebellious, profane, or perverted characters, especially females, they utilize madness. Sane characters, however, can only do so by "traveling"—either in "reality" to a foreign land or in their imagination and dreams. Sharifa has, for example, written a short story called "An Ideal Chauffeur" in which the protagonist is a prostitute. Sharifa, acutely aware of social restrictions on the creative process, has set her story in a foreign land. But that could not protect it from being rejected for publication in her country (although it was accepted for publication in Kuwait).

However, women can challenge the normative mode of interaction, although to a limited extent, even when they are in concealed spaces, such as in a room. While the management of space may ensure the isolation of women in fictional settings, the content of this isolation is remarkably transformed through "traveling." Travel allows these women to wander, thus extending the boundaries not only of space but also of time. Najwa's setting, for example, ensures that the woman is inside, that she conforms to social norms of concealment and segregation. But her character wanders, through "dreaming" and "travel." She is presented as concealed but only visually. Aurally, however, she is revealed—she speaks, writes, and in fact can be "heard." In Najwa's story, norms of physical concealment are sustained, but only in form, to solve the contradiction embedded in her character's existence. On the one hand, the character is portrayed as free-spirited, a rebellious soul who is discovering her need and desire for freedom. On the other hand, the limitations posed by the social management of space (the house, the room, and the corridor) are too constraining to the character's aspirations. Najwa's character is granted her "freedom" through "travel" and "dreaming." As a mobilizing metaphor that is by definition antithetical to norms of immobility, travel is the metaphor most commonly used by women writers to challenge the social demarcation of space. Moreover, not only is travel a leap over space but also over time (to the past as well as the future).

Venturing in Concealed Spaces: Practical and Symbolic Functions of Setting

The detailed descriptions of the rooms in these stories reveal their two functions: one as reality, the other as symbol. In Ḵhayriyya's story, for example, the room has a bed, a closet, a small desk, a fancy rug, a window that is closed and veiled by a thick velvet curtain, a fly, and a pair of shoes (unworn, symbolizing lack of mobility). The room, as the character sees it, is "inhabited" simply by boredom. But it is in the room that this character, as well as Najwa's, have indeed practiced the utmost freedom by venturing in time and space. The room becomes the setting in which selfhood is developed through contemplation and reflection. To be segregated and separated (by choice) is to establish a place in which to be free from social entanglements. That the room is often described as having only a bed and a window, almost like a prison cell, points to its symbolic function.

In reality, however, the room seems to be "the" site for self-revelation. The opportunity it allows for exploring the unconscious reveals the room as an essential means of self-knowledge, and a vehicle of empowerment, independence, and autonomy. But the room, as other surroundings in general, is more often than not manipulated symbolically. A corridor may function as a symbol of transition from one "room" to another. A room may symbolize a prison. A prison may symbolize women's confinement or the dilemma of the individual's alienation exacerbated by social change. A hospital, by the same token, may symbolize a state of dysfunctionality and pathology in society. Abnormality (i.e., madness) may signify a certain perception of "reality" or separation from reality.

The same can be said of the traditional women's black cloak or outer covering, the *'abaya*. The *'abaya* lurks in the background of the stories as women attempt to venture outside the home. It is more pronounced in Khayriyya's and Sharifa's stories, because Najwa's character does not leave the house. While it seems to function as an unmistakable indicator of space, the *'abaya,* as the room, has a symbolic as well as a practical function. As a pretext as well as a vehicle for legitimizing their access to public space, women seem not to express any resentment toward it. In Sharifa's story "Nawal," the symbolic as well as the practical purposes of the *'abaya* intertwine. The *'abaya,* in fact, plays a detrimental role. The tragic death of the child seems to be caused by the blazing sun, the lack of air, and probably the exacerbation of heat by the black color of the *'abaya.*

Temporal Metaphors as a Means of Control over Time

While in their fiction women writers practice a degree of control over space through the manipulation of spatial metaphors, they also practice a comparable control over time. The use of techniques of stream of consciousness and flashback allows the characters to stretch their memories, and to make sense of the present by making sense of the past. These women practice the art of memory through the technique of flashback. The dominant use of these narrative techniques among the writers—supported by such devices as the photograph album in Najwa's story—highlights their belief in women's ability to use memory as a means of establishing continuity and a sense of history in their lives.

In Sharifa's "Sections," discontinuity of her character's life is both spatial and temporal. Discontinuity manifests itself in the protagonist's life being "sectionalized." These sections are "rear," "horizontal," "small," "last," "first," "another." They are also experiential: "a section of pain." The protagonist is acutely conscious of time (she knows her age, how long she has been in the hospital, the planting of a palm tree every year, the month of Ramadhan, and the Eid). The mad Zahra in "Secret" remembers the days of meetings with her lover: Thursdays. She saw forces of modernization as forces of uprooting, of divorce from history. That sense of human beings being divorced from their history is echoed in "Nawal" where the protagonist is made to suffer amnesia in which she either cannot or does not want to remember.

A Night of One's Own

In contrast to Sharifa, and to a lesser extent to Khayriyya, in most of Najwa's stories events take place not only in a house and a small room but also during the night. Night has its hold on Najwa both as actuality and as symbol. Five of Najwa's nine stories in her collection take place during the night. In fact, not one story is devoid of the night's presence (in one story alone night is mentioned eleven times). Night is usually seen as a time for "rest," but traditionally it is also known as a time of subversion.[15] If Najwa's stories present a challenge to the mode of interaction between men and women through her use of "travel," she presents another challenge by her choice of night as a time for interaction. Najwa transforms the night, for women, from a time for romance to a time for the exercise of independence, for self-confrontation, for reflection on her history, for hard work, and for building courage. This notion of night as a means of self-empowerment and of making history captures the Sheherazadian model of the woman. Sheherazade's and other women's salvation was accomplished by working at night, through memory and by means of the word. As exemplified by the letter in Najwa's story and working at night, a total Sheherazadian scenario emerges.[16]

Like the color of the *'abaya*, the darkness of the night (*dhalam*, which shares the same root word as *dholm*, or injustice) may also stand in allegorical relationship to women's conditions. But to invoke night is not necessarily to make a pessimistic statement but rather to invoke hope. The potential of awakening, of morning light, carries the promise of change. As a metaphor, night suggests the inevitability of cyclical change as a rule in the dynamics of the universe. It is light that comes after dark, and it is awakening that comes after dreams or perhaps nightmares. The morning has in fact begun for Najwa's protagonist. It was already one o'clock in the morning!

4

Redefining the Issues:
The Politics of Re-vision and
the Production of Difference

This chapter examines the works of Juhayer Al-Musa'ed, Fatna Shāker, and Sohaila Zain Al-Abedin. These women writers are the most widely read female Saudi Arabian essayists, having persisted in the writing scene exclusively as essayists for more than a decade.[1] The selections are intended to provide an overview of the subjects these writers define as issues or problems their society faces, but they also reveal within their various narrative structures and communicative techniques a diversity of styles and cultural positions, as well as ideological orientations. The variety of issues, themes, and emphases of these writers reflect their broad interest in the problems of the society as a whole, and a tendency to question and redefine what the dominant discourse calls the "woman's issue." The articles document the subtleties of the cultural debate on women and reveal the nuances of discursive formation in society.

The analysis of their writings will focus on how these women conceptualize and understand their relationship to men, to the postulates of the dominant discourse, to tradition, to religion, and to the West. Their writings demonstrate a highly developed sense of the intertwining nature of all these elements. The politics of the production of difference in which these women are engaged is tightly connected to the mastery of the art of asking the right questions, whether in relation to the local or the global discourses on women and their place in society. In their definition of the issues they provide a re-vision of the postulates of their society and challenge its responsibilities to women. As women they assert their differences from men; as intellectuals they provide a critique of cultural institutions; and as Arab Muslim women they speak of the forces that dominate them, without slipping into a Western garb or adopting a Western definition of their situation for which they mock other Arab women.

The analysis will also show how the writers utilize a certain logic or strategy in arguing about the issues and how this has affected the writers' conceptions of the causes of social problems. Moreover, the ability of these women writers to appeal to both religion and tradition is only matched by their profound insights into the basis of social institutions in a way that facilitates the disentanglement of the religious from the social. Almost an attempt at the impossible, this disentanglement, as will be seen, is critical for women in order to counter the tendency of the dominant discourse to blur the two as a means of controlling women.

Juhayer Al-Musa'ed: Selections from Her Writings

The Creator and the Victim[2]

It seems to me that journalists in all other societies have given special attention to women . . . Foreign journalists and Arab alike have dealt with women as objects of commercialization by depicting them in colored posters. Even the so-called women's magazines have exploited women by distributing these pictures among men . . . What becomes clear is that the woman becomes no more than bait to attract men . . . But journalism has also exploited women in another way; that is, through [talking] about women's roles and their commitment to their society. Every topic, no matter how marginal or insignificant, has been made an "issue," to be inflated by sensational rhetoric . . . The topic becomes a big "issue" and every change that occurs in society is seen to have an effect on women. Some of those topics exhausted in discussion are women's work outside the home; women's education; women college graduates who are looking for husbands; spinsterhood; foreign maids and nannies; and so forth. . . . Many topics are discussed as "women's issues" whereas in fact they are not. They are simply issues of a society that is experiencing development and change . . .

For example, when we deal with a woman's work outside the home, as a teacher, for example, not only do we see it as a problem but we also deal with the subject in terms of allegations and warnings to women that work is the cause of all family tragedies. We do not think of how to enable women to work and take care of the family, either by reducing their load of work hours or by allowing women to choose a certain number of hours in which to work. We all know that education of girls cannot be maintained without women teachers . . . , why then don't we make our discussions more fruitful? The same thing goes for the woman doctor . . . The existence of women doctors is no doubt hailed as a great achievement for our developing society. But this achievement is seen as a sign of personal failure, for which the woman has to be held accountable. We hear the woman doctor cry out because she cannot find a husband, and we consider this to be a failure. We raise questions about why women college graduates are not getting married, and we never ask why their male counterparts are not getting married either. There are men who have reached their thirties, and even beyond, but have never married; yet we never disturb their bachelorhood and ask why they don't get married . . . Why do we concentrate on women, and consider education in medicine or work as a doctor, for example, to be the cause?

Journalism concentrates on the woman as she goes to school and gets an education, as she works, as she eats, as she gets married, as she brings up her children, as she gives birth, and so on . . . The woman becomes the "creator" of journalism and also its victim.

Swallowed by This "Mystical Giant"[3]

Lately . . . and for some time now, the press has been suffering from a fever . . . As a result of this fever, many issues have started to arise; that is, if we can call them "issues." Is this feverish talk an attempt to win readership regardless of the means? Will Mr. Chief Editor allow me to dig with my clipped nails and "tied" tongue, and will he allow me to dig into the pages of the newspapers to reflect my own view of the press's role in the life of the Saudi woman? Will my (male) colleagues be angry and think I am feverish, too? That is fine . . . But I expect that they will be noble enough to let me participate in the battle of opinions, and I hope I may be forgiven if I am mistaken.

Whoever reads newspapers these days will have no doubt that what Saudi women suffer from is a number of problems that do not extend beyond such issues as girls' clubs, women and driving, high dowries, and so forth . . . I would like to pose a naive question . . . What kind of image is our media presenting to those who read it abroad? As women, we do not dispute the necessity of discussing matters related to the role of the woman in society, or her needs . . . We agree with the principle but disagree with the manner and the way in which it has been conducted.

Journalistic sensationalism is the method our newspapers prefer. The paper does not cover the subject from all sides—within what is possible and allowed—giving the reader a chance to voice his or her point of view. Rather, the discussion of an issue starts with a personal opinion from a reader (regardless of his or her level of awareness, education, or age), which is then followed by a response from another reader, then still another, endlessly. In the end, views remain diverse and no agreement is reached. And because the topic has previously arisen and has been discussed continuously dozens of times . . . our virtuous respected *'ulama* interfere and bring the *fatwa* [religious judgment] on the matter in terms of what is permitted and what is forbidden. In their *fatwas,* they truly try to take readers' views into consideration. But these views are often one-sided, ignoring other views and turning their backs on opinions that are most obvious and clear. The final word is reserved for our *'ulama*—may Allah save them—who try to do the right thing for the safety of Muslim society. They judge from what they see, hear, and read.

All this keeps happening, and the press stands there watching. It does not "participate," nor does it see itself as a partner in the issue. All the media cares about is sensationalism and the readers' response. It does not take a stand on the issues, and acts as if the issue does not concern [it] at all. I think that the press does not want to serve the woman but rather wants only to serve its own needs . . . I hope I am mistaken, but let's take a look.

When the idea of clubs for women was discussed, it faced overwhelming rejection even before the designation [club] was explained—as if it were a "good opportunity to attack women." Because of the magical effect and hegemony of "sports" on people's minds, and because we are really "good sports," the clubs were interpreted as "athletic clubs," as if the word *club* can carry only a recreational meaning. There are many known literary clubs [in the country], which as far as I know include women in their memberships. Have these clubs led to women's deviance or perversion? God forbid . . . or do these women have special privileges over other women?

Some wrote "No to perversion" and said that clubs are a means to spread the plagues that smear women's purity and virtue . . . The question to those who lecture us about perversion is, would perversion wait until it appears in women's clubs? Does that mean that because there are no women's clubs now, that perversion is nonexistent among girls? I wish this were true . . . it would—by Allah—be the greatest news. Why, then, do we have institutions for fallen women and juvenile halls for girls? Why would this happen if all our girls were virtuous and had never been to clubs before?

Some said that, from a religious point of view, the woman is all *owra* [private, not to be seen] except her face and palms. Yes, the woman is *owra* . . . it is true . . . but to whom is the woman *owra?* It is only to the man. How could a woman among other women be *owra?* I don't want to say, in the name of the religion, something I have no right to say. If there is a mistake here, it is from me, and probably caused by Satan. But religion is innocent of my mistakes, it is innocent . . . innocent.

Does religion forbid religious learning? Aisha—may God be pleased with her—taught a generation of men, and we have the best examples in the mothers of the believers. If a club were opened for the purpose of religious learning and cultural discussions, would our *'ulama*—may Allah save them—object to that? I never heard they did before . . . So why would they object to everything that concerns the woman? Why do girls' clubs face all this anger and attack, and why are they considered a danger and a threat to society?

Another example . . . When [Arabian] supermarkets were opened, both sexes could mix freely. Let us hope they do not close them or, even worse, put up a sign that says "women are not allowed" (may Allah take care of us and guide us to the right path). But the fact is that when supermarkets opened we all agreed, my grandmother and yours, my mother and yours, and my father and yours. We even, my dear reader, have called them [by their Western name] "supermarket." Allahu Akbar . . . God is great . . . our Arabic tongue has even been [twisted] and nobody objects . . .

I am not for or against clubs for girls . . . but I object to the way journalism deals with topics that concern women. All the newspapers have done is to watch the situation and cheer for more distribution. The woman is always the victim. Have you ever read any subject more sensational than the one in which the woman is portrayed as a victim? I ask one question and wish for an answer . . . how do newspapers serve women? How do women benefit from these issues? Have any of these issues ended in their favor? Any one at all? Of all the many issues that have been tackled?

Do you remember the issue of women and driving? Our *'ulama* were asked about whether is was permissible for women to drive cars. But [correspondingly] the newspapers neglected to ask them about the statement that "men are *qawwuamoun* on women [caretakers of women]" and what this guardianship in fact means. For if every guardian faced his responsibilities and every man practiced his *qiwama* caretaker role, and drove women to work and every other place, then absolutely no problem would exist. But if he is busy or lazy (or whatever), what is the solution? Should half the society be paralyzed? Or should the [foreign] driver be the solution? It is a grave injustice for the woman to take responsibility for all this . . . Let every man face his responsibility and after that women can be held accountable [for their own]. Some men think women should drive cars, breaking traditional barriers, just so they will not say to the man, "Move it, it's your turn now to take responsibility." Don't you see this is an injustice?

I think that when the newspaper takes up an issue, it should be covered comprehensively, and readers should be given the opportunity to participate. Dear Journalism, may you accept—from a woman—prayers of [good health] . . . be just . . . this Mystical Giant that swallows the woman in the name of Journalism, causes women such a great injustice.

Female Journalists and Women's Liberation[4]

I have read something in the newspapers that made me change the topic I originally intended to write about today. If this article is incoherent, it is because I am writing in a hurry.

One of the newspapers has published the following: a group of female Arab journalists is convening [in Cairo] under the banner "Arab Media, in Service to Woman's Liberation." Since the topic concerns both the Arab Media and women, it was only natural that it caught our interest and captured all our attention!

I understand that Jerusalem is in need of liberation . . . Palestine is struggling for liberation . . . Afghanistan is impatiently waiting for complete liberation . . . So are other parts of the Muslim world struggling for liberation . . . I understand that and I think we all agree on this . . . But what we do not agree on is what the woman wants from liberation? Who is "occupying" her and from whom is she seeking liberation? Why does the woman complain of oppression? And who is she complaining about? I expect that the thought is widespread [among Arab women] that the woman is suffering from man's oppression of her

. . . These expressions are not only widespread among Arab women but have also become a part of our parlance that we imported, among other things, from foreigners . . . As such, we hear a lot about man's oppression [of woman], man's enslavement [of woman], and woman's equality with man . . . The woman wastes her life thinking about the man . . . how to antagonize him or to get even with him, and so forth . . . But at the same time we find that the woman marries the man, loves the man, and bears him children!

I can envision the speeches [of these convening women] . . . One woman stands up and calls for woman's liberation from barriers of oppression and pitfalls of enslavement . . . She kicks off all conceptions that shackle the woman . . . She bangs on the table protesting all attempts that halt women's liberation . . . She turns her back on all values of love and loyalty to the man . . . Then she goes home where she eagerly inquires about her children and takes refuge in her husband . . .

All women have men in their lives, and all men have women in theirs. This is the human nature that Allah has created . . . I agree with some women who suffer from man's authoritarianism, for some men do not recognize the just content of Islamic principles. The man is required [by Islam] to hold the woman with the utmost kindness or else release her with dignity. But not all men are oppressors or cruel, and they are not prison guards of the marriage cage . . . Even if that were so, the solution is not to raise the slogan of "liberation" or "equality" . . . rather, we should choose a slogan with which we can work and reach our goals . . . If the slogan asserts that the woman is a human being with rights and duties, this will be understandable . . . and if slogans say that the woman is a first-class citizen, this is also good . . .

But if they mean by "woman's liberation" that the woman should be freed from man's authority at home, then qualifications are needed . . . They are required by the true woman herself! Who wants a man who is half and half? In other words, what kind of a woman desires a man in whose home she plays the role of the man? No true woman does not want a true man . . . The true woman loves and finds pleasure in a man who takes responsibility for her and who carries this responsibility with adequacy and in a manly way.

The man has a right to rule his home, and the woman has to rule with him and not just be ruled by him. What exactly is meant by liberation? Freeing the woman from man's oppression? Or does it mean freeing the woman from her responsibilities of home, husband, and children? Or does it mean freeing her from the burden of homemaking, so she will have more time for her husband and children?

The truth is that the woman, especially the Arab woman, when she wanted to lighten (not get rid of) the burden of homemaking, used a housemaid, a woman just like herself, to help with her home and children . . . Raising children has always been the woman's responsibility (whether as maid or as mother). This means that we women are in fact convinced that raising children is the woman's responsibility in the first place . . . That is why we bring in foreign nannies and housemaids instead of making the man share the responsibility for raising our children.

It is a shame that we sometimes copy expressions or imitate slogans coming from the West, via other Arab countries, as if they are worthy of being followed or could stand as examples for us . . . The expression "woman's liberation" is imported blindly from the foreign West . . . The question is, how fruitful are its results and how much has been accomplished for women since the expression began to invade us?

The foreign woman has called for liberation and equality. She believes in this lie. But she is also paying dearly for it, especially in her relationship with the man as a husband or even as a son. Under the "personal freedom" slogan, family relations have deteriorated in the West and the word *family* has lost its meaning. Do you know why? Because it violates human nature . . . The man no longer feels nor does he practice his manhood the way he should. Neither does the woman feel her womanhood nor actualize it the way it should be actualized.

Now the foreign woman discovers the high price she has to pay for the equality lie. The Arab world and some Arab women imitate the West. They are going through the same phase and making the same mistakes for which the Western woman is still paying dearly . . . The foreign woman, even after all she has done for her society, still faces the accusation that she is responsible for the loss of men's jobs . . . We should not think that the foreign woman has accomplished what we haven't . . . On the contrary.

Oh, convening Arab women! What a "disaster" to have you [among us], and this time, I am not even going to apologize!

A Personal Sketch of the Writer Juhayer Al-Musa'ed

Juhayer Al-Musa'ed was born in 1955 in Ar-Riyadh. Coming from a middle-class Nejdi family, she was the first woman in her family to graduate from college. She obtained her B.A. in education from Ar-Riyadh University, where she also received an M.A. in administrative education, the field in which she now works. She has studied and spent all her life in Riyadh. She started writing at age fourteen when she was in preparatory school. Her first writings, which she describes as romantic reflections, were dedicated mostly to exploring the feelings of a teenager through themes of love and romance. She sent these pieces as reader mail to be published under a female pseudonym. She has written for various newspapers—*Ar-Riyadh, Al-Yowm, Al-Jazeera*—and for *Al-Yamama* magazine.

The first time she used her real name was with the publication of an article entitled "The Bare Face of America" in the late 1970s. Parts of the article were broadcast on "Voice of America," where she was referred to as a male. This reference to her as a male was a common mistake that persisted well after she had become an established writer. When her name first appeared, Juhayer was thought to be a man's name—not only because it was rather uncommon but because it does not indicate the sex of its holder like other names. However, it was perhaps what her readers perceived as a direct and daring approach to social problems, seen as "manly," that created this misconception. Although she explained on many occasions that she was in fact a woman, and many are now convinced of this (especially after she wrote about her engagement, and later about her marriage), readers still sent her mail daring her to reveal her true identity.

I conducted the interview with Juhayer during her visit to her father's house in Ar-Riyadh. The house was spacious and seemed to have been built rather recently—newly furnished, as was the case with most of the homes in Riyadh. The interview took place in the reception room with little or no interruptions. As in most Saudi Arabian houses, the reception room, which is referred to as the "salon," was located near the entrance to ensure maximum privacy. Juhayer provided me with two huge bound volumes, one containing all her articles published since the late 1970s, the other including what was written about her, either by critics or readers, as well as the responses of officials to her writings. I was impressed with the effort, and she immediately gave credit to her husband, whom she said laboriously collected the material. The volumes were an invaluable source of material on her and the society as a whole.

Juhayer the person seemed as energetic as her writings. I could not help but notice that she writes as she speaks, and she speaks as if she were reading one of her articles. Juhayer writes a weekly column in *Al-Jazeera*, a daily newspaper in the eastern province, and has written occasionally for *Ar-Riyadh*. Juhayer's style is characterized by its catchy titles and flaring language, which engages the reader in her lengthy articles. Her appeal is less to the intellectuals than to regular readership. Juhayer is famous for her argumentative style which forces the reader to engage in the argument, provoking them to take a stand, frequently addressing them as "dear reader." Because her aim is persuasion, she makes use of logic and analogy and tends to pass messages in many different ways. This may have led to lengthy articles but it reflects her awareness of the diversity of her audience and her keen interest in securing a level of communication with all of her readers.

Juhayer is most popular among the Najdis, who seem to be protective of her and consider her their pride. For some of them, she conjures up an image of the traditional Arab woman who can speak her mind and be heard, without questioning her loyalty. And indeed Juhayer assures her loyalty to the culture through her commitment to its norms, including wearing *hijab* (veiling) abroad. Juhayer also often expresses loyalty to the royal family by saluting this prince or that princess. On one occasion she calls King Fahd by his first name and then as "Fahd Al Fahod" or the "Leopard of all Leopards." Some have even suspected that she might in fact be a member of the royal family hiding behind a pseudonym. They reason that in order to protest what happens in society or to engage in discussions with religious leaders in the manner that she does, one has to be "protected."

The scores of articles Juhayer has written during the past ten years reflect a broad interest in "social problems," addressing especially such issues as marriage, women and men, and problems of youth. But she also tackles problems of human services (e.g., medical centers, schools, airports, tourism), especially in the city of Ar-Riyadh. She addresses officials directly, including the king himself, demanding solutions. Very often the officials respond to her writings, which has gained her the trust of many readers, both men and women, who often sent letters urging her to be their voice. Because of her highly developed journalistic sense, her writings reflect the urgency with which certain issues are discussed at a particular time. With few exceptions, rarely do we find instances in which Juhayer chooses to be silent on the "issue of the hour"—be it global or national politics or historical events. The selection of articles included here reflects her keen sense of what is "worth" discussing and her sharp observations of the purpose to which journalistic discourse on women should be put.

While Juhayer tends to critique the practices of men, women, government officials, and the religious *'ulama*, she rarely resorts to confrontation. This is partly because Juhayer often reduces "social problems" to psychological differences or miscommunication between men and women. She does not tend to question the system or suggest structural changes. This is also perhaps why her approach to a problem is often seen as down-to-earth, if only by virtue of her search for immediate causes. Even when she speaks openly of censorship (which she does more openly than any other woman writer), she tends to see censorship as "more a function of timidity [of the editor] than of real rules or regulations" (personal communication, 1989). Such a conception enhances her loyalty to the state and engenders its view as tolerant of intellectual freedom.

But lack of confrontation is also a function of Juhayer's style. While she protests probably more often than others, and some even see it as "too much," Juhayer uses a style that is based on persuasiveness as well as on a kind of theatrical performance and self-effacement. The selections presented here reflect how she refuses to take sides on issues that are "too sensitive," either religiously or politically. Many times she laces her critiques with wit and sarcasm.[5] Her vivacious style is sprinkled with terms of endearment and humility, especially when she speaks to or about religious leaders. Although her reputation for daring is seen as testing censorship limitations, her sarcastic style, coupled with her humility, have in fact succeeded in working as a disarming device even when she engages in exchanges with the *'ulama*. In religious matters she tends to speak humbly, with a "correct me if I'm wrong" type of statement that often gets her off the hook. This humbleness, usually mixed with her penchant for sarcasm and wit, is a double-edged device. At times it may prove to be an effective way of presenting serious messages. But this underlying attitude of "don't take me too seriously" or "I'm just kidding" may also undermine her message and defeat her argument.

Juhayer demonstrates little concern with these stylistic and ideological matters. As a writer her priority is to win the reader's loyalty, and she finds her style effective in this regard. But she explains that her intention has always been "to tell the truth, honestly. No matter how careful we are in telling it—it is always risky. It is never my purpose to make people like me" (personal communication, 1989). Juhayer is responding here to women readers who have asserted that while she sometimes criticizes men, she also often defends them. What Juhayer sees as the pursuit of "truth" is seen by her female readers as siding with men. At times she seems keen on winning men's trust—either by focusing on their problems with women or even by adopting their point of view. Juhayer tends to see men not as subjects of attack but rather of discovery, suggesting that the man is like a new continent that needs to be explored. One of her articles that was most disliked by many of her female readers was one that tells of a woman who was faced with her husband's decision to take another wife. After she recounts the experience of her pain, agony, puzzlement, jealousy, and deep sense of betrayal, the woman, in an effort to find out what went wrong, tells us:

I discovered that my work, my home, my child have taken all my interest and attention, they became my first priority, over him . . . Damn woman's arrogance! . . . Damn to all the empty slogans that deprived me of my happiness! . . . I ask myself how was he ever able to put up with my soldierlike walk, with my body that was expanding and getting fatter in every curve . . . How patient he was watching me taking pleasure in everything except him . . . I have discovered, perhaps too late, that there was no woman in our home.[6]

The story of a woman whose husband has taken a second wife is one that happens every day. But what antagonized Juhayer's female readers was not the story but the plot. The plot asserts that what happened was the woman's fault rather than the man's abuse of his right to take another wife. This plot was unacceptable to the female readers who see Juhayer blaming the victim. They see Juhayer as declaring her alliance with men, hence emphasizing the premises of the dominant discourse.[7]

The female readers' reaction did not disturb Juhayer who was quick to point out: "I know that many women will be angry at me . . . will burn my words and be suspicious of my identity as a woman . . . But you can be sure that this will not shake me one bit . . . We have to think seriously and justly . . . We are together hand-in-hand, with one condition, that we think with justice and objectivity."[8]

Her squabble with female readers did not end there. When Juhayer wrote about her own personal experience of marriage, her female readers were her most ardent critics. Between the months of February and

March 1986, newspapers carried frequent attacks on her by female readers for disclosing her private feelings. Some said that Islam does not permit a woman to do so, a view also shared by a fellow writer Sohaila Zain Al-Abedin. Writing favorably about marriage and emphasizing the contrast between the pleasant life of the married and that of the unmarried displeased other women for other reasons. A woman protesting Juhayer's veneration of the institution of marriage itself angrily asked, "Must the woman who is not married be in despair, be unable to smile, be a vagabond who has no harbor, someone who knows neither sleep nor awakening?"[9]

But Juhayer is not uninterested in securing the loyalty of both male and female readers because she believes that the writer should establish her readership as a means of independence and of control over the conditions of writing. She explains that she might have started more provocatively or have spread her wings to topics of general interest to the public in order to ensure a wider and stable readership. She believes that this is the best strategy for her as a woman: "Today when I have my own readership, I can negotiate the terms of my commitment with any editor. I now speak from a different position than when I first started. . . . now that I am an established writer I can do more for women" (personal communication, 1989).

And indeed Juhayer was in a better position to do more for women when she debated on their behalf with religious leaders. Women, she observes, should not be timid when it comes to discussing religious matters that bear on women. But that means that they should have a firsthand knowledge of their religion by carefully studying the Qur'an and the Sunna, which is exactly what gave her an advantage when discussing the woman's right to her earnings. Shaikh Ali Ṭanṭawi, through his popular Friday television program, has expressed the opinion that women who work outside the home are obliged to give all or at least part of their earnings to their husbands as compensation for giving up their rights to the wives' time. In response to this opinion, Juhayer vehemently argued that this would contradict the basic principle of financial independence that Islam granted women. She alluded to Qur'anic verses, as well as to evidence from early Islam that testifies to this fact. The readers were divided over the issue, until Shaikh Abdul-Aziz Ben Baz, the Mufti who is often perceived to be anti-women, declared that "the woman is right, and Shaikh Ṭanṭawi is wrong,"[10] that in fact there is nothing in Islam that warrants Shaikh Ṭanṭawi's conclusion that men have any claim on women's earnings. Although the Mufti does not support women's work as a matter of principle, he testified that, Islamically, "*qiwama* [caretaking] is the man's responsibility, and providence is his duty" (Al-Qiwama Rajul Wal-infaqu Rajul). To the relief of many working women, Shaikh Ben Baz, thanks to Juhayer's determination to carry the issue as far as was needed, left no doubt that women's wealth is theirs alone, whether generated by work or by inheritance.

Although this exchange gained Juhayer a great deal of support among women, it did not in fact affect her popularity and enthusiasm among men. The following commentary on her writing by a male writer captures the general enthusiasm that she sparks:

> Juhayer Al-Musa'ed is a name that has answered a question that remained unanswered for years. That is, "What are the chances of finding a Saudi woman writer who writes on hot tinfoil, a writer who interacts with political and economic events on the local, Arab, and global levels?".
> . . . . Juhayer declares the end of a phase of [women's] sections that are only read by the editors and the printing workers. She inaugurates the beginning of an era of lengthy writings, but with a color, aroma, and taste. A salute to the writer, . . . the beginner of an era . . . who made herself heard by the largest possible number of those who are looking for hot words from a woman. The woman [writer] for years offered only "the dish of the day," usually copied from books and magazines.[11]

Textual Analysis

Social Problems Revisited

Juhayer's work reflects an extraordinary consciousness of the discourses about women over at least a fifteen-year period. One indication of the persistence of the discourse on women since the mid-1970s to the present is that Juhayer's two selected articles "Swallowed by This 'Mystical Giant,' " and "The Creator and the Victim" can almost be read as one—despite the fact that their publication dates are seven years apart. In the former, which was published in 1982, as in the latter published in 1989, she addresses the same theme of the media's "victimization" of women, and questions its purpose and the manner in which certain issues are defined. In fact, Juhayer was not alone, and we also find that during that period, other women writers have also addressed the same issues. But the subject of the media and how it deals with women has been Juhayer's main concern over the past ten years.

While she has no quarrel with the principle of discussing matters that pertain to women, she disagrees with the selection of certain issues for discussion, for in her opinion they do not reflect the "real" issues that Saudi women face. In both articles mentioned above, Juhayer exposes the many ways in which the media exploits the so-called women's issues and its vested interest in sensationalizing them. According to Juhayer, the media's exploitation of women is nothing new, nor is it peculiar to her society, but rather it is a universal fact. The foreign media has long been using women, through their "colored posters," to advance financial gains and high profits. The local media does not seem very different in that respect. Juhayer brings the analogy between the world media who "exposes" women through posters to attract readers and the local media who, being prohibited from physically "exposing" Saudi women through posters, has found a way of "exposing" them through discourse. Juhayer believes that the local media has in fact succeeded in creating a sensationalism comparable to that created by the Western press. She goes furthur and establishes a more subtle common ground between the foreign and the Saudi media, suggesting that women are in fact used by both as "bait"; that is, women are used by men to "hunt" other men. This image of women as "bait" is especially revealing of Juhayer's contention that the dominant discourse uses women not only as an object of control but also as a means of controlling men.

Juhayer then turns to the local context to discover that not only is the media's interest served by all this talk about women but male writers also boost their careers on the subject of women. This point can best be illustrated by an article written in 1979, entitled "Man, the New Continent":

> The woman has formed a center of a closed circle. On its edge stood those whose names have found their way to the media simply by being "woman supporters" and by virtue of writing on a dark planet . . . Man's existence does not seem to be an "issue" . . . not because he is less "problematic," but because he is seen as not "complicated" enough to

make writing about him a form of heroism, or on whose shoulders male
writers would be able to be classified as intellectuals. . . . . . . Imagine,
. . . that [with my pen] I cross the boundaries called "man's mind,"
"man's problems," "man's needs," "man's aspirations." . . . . [But]
man's independent continent is surrounded by thorny wires . . . stepping into it would no doubt be wounding [to the woman]. [12]

Despite her awareness of the dominating nature of the discourse
about women, she seems to be either unable or hesitant to go further
than to identify the media as the sole agent that runs this verbal
machinery on women. Juhayer invokes a sense of discourse as a pervasive
force that is capable of committing what amounts to symbolic violence
against women. While she uses the image of "bait" to capture the
essence of woman as victim, she uses the image "mystical giant" to refer
to the discourse. The metaphor "mystical giant" reflects a view of the
power that drives the discourse as anonymous and faceless—a power
that, since it is "mystical," by definition must defeat all attempts to
explain its sources or identify its actors.

Juhayer, however, attempts to explore the process by which a topic
is raised to the status of an issue. Although Juhayer hints at censorship
when she speaks of "tied tongue" and "clipped nails," in "Swallowed
by This 'Mystical Giant,' " she describes this as a "feverish," irrational
process, because subjects such as work and education are discussed as
"women's issues," while in fact they are "issues of a society that is
experiencing development and change." The discourse is contradictory
at best for while, on the one hand, the existence of women doctors, for
example, is "hailed as a great achievement of our developing society,"
on the other hand these very achievements are seen as signs of women's
failure. If the woman is married, her work outside the home is seen as a
cause of her failure as a wife and mother. If she is unmarried, then her
failure to marry is seen as a result of her education and most definitely
of the demanding nature of her work. [13]

Juhayer takes another step toward identifying major players in the
media game. She identifies two other groups of actors—the readers and
the religious leaders. The former are responsible for initiating the issue
and the latter for allowing the talk before determining its outcome,
usually after the damage is done. A subject is initiated by a reader or a
number of readers and becomes a hot topic because of persistent discussion of it over a period of time that may extend to months or even years.
Finally, the religious leaders are invited to give the last word. The

'ulama, according to Juhayer, "judge from what they see, hear, and read." Because women's voices are either not heard or seem to be lost in the "fever," the opinions of religious leaders, she asserts, tend to reflect a partial and "one-sided view of the issue." But Juhayer is not accusing the *'ulama,* for they, "may God save them all," always have the good of the society at heart.

While Juhayer pays her respects to the *'ulama,* she implicitly warns the religious leaders that they themselves also seem to have been exploited by the media, which "stands there watching" everyone, including the *'ulama,* as the issues are discussed in the direction the media wants—which many times is incongruent with Islamic principles themselves. Juhayer supports her view with a number of examples drawn from such "issues" as "women's clubs" and "driving." In relation to women's clubs, for example, she charges that the discussions are totally beside the point, for the discussants have taken the athletic (for women also negative) connotations of the word *club,* and left aside the idea of women getting together to further their religious beliefs. Juhayer is aware of how deeply ingrained are the negative notions of athleticism for women, given the restrictions on women's physical education even within schools. But Juhayer's penchant for sarcasm seizes the opportunity to poke fun at men's obsession with sports, while they at the same time lack the merit of being "good sports"!

Juhayer's strategy is to attack what she sees as the source of the problem and to point to the bias involved in its approach. Aside from perhaps developing muscles, one of the objections revealed by the discussions of "girls' clubs" was based on the assumption that these clubs are detrimental to women's virtue because they are conducive to perversion. The emphasis on the athletic dimension of the "club" has conjured up images of women's bodies not properly covered and has raised the religious issue of woman's body as *owra*—to be concealed at all times. Juhayer has no quarrel with the notion of the woman's body as *owra,* but she asks the question that almost everyone was ignoring: Does religion stipulate that the woman is *owra* in relation to other women or only in relation to strange men? Juhayer, in all probability, believes the latter to be the answer, but she deliberately declines to state her opinion, acknowledging in all humbleness that it is a matter to be settled—although it has first to be faced—by the religious leaders themselves. While she faces the religious leaders with this question,

Juhayer does not deny or shy away from confronting the charges that clubs may lead to women's perversion. Taking the offensive, she first points out that women have already participated in other types of clubs, namely literary, but that neither these clubs nor women have suffered negative consequences to their reputations. Moreover, she not only ridicules the idea of perversion but also shocks everyone by simply stating that perversion is already occurring anyway, with or without clubs. Otherwise, "why do we have institutions for fallen women and juvenile halls for girls?"

This may sound like common sense, but it is by no means so common, if only because Juhayer breaks one of the rules of the dominant discourse based on the exclusion of certain facts such as these. The acknowledgment of existing moral decadence among women is a source of disquietude for religious leaders. It attacks their sense of security and upsets their congratulatory attitude regarding the degree of control they have so far managed to maintain over women. It also may reflect "badly" on Saudi women's image abroad—for which Juhayer herself often expresses concern. But the most serious consequences of such facts lie in feeding the general apprehension in society about women's grow-ing mobility, provoking the need for more vigilance in regard to women and justifying restrictions against them.

Despite the seriousness of Juhayer's message, it is not said in an antag-onizing spirit to the *'ulama*. When she speaks of the girls' clubs, note how her reluctance to assert authority in matters of religious interpreta-tion works as a protective and disarming device. In fact, she believes that "she has no right to speak in the name of religion," but she will try any-way, with an attitude of "correct me if I'm wrong!" Moreover, her use of terms of endearment, her witty injunctures, her professed loyalty to the culture and the political system, as well as her perceived sincerity, allow such messages to pass without serious repercussions.

The Art of Asking the Right Questions

While Juhayer conveys the selective nature of the prevalent discourse in which certain elements are either excluded or transformed, she is not concerned about taking a position for or against the establishment of girls' clubs. Juhayer's skill is in the art of asking the right questions without necessarily providing the answers. In regard to the issue of girls' clubs, Juhayer poses a logical argument that shifts the question from the form to the content of the clubs. What if these clubs were turned into centers for religious learning? Would the *'ulama* object and still consider these clubs a danger and a threat to society? Posing the questions as such allows Juhayer to turn to Islamic history, which provides facts about analogous institutions. "The mothers of believers," especially Aisha, led an active role in teaching generations, not only of women but also of men, "half their religion." Aisha, the wife of the prophet, who led an army against Ali in the seventh century, is also a symbol of leadership. As such, the idea of a "club" as a center of learning is not then foreign to Islamic history, both in form and in content.

If historical analogies are unconvincing evidence for some, then other analogies can be drawn from contemporary life. If the issue is women's deviance and the desire to prevent it, then why did no one seemed concerned about perversion when supermarkets opened. Not only was the idea of supermarkets adopted but they were also called by their Western name. Not only was the Arab tongue "twisted" but the rules of segregation of the sexes were also abandoned inside the supermarkets. Men and women, she asserts, have mixed freely in supermarkets, and inside them women do not even observe the rules of modesty regarding the total covering of their hair.

The contradictory nature of the discourse on women and its tendency to ask the wrong questions is also revealed by another example given by Juhayer. Although the issue of women driving cars has been vehemently discussed for the past ten years, Juhayer believes that the issue was lost between the pros and the cons and never resolved. The reason is that both camps were not asking the right question, which is, "Whose responsibility is it to drive a woman?" No one doubts that it is men's. But why would a question of men's responsibility be transformed into a question of women's "rights" or "privileges" or the lack of them? The answer for Juhayer is simple; women's need to drive is born out of men's lack of responsibility toward them, which the Qur'an captures in the word *qiwama*. Juhayer conveys her astonishment that no one has pointed a finger at these men who leave women with two choices: either to remain completely immobilized at home or to rely on a strange driver with the possibility of compromising her morality and possibly her life.

Aside from the violation in such situations of a basic Islamic stipulation that women should not be left alone with strange men, this is hardly what the Islamic principle of "men taking care of women" is all about. Implicit in this is a warning to the religious leaders that approaching the issue of driving as a matter of "religious permissibility" or the lack of it may not be compatible with—or may even constitute a great deviation from—the Islamic principles concerning men's responsibility for women. Her message also carries a warning to women that the way the media formulates questions and defines the issues should not be taken at face value and that they should learn how to ask the right questions. Since driving is man's responsibility, women should remember that it is also his problem, not woman's. Women's view of the issue as a "right" or a "privilege" is for Juhayer a false conception, for driving is a new burden for women, pure and simple. Juhayer stops short of accusing men of conspiracy to cajole women to see driving in terms of a "right" or a "privilege," a ground on which women can never win.

Global Discourses on Liberation: Asking the Right Question

Juhayer is equally concerned with asking the right questions in relation to the global discourses on women, which she believes touch the lives of Saudi women. In her article "Female Journalism and Women's Liberation," she critiques those women who do not stop to pose the question: From whom and from what ties does the woman want to be liberated? She first asserts that the notion of liberation is a foreign concept and was imported by Arab women from Western culture. She also points out that those very Arab women who were convening to discuss "women's liberation" contradict themselves, since in reality they all have men in their lives whom they love, marry, and for whom they bear children. Quoting a Qur'anic verse, Juhayer believes that men and women have no reason to be antagonistic toward each other simply because men are required to treat women with "utmost kindness or to release them with dignity" (Qur'an 2:229). Those men who exhibit oppressive or abusive behavior are, by definition, deviants from Islam.

According to Juhayer, adopting the slogan of "liberation" in the Western sense is not the solution or the remedy for such deviations. Moreover, the slogan does not meet the needs of the Arab woman herself. For the idea of liberation asserts notions that the "true woman" would not accept, such as playing the role of a man at home. Juhayer believes that a "true woman" has certain expectations of what constitutes a "true man." A "true man" should carry his responsibilities toward the woman. Ideally at least, a woman should have no reason to seek liberation from men because she is not "occupied" or enslaved by him. The man may have the right to "rule the home" but not to "rule the woman."

If playing the role of a man in the home is not what some mean by women's liberation, then do they mean freeing women from their responsibilities of caring for children, husband, and home? If this is the case, then these women contradict themselves in yet another respect. According to Juhayer, they then place this burden on maids, who are woman like themselves. If these or any other women are sincere about freeing "women," then they should instead get the fathers to share the responsibility of raising children. Here again, as in the case of driving, Juhayer sees women as systematically overlooking men's responsibility. Instead of obligating the man to carry his responsibility as a father, they take it upon themselves to find a replacement for him, in this case a nanny, and in the case of driving, a driver. The connection she makes between the driver and the nanny is noteworthy because they are both seen as problems that women cause as a result of working outside the home.

The West, Women's Liberation, and the "Equality Lie"

Foreign nannies and drivers are perhaps more specific to the cultural scene in Saudi Arabia than to other Muslim countries, but Juhayer makes a case against them in order to ridicule both the Arab media and Arab women. Juhayer's critique of Arab women centers on their failure to recognize the cultural differences between Arab and Western women. She makes the point that Arab women, instead of learning from the mistakes of Western women, practice "blind imitation." They have not even asked themselves: What have these slogans accomplished for women in the West? "Liberation" and "equality" are just "lies" for which Western women pay a high price. According to Juhayer, the Western woman has lost her sense of self and family, and faces man's antagonism for stealing his jobs.

For Juhayer "the truth in the heart of the equality lie" is that, whether in socialist or capitalist Western societies, Western women have not accomplished anything that can be proudly exported to others. They cannot be models of change for a number of reasons. First, they have not been successful in their own backyard in practicing what they preach; second, their reality differs in nature from that of the Arab and the Arabian woman. The Western woman is in no position to be a judge of women in Juhayer's part of the world because Western (and other foreign) women demonstrate total "ignorance" of Arabian women and the role they play in their society:

> They [the foreigners] imagine the Saudi woman . . . . . as a bundle of backwardness, a disgrace to humanity in the twentieth century. . . . . who still thinks in past centuries' mentality . . . That is what they think of our women. But that is because they have not read our papers. . . . . they should have because they think they are more advanced, and if they are they should have known more and better [about us]. When they read, they would certainly discover that among the Saudi women, there are those who love thinking . . . . . [whose] situation did not kill thought but rather revived it, gave it life, depth, and meaning . . . They have established themselves in the [literary] field and proved their distinction . . . let us read what is coming to us [from outside] and [compare] how many of these foreign feminine names have shined apart from dress, fashion, and . . . . . smiles.[14]

Juhayer represents the Arabian woman's notion of liberation as one that is based on deconstructing the very categories by which Western discourse establishes its hegemony on local discourses on women:

> The Saudi woman wants to express herself and give her identity a distinct color . . . The slogans that she hears in the East and the West are still for her a crossword puzzle, needing to be solved . . . Before she enters the maze . . . . . [the Saudi woman] has to know the sources of Western cultures and the roots of its slogans [she should also examine] the source of fascination with which they are held [in other parts of the world].[15]

Fatna Shāker: Selections from Her Writings

On the Edge of the Magic Bottle[16]

"Woman's rights as human rights" is a complicated topic—easy to talk about but difficult to practice.

The United Nations thought it would solve the problem of "human rights" . . . and made a prospectus of what it thought to be basic and necessary, which of course was within what the members were able to agree on. But despite all that, the human being is still subordinated, nationally and internationally, to the authority and domination of customs, rather than laws that define his or her rights. Customary law in its different political, economic, and social forms often prevents the human being from enjoying rights legitimated by religion, as well as by human laws.

The subject of "woman's rights" has remained separate and almost independent. The woman probably has, since time immemorial, been a "puzzling problem" for her society, and society has not known what to do with her. On the one hand, she is the fountain of life, the rearer of children, and the one who molds the minds of men and children. On the other hand, there is something that society fears from women, or maybe fears for women. It is probably that incredible power that the woman possesses as a maker of generations, and that fear ingrained in society that portrays her as a "magical giant" that has to be put back in the magic bottle . . . but can also be taken out of the "bottle" from time to time to serve some basic and necessary functions.

But when we place women under interdiction, whether in the name of protection or to limit their ambitions and aspirations, is not that limiting the visions, dreams, thoughts, and ambitions of that blooming mind? How would a flower or a tree grow in unexposed soil—or if it were exposed once to the sunlight—only to be neglected again dozens of times? I think that it would be withered and deformed.

The attempts of women to continue searching for their rights are only attempts to get out of the "magic bottle." The characteristics and shape of the "magic bottle" are but a reflection of the staid and archaic customs of the society.

Customs may or may not be correct, they may or may not be fair or just, they may or may not be logical. The woman's wisdom is in her ability to distinguish between right and wrong. She should not throw out everything in order to overcome the obstacles that have for some time constrained her freedom and abilities. Our responsibility is great, and the ability to put this to practice is not as easy as talking about it.

A Salute to a Man [17]

When the Saudi woman insists on knowing the Saudi man's view of her situation, she does not do this in order to obtain a ticket to pass to a new field in education or work. The man who thinks this is mistaken. She seeks his opinion because she believes that the movement of her society is tied to the movement of both man and woman. She believes that the core of society is the family . . . that family strength and stability is society's strength and stability . . . These cannot be maintained except by maintaining the humanity of both men and women.

The humanity of women was established by Islam when it freed her from "female infanticide" and acknowledged for her a human existence independent of men. Islam made her a partner and not a subordinate . . . and there is a big difference between partnership and subordination.

Although religious laws and regulations may change [the definition of woman's existence] in reality, they do not easily change the individual's oblique soul. "Female infanticide" may have stopped physically but still be practiced, however differently, in kind and degree. The gracious prophet Mohammed—peace be upon him—set a good example of how to treat women and respect their minds, bodies, and actions. He meant to free man's mind from pre-Islamic customs, and to enlighten his soul to see the complementary meaning of humanity, which is male and female. Each is independent, yet they are created to be partners, complementary to each other. This is how the contemporary Saudi woman views her place in the [man's land]. She does not see herself as a separate issue. Her problem is man's problem. And their problems together are the problems of the whole society . . . The most beautiful comment made in one of those dialogues between men and women in the university was Hamad Al-Jasser's phrase: "What a lucky [happy] nation that allows women to write its history."

Does the Man Have an Issue? [18]

The human being faces an issue in life when an imbalance occurs between rights and responsibilities. One faces an issue when one suffers from a gap between one's legitimate rights and the rights that are socially permitted—or when one is given great responsibility in life without having the proper environment that fulfills the conditions for preparing one fully for bearing the responsibility.

The human being faces an issue when he or she is branded as a failure by the same society that helped implant the seeds of failure in that individual in the first place. Often we hear about the woman's issue, the child's issue, the minorities' issue, but rarely do we hear of the man's issue! Does that mean that the man does not suffer from imbalance in his rights and his responsibilities? Or is it because the man controls all affairs and, as such, works automatically to remove imbalance, if any exists; hence he does not need the society's interference to discuss his issues? For the woman, it is different; she had to seek her right to education, her right to work, and her right to voice her opinion and to choose her life partner. It was in this context that she began to have an issue, which is often called "the issue of woman's liberation." And when the woman is asked about the things from which she intends to liberate herself, she replies that she wants liberation from restrictions and conceptions that hinder the practice of her legitimate human rights.

The meaning of this reply differs from one society to another and from one woman to another. The degree of women's awareness also differs according to the indicators and consequences of the issue.

If the man is asked about the things from which the woman wants to liberate herself, he replies that it is the home, the children, the marriage responsibilities, and motherhood. The man rarely acknowledges that the woman wants, through education and work, to be liberated from her intellectual hegemony and economic siege.

Why can't the woman's goal of liberation simply be understood— that she wants to become certain about herself and the truth about her needs, as well as her relation to the female in her, to the man, and to the child?

Some men may choose a shortcut and say: "The only certainty is that the woman is created to bear children, give birth, and bring them up." This is an inevitable biological fact, but the issue for the woman goes much deeper than that. And as long as the woman has an issue, the man too has an issue, and a deeply rooted one at that.

The Man and the Woman [19]

The man and the woman, are they enemies or companions? The woman knows man first as a father, then as a brother, then as a partner in her life, then as a son. The man knows woman first as a mother, then as a sister, then as a life partner, then as a daughter. And in spite of this, the dialogue often takes the form of a challenge and competition which reflects the attempt of each to prove his or her importance and capability over the other. With this, the dialogue turns into a battle.

Battles between men and women are not characteristic of only one epoch. Many myths, stories, and poems are filled with serious as well as comic images of the traps each sex has set—rather creatively—to trick the other into battle.

And in spite of this, the man and the woman certainly know that life cannot be complete without both their existences. It is through them both that unity of creation and human meanings become visible and able to cross all barriers.

Is it out of arrogance, then, that each would try to prove that he or she is the most powerful, the most competent, or the most intelligent? Yes, it is an eternal arrogance, because in each of them exists an ego that says "Me" . . . The arrogance and collision are often between their two egos.

The happy woman, some say, is the one who has not discovered her ego [herself]. That is because "ego" occupies only limited space in women. It is dominated by the existence of others in her life, the most important of whom are her man and the children she had with him. As for the man, his ego has from the time of his creation been inflated, and has dominated the existence of those with whom he shares his life, the most important of whom are his wife and the children he had with her.

The misery occurs for the woman when she discovers herself, and her ego develops, which becomes the basis of dealing with her man. Here enter arrogance and collision. The man cannot bear another self [ego] to rival his. He wants to spread out his ego like a blanket, as he has always done. He wants to spread it out and use it to shelter his needs, his interests, and all the requirements of his security and comfort.

But now he collides with her ego, when she says, "What about me? What about my needs and my interests and the requirements of my own security and comfort!?"

The man is surprised, even astonished! "What needs is she talking about? Have I not been the source of all her needs and security?" The man's pride is wounded, and he may refuse to acknowledge the voice that comes from his wife's inner self. He is afraid that his ego will have to shrink in order to allow space for his wife's.

They both suffer, and the suffering may become a source of male and female battles. The suffering may lead the man to extend his hand to his wife, to try to reach out to her even half way. It is the man's step toward understanding and giving that can turn this suffering into beautiful meaning, and into a feeling of psychological unity. The woman's life becomes beautiful, joyful, and happy, even if tears were shed along the way.

Whatever the result [of the dialogue], man and woman will always exist. One complements the other, as the Qu'ran says: "One of Allah's signs is that he created from within you a spouse with whom you become at peace and He has instilled among you love and mercy."

I Practice Reading Secretly[20]

This was a telephone conversation between me and a female reader who chose to remain anonymous:

READER: I have read (your column) for some time, but I read it secretly!

FATNA: I don't understand.

READER: I am a married woman and my husband cannot bear seeing me with a serious book, or a good article.

FATNA: How did you reach this conclusion?

READER: Because I observed what has been going on in one instance after another. First he brings home only a small number of magazines and newspapers. Some of these he puts aside for himself, and the rest for me. Those he brings especially for me do not go beyond fashion, celebrities, food, and other simple topics.

FATNA: As long as he brings home other subjects, you can always take a look and read those.

READER: Yes, that is what I do, but secretly!

FATNA: How can you read "secretly"? I still cannot comprehend.

READER: As time went by, he noticed my interest in some serious writings and in some male and female writers. I wanted to show him my interest in what I had read, and to try to find out what he thought. He was not interested, and if he had to comment it was negatively. He made remarks like, "What do you care about these subjects?" or "Don't forget that you're a woman and your home and children are more important than this talk." I did not pay much attention to his remarks. But when he started to notice my absorption or my thinking about what I had read, and that I was continuing my reading, his reaction turned from mere negative remarks to annoyance.

FATNA: What kind of annoyance?

READER: He does not bring home, for example, the papers he knows I am interested in, or if he brings them, he hides them from me. I had to face him with the truth, and to tell him frankly that I think he does not want me to read or add to my knowledge. I also told him that I think he is afraid of developing my mind.

FATNA: It looks like you hurt his feelings, or touched a nerve in him. How did he react?

READER: He threatened . . . threatened with many things if he caught me committing the reading act—

FATNA (*interrupting*):   Now I am beginning to understand.

READER: To tell you the truth, I decided to put his mind at rest. To give him what he wants, while accomplishing what I want. I stopped reading anything in his presence except what he chooses for me, while I secretly collect all the topics I want to read, the writers I prefer, and read them in his absence. In fact, I eagerly look for whatever I missed of those writings and get them from friends.

At the end, the reader said something that is worth a pause for thought: "I wished I could read, and do other things, in front of him and with him. I wished an idea here or there would bring us together and renew our life together. But he drove me, intentionally or ignorantly, to practice my hobby secretly and away from him. For me, citizenship is the right not to exercise my humanity in the dark."

A Personal Sketch

Fatna Shāker was born in Jeddah in 1940. She received part of her education there, but continued her studies in Egypt until she graduated in economics from Cairo University in 1962. In the early 1960s Fatna was the first woman to supervise a woman's section in the newspaper *'Ukaz*. She was also the first Saudi female voice in Saudi broadcasting, establishing a program for women called "The Happy Home" in the early 1960s. She continued her graduate studies in the United States, obtaining her M.A. in 1966 and her Ph.D. in 1972 from Purdue University. After her return to Saudi Arabia, she taught at the department of sociology in King Abdul Aziz University in Jeddah until 1980 when she was appointed the chief editor of *Sayyidaty*, a Saudi-owned woman's magazine based in London. During her stay in London, Fatna wrote a regular column entitled "Hiwar" (dialogue), in the affiliate daily newspaper *Ash-Sharqul-Awsat*.

    I first became acquainted with Fatna in 1986 while she was on a sabbatical at Berkeley. When I contacted her in Jeddah and told her about my field research, she expressed her desire to see me as a friend but not as a researcher since she did not consider herself a literary figure, only a writer. I told her that I accepted her definition of herself but nevertheless that I would like to see her in that very capacity. In all fairness she was truly busy, but I insisted on including her in my

research because my sample would have been incomplete without someone of her stature. Fatna has, for the past three decades, been one of the
most energetic of Saudi women writers. She has left her mark on the
institution of writing, and constitutes a part of its history.

After much insistence on my part, she agreed to meet with me in her
apartment in the King Abdul-Aziz University faculty complex in Jeddah. In the interview, which lasted about four hours, she explained that
she had hesitated to be interviewed because she had some reservations
about most of the research done in the West on her country. She had
just returned from a conference abroad, and had come back with
haunting ethical questions regarding the direction and purpose of Western scholarship on the Third World in general, and on her own country
in particular. "Sometimes I lose faith in Western academia and its
ability to understand others, let alone help them. People who are
participating in a study open their hearts and their minds to researchers
and foreign agencies, but they have no control over the use of information extracted from them. I am haunted by the possibility of that
research being used to oppress these people or harm them." As an
anthropologist, I was haunted by the same issues myself. I explained
that despite the existence of ethical codes, control over the use of one's
research admittedly remains an ethical dilemma for many conscientious
researchers.

In that hot, humid April night that was typical of Jeddah, I immediately felt comfortable in her small but cozy apartment. Different in
that respect than other (huge) houses in Jeddah, it revealed in its
organization, decor, color, and aura a soft taste as well as a gentle
personality. It also reflected an unmistakable appreciation of other
cultures. Artifacts and souvenirs with Islamic motifs were displayed
beside pieces from England, Egypt, America, Yemen, India, and Africa, especially from Kenya where she had lived for a number of years
with her husband.

The numerous floor pillows, stuffed animals, plates, the wall decor
were so meticulously placed that, despite the apartment's small size,
each item seemed to secure the right place for itself. Collectively, these
pieces constituted a harmonious whole, and were in a mysterious way
pleasant to the eye as well as to the heart. When Fatna spoke of her
concerns about the relationship to the "other," I immediately realized
how the setting itself symbolized her own conception of a world in

which the freedom to be different becomes, if not desired, a recognized right.

Fatna's first attempts at writing were mainly expressions of her feelings as she was coming of age, in the newsletters posted on the school walls. When she decided to publish her writings, she used her real name for which she received much encouragement and support from her father who was in the army, and from her Egyptian mother, of whom she spoke with awe. To her mother Fatna also owes her strong values of independence, authenticity, and self-esteem. These values were to affect her view of writing and of the writer's responsibility, and were to make her aware of the special position of the woman as a writer. Whatever Fatna spoke about, she seemed always concerned with at least three issues: the relation to the "other," especially to Western civilization; the contradictions within her society, in which a great confusion of values existed; and her country's alarming tendency toward consumerism. Fatna spoke of these concerns, which are all connected and intertwined:

The writers of my country are preoccupied these days with the . . . ongoing debate on religion, literature . . . and our perception of Western civilization. Unfortunately. . . one of our problems is the tendency to practice one thing and believe another. We are infested, for example, with consumerism, but we advocate contrary values. This divorce between the real and the ideal . . . leads to weakness and defeat even if no challenge exists. But we do face a challenge from the outside, and a big one indeed . . . for which we have made ourselves vulnerable. . . . While opening to Western civilization is unprecedented, restrictions on women is also unprecedented. . . . I was less restricted twenty years ago in Jeddah . . . Today men have problems understanding what is happening to women. They are astonished at what women have accomplished. Girls are excelling in schools and universities in comparison with boys. They are entering many domains. Men do not know how to deal with this female success. How should they categorize it? How can they fit it in with their previous beliefs about women? How are they to interpret it . . . it scares them so they [resort to oppressing women].

Fatna believes that forces that oppress women can only be combatted by the woman herself because they are "her own making. . . . the male chauvinist is after all raised by a woman whom he loves and respects." Also "women . . . because they leave [religion] for others to interpret for them, many times they are victimized by their own ignorance."

Fatna does not shy away from confronting religious issues when the occasion demands, especially in response to the readers' letters to her weekly column in *Ar-Riyadh*. Fatna's collection, entitled *Nabt Al-Ardh (The Earth's Plant)* (1981), contains about 150 short articles on a variety of topics, themes, and issues reflecting Fatna's broad interests. Approximately a third of the articles are devoted to issues related to women and men, family, marriage, and work, in which she had to deal with religion extensively. She also has written on human values, change, development, human services, travel, spirituality, global politics, love, philosophical problems of human existence and its purpose, relation with the land, patterns of social behavior, writing, politics, childhood, relation with the West, development, and other topics. Fatna was also engaged in journalistic reporting during the years in which she was working in London. She conducted an interview with Indira Ghandi, the late Prime Minister of India, which paved the way for Ghandi's first visit to Saudi Arabia in 1981. Fatna also traveled to Yemen for the purpose of reporting on the use of the narcotic substance *Qat* in 1982.

Considering the variety of Fatna's interests, the selected articles are mainly representative of Fatna's style and logic of argument. Her articles were most yielding to translation, which made the selection process more difficult, because each piece was as worthy and as potentially possible to translate as any other. This perhaps is because of her clear, simple, unpretentious, precise yet highly literary style, which is also an element in the attraction her writings have for readers of diverse educational levels.

Fatna speaks with the authority characteristic of a teacher. She presents her ideas calmly but with confidence; her tone is detached and her style is reconciliatory, geared toward persuasion rather than confrontation. However, she never leaves the reader with any illusion as to whose side she is on or what she personally thinks. During the period in which she was chief editor of *Sayyadaty* magazine and also its equivalent "Dear Abby," she responded to the readers' problems as a mediator or a cultural broker between individuals and their society using her own experiences and those of others.

Fatna's influence is mostly on university women and men. She is less warmly received by conservative elements than Juhayer although she appeals to Islam in her writings, and represents reasonable interpretations without undermining the authority of the *'ulama*. This may have something to do with her cultural position. In contrast to Juhayer's almost total conformity to cultural rules, Fatna's application of the cultural rule of hair-covering had not been carried out to the letter during her years of education and work abroad, which made her a subject of criticism.[21]

It is probably no accident that her collection, *The Earth's Plant*, came to emphasize her sense of belonging and dedication to her country. The content of the collection not only reflects her personal loyalty to the land but the title seems to refer to and emphasize the loyalty of all Arabian women to their land despite accusations to the contrary. This is especially noteworthy considering how changes in the position of women are seen as a sign of betrayal to their roots, and of alliance with Western values. On the other hand, she also does not hesitate to accept premises of women's liberation and equality despite their connection to the West. However, her writings always recognize the *'ulama*, although she tends to provide her own reading of the religious texts themselves without reliance on them. Her critique of social institutions is mostly on the basis of religion and, as a result, contributes a great deal to the disentanglement of religion from tradition.

Fatna believes that women can make these contributions if they do not work with assumptions of censorship. Although women writers face many restrictions, she thinks they should always test their limitations:

It is true that women writers face many challenges, that they are still on the margins of the institution, and cannot penetrate it. For example, it sometimes takes a great deal of courage for a woman to engage in discussions or literary debates with male writers. Social mores render any dyadic relationship with a man suspicious, and women can still pay the price for this with damaged reputations. But we also have to admit that we have made headway during these years. We can now explore many issues that were previously assumed to be taboos, either in the political, religious, or social sense. Women can criticize officials, present contrary views—even on religion, and indulge in a critique of social institutions.

Textual Analysis

Defining the Issues: Men, Women, and Liberation

While Juhayer's analysis focuses on the process by which the discourse has turned the woman herself into an issue, Fatna, on the other hand, shifts the focus from woman as an issue to woman as *having* an issue. The title of her article, "Does the Man Have an Issue?" does even more. It shifts the question from women having an issue to men. Fatna defines the issues of men as inseparable from those of women. Men or women face issues, she points out, not because of an inherent tendency in one sex to develop more problems than the other, but rather, because these issues are born out of specific social conditions and structural relations to which both sexes are subjected. Fatna's background as a professor of sociology is apparent in her formulation of the issue in terms of a sociological law that reflects the nature of affairs in human societies as a whole. For her, the problem can only be solved if understood in broader terms and explored in terms of structural causes. It is the "imbalance between rights and responsibilities," and the "gap between the legitimate rights and what is socially permitted" that causes social and psychological anomie for all human beings. By defining the issue as such and placing it within the "human" context, her message has a better chance not only of being better understood but also of being received favorably. To establish that men as well as women, regardless of time or space, are prone to suffer from the same imbalances has a comforting effect on those who feel defensive about their specific social conditions.

Fatna believes that the reason we hear about the problems of minorities, of children, and of women, but never of men, lies in the asymmetrical power relations in society. Men are situated in positions of control that allow them to "remove" any obstacles. Men are granted the right to be educated, to work, and on occasion to choose their life partners— but women have to win these rights, because these were not considered "human" rights for both men and women.

When women pressed for their basic rights, the name used for such attempts was "woman's liberation." Fatna does not dismiss the concept of "liberation," in fear of its Western connotations. Rather, she takes the opportunity to "liberate" its definition—not only from men's hege-

mony but also from its Western roots. She emphasizes that Saudi
women do have a reason to liberate themselves, but contrary to men's
assertions, not from home, children, and family. Rather, women seek
liberation from man's hegemony over their existence and his definition
of the issues for them—and of their wants. A woman wants to know
herself, and men should not be alarmed by this desire or fear that this
might lead to a kind of separatism. For not only are men's and women's
problems entangled but their existences are also inseparable.

Men, Women, and Society

This conception of the intertwining nature of men's and women's
existence permeates most of Fatna's writings. In her article, "A Salute
to a Man," the same sentiment is emphasized in which she states that
"[the woman] does not see herself as a separate issue. Her problem is
man's problem. And their problems together are the problems of the
whole society." While the issue for Juhayer is conceptualized as discursive, in which reality forms a circle with women occupying its center,
the reality for Fatna is conceptualized as the triangle of men, women,
and society. Fatna is concerned with exploring how men and women
relate to each other and how they relate to society. The "movement of
society is tied to the movement of men and women." Their relationship
is mediated by the family, which is "the core of the society," the
strength of which can only be maintained by "maintaining the humanity of both men and women."

But Fatna sees the belief in woman's humanity to be shaken in
society, despite Islam having guaranteed these rights for women, both
in theory and in practice. Islam made the woman a "partner" for the
man, not his subordinate. Here Fatna does not hesitate to speak of
"woman's rights," defining them as part and parcel of "human rights."
Denying these rights to women is rooted in the hegemony of social
practices, dubbed by Fatna as customary laws or tradition rather than religion.

Women and the Dialectics of Fear and Protection

For Fatna, it is not a more or less defined group of actors that exploit
the subject of women in discourse, as Juhayer believes; rather, the

villain is a vague entity called "society" or "tradition" or, more precisely, the conceptions of women within society. The conception of woman as a problem lies in the contradictions and ambivalence embedded in social perceptions of women both as objects of fear and of protection, simultaneously—a perception of women both as the source of an overwhelming power and at the same time of an overwhelming powerlessness. Fatna captures the essence of this ambivalence in her metaphor of the "genie in the magic bottle." But Fatna's use of the metaphor also points to how women are not only subordinated to the needs of discourse but, more important, to the needs of society. Society exploits women because they are not granted rights as a basic principle but instead are occasionally taken out of the magic bottle "to serve some basic and necessary functions [for society]."

When women were given the right to education, for example, there was a general apprehension about the "blooming" of women's minds that would come with education. The perception of woman as a genie came out of society's lack of understanding of her, not as a function of any extraordinary powers with which the woman is endowed or even has recently acquired. But Fatna's use of the genie metaphor, while it retains for women the belief in their power, exacerbates for men the sense of alarm and emphasizes the need for the power of this "genie" to be controlled. For women to be on the "edge of the magic bottle" means that society has to be on guard. What complicates the issue even further is that Fatna asserts that this power is needed for development purposes, an implicit reminder to the traditional elements of their decreasing or possible loss of control over women.

On another level, Fatna establishes that a double jeopardy is involved in the fear for or of women. On the one hand, while the responsibility of molding minds rests with women, they are seen as mindless. When society exhibits a fear of women, it strips them of their basic human rights and renders them in need of control. And when society fears for women, it renders them vulnerable and in need of protection. Women's rights to a free existence, seen from either perspective, are lost somewhere between these two contradictory conceptions. Fatna's purpose, more implicit than explicit, is to advance a definition of "liberation" based on a condition in which women cease to be either objects of fear or of protection. A more calming effect on the perceived power of women which the metaphor of "genie" might invoke, may be achieved by Fatna's likening the woman to a flower or a tree. *Flower* or *tree* are terms commonly used in Arabic literary and popular culture to refer to women. Although the second emphasizes the woman's procreative and nurturing attributes, the first seems to invoke women's beauty and fragility, and emphasizes the woman as an object of pleasure. These are more appealing and comforting terms in which to think of women, at least for centers of power who have a vested interest in controlling perceptions of women.

Society as Villain

While Fatna targets that vague entity called society, and its tradition, as the source of ambivalence in the perception of women, she holds that these societal beliefs trickle down to the relationship between individual men and women. In her article "The Man and the Woman," Fatna moves from the social to the psychological plane and begins to examine the relationship between the sexes as purely a function of communication on the interpersonal level. She observes that antagonism between individual men and women does exist as a characteristic of a specific dyadic relationship. But if the woman knows the man in relationships that are traditionally not known to be antagonistic (i.e., as a father, a brother, or a son), then why does antagonism exist and at what point does it begin?

Fatna confines the occurrence of antagonism to the marital relations between husbands and wives rather than to other familial relations. The invocation of relations of women to their fathers, brothers, and sons serves as a reminder that antagonism between the sexes is not a natural state of affairs. Antagonism arises as a clash of the husband's and wife's egos. She points to men's sense of insecurity, and their tendency and constant desire to be the source and the center of love, affection, need, and security for their families. Man's sense of security is threatened by women who undertake the journey of self-discovery.

In "I Practice Reading Secretly," Fatna provides an example of the nature of the obstacles that individual men create for their wives. It reflects a great deal of fear and apprehension on the part of the man about women's reading, both in the literal and perhaps the figurative sense. Reading of material that leads to "developing her mind" is seen not only as an "act" but also as a crime "committed," insomuch as it is

not confined to material that make her a better wife and mother. Men—
but also women themselves—may think that a woman's self-discovery
will lead women to engage in a battle of competition and challenge to
men in order to prove their newly developed selves. Despite the husband's constant attempts to stop her, the wife succeeds, pointing out
that it is not man's oppression but rather woman's subordination and
lack of will that deprives them of the opportunity to develop themselves
as independent human beings.

Through the success of the woman who practiced "reading secretly,"
Fatna conveys the sense that women's journey toward self-discovery is
unstoppable, inevitable, and irreversible. It can no longer be controlled
because it can be done secretly and without man's help or permission.
Men have no choice but to accompany women on this journey. Fatna
promises men the sweet fruits of understanding, the beauty of sharing,
and the joy of the psychological unity to which reading may contribute
to the relationship between a husband and wife.

Vive la Difference: Quality Versus Equality

This psychological unity between a man and a woman is imperative for
Fatna. In the heart of her conception of the relationship between a man
and a woman is that they are indispensable to each other. But despite
the fact that certain problems can be traced to the dyadic relations
between men and women, for her the problems are largely social in
nature and structural in their causes. This social approach permits her
to see man not as an oppressor (in psychological terms) but rather as an
ally in the battle to change social conditions that oppress both men and
women. Fatna is able to relate these profound messages by making
visible the fine line between difference and opposition. Juhayer asked
the important questions of liberation—of whom, from whom, and
defined by whom—emphasizing the Western roots of both concepts of
equality and liberation. But Fatna does not see them as Western but
rather as "human" concepts to be adopted, although to be redefined in
accordance with her own society.

Equality and liberation become synonymous—not with separatism
but rather with the qualities of self-worth, mental strength, and will.
In her articles, the concept of liberation is defined within a context that
celebrates women's nurturing and affiliation and loyalty to kin, and

voices their commitment to such social institutions as family and mothering. The celebration of these female qualities is important if women are to keep a positive gender identity and a sense of pride in being a woman, which Fatna sees as vital. Fatna's proposals for equality and liberation do not require demolishing a woman's world but rather keeping her world intact. Her attempt is to emphasize the "conditions" of oppression in society that men and women share, not their shared qualities. The direction she would like women of her country to take is not to threaten the position of men but rather to re-position them in the battle against society. This not only provides women with the means of empowerment but also is not defeating to their self-actualization.

The Appeal to Authority of Religion and Tradition

What is remarkable in these messages is that although "equality of women" and their "liberation" are seen by the dominant discourse as Western ideals, Fatna succeeds in connecting her proposals to Islamic ideals. In her articles she emphasizes justice in a relationship of partnership and complementarity between men and women. The idea of men and women complementing each other is advocated in the Qur'an. Men can only maintain their *qiwama* (caretaking) under one condition—by meeting their economic responsibilities for which they are endowed with certain qualities, as stated in the Qur'an. According to Fatna, men have to understand the model the prophet provided as a husband; the prophet perceived that the difference in the roles of husband and wife had the single goal of maintaining the family. Whatever division of labor is agreed on, the humanity of both men and women, mercy, and justice are principles never to be compromised.

The ideal of justice as a result of men and women complementing each other is the meaning Fatna generates through a new definition of the notion of liberation, which also creates a new awareness of social reality and points to the contradictions in which it is embedded. In her effort to disentangle traditional elements from the religious, she points to a general regression in society toward practicing pre-Islamic customs. The reality of contemporary women, she charges, is reminiscent of the pre-Islamic practice of infanticide. The metaphor of infanticide invokes a sense of betrayal to Islam by a society that adopts a religious ideology considered to be puritanical. It is perhaps that sense of betrayal of the religious leaders to "real" Islam that leads her to invoke the authority of Hamad Al-Jasser, a respectful historian who is a cultural rather than a religious figure, to testify on women's behalf. That she recognizes a cultural figure over a religious one has probably conveyed a view of religious scholars that is not as deserving of salutation.

Sohaila Zain Al-Abedin: Selections from Her Writings

Unveiling Emotions Is No Less Dangerous Than Unveiling the Face[22]

Islam has intended for women to be protected from any abuse. Prescribing *hijab* (veiling) is but one means to establish that protection. If we look deeper into its meaning, goals, and dimensions we find that hijab is meant to protect women from whatever arouses [men's] sexual desires, which leads to impiety and error. It leads those [men] who are sick at heart—and there are many—to be infatuated. If the woman's physical beauty is arousing to men's desires, her emotional expressions toward a man are also arousing.

Unveiling emotions is no less dangerous than unveiling the face. The woman's expression of emotion is just like her other beauties, which she should not show except to her husband, in their own privacy; they are not to be revealed to others. Unfortunately, that is what one of the Saudi women writers has already done. She has turned her intimate exchanges with her husband into material for her writings, in which she uncovered her minute feelings about her marriage.[23] She should have been more careful to keep her emotions only for him, instead of turning them into a public matter available in a widely read newspaper. By doing this she was not particularly creative, and it would have been much better for her had she said nothing at all. For she has hurt the feelings of all women who are [religiously] committed.

Worse yet, when she tried to justify her action, she told us that her example was May Ziada, who was sending love letters to Khalil Jibran.[24] May Ziada was not even a Muslim in the first place, and she was not even married to Jibran or any other man. As such, she is not an acceptable model for us Muslim women. If her intimate letters meet with such admiration, then what a shame! We have indeed lost our morals and good deeds! How can this "lack of politeness" be considered the highest form of "literature"?[25] This is just like viewing Simone de Beauvoir as one of the most famous woman liberators in the world because she has liberated herself from whatever is legitimate and religious. She allowed herself to live with a man illegitimately. And no one has seen her as a fallen woman or was concerned about the fact that this makes her no different than prostitutes, stripped of all virtues and human values! I was deeply disappointed in one of our male writers who (on the occasion of her death) wrote: "Until the last moment of her life, de Beauvoir did not stop struggling for her principles and the values for which she had lived." These and other glorifying words portray her as an example to be followed. I should like to ask the writer, "What are the values for which she lived, when she allowed herself to live illegitimately with a man? What principles and ideals did she hold? Existentialism? Is existentialism a constructive philosophy?" It is regrettable that we find this kind of glorification for such existentialists as de Beauvoir and Sartre, with whom she shared an illegitimate relationship.

The most important question is: What effect would the male writer's article have on those female writers who are just beginning? They will certainly see de Beauvoir as a model and try to follow in her footsteps, especially when they read such writings about her as the one that appeared in one of our newspapers under this title: "De Beauvoir, or When History Possesses a Wise Girl." I deplore such glorification of her because our press should have given us an accurate account of her background and clarified the hidden dangers in her thought.

Creativity, I believe, should not uncover intimate confessions between wife and husband. A woman is usually embarrassed to tell such things, even to those closest to her. Now this woman writer dares to confess them publicly, despite the fact that they are the most private of her private things that she should keep for herself and her husband. This is not creativity. Creativity for women writers is to bring out the meaning of marriage and its constructive effects on their literary contributions. The woman writer should understand this and not listen to those who tell her, "It is within your rights as a human being to express your feelings and this will make you a creative writer . . . you can do it because the man can." Or they ask such questions as, "Why is this permitted for the man but not for the woman?" The wise woman would not pay much attention to such issues, for men and women are different. Their roles are different. It is true that Islam has granted rights and duties for both of them as human beings, but essential differences exist between them. For example, the woman cannot marry more than one man at the same time, whereas the man can marry up to four women. *Hijab* is prescribed for women but not for men. Why? Because the woman is a source of infatuation for the man. It is women who have something to fear from men, not the opposite. And it is the man who asks to marry the woman, not vice versa.

This woman writer should not forget that she is also a mother and an educator . . . She should not forget that she is not like a man. If the man flirts with a woman in love poetry, this does not mean she can do the same . . . She has to understand that her emotions and feelings, like her body, have to be protected. The unveiling of feelings is like the unveiling of the face. The woman's *hijab* can be completed only by veiling her emotions, and not revealing them except to her husband. Lastly, the woman writer has to remember that her familial duties stand above her creative writing. She must thank Allah for his blessings, for the status she has reached under Islam. All the women of the world envy her. If she wants to be really creative, she should be satisfied with her home, and her *hijab*. She should put her energy into increasing her knowledge. Creativity, in a word, is not achieved by unveiling or working outside the home.

The Issue of Woman and Creativity: Commentary on *'Ukaz's* Literary Supplement[26]

I would like to comment on what the poet Thurayya Gābel has said about the nature of the constraints imposed on Saudi women writers. According to Thurayya's views, "We write from our homes, and work from them, and we do all that from behind seven vaults . . . But despite all the obstacles that we all know of but cannot talk about, we work, and we will continue to work until relief arrives."

May I ask Thurayya Gabel to allow me to discuss her views? As a fellowSaudi woman writer, I disagree with her on all counts. First, if we do not write from our homes, then from where should we write? What is wrong with writing from home? All [men] writers do in fact write from their homes, and if they do not, then where do they write from? Their work place? How can they work with ringing phones and streams of visitors?

I am personally satisfied and happy with what I have accomplished by writing at home. I am proud that those so-called home writings have reached the different corners of the world. My views have been discussed in the American press, and my books are taught at colleges and have become sources for researchers. They are requested from Algeria and I have received many letters of praise from Egypt. In fact, they were all sold out in the Cairo International Book Fair. My "home" writings have qualified me to be a member of the Islamic Literature Association in India, which has only two female members. Given all this I do not see how writing from home constitutes an obstacle. I suggest that it is even more productive because it is not limited to certain hours or topics. I write what I think is important, and for specific goals and according to my own method . . . This feeling of freedom is the most important factor in creativity. I do not understand why Ms. Gābel and many others want to transform writing from a mission to a profession that can constrain women's contributions.

Second, she says, "and we work from them [our homes]." I suggest that the fact that a Saudi female writer can work from her home as chief editor of a magazine or as supervisor of the woman's section of a magazine should be considered a privilege that distinguishes her from all other female writers in the world. For it does not force her to leave her home and face the problems that other women suffer when working outside the home. She saves the time of commuting between work and home, and the time she would need to spend getting ready for work.

Third, Thurayya speaks of home as "seven vaults." Who can say that the home is a vault? To what degree has the woman become seduced into leaving her home that she imagines it to be a vault? And worse, not only one, but seven vaults? I have no doubt that Thurayya Gābel has not chosen the "seven vaults" metaphor haphazardly. She surely intended it to hint at many issues she did not have the courage to reveal. Or why would she say, "despite all the obstacles that we all know of but cannot talk about"?

No doubt she meant to include *hijab*, segregation, and limiting women's work to certain fields, among these "vaults" and obstacles that she cannot talk about. She cannot talk about it because to object to it is to object to Allah's laws. If she means by "relief" to discard *hijab* or disobey the Islamic law, then this is not a relief but rather a calamity that we pray to Allah not to inflict on us.

It is regrettable and painful that some Saudi women writers are dissatisfied with the Saudi woman's position and think it abnormal in comparison with the position of Arab women whom they consider normal. They are affected by the so-called woman's liberation movement and by ideas of woman's equality with man.

This kind of thinking deprives the Saudi woman of her true Islamic identity . . . It is one of Allah's blessings that the Saudi woman has been educated and reared in the protection of *hijab*. For *hijab* was never an obstacle to her reaching the highest levels of knowledge. That is what Islam wanted for her. Our enlightened government has proven to the whole world that *hijab* and segregation of the sexes do not prevent the woman from gaining knowledge. The Saudi woman should acknowledge this blessing and thank Allah for it . . . I do not know what the woman writer aims at by calling for other women to leave their secure castle, their kingdom, their home, in which their creator ordered them to "stay." I don't know why we leave Allah's prescriptions and respond to satanic calls.

On Woman's Writing [27]

I hope that the literary supplements and literary sections in our newspapers will adopt my suggestions. For it seems that the feminine voice does not easily reach the ears of men. Even if it is convincing and finds its way to their minds, and even if they secretly agree with it, they will still not announce their agreement because the voice is that of a female, not a male!

But is it my fault that I was born female? This is Allah's will, and what Allah has created can never be changed. But since I am a female, I am proud of it and I praise Allah and thank him thousands of times for it. Many times I ask myself, what if I dropped the feminine ending from my name—what kind of effect would my writings have on people? But if I did this, I would lose my self-respect, my soul, my mind, and all my being, for I am not used to changing colors or appearing in different garbs.

This idea occurred to me recently when an official suggested that the value of any opinion depends on the value and status of the person voicing it. I looked at myself and found that I have no important official position and do not carry a great academic title. I only carry a feminine name. It is unfortunate that the female is seen as shallow, incapable, and insignificant. If she has ideas or points of view, people tend to suspect that a man has in fact written them for her. They will say that a man is hiding behind her and even start to inquire about his identity.

This is a great injustice that befalls the female in our land at this

time. If confidence in a woman's intellectual capabilities is so severely
lacking, then how can her views be taken seriously? I often think about
this painful fact when I approach an important issue which, in man's
view, women have no business approaching. I say, "Do not look at the
identity of the speaker but look at the content, for it is the content that
matters the most." I suffer from this sad state of affairs, for there are
those who suspect that someone else is writing for me . . . I feel this as
a stab in my heart . . . It forms an obstacle between me and my
readers, to whom I give without any expectation of return, except to
communicate with them in my own style and my own words. If it pains
me to find that the editors have changed some of my words, how then
can I be capable of claiming for myself the intellectual effort and sweat
of others? . . . What kind of a person am I, in their view? I do not know
what kind of people can think that way. All I can say is that suspicion is
a great sin!

On the Woman's Literary Movement in Saudi Arabia [28]

The Saudi woman has proven to be courageous when she knocked on the
door of literature, despite her short acquaintance with knowledge and
her long journey in illiteracy. The doors were all closed in her face, but
she was able to find openings through which to share her intellect with
the world. This was a great achievement, and a revolutionary step against
the residual ideas in society that put her intellectual abilities down and
demeaned their value. We all know that the literary path is full of
obstacles and thorns, and full of pain even for the man. If the man's path
is that difficult, the woman faces even greater difficulties. If [some men
have] in fact obstructed the way to literature for other men, we can only
imagine how they can, through their masculinity with all its pride,
authority, dominance, and arrogance, stand against the feminine nature
with its weakness, helplessness, and submission. As a result, women's
problems in the literary domain can only be doubled.

In fact, the problems of the literary woman are exacerbated by the
man's view of the woman! The man often views the woman as being
created for his own pleasure. She is but a body that satisfies his needs
and desires, not an intellect that seeks dialogue with his intellect or
stands on an equal footing with his. As such, he is ready to reject, object
to, or foil the woman's literary attempts.

When a man marries a literary woman, we find him rejecting the idea
of her continuing to write. He does not care much about the suffering

and pain she experiences when he buries her intellect alive. The fact is that all difficulties of life are bearable compared to the assassination and burying of one's intellect . . . Does a woman's [literary] contribution bring shame to her or her husband? If that is true, then the prophet (prayer and peace be upon him) would not have proclaimed his wife Aisha as the ultimate religious authority when he said, "Half of religious knowledge [resides within] this red-faced woman [meaning Aisha]." Also Omar (the second caliph)—may Allah be pleased with him—was not ashamed to announce to the people that he, as a caliph, had made a mistake in his religious judgment (regarding woman's marriage gifts), and that he had been corrected by a woman who had the right Islamic view. He never objected to her participation or to that of other women.

Those who object to women's literary participation are not guided by Islam. Not only is it not at all shameful for a woman to write and sign her own real name, but for her to do so is in fact a religious duty. I consider it a duty for the woman to guide others to the Islamic way . . . In our time, writing is an effective means of such guidance. If the woman declines the opportunity to give guidance, then she is weak in her Islamic beliefs. For the prophet (prayer and peace be upon him) said: "Whoever sees wrongdoing has to change it, by hand; if that is impossible, then by tongue; if that is impossible, by the heart, and this is the least a believer can do."

But if the man finds signs of subversion in the woman, then he, as a husband, a father, a brother, or a son, has not only the right but also the duty, and it is the duty of all in society, to shut this pen up and bury it alive, because it has deviated from the right path and is aimed for the destruction of all society.

We also find that many men have chosen not to take any stand on the issue of a woman writing. No one has subjected her work to serious study; all that is said of her contribution is nothing more than personal opinions.

Those who object to a woman's literary participation, however, often want to restrict the woman writer's concerns and interests to what they see as suitable subjects. When the woman speaks of political, economic, educational, or academic issues and has delved into books, thinking and deducing and drawing conclusions, these men would say, "I do not want a woman who thinks . . . I prefer a woman who touches my heart and my emotions, not my mind." Here, a man wants to exploit the woman's undeveloped intellect for his own pleasure, as he has already exploited her body.

This kind of thinking is the highest form of exploitation, in which the twentieth-century man exploits the woman as a mind, a soul, and a body. The man has not yet understood that the woman is an inseparable part of this world. Anything that happens in it is felt by her, just as it is felt by him, if not more so. Its developments affect her just as they affect him, for she does not live in a world different than his. It is her right, as a human being who possesses an intellect, to participate with her views in whatever is happening in the world . . . Who can say that the woman is not as affected by inflation as everyone else? Who can say that the woman is not affected by the wars with Israel, by Camp David and its consequences? Who can say that the women in Syria and Lebanon are not affected by the domestic problems in their countries or by the Israelis' annexation of the Golan Heights? Who can say that women were not affected by the Iraq-Iran war? Or who can say that women are not going to be affected by a third world war? How can we say that women have no business tackling this or that issue?

I do not condone a woman's interference in political affairs or her seeking political rights. In fact, I reject such notions because Islam did not give her this right for reasons we all understand. What I believe, however, is that she has the right to voice her point of view about the events around her. Voicing an opinion is vastly different than interfering in the business of politics or authority. The woman never said to the man: "You have no business discussing or thinking about my affairs as a woman." Our bookstores are in fact filled with books written about women by men. Women have never objected to that.

We may ask, why does the man tend to undermine the woman's intellect and deny her good thinking? Why does he see her as shallow, extravagant, and concerned only with fashion? Why does he accept her beautiful appearance while rejecting the beauty of her mind? I cannot deny that the woman is responsible for man's view of her as a sexual object. She has made it a vehicle of man's pleasure. She took care of her appearance and neglected her mind. But she is not the only one responsible for this state of affairs. The literature written by men on women has also contributed to this image. The woman constitutes a major element in that literature, whether as a source of inspiration or as a heroine. The content of that literature has concentrated on her beauty and appearance.

We cannot deny that the literature written by Saudi women has not yet reached a level of excellence comparable to that of men. But why? To do justice to this question, we have to look at the process of evaluation. We have to pose the question in terms of the following inquiries: Is it related to a woman's intellectual inability to form a comprehensive view of life or to describe what wavers in the human soul? Or is it because she lacks sensitivity to human pain and suffering? Is it because of her isolation that she lives sometimes unaware of the intellectual and social movements that touch her life and the lives of others? Are these the reasons why her literature has been discarded and classified as feminine or "womanly literature," literature that does not compare to men's literature? Or do other explanations account for the low status of women's literature? I would like on this occasion to summarize my views on what some of the reasons might be:

First is the infanticide practiced against the woman writer which buries her in her infancy (within about six years of her birth as a writer). In this short period, whatever she produces is only the beginning. As she starts to mature, she suddenly disappears. Six or ten years are not enough to produce a literary person in the full meaning of the word. The literary person has to maintain encyclopedic interests in different sciences, arts, and literature. He or she cannot be limited to only certain areas of interest. For it is important to understand all the different aspects of issues, whether popular or literary, political or economic, religious or social. In addition to this, the literary person has to be more attached to and involved with people, for he or she is the mirror that reflects their pains, hopes, struggles, and aspirations. He or she has to understand people's psyches, has to honestly express their feelings. The literary individual also has to know the nature of their occupations, to present their concerns and problems and facilitate their solutions. All this is still not enough. He or she must also be a good diver into the deep waters of the Arabic language and its arts of expression. This cannot be accomplished in just a few years. As I have already said, just a few years cannot establish literature or produce a literary person.

Given these facts, I will be frank and say that women's literature has not been and will not be elevated to a higher level as long as the career age of our literary women is quite short—and it will stay short as long as the woman writer's intellect is buried in infancy as soon as she gets married. When this happens we are deprived of the literary woman's intellect; it is buried in her identity as a wife and a mother. No doubt, as a wife and a mother, she is more capable than others in describing the feelings of motherhood and of married life. When the woman marries, she becomes more mature and understands life better because of her new responsibilities and her newly formed ties with people she did not know before but with whom she becomes closer than with her own original family. The new life, with all its new dimensions and responsibilities, helps the woman writer evolve and mature. The literature of Saudi women lacks this contribution, and if writers who are married and are mothers exist, they are very few. The solution, in my opinion, is in the hands of the husband. He has to be convinced that his wife's practice of any literary form does not touch, in any way, his name, person, or manhood, and that her literary work is highly committed to the ethics, the stipulations, and the principles of our religion. Practicing literary writing does not, in my view, oppose or interfere with a woman's responsibilities as a wife and mother. For insofar as she does not consider it to be a profession, she will not be constrained by certain working hours.

The irony is that when the woman writer marries, her husband does not object to her continuation in any other job, but he does not encourage, or he objects to, her literary production. This is despite the fact that our society is more in need of her intellectual production than of her employment in jobs outside the home. A teacher could be born every day, but this is not the case for a woman writer. I hope that marriage is not the ghost that runs after the woman's intellect to assassinate it.

The second point I would like to make is that Saudi women's participation in literature has only occurred over the last ten years, whereas Saudi men's involvement with literature has existed for more than half a century. In fact we commit a great injustice if we compare men's work with women's. Furthermore, the number of Saudi men writers is much larger than the number of women writers. For every hundred male writers, there are only ten female writers. Even if we overlook how brief the period has been since women started to contribute to literary production compared to the contribution of men, we cannot ignore the fact that the more women writers we have, the better the chances are for women to produce literature of a higher quality.

Thus any comparison between men's and women's writings should be eliminated, because it has no basis in reality. Rather, we should sift through women's literary production and define its premises, goals, and direction. It has to be subjected to scientific study. We have to follow through with each female writer and evaluate her writing not only in terms of her talent but, more important, in terms of her commitment to the principles and prescriptions of Islam. Islam, in my opinion, has to be the backbone on which our literature should be based. If we find that one of the women writers has gone beyond these boundaries, we should seek to stop her despite the quality of her writing. Studying women's writing should not be seen as a waste of time. I suggest that we start studying it now, so we can protect our literature from subversion.

I have a third point I wish to make. In evaluating women's writings, we have to consider the lack of cultural centers and libraries available to women. The woman writer is isolated from the literary movement in our country. The literary clubs have not yet incorporated women as participants in their literary events via closed-circuit television, or even by sending brochures containing details of the events.

Lastly, I can say that the talented Saudi Arabian literary woman who has the mind of a genius and a gleaming intellect has yet to appear. One with such qualities would ultimately be better than a hundred others.

Personal Sketch

I became acquainted with the work of Sohaila Zain Al-'Abedin early in the 1980s, when I stumbled upon a book of hers in the bookshelves of a Saudi female friend in the United States. When I was in Jeddah I called her in Madinah and she was very receptive to me and my project, something that may have had to do with my being the guest of a scholar with whom she shared a mutual respect. That first call lasted about an hour and a half, after which we agreed to meet in Madinah. During that first visit to Madinah, Sohaila was unable to see me because she was attending to her mother who was in the hospital at the time. During my second visit, however, her mother was better, and Sohaila was accommodating to my time constraints. The interview took place in late evening during Ramadhan, in her family home not far from the prophet's mosque. She was a gracious hostess, a perfect interviewee whose desire to express her views on the various issues not only was informative about her personally but also shed light on the entire cultural scene.

Sohaila takes pride in being a native Madinan. Madinah is the second holiest city in Arabia, located in the western province. She was born and raised there, and received her early education in its local schools. She obtained a bachelor of arts degree in history from Ar-Riyadh University by studying at home and attending the finals in Riyadh. Sohaila not only writes but also works at home as the head of Qur'anic women's schools in Madinah, a project affiliated with Imam Saud Islamic University. She is also an active member of various associations, such as the Islamic Literature Association in India and the Association of Arab Historians in Baghdad.

She writes for various newspapers but especially for *Annadwa,* the conservative Makkan newspaper, and *Al-Madinah,* published in Jeddah. Sohaila first became known in the field in the mid-1970s and has been

an active writer ever since. According to Sohaila's vitae, she has published, so far, twenty-four items of literary and historical research, some
of which were later collected and published in book form. At the time
of my visit, Sohaila had published six books, five of which are on the
subject of women and family in Islam. One, *Maseerat Al-Mar'a Assaudia
Ila Ayn?* (The Saudi woman's march: To where?), was first published in
1982 and appeared in a third edition in 1984 (the number of editions is
in itself a unique occurrence). The others are *Al-mar'a baina Al-efrat
wattafree'at* (Woman between exorbitance and intemperance [1984]);
Dowr Al-mar'a Al-muslima fi wadh'ena Al-rahen (Role of Muslim women
in our current situation [1987]); *Binaa Al-usra Al-muslima* (Building
the Muslim family [1984]); *Min omqul-rouh wasol-bul-fikr* (From the
depth of the soul and the essence of the intellect [1985]); *Al-mar'a Al-
muslima wal-ibda'a* (Muslim women and creativity [in press]). One of
her books has been assigned to be used as a text in the Women's College
in Imam Saud Islamic University.

Sohaila owes much of this accomplishment to the support she has
received from her family, and she speaks with great affection of both
her parents. Her mother gave her the space and the time to develop her
writing skills and believed in her ability to achieve excellence. Her
father was a religious scholar who had refused to assume the responsibility of a judge, in fear of compromising his piety. The dedication of her
first book was to her father, and speaks of a sensitive and kind man with
whom she had a special relationship:

> Every word I read or write now reminds me of you. It reminds me of you
> when you were with us, my sister and I, in that hotel room in Riyadh
> that we used to take during the final exam periods at the university. It
> reminds me of you walking under the burning sun of Riyadh, to bring
> us the lecture notes from one of the regular students, and copying them.
> . . . . . When we had finished our exam we would find you eagerly
> asking, "How did the exam go?" I still remember you, searching in
> Riyadh's restaurants for the tastiest and the best food to bring us,
> because the hotel food was not to our liking. I still remember all the
> pain and hardship we have caused you when you accompanied us on
> those trips.[29]

Sohaila, in addition to her books, had generously provided me with
thousands of pages of manuscripts and newspaper clippings. Although

five of her published books concern women and family, Sohaila's approach often tends to deal with the broader contexts in which women and family are embedded. Religion, politics, architecture, the media, literacy, literature, and other topics of social commentary constitute the bulk of her sixth book. Taking pride in the designation "Islamic writer and thinker," Sohaila is increasingly becoming involved in issues of greater universality, such as Islamic thought, Islamic literature, Islamic architecture, Islamic cities, and Islamic history. In fact, of the seven other books planned for future publication, only two are related to women.

Sohaila's interest in social issues as a whole has to do with her belief that every issue, no matter how far removed it seems to be from women's issues, from a man's point of view, touches women in a profound way. Moreover, Sohaila has asserted on many occasions that, as a matter of principle, women have the right, as well as the ability, to speak on any topic or any issue. As her selection reveals, she has voiced a bitter protest and resistance to limitations imposed on her as a woman writer, who is seen to have "no business approaching certain issues." The selected articles reflect the views she expounds in her books, interviews, and talks, and also provides an insider's view of the nature of the constraints placed on women in the literary field. They also reflect her ideological orientation, and her style of presentation.

Sohaila, and not wholly illegitimately, is often perceived by other literary men and women as being in line with the dominant discourse. By placing *hijab* and women's immobility at the center of her works, by emphasizing "difference" between the sexes in a way that establishes man as superior, and, most important, by her advocation of discipline and punishment for those—whether men or women—who cannot see the "light," Sohaila lies on the far right of the ideological continuum. When engaging in confrontations with other women writers on these issues, ideology for Sohaila always takes precedence over gender.

Because of Sohaila's assertive rhetoric and her style of presentation, as well as her tone, which seems, to some at least, too authoritative, women writers perceive her language as being "manly." Sohaila is not unhappy about this perception of her writing, as long as it does not go so far as to assert that a man is writing for her! In her view, she attempts to "practice control over meaning. I say what I mean, and mean what I say. I like to write in a way that is understandable to my mother." She writes with the confidence and fervor of a "true believer" who does not speak for Islam but rather, through her, Islam speaks for itself. Unlike Juhayer, who always assures us that her writings reflect her opinion and that she may not be right, Sohaila states her views in a matter-of-fact fashion, confident that she presents "Islam." Her choice of essay writing or historical research over poetry, for which she professes a great appreciation, may be related to her commitment to the "right" or religiously suitable form. Sohaila is concerned about what she sees as a weakening commitment to Islamic ideals, which she attributes to the influence of Western ideals, especially among women. Her preoccupation with this issue is reflected in her relentless opposition to what she terms *modernism*. The issue of modernism haunts Sohaila, and her antagonism toward modernists reaches its peak when they are also women. Sohaila sees the actual danger of this modernist trend in its hegemony over literary institutions. She charges that literary sections and literary supplements of major newspapers and magazines are taken over by the "modernists" whose "bias against the 'Islamicists' reached such a point that at one time I was unable to publish my writings . . . They even tried to stop publication of a series of articles on one of their symbols, Tawfiqul-Hakim [a prominent Egyptian writer]."

Sohaila, who is both strong-willed and self-disciplined and harbors the conviction that the Muslim writer should see writing as a mission, intends, along with her brother, to establish a publishing house to combat what she sees as increasing censorship of her writings by the modernists.

While Sohaila sees infatuation with the West as the major danger threatening Islam, and fervently undermines Western symbols, she in fact believes that the real danger is seated in those Muslims who imitate the West. Sohaila, who made a trip to the United States some years ago, at which time she visited California, was impressed with its natural beauty and the value people attach to time and hard work. But she sees no reason for Muslims to have their self-confidence and their religious convictions shaken by the West: "Muslims already have proof that their civilization is, as it was in the past, capable of leading the world. It is common knowledge that the basis of Western civilization was built by the Muslims in every conceivable field: mathematics, astronomy, medicine, philosophy. Muslims can reclaim these roots." Her main message is that if people of this generation are "fated" to be imitators, then rather than imitating the West, they should model themselves after their own "golden past."

Textual Analysis

Defining the Issues: Islamic Institutions and the West

A noticeable facet of Sohaila's writing is that, whether the subject is literary, religious, or political or related to creativity, history, writing, or even architecture, the discussion always shifts to matters pertaining to two issues: women and the imperatives of veiling, immobility, and segregation from men, and the necessity of combating the encroachment of the West. In an article dealing with the architectural design of an Islamic city, for example, Sohaila demonstrates how these preoccupations are intertwined in her thinking: "[our houses] were designed to suit societies in which women are stripped bare in front of men. . . . . Even in the two Holy Places, women can still be seen by men. Because of lack of dividers that would prevent men from looking at women, many times men mix with women in prayers and even invade their space." [30]

Sohaila's emphasis on such institutions as *hijab* and segregation reflects her deep consciousness of the Western presence in her world, and the tension in the relationship between the West and Islamic civilization. It also reflects how the West itself has become an element in the definition and conception of what becomes or constitutes a problem or an issue in her society. In her book *Maseerat Al-Mar'aa,* Sohaila points out that "the West in its attack on Islam has focused on the *hijab* . . . Those Arab women who have discarded their *hijab* have in fact taken Western women as a model." For Sohaila, if the West applauds the discarding of *hijab,* then *hijab* should be advocated and considered a defining attribute for Islam and a source of its future empowerment. That issues of concealment, immobility, and segregation assume special significance not only in Sohaila's writing but also among those she calls "Islamicists" seems to be more a response to the Western perception of Islam than to an intrinsic significance of these issues within the religion itself.

Home Sweet Home: Mobility and Its Discontents

In one of the selected articles in which Sohaila comments on the issue of woman's creativity, she engages in a noteworthy exchange with a female Saudi poet, in which the issues of *hijab* and mobility take center stage—despite the discussion having originally been about literary creativity.[31] The poet Thurayya Gābel asserted that women's lack of mobility, and their writing and working from home, are major constraints on women writers and hinder their creativity. Sohaila tries to prove the contrary, stating that what Thurayya perceived as constraints were not detrimental to the quality of literary work, and judging from her own experience, seem to have had positive effects. Sohaila, who is in reality more voluminous in her writing than probably any other woman writer in her country, expresses a sense of pride that her work, while having been accomplished at home, has "reached different corners of the world." She sees writing from home as more productive and yielding to a sense of freedom rather than as a constraint. This sense of freedom is enhanced by her conception of writing as a "mission," not a "profession," and by what writing at home entails in terms of the writer's control of time, space, and the content of the writing.

Islam, in Sohaila's view, has advised women to stay at home in order to spare Muslim women the same problems professional women face all over the world. On one occasion she criticized the short-story writer Khayriyya As-Saggaf, for endorsing the idea of professional women journalists through the opening of a women's office in the Riyadh newspaper. Despite the fact that rules of segregation were strictly observed in the women's office, Sohaila rejected it as a type of professionalism that poses a challenge to women's commitment to the home.

Home, for Sohaila, is the "woman's castle" and her "queendom." To work in it is a privilege, not a constraint, and certainly not "seven vaults," as Thurayya sees it. Here Sohaila takes Thurayya to task for her use of this metaphor, speculating that the hidden meanings behind it have to do with the issues of *hijab*, segregation, and work in certain fields, which Thurayya admits "we . . . cannot talk about." Sohaila ignores the manmade religious censorship at which Thurayya hints, and sees it as "Allah's laws" to which no one should object. While Thurayya points to those constraints as matters of a specific mode of interpretation, Sohaila does not draw this distinction between Islam and its interpretation by different doctrines. For her, the Islamic laws are immutable. Any other view is either a function of "satanic calls" or of infatuation with the West. The two, however, are viewed by Sohaila as not fundamentally different.

The West and Its Models

Sohaila, who is highly conscious of the effect of the West, is also extremely aware of the role that Western symbols play in Muslims' infatuation with the West, especially Muslim women. Thurayya's views on the nature of the constraints on Saudi women in general and on women writers in particular, although provocative, are in fact shared by many other participants in the discourse on the issue—both men and women. Although Sohaila strongly disagrees with Thurayya "on all counts," she seems to have chosen to debate Thurayya more for what she symbolizes as a person than for what she has said or the way she has said it. Thurayya, whom I interviewed in Jeddah, is a leading Saudi literary figure and, as such, is a household name whose love lyrics are sung by the most famous Saudi singers. She lived and studied in Lebanon for many years and published her first collection of poetry there in 1963. A sensitive poet, as well as a strong, outspoken, and confident businesswoman, she comes from a prominent family in Jeddah. She presided for a short period over a women's magazine published in Paris called *Zeena,* which Sohaila viewed as being unrepresentative of Islamic values. Thurayya, who apparently has enjoyed a high degree of mobility since her early years, is for Sohaila a model of the *liberated* woman in the Western sense of the word. It is this model which Thurayya represents that Sohaila feels challenged by and toward which she directs her attack. Thurayya represents mobility and challenges mores of modesty if only by revealing emotions through love songs. Topping Thurayya's sins in Sohaila's eyes is her wish for change and her expectation of "relief."

Sohaila seizes the opportunity in her writings to assert her opposition to Western symbols, such as Simone de Beauvoir. She launches an attack on de Beauvoir, whom she views as being stripped of "all virtues and human values." Sohaila views de Beauvoir as an embodiment of Western values of sexual permissiveness and a symbol of the moral and intellectual decadence of the West. But this frequent invocation of Western models, even for the purpose of undermining them, has the consequence of forging a connection of contemporary Muslim women to the West, if only because Western models become the yardstick by which women are evaluated. "Good Muslim women" would naturally be those who prove their distance from Western models, and vice versa. But Sohaila sees this distance from the West as only half her mission. The other half is to provide "positive" examples, which Sohaila selects from the Arab Muslim history of women, and present them as models. These models include early Muslim women, such as "the mothers of the believers," 'Aisha and Khadija.

Sohaila goes further and presents her own experience as a model for Muslim women. When Sohaila speaks about herself and her accomplishments, one may think she is merely boasting about her own achievements. But in fact she does not speak of her own personal accomplishments in order to gain personal prestige but rather to present herself purely as a model. When she speaks of how much she has accomplished—without giving up "Islamic" stipulations—she speaks of how much the Islamic model she represents can accomplish, not how much Sohaila the person can do.

Given her awareness of the role models can play, she realizes that, as a successful model, she can cajole women to imitate her. It was probably this awareness that allowed her to study a young male poet from Abha, Abdul-Rahman Al-'Ashmawi, and present him as a model of an Islamic poet whose work she views as conforming to Islam both in form and content. As Fatna Shāker previously pointed out, most women writers would hesitate to engage in such an enterprise for fear of harming their reputation. But Sohaila is confident that she will be understood as simply giving recognition to an "Islamic" poet who stands as a realization of her conception of "Islamic literature" and one who deserves to be presented as a model for others.

However Sohaila's writings are perceived, her presentation of Muslim women as models for action has the effect of drawing confidence from their history. This puts Sohaila in tune with Fatna and Juhayer, as well as with other women writers, in their battle to forge continuity between contemporary women and their history. Moreover, by presenting herself as an example of a woman who stays home but can still be productive, Sohaila has in fact aroused feelings of pride and instilled a positive gender identity in those women who stay at home but whom others characterized as idle. Although it is men who often respond to her work favorably, a segment of her female readers see her as one who is concerned with maintaining the dignity, as well as the "purity," of Muslim women. Yet, others perceive her as an advocate of women's rights, since on occasion she even opposed religious leaders in support of women's education. Also, although Sohaila supports polygyny as an Islamic institution, she criticizes its abuses, especially in regard to taking young brides as second wives.

Ideology over Gender

In regard to any of the issues Sohaila discusses, one must realize that she derives her authority mainly from the content of her writings, which she presents as being "guided by Islam"; from her belief that she has a mission; and from her ideological orientation as an ardent advocate of the Wahhabis' mode of interpretation. In her own relationship to other women writers, as well as in her treatment of the issues that concern women, ideological considerations are given priority over being a woman. Sohaila has often indicated her pride in the media's designation of her as an "Islamic writer." While it is generally rare for other women writers to engage in harsh criticism of one another, Sohaila does not hesitate to speak her mind on whatever and whomever she believes to be "deviating" from what is "truly Islamic."

In the article "On the Woman's Literary Movement in Saudi Arabia," Sohaila states: "We have to follow through with each female writer and evaluate her writing not only in terms of her talent [but also in terms of] her commitment to the principles and prescriptions of Islam. . . . If we find that one of the women writers has gone beyond these [Islamic] boundaries, we should seek to stop her despite the quality of her writing." The responsibility of disciplining these women is in the hands of the males in their families, namely their fathers, husbands, brothers, or sons.

When she speaks of "deviation" and punishment, Sohaila does not only mean women but also men who voice different views. She has had numerous confrontations with male literary figures, whose Islamic beliefs she sometimes undermines. These men argue that one cannot easily disagree with her without being portrayed—if not as antithetical to "Islamic principles"—then as being pro-West. As a result, those whose beliefs she criticizes rarely, if ever, respond to her. In the interview,

Sohaila defended her tendency to question the beliefs of others: "Those to whom I objected in terms of the purpose and style of their literary endeavors may be believers in their hearts but not in their minds or conscience. The Muslim should believe in both heart and mind."

Sohaila derives her authority to speak in this manner from her appeal to the "truth," which she believes is embedded in the Wahhabis' mode of interpretation. Often Sohaila tends to use strategies of persuasion. In her response to Thurayya, for example, when speaking of veiling and immobility she discusses these issues as "an advantage," as "freedom," as a "blessing," and as "protection," or all these combined. It is only when Sohaila feels that her logic is failing that she presents her points as "Allah's laws." But her strategy is seen as one of intimidation because if she fails to invoke the "fear of Allah," then she often provokes the state to use its power to enforce the "laws" by whatever means.

It is this play on the balance of power between the state and the religious leaders that contributes to her strength in both centers of power. Sohaila sees it as the state's responsibility to withhold or mini-mize its support for any institution that gives women new opportunities to leave their homes. Sohaila invokes the state's power by calling on it to introduce certain measures and by praising it for introducing them. While this may be understood mainly as a tactic to solicit the state's support, it also poses an implicit challenge to the state. For it is testing the state to prove its allegiance to and "custodianship" of Islam, especially as the King calls himself "the Custodian of the Holy Places." Because of the state's openness to the West, it is necessary politically that the state prove its alliance with the religious leaders.

While Sohaila charges the state with the ultimate responsibility for discipline and punishment, she always maintains amicable terms with the state while exhorting and coaxing it into more restrictive measures regarding women. As a result, she is an asset to the religious leaders, not only in ideological terms but also politically. Their diminishing political power makes it difficult for them to always keep the state in line without them being subjected to its oppression. Sohaila's writings also prove to be useful to the state. The state's image is often polished through Sohaila's constant praise of its many restrictive measures on women. The state, constantly needing to secure the *'ulama'*s support, uses these measures regarding women to make symbolic statements about its commitment to "Islam."

Sohaila's Conception of Men and Women:
Vive la Difference

Sohaila, in these articles as well as in others, advances a conception of women as essentially different than men, and accords women lower status by virtue of their very nature. They are weak, emotional, submissive, "deficient," and in constant need of men's protection. Men, on the other hand, are strong, rational, authoritative, and dominant. Their nature places them in positions of superiority to women and gives them the responsibility of protecting women, even through discipline. Sohaila's conception, which is consistent with most of the Wahhabi male scholars, relies on the juxtaposition of such characteristics as superiority/inferiority, strength/weakness, rationality/emotion. The uniqueness lies in the contradictory propositions and inconsistencies that emerge when these topics are treated as binary oppositions in relation to men and women. Sohaila's perception of man as superior, for example, poses problems for her very argument about protection. She proposes that by enforcing *hijab* on women, the man is protecting the woman, obviously from other men. This implies that women should veil themselves in order to protect man from himself, to prevent him from committing "impiety and error." To push Sohaila's argument further, it is the woman's, not the man's, responsibility to curb those tendencies in men. Her logic establishes the reverse of her proposed binary opposition of men as strong and women as weak. Here, not only do men demonstrate weakness but in fact women are also in a position of having exclusive control over men. Men emerge almost as invalids who should not be held responsible for their acts: in a word, they should be protected.

An important result of this logic is that should an "error" occur between a man and a woman, it is automatically seen as the woman's fault. Man and society become the woman's victims. Given the logic in this part of her argument, it is no wonder that Sohaila views women as the "key" to all social change, as well as the one to blame for society's ills. In contrast to Juhayer, who views women as victims of discourse, and to Fatna who sees women's situation as a consequence of "real" forces in society, Sohaila views women as the victimizers of the whole society, thanks to the West's influence over them.

Also in contrast to Juhayer and Fatna, who by no means see women as the cause of men's "real" battles, Sohaila clearly exonerates men and shifts responsibility to women not only for local problems but for national disasters, even the loss of Palestine. The encroachment of the West, according to Sohaila, has always been through one gate: women. In her book *The Woman Between Exorbitance and Intemperance,* she calls on the Saudi Arabian government to sponsor a conference to "mend" the situation of Muslim women, which she says is no less important than any other issue, whether political or economic, ". . . no less important than the liberation of Jerusalem . . . Regretfully, we pursue a goal without a concern for the key that opens the door to reach it."[32]

Concealment and Revelation

Sohaila's writings seems to exacerbate the need for women to be controlled, rendering it an imperative for the survival of Islam itself. The means are to be by more concealment of women through veiling, as well as more vigilance, scrutiny, and even exposition of their activities. In her revealing article "The Unveiling of Emotions Is No Less Dangerous Than the Unveiling of the Face," Sohaila reiterates the meanings of *hijab* as blessing and protection. But she carries the idea of veiling even further, using it also in relation to women's expressions of emotions and intellect, and establishing her own definition of what constitutes "the private" and "the public" in relationship to women. Not only is "woman's physical beauty" a source of infatuation for men, and hence to be concealed, but her "emotional confessions" also must be hidden. They, too, are "ornaments" that must be concealed.

Here, Sohaila is referring to Juhayer but without mentioning her name. Unlike her naming of Thurayya, Sohaila chooses not to name Juhayer because she does not stand as a symbol for the liberated woman in the way that Thurayya does. But Sohaila feels compelled to use the occasion to make a point about the newly developed dimensions of *hijab,* and the notion of concealment for women. Juhayer, who was a newlywed in 1986, wrote about her personal experience with love and expressed her happiness in finding her long-dreamed-of "knight." Sohaila viewed these expressions as "personal experiences," intimate confessions that by no means constitute literary "creativity," and that it is not religiously permissible to disclose.

Women's personal experiences, according to Sohaila, must be concealed, for the expression of personal feelings is an emotional matter that has no bearing on "guidance." However, women's expressions that lend themselves to the intellect are of a different nature. In fact, women "stand on equal footing" with men when it comes to the intellect. In her two articles on women writing, Sohaila's argument reveals a change of heart and tone in speaking about men. Here, she criticizes men for "burying women's intellect alive" and speaks of their "exploitation" of the woman's mind as well as her body! This time, instead of the man, it is the intellectual woman who emerges as a victim of man's "exploitation," "infanticide," and "assassination."

This strong language can hardly be reconciled with Sohaila's view of man as both a victim and protector of women. But her emphasis on the woman's intellectual capabilities becomes even more problematic when it is set against her views, expounded in almost all her writings, of women as "lacking in mental capacity and piety."[33] In establishing women's lack of mental capacity and religion, and relating these to causes that cannot be remedied (i.e., physical causes), it is remarkable that Sohaila emerges in these articles as an advocate of women's "possession" of both intellect and religion. She, for one thing, is a woman who, by virtue of holding and practicing "Islamic" principles, sees herself in a higher position than men who do not. Here she draws evidence from Islamic history, in which women not only have carried knowledge as a part of their religious duty but have also used it as a means of furthering women's causes. She alludes to this despite the fact that her articles always end with establishing men in a relation of superiority to women, and place them in charge of women's body and intellect, even to the extent of giving them the right of discipline and punishment.

Of Religion and Tradition

Men, according to Sohaila, have a tendency to undermine women's intellect, either as a matter of their perception that women neglect their minds or because of the "residual ideas in society" that yielded such a perception. Because of her reliance on the Wahhabi *'ulama* as "the" religious authority, with its apparent tendency to diffuse the cultural with the religious, Sohaila, in a similar manner, deals with such institutions as concealment, segregation, and immobility as matters of Islamic law. While they are social institutions sanctioned by religion, they are seen to be enforced rather than transformed by social practices. As a result, Sohaila's loyalty to religion is inseparable from her loyalty to culture and society.

It is that loyalty that drives her underlying assumption that, just as men are victimized by women, society, in Sohaila's view, is also a victim of women. By invoking the social to explain men's perceptions of a woman's intellect, Sohaila attempts to resolve the dilemma created by her biological explanation. But she is trapped by her own conception of women. By adopting biological explanations, her own existence as a woman writer, who no doubt has intellectual capabilities, cannot be justified. For she herself is living proof that the very claim of a woman's "deficiency" that she so vehemently defends is invalid. By oscillating between the biological and the social, Sohaila attempts to keep the notion of "deficiency" intact as a rule that governs all women, while at the same time establishing her own existence as an exception that does not disprove the rule. The logic of her argument establishes that while women are "naturally deficient," she personally possesses both mind and religion, not only over other women but also over some men.

Sohaila seems unsure of how to solve the contradiction. In her article "On Woman's Writing," she reflects her hesitation on whether to assert herself in terms of the rule or the exception. While her views may coax other women to accept the existent definitions and theories about them, men's views of women as "incapable, shallow, and insignificant" gives "pain" to Sohaila. But she shifts her strategy from defending women's capabilities in general to pleading with her reader: "Do not look at the speaker's identity, look at the content, for it is the content that matters most." She seems to suggest here that only by denying her identify as a woman can she find a way out of the trap that she herself has created—as if the price women must pay for their words to stand on their own merit is nothing short of total concealment of themselves as creators of these words.

Literary Marginalization and
the Privatization of the Public

Alkalamu untha wal-jawabu thakar.
(Speaking is female, response is male.)
—Old Arabic saying

While it is a function of being a writer to be allowed to "escape the prison of language," from what has so far been demonstrated by Saudi women writers, it seems that a function of being a woman writer is to always end up being "recaptured."[1] As intellectuals or even as highly educated individuals, these women can no longer be accused of "lacking" knowledge. But the rules of the game have been transformed in such a way as to ensure that, while women's knowledge can be "displayed," it also, through critical reviews, becomes discredited and disqualified if only by rendering it personal. Publishing is no guarantee that a matter will be made "public," since within the process of review, a "published" matter may be pulled back to the domain of the private. This chapter's objective is to show how imperatives of control have shifted the emphasis of the dominant discourse from "the woman as private," yet nevertheless a subject of public discourse, to a situation in which the products of women's minds, their words, which are made public, are privatized. Not only do their words become objects of study, of analysis, and of judgment by men but women writers themselves are restructured in a way that is consequential for the perception of their works.[2] In what follows I present a number of reviews of women's literature written by men, which I consider representative of how these reviews function in mediating women's writings to the general public, and of the criteria by which these writings are judged. Women's literary products become the field of another power game, the objective of which is to put women back in their "place." The common thread in these reviews is the tendency to systematically discredit women's knowledge and to invalidate women's experiences by relegating them to the private.[3] They are described as personal, or at best "feminine," not only in terms of form, scope, or the nature of the experiences they explore but also in terms of symbols, themes, settings, and styles. Very often, this means stripping women's writings from their important political context.

Reviewing, Literary Criticism, and Cultural Considerations

Attempts at representing women's writings through reviews are alive and well in the Saudi newspapers. The reviewers form a loosely defined group of people, the majority of whom are male social commentators, columnists, religious clerks deemed experts on linguistic matters, or simply readers who comment on women's writings. I call them reviewers—as distinguished from critics—advisedly, because of the lack of agreement in Saudi society on what it takes to be a critic in terms of competency or legitimacy. Despite the existence of a handful of specialized male critics who are mostly university professors working in the field of literature, and who have produced sophisticated works applying both Eastern and Western principles of literary criticism, this occupation is still not a fully established institution. Those who hold degrees in literature or literary studies are considered more legitimate than others and probably are expected to be more competent. But practically speaking, any writer with sufficient knowledge of language and of literary tradition can legitimately voice an opinion on a literary issue, piece, or writer, and such opinions can influence readers. In fact, readers, columnists, university professors, and even religious clerks may enter the literary debate at any time. As a result, the reviews written for the daily newspapers and magazines by these diverse contributors may be more revealing of the predominant tastes and needs of the general readers than the reviews by more specialized literary critics.[4]

So far, however, literary reviewing or criticism is an institution dominated by men. Women writers are yet to enter the field of criticism although some have made a few attempts at critiquing one another or other, male, writers. The only woman to whom I found a reference as a "critic" in the literary circles is Maryam Al-Baghdadi, a professor of literature who published a collection of poems that followed the traditional Arabic Qasida in form but was poor in imagery and emotional import. Recently, the poet Fowziyya Abu-Khalid has been engaged in critiquing literary works of both men and women.

Considering that literary criticism is a field still dominated by men, one must keep in mind that criticism between men and women is not free from the social restraints that govern the relationship between men and women in general. Historically, women in Arabia, whether as critics or as subjects of critique, have been excluded from the institution of criticism, formerly composed of the poets themselves, as well as consumers of poetry. As symbols of family honor, women could not be part of this institution since, although it ensured poets a degree of recognition and the rapid transmission of their literary contributions, it also incurred a degree of exposure and scrutiny deemed unacceptable for women. Criticism was practiced in the settings of the *majalis,* a pre-Islamic phenomenon that continued after Islam and was adopted by the caliphs, some of whom were themselves poets or authorities in literary taste. As literary "salons" that were exclusively male, it was inappropriate for "free" women to attend the *majalis,* although slave women (*Jawari*) who were trained in literary skills were an indispensible part of these *majalis.*[5]

Another factor in excluding women from the enterprise of criticism has to do with the subject matter of poetry. The poetry of praise (especially of the caliphs) and of unfulfilled love, which constituted the main subject matter of most of the literary production in earlier times, were seen as socially inappropriate for a woman to express, for fear of compromising her reputation. Although some women have managed to become known historically as distinguished poets, orators, or political speakers, they probably have been acknowledged as a result of meeting the sociocultural criteria of what was defined as acceptable subjects for women—such as eulogy and family relations.[6]

In contemporary Arabia, remnants of these factors are still alive. Women writers often acknowledge that the type and amount of critical attention a woman writer receives has to do with the reviewer's age and status. It is noteworthy that younger male critics tend in their critique of women writers to be harsh, perhaps as a means to ensure adequate distancing from these women and to avoid suspicions of personal interest. On the other hand, some women writers charge that older critics tend, as a form of encouragement, to call them "daughters," to praise them at the outset, and to treat them as important, placing high expectations on them. If women writers, for whatever reason, stopped writing or disappeared from the writing scene, this was considered as one of "woman's failings." Ironically, those women who have withstood the pressures and demands of a writing career, and have persevered, have often been, for one reason or another, the subject of severe criticism and even personal attacks.

Depending on their age, the male reviewers then tend to respond to these social constraints either by appearing overly antagonistic or overly protective of women writers. Neither tendency is acceptable to women writers who as a result increasingly take the enterprise of criticism less seriously. Not only are women writers annoyed by their belief that women are held to higher standards in terms of their commitment to writing than men are but that they are placed under constant surveillance—a circumstance they believe denies them the opportunity to grow, as male writers can. These problems cloud the relationship between local critics and women writers.

But there are many male reviewers who are not Saudis; some publish reviews in their home countries, others write regularly for Saudi newspapers and magazines. The latter, although they have the advantage of being free of local social considerations, are not free of political, ideological, or financial interests. These foreign critics are less likely—even if they reside in the country, but especially if they reside abroad—to be suspected of personal interest in reviewing a woman writer's work. Many women writers, however, do not take these critics seriously. In fact, one Saudi woman writer called them "suitcase critics" who perform superficial critiques just "to fill pages" and perhaps to fill pockets as well.

Men Reviewing Women

Three examples of critique by three different Saudi male reviewers of a Saudi woman writer, Najwa Hashim, are representative of the main patterns reflected in men's critique of women writers. One can only infer the reviewers' qualifications, means of recruitment, or ideological orientations from the tone and nature of their writings. However, regardless of the diversity of their ideological orientations or the variety of critical methods they utilize (which one may or may not be able to detect from their critiques), it is the patterns that emerge that are of primary interest. The selection is followed with an analysis of these major patterns.

The first example comes from a male writer who is currently the chief editor of a woman's magazine published in London. He is known for his "light" writings and social commentary:

> We may agree or disagree on the existence of "women's literature" . . . but certainly [something called] "feminine expression" exists . . . Words, expressions, phrases, and styles clearly [distinguish] the stories of women writers. . . . For example, these stories are characterized by an excessive expression of emotions, screaming in sad situations, "hysteria" in expressing inner dilemmas, and by colors, sadness, candles, tears, and goodbyes. The stories are more imaginative and contain more dreams . . . If all that is true—and it is—then our author Najwa Mohamed Hashim reflects these merits—or faults—of women's literature in her collection, *Travel in the Night of Sadness*. Even the title carries the same weeping tones . . . Travel is good-bye and pain, and night is darkness and sleeplessness. . . . .
>
> As I have said, we may agree or disagree on the subject of "women's literature," but the features of the feminine pen are clear, whether in her choice of [the subject of] man and woman. . . . or in the constant choice of the protagonist as the narrator . . . Najwa certainly is capable of attracting [the reader] strongly to her artistic world; she is a promising writer with a special flavor that deserves our attention, our caring, and our asking her for more.[7]

In Al-Faisal magazine, the writer of the following piece was not named but seems to have knowledge of Arabic literature, and his more conservative bent shows in his use of religious and classic literary expressions:

> A wild wave of stylistic innovations [*bid'a*], coming apparently from the North [Lebanon and Syria], is sweeping all young women writers in the Kingdom, . . . in which one can now substitute the word *torture*, for example, for the expression the "mills of tearing and pain," etc. . . . The pages of newspapers and magazines are filled with all these innovative and imprecise expressions. . . . I am sure that these stylistic innovations are symptoms of artistic failure, . . . and immature attempts that take on the appearance of modernism . . .
>
> I say this after having finished reading nine short stories by the writer Najwa Hashim. . . . In her poetic dedication she complains of being born into an environment that lacks love for the word, although it was the same environment that produced Omar ibn Abi-Rabi'a and Jamil Bothaina [poets from classical times]. . . . I personally did not understand one thing from the dedication [of the book] . . . She talks about birds of night. To me birds of night are the owls or the crows that live in the ruins. . . . Despite her incoherency [hallucination], in the tradition of the failed pupils of Colette Khouri [a contemporary Lebanese woman writer], she has a heart that is full of love and warmth, even when wrapped in darkness . . . She uses a great many surrealistic images . . . "My nerves are in my hand. I squeeze them and they pain me without pain" . . . (praise be to Allah who has power over all things) . . . Or "sadness is a joyful thing that sweeps us like a plague" . . . (may Allah save us). . . .
>
> I suppose she is yet to discover herself. From what we have mentioned so far of her dialogue with herself or with the other—for she is always the heroine of her stories—we can form of all her writing a complete and concise biography of her own self . . . She seems to be in a struggle to survive, first, and then to present her icy pen to announce that she is the knight of the new form of expression . . . All the stories resemble one another, all take place in a limited field of interaction . . . to the point where one can see them as one subject. . . . The verb *inhabit* is one of her specialties, in addition to other terms [that are not in accordance with classic Arabic] . . . Every story becomes an outburst of sadness and darkness . . .
>
> In this context the plot is bound to become easier, and that is probably the writer's only success . . . But for variety's sake, she should change the subject of her stories. . . . and do away with long dialogues

with the night, the cat, the crow, or with someone who is unknown or does not exist . . . Her style is excessively romantic . . . and she soars too high . . . Therefore, realism would be a good alternative that could protect her from unrealistic imaginative illusions and would probably provide a means for her characters to develop according to the development of events.[8]

In the newspaper *Al-Yowm,* under the title "The Image of Self: A Preliminary Impression of Najwa Hashim's Collection, Travel in the Night of Sadness," this reviewer, unlike the other two, is known to be a literary critic:

What I have read so far about the writer Najwa Hashim does not exceed the special compassion rendered the woman writer herself rather than critically examining what she has written. . . . . As a Russian critic once said, "the writer does not need praise as much as he or she needs hard criticism to strengthen his or her talent." I have no doubt that she has a talent although this confession on my part may anger others . . . This talent is revealed in her strong and poetic language . . . although what she writes about is very much a personal concern. She has an ability to express her personal concern, which is a romantic concern, where love and the relationship between men and women constitute the center. . . .

However, this could be a phase that all writers go through, in which personal concerns take priority at the beginning, and words of passion may bury the talent. . . . The truthfulness of experience is a very important condition for talent, and that is what gives power to her words and her resentment of oppression. . . . She soars in the skies of freedom . . . Freedom and will are the two poles on which Najwa's tent is built. . . . But this tent is only large enough for two people. . . . "The will, the will, where is the will?" But this question is constrained by her view of human existence as "me and him."

We should not look for excuses for Najwa, but we have to remember that she is a "woman," and under the circumstances that surround her, her relationship with her milieu is bound to remain on the level of personal exchange. . . . That is, between a self surrounded by paternalistic [feelings] and an outside that requires her to defend her self and her right [of existence] . . . the writer knows that . . . she speaks of freedom, love, will, and justice . . . and she tries to tackle social problems such as spinsterhood, divorce, and familial oppression. . . . Change for her means to change self to confront the outside, but this is a personal rebellion, and the world for her becomes merely a man. She does not seem to be aware of the real subject, which is what makes this man a man? . . .

This is one of the basic flaws of her writing; the other is that her short stories are lifeless, for she does not provide characters that are well developed. . . . Najwa has a talent, and her linguistic abilities should not be underestimated . . . this is despite her indulgence in self-expression . . . She in fact contributes to the defending of her existence, and we don't lose anything by acknowledging that she makes more sense than many others (males) who make noise with no substance. . . . Thousands of women and men read Najwa Hashim. We have to acknowledge this fact, and instead of leaving her running around troubled on the fringes of her personal anxieties and romanticism, we have to clarify why her writing is not taken seriously by educated [readers] and other writers. . . . .

Najwa Hashim is involved in confession and self-expression . . . a reflection of the female as she sees her under men's hegemony. But this is the first step [for her] to know the world. . . . The writer exists, and she writes about what is important to her. If we keep silent about her work we will not be able to correct it or tell her that . . . these issues are not the world, that her dreams and her personal concerns are not the dreams and concerns of other women. . . . writing is pain and suffering and I have no doubt that Najwa Hashim is in pain and that she suffers . . . This is clear from the strength of her language and the transparency of her images. That is because, as she herself has said, "Travel on the edge of glass and under the burning sun is something that can only be felt by the traveler."[9]

The Idea of Women's Literature

Whatever interpretive methods these reviewers followed a consensus seems to exist among male reviewers that women's writing cannot be ignored. To ignore it is to give up control over its reception and run the risk of letting the "genie out of the magic bottle," to recall Fatna's metaphor. In their reviews, not only are individual works or individual writers discussed but the whole tradition of women's writing is examined under the rubric of "women's literature." The idea of "women's literature" has in fact been a lively issue for discussion at least since

1982, an issue to which entire literary supplements have been devoted.[10] In these discussions, the question of "women's literature" is approached in terms of a debate on whether style and subject matter can be seen as the defining characteristics. Women's literature is distinguished from "the literature" in a way that men's literature is not, and it is gauged in terms of differences between men and women that are presented in themes, styles, vocabulary, metaphors, settings, and characterizations. The debate has reflected the general view that women's literature is considered feminine, and described as being poetic, emotional, personal, or biographical.

But women writers, almost in their entirety, have resisted the idea of separating literary works into "literature" and "feminine literature," and have insisted that literature is literature, that women do not write with their "lipsticks" (as Juhayer once commented). Women exposed the vagueness embedded in the assertion that women have a certain style and a certain distinguishable language, and attempted to uncover the ambiguity surrounding the concept of women's literature. At one time the term *feminine* has been applied to what is written *about* women, at other times to what is written *for* women, but it is most commonly used to refer both to what is written *by* women as well as *for* women. Women insist that if, by "women's literature," men refer to what is written *on* and *about* women, then men have written more women's literature than women have themselves. But if "women's literature" refers to the writings produced by women on women, what happens when these writings pertain to problems of society as a whole, rather than to women as a category?

Despite attempts (mainly by men but also by some women) to advance arguments that the styles of men and women differ, no clear formulation has been made of what exactly distinguishes the two styles. One reason the distinction remained vague is perhaps because no indigenous tradition of literary "detection" exists that is as highly developed as, for example, that which exists in Western cultures. In the West, in the Victorian era, the use of male pseudonyms led to the refining of techniques of literary detection.[11] But in Saudi Arabia the opposite phenomenon exists in which not only do some male writers use female pseudonyms (mostly when writing on what are considered women's issues) but women, too, when using a nom de plume, always use a feminine name. That men had actually produced writings under women's names has only recently been publicly revealed, and to my knowledge no serious attempts have yet been made to analyze these writings with the intention of determining their inherent masculine or feminine qualities.

A journalistic tradition has existed in the Saudi newspapers, as it has in other parts of the Arab world, that "separates," rather than "distinguishes," women's writings from those of men. Early attempts at separating women's writings from men's took the form of "physically" segregating women's writings by allocating them to certain spaces designated as "women's sections" in newspapers and magazines. In the last decade or so, women have persistently fought these attempts, demanding that their writings be placed in sections designated by their subject matter (e.g., literary or social sections) rather than by gender as "women's sections." In an effort to resist this attempt to segregate their writings, women writers have at times avoided topics that could easily be classified as feminine, to preclude the possibility of having the piece assigned to "women's sections." Although they have yet to secure a place for themselves on the front pages (usually devoted to important local and global political developments), women writers seem to be succeeding in undermining the type of physical segregation presently imposed on their writings.[12] Women's sections are still included in major newspapers, but they have been considerably reduced in number and their subject matter has been almost entirely limited to homemaking subjects. The majority of Saudi women writers reject the idea of "women's sections," preferring to write their own columns that allow them more freedom to tackle various issues. They also alternate with men in writing for literary supplements, which allows them to occupy the most prestigious and important spots in the newspapers and magazines.

It is noteworthy that women's attempts to go beyond the borders of their "space" by writing about broader issues at times are met with direct resistance from both men and women. Letters from women readers reflect an expectation that women should write about women, and these readers register protest when women writers place their priorities or concerns elsewhere. For example, Juhayer's mail is filled with critical letters from female readers complaining about her "honoring" a "man's point of view" or focusing on his experience. Men also express disdain for women's tendency to write on issues other than "women's issues." This may be partially explained by men's desire to know more about women. The letters from male readers suggest that women writers spark continuous male interest in knowing and having an "encounter" with women other than their immediate kin. This may also explain the high rate of response to women's writings from male readers in comparison with female readers.

It is against this background that one can understand why almost all women writers have, at one time or another, protested these pressures to "confine" themselves to issues pertaining only to women. As a result, they constantly have to assert their right, as well as their ability, to speak on topics of general interest. Women have attained immeasurable success in integrating their writings into the general organization of newspapers and magazines—at least in terms of physical space. But the idea of "women's literature," as expressed by Najwa's critic, or "women's sections" is more than attempts to make distinctions; they are the means used to put women back in their "place." The attempts at separating women's literature from literature in general seem, more or less consciously, to be geared at minimizing the intellectual "intermingling" between men and women, following perhaps the cultural contours of segregation and concealment in relation to women.[13] Within a society that places great emphasis on segregation of the sexes, literature is perhaps the only domain in which, both literally and figuratively, women's works are put "side by side" with those of men.

In short, the insistence on the part of Najwa's critic on the categorization of "women's literature" seems to secure the removal of women's writings from the domain of literary competition with men, while at the same time have limiting effects on women's enterprise.

Fact in Fiction: The Autobiographical Critique

In addition to being a means by which men avoid competition, one important result of reviewers' tendency to designate women's writings as "women's literature" has been the limiting of its scope so that the experiences women represent somehow become less worthy of being considered universal or human. By rendering women's literature "feminine," not only is women's contribution to the human experience concealed but that part of human experience is rendered private. Women have constantly appealed to readers and reviewers to see the content of their writings as pertaining to human beings in general, rather than reflecting feminine experience. For example, Ķhayriyya As-

Saggaf, aware of the prevalence of this tendency, appeals to the reader in the preface to her collection, *Sailing Toward the Dimensions,* to read her stories as an account of human experience, rather than as a strictly feminine experience. Her reviewers, as in the case of Najwa Hashim, nevertheless insisted that the experiences she portrays are "about" women, despite the fact that almost half her stories describe events experienced by men. In fact, women writers include these male experiences in their works because they are acutely aware of addressing an audience that is primarily men. As a result, going beyond the "womanly" may not only be seen as a leap to include human experiences but also as an attempt to appeal to the wider audience of men.

As can be seen in the above three examples of critique, the reviewers tend to narrow even further the scope of women's experience as portrayed in fiction. Not only are women denied the status of writing about the human experience but their writings are further transformed from the feminine to the personal. That is, women's works lose their validity as a reflection of or on human experience, first by rendering them true only to the reality of women, and second by viewing them true only to the experience of the writer herself. This autobiographical type of critique is one of the most common interpretive methods used to explain away women's writings. The main thrust of the autobiographical critique follows these rules: first, the writer's imaginative literary work is subjected to the rules of proof as reality, rather than as fiction. Second, the writer herself becomes the subject matter of her work. And third, as personal experience, the "truth" value of her writing is made ambiguous, and may be used in contradictory terms. As can be seen in the responses of Najwa's critics, while the experience she portrays is deemed "true" of the writer herself, it is not deemed by the critics as true of "other women." The result is that the writer's experience is not only discredited as representative of human experience but it is also deprived of being "feminine."

The confusion and the ambiguous manner in which the notion of "truth" is defined in Najwa's writings suggests that the fictional nature of women's works is not determined by an intrinsic quality of the genre to which the text itself belongs (i.e., fictitious story) but rather is seen as a fiction because of the reader's attitude toward the text. This may have been partially related to a general tendency, especially among the theologically oriented interpreters, to subordinate works of imagination to rules of evidence, in which whatever is imagined has to be consistent with reality.[14] But underlying this confusion of the real with the imaginative is the implication that women lack creativity. The definition of "reality," in fact, can become crucial in cases where readers may be so alienated from their own reality that even what the writer intended as a "realistic" depiction may end up being read as fiction by the reader. Readers, as Najwa's critics in their assertion or imposition of the status of fiction on a certain work, and stripping another work from it, exercise the ultimate control over the text.

It follows that forms of literature, especially those based on imagination, cease to provide the writer with a way of expressing those points of view that cannot be expressed in nonfictional forms. Fiction treated as personal history tends to present the writing as expository of the woman writer herself. Generally, writing about one's own experience is, as Najwa is accused of doing, viewed negatively in the culture as a practice of self-exposure, but for a woman writer to indulge in what is perceived as self-exhibition and self-revelation is, by definition, seen as an immodest practice, and as something shameful for the woman. This view is reflected in the common charge leveled against unmarried women writers that their writings are attempts at advertising themselves as potential marriage partners, and that it is for this reason that women writers tend to disappear after marriage. A good example of how "personal" experience is seen as a form of immodest self-revelation, even from the point of view of another woman writer, can be seen in chapter 4, in which Sohaila Zain Al-'Abedin takes Juhayer Al-Musa'ed to task for her "unveiling of emotions," implying that her writings are "confessional" and self-expository, and as such represent a breach of modesty.

Privatization of Themes, Styles, and Narrative Modes

Najwa's reviewers, as well as reviewers of other women's writings, tend to locate proof of the private nature of women's experiences even in the themes they choose, as well as in the concerns and narrative styles these women writers employ. For example, the theme of the relationship between men and women (e.g., marriage, love, divorce) is considered private or, at best, a feminine concern. Najwa's critics reveal that the theme of love between a man and a woman, when approached by a woman, is seen as worthless romanticism from which women writers have to move away if they are to enter the main literary discourse. Love as emotion is often seen as a private matter that, in order to be discussed in public, must be cast in acceptable terms (i.e., love of country, love of father, sometimes love of husband). Men have more freedom to speak of the love of a woman, and even traditionally, love has been one of the most predominant themes in the Arab classic poetry written by men.[15]

Not only women's themes but also their narrative modes and styles are seen as proof of the private nature of women's literature. In most of the short stories and poetry written by women, the point of view is usually revealed through the first person, who often happens to be a woman (this is especially true of Najwa). The use of first person narrative with a woman as the narrator leads to the impression that the story is realistic and "true" and to its identification as autobiographical. By the same token, the choice of stream of consciousness by women writers as a favorite narrative technique—with its built-in power of reflection and of revealing mental processes—has led to viewing this technique as inherently feminine. Moreover, even when women writers use the first person narrative with a male as the narrator or present a male as a main character in the third person, they are accused, as was Najwa, of lacking the ability to develop male characters.

The reviewers see women's style in expressing emotions as itself highly feminine. One of Najwa's critics states: "For example, these stories are characterized by excessive expression of emotions, screaming in sad situations, "hysteria" in expressing inner dilemmas, and by colors, sadness, candles, tears, and goodbyes." Another critic also sees these elements as expressions of a "real" pain with which the writer herself is struggling. Thus the woman writer herself becomes a field of investigation, in which psychological explanations (usually psychoanalytical) are advanced to penetrate her unconscious, especially to see what is behind her language, her vocabulary, and her metaphors. Najwa's emphasis on night, for example, seems to irritate the second critic. Although Najwa uses night as a setting or as a symbol for broader realities affecting women and society as a whole, this critic sees it as a reflection of the writer's dark inner self, not as a metaphor for the general "dark" state of affairs in her society. The reviewers either project their own romantic view of night or the cultural apprehensions about night as a time of subversion. Night for Najwa was not a time for romance but rather a time for self-confrontation and self-knowledge, a time to practice full humanity.

As is the case with other women writers, Najwa's reviewers have often described her language as "poetic." This may appear to be high praise, for poetry is the most pure of Arabic literary forms. But within the context of a short story, "poetic" implies a tendency to emphasize the formal and stylistic qualities of the work while undermining or completely ignoring the message. This is one reason why most women writers are not happy with such a description. The emphasis on the aesthetics of the work rather than on its message is, for many reviewers, especially the non-Saudis, the "safest" aspects of a woman's literary works. While this has brought attention to women's works, these critics, by considering the aesthetic qualities of the texts in total isolation or exclusion of the content, have not only concealed the serious political messages embedded in the works but have generated an assumption that women are incapable of producing works of substance.

Other Examples of Critique: Questioning Women's Morality

While some reviewers often emphasize the aesthetic aspects of women's writing as a means of blurring or devaluing the content of their writings, others emphasize the message so that the text, as well as the writer, is ideologically exposed. These critics use a mix of moral, social, theological, and ideological interpretive methods to explain the works of women writers, especially those who do not seem to entirely assume the values of the dominant discourse. In this type of critique the aesthetics of the work, in terms of style, symbols, and imagery, become themselves subjects of criticism as part of the message or as messages in their own right. Moreover, the morality of women writers, unlike that of men, becomes an important evaluative criteria and thus a critical aspect of their work.

Examples of this type of critique can be drawn from a book, published in late 1988, entitled *Modernism in the Scale of Islam*. The writer, Al-Qarni, is an ultra conservative, who was not known in literary circles before the book was published. The book adopts a sensational journalistic style, expounding free-floating generalizations and leveling personal attacks at writers whom he designates "modernists." The author's net was wide enough to include all those writers, men as well as women, whose style he judges to be "obscure, uncanny, or ambiguous." He rejects all attempts to use metaphors, symbols, myths, or terminology borrowed from the West or even from periods in Islamic history or from traditions he does not consider "representative" of history or Islam. He considers Sheherazade a symbol of idolatry, and he charges that words such as *night, conflict, collision,* and *crucifixion* are all "subversive" terminology, used as a code among the "conspirers" against the Arabic language and Islam.

He also sees those who promote colloquialism or even those who use classical Arabic but modify its structure (as is done in modern Arab poetry) as undermining the Arabic language. Not surprisingly, the author of the book positions a woman writer, Sohaila Zain Al-'Abedin (see chapter 4), as his weapon against other women writers whom he brands "modernists." He quotes Sohaila's characterization of modernism as a

> materialistic, atheistic ideology that seeks to take Arab thought back to the era of idolatry . . . Modernism has announced its rebellion on everything religious, ethical, and moral. It is a revolution against religion and history, past, tradition, language, and morality. It started with modification of form as the first step in an atheistic revolution [to destroy religious content]." [16]

As an example of "idolatry symbolism," Al-Qarni quotes this passage from one of Khayriyya's stories: "Balqees raises her brows, what led you to wear Sheherazade's garb . . . Tell us, but not Shahrayar's stories. Shahrayar is a symbol of blood . . . Sheherazade is the symbol of worldly play." [17] How Sheherazade or Balqees can be considered symbolic of idols is not clear, but it seems that this characterization reflects a deep antagonism toward these two women as symbols (see chapter 2).

Although some women writers are classified as modernists, such as Khayriyya and Ruqayya, their choice of themes and topics, and at times even their points of view, reflect culturally proper subjects (e.g., marriage, motherhood, women, women of Islam). The use of symbols, metaphors, or myths that are deemed ambiguous, or the choice of a literary form or genre that is not indigenous, are decisive factors in classifying a woman writer as a modernist.

Al-Qarni's strongest attack, however, was launched against three of the women writers, two of whom are discussed in this book—the poets Fowziyya Abu-Khalid and Khadija Al-Amri and the playwright and short-story writer Rajaa 'Alim. The author first takes issue with the two poets who, along with other male poets, apparently represented the country in a literary event in Kuwait. He takes Fowziyya and Khadija to task for uncovering their hair in public, designating them as *mutabar-rijat,* for having their pictures taken and printed in newspapers (one of which was local), and for "reading poetry in public, allowing strangers to hear their voices." But, most important, he criticizes them for "mixing" with men in public (the pictures showed them "sitting side by side with men," one of whom was Khadija's husband, the well-known poet Mohamed Al-Harbi).

Regretting that Saudi Arabia was represented by Fowziyya Abu-Khalid in the Kuwaiti event, the author charges that "if Fowziyya has taken off the clothes of modesty [referring to the uncovering of her hair], has stood on podiums with men, has sat among them with no protective veil, she should also be in a hurry to take off her heritage."[18] He cites other evidence against Fowziyya, charging her with sensationalism and the use of suggestive language full of "sexual implications." He cites her answer to a question in a magazine interview: "This is a beautiful question, as beautiful as children's experimentations under the stairs and on the roofs, to discover the secret of the whispering of last night and the sudden rapport developed between the adults after a day of cursing [name calling]."[19]

In another interview, Fowziyya goes further and challenges the conservative elements openly: "This is an atmosphere that is afraid of nature, trying to protect itself by offerings to God, and by the use of amulets of protection and divination."[20] Al-Qarni makes a point of reminding everyone that "she is a lecturer to our daughters in one of the universities."[21] This incitement to discipline the poet was to show results only a few months after the book's publication. Fowziyya was barred from lecturing and was given a nonteaching job in the same college.

Rajaa 'Alim did not attend the event in Kuwait, and thus was spared the reviling Fowziyya had faced. But, along with the two poets, she was criticized for using "symbols of modern atheism and old idolatry," for writing uncanny stories, and for her ambiguous style. Although the book asserts that the spread of modernism in the Arab world was an effect of the spread of Western "ills," the author also sees it as being rooted in what he calls "heretic sufist" trends that appeared in some periods in Islamic history, which he deems "unrepresentative" and thus unworthy of recognition. Rajaa tends to use numerical symbols that are seen to be derived from those traditions, such as the use of the number 9 by some sects. But Rajaa also presents a challenge: she cheers for those "ad-libbers" who read "outside" the text; she advocates a new and different reading of history, religion, and tradition; and she tends to encourage a break with patterned thought. All these characteristics are embedded in the Sufi tradition of Islamic mysticism (see chapter 2).

The hostility to Rajaa's and Fowziyya's works can be explained by their adoption of certain styles of representations (e.g., symbolic, allegorical) in the modern composition of poetry and short stories, and their presentation of new structures of language, all of which disturbs those who appoint themselves protectors of the language. These two women, as well as most other women writers, present the traditionalists with texts that are written in their same language but that are constructed in a way that limits the traditionalists' ability to understand the texts. Here, the traditionalists' fear of losing control over women is exacerbated by their fear of losing control over the language. These critics respond by declaring that these women's style of writing is incomprehensible, and thus is relegated to the status of the private. Najwa's critic called it personal "hallucination."

As mentioned above, Al-Qarni wrote his book of criticism as a campaign in the war against those he terms *modernists*. That women have taken positions, or seen as positioned by others, as weapons in the battle over modernism has important consequences. On the one hand, women's participation in the battle is indicative of the growing consciousness on the part of the dominant discourse of the significant role women play as codifiers of culture. It reflects the fact that various forces in society are actually competing for the services of women writers. Most important, the fact that the battle over modernism has included women on both sides has placed women on the same footing as men in the intellectual domain. Despite the personal price they have to pay as women, for the first time they were allowed to escape the evaluation and marginalization of their work as "womanly," and the way was paved for their writings to become a part of the wider literary discourse. On the other hand, it has divided women writers along ideological lines and weakened their consciousness of their collective womanness. The danger is that women are often jettisoned should ideological calculations deem it necessary. The possibility of men defending or backing women up is socially risky, and as a result those women who are attacked are usually left alone in the field to fight their own battles.

That women are expected to be calm and to write calmly has limited their ability to respond in kind to those attacks that not only distort their writings but also distort their personal reputation and stigmatize their families. Women are left with few choices; they either ignore these attacks, resort to silence for a while, or stop writing altogether. Many women who have stopped publishing their works are presumed to do so for familial reasons, and the media refer to this as disappearance or silence rather than as silencing. But some women writers have started to write, both explicitly and implicitly, about the various forms of censorship that attempt to silence them in their writings, whether that censorship is political, cultural, or religious. Having recognized and used the power of language, these women have come to use the power of silence as well. Women writers may threaten to stop writing their weekly columns and use silence as pressure to gain more freedom in writing what the editors may view as nonconformist literature. A measure of women's success in disarming the dominant discourse and in turning silence to their advantage is that more readers think these women writers were silenced before they think that they simply "disappeared" for familial reasons.

Regaining Control over Literary Products: Women's Response

The various forms of constraints on women as writers exacerbate the woman writer's sense of the cultural dilemma of being both a woman and a writer. They must constantly face the difficult question of how a woman can be recognized as a creative writer without compromising her morality and her identity or undermining the value of her literary works. Women find no easy way out of this dilemma but nevertheless use certain strategies to avoid the personal reviling, while at the same time undermining the dominant discourse's control over the interpretation of their texts.

We have seen how the reviewers, as well as other readers, first assert their authority over the text by determining its genre as either fiction or a reflection of the writer's actual experience. In doing so they assert their authority over the writer by making moral judgments of her through their reading of her text. Recognizing this power that reviewers exert and the assertions that are made regarding her intentions, the writer's only way of regaining authority over her text is by depriving the readers of that power. These writers accomplish this through a variety of means.

The fear of impropriety, and the desire to explore their creative potential away from social considerations and ethical interpretations, has led some women writers to adopt pseudonyms, albeit temporarily. Although few in number, those who adopt pseudonyms are relatively more able to free themselves from the immediate constraints of family, relatives, and friends. Portraying experiences such as intimate love, drug and alcohol abuse, or prostitution have stigmatizing effects—not only on the writer's own person but also on her family, simply because they are believed to be true experiences of the woman herself or of her surroundings.

Some of those who insist on using their real names tend to remove any autobiographical perception of their writings by concealing their involvement in the lives of their characters. They use strategies of camouflaging and "jamming" techniques, such as abandoning the first-person woman narrator or by establishing a male narrator. But even in fiction, a compelling literary portrayal of these experiences, rather than being seen as a sign of her creativity, subjects the woman to accusations that she knows more about the stigmatizing topic than "good" women would normally know.[22]

Resistance to claims of biographical experience leads women not only to conceal their personal identity but to deny their experience as women. Some writers, seeking to be creative and to join the literary discourse on an equal footing with men, may have found it useful to avoid explicit feminine experience as a way of incurring value on their literature. This denial or dissociation from "feminine experiences" may, by implication, perpetuate the conception of women's experience as private and unworthy of literary recognition. Indeed, the woman writer is in a position to have to sacrifice her "self" in order for her work to live. The choice for some women writers to "die" as authors in order for their words to survive is exemplified by Fatna Shāker. Fatna appeals to the reader of her collection:

> Do not make a connection between me and my words . . . Forget who I am, so you will not be preoccupied with my identity and lose interaction with what I am giving [writing] you . . . You cannot reach me unless you jump over the borders . . . remember that I am a human being, I love and hate, give and take, smile and cry . . . There is only one difference. The smile does not reach its transparent stage until eyes have poured enough tears to fertilize the endless desert.[23]

Women writers, in order to limit the reviewer's control over their texts, have at times even chosen to sacrifice their writing styles. That the various constraints placed on women writers has taken their toll can be seen in the number of writers who have altered their writing style— at times even beyond recognition. Najwa Hashim is a case in point. She has often been criticized for indulging in "romanticism," in "self-reflection," and for being overly concerned with the single topic of the relationship between men and women. The later developments in Najwa's work reflect a major shift away from these subjects. In Najwa's later works women are still the main characters, but instead of being young, educated, suburban women dealing with personal and social dilemmas, they are Jaizani women who speak a Jaizani dialect, and whose lives are depicted as a group rather than as individuals. Although her use of a local dialect that readers had difficulty understanding was a subject of criticism, the change has been hailed by reviewers as "a realistic turn" away, presumably, from "hallucinating" women.

Rajaa 'Alim is a second case in point. Whether to minimize the reader's control over her writings or perhaps to appeal to the ordinary reader and thus gain a wider readership, Rajaa's powerful symbolic thinking and vivid imagery have been transformed into a more direct and even journalistic style. In her later writings in Ar-Riyadh, she adopts an uncharacteristic, straightforward language and writes on themes that widen the circle of her target audience to other than the cultured elite.

Within these constellations of constraints on women's creativity, the effectiveness of the Saudi Arabian women writers should not be judged on the basis of a definition of creativity in the purely literary sense. For "plunging" in this sea of constraints may have produced only "half-drowned" literature.[24] Although at times women resort to self-defeating and women-defeating tactics, their creativity is evident in their skillful use of the rules of the political game and in their consciousness of the nature of the participants in the discourse and the positions from which they speak. Their writings are special if only because, in their attempt to regain control over their literary products, they make sure that they are not subordinated by the rules of the language game but rather that they see themselves and act as full-fledged players who—although under scrutiny—are capable of placing others under scrutiny as well.

Conclusions and Implications:
Contexts of Resistance and
the Dialectics of Protest and Affirmation

The purpose of this study has been to highlight the complexity and the different dimensions of the phenomenon of being a woman and a writer in Saudi Arabia. Specifically, the objective has been to understand the role of women writers in the process of their society's ideological formation as they make the connection between the poetic, the political, and the personal and contribute to the interpretation of major cultural institutions and revisions of values, ideas, and meanings in society. But women writers, by using aesthetics as a political strategy for providing new visions, have also transformed fundamentally the way women are defined and perceived by dominant discourses in their society. In fact, by gaining control over means of interpretation, these women not only have disturbed the conceptual machinery in charge of theorizing about women but have also carved out an important political role that affects the power structure in their society.

For the issues that constitute the center of gravity for the writers' intellectual activities are issues of concern to the society as a whole. Their texts reflect a concern with the widening gap between the real and the ideal, and with the interplay of time and space, and how women are caught in the middle. The texts also reflect a concern with women in their relationship to religion and to tradition, as well as to the West. In expressing such concerns these writers strive to provide their visions of an identity for the present that differs from that of the past (as defined by the centers of power); an identity for their civilization that differs from that in the West; and an identity for themselves as "real" rather than as mere symbols, and one that portrays women as being different than men but not in opposition to them.

What follows is an exploration of the main characteristics of their enterprise and points of challenge and revision they provide to major concepts and values in their society. Cultural explanations of why certain points of view rather than others exist in their writings are then offered. Also, in tracing the cultural and ideological premises underlying the thought of these women writers, the extent to which these premises diverge from or converge with Western feminist premises regarding patriarchy, consciousness, and resistance is examined. The chapter ends with theoretical reflections on the notions of power and resistance, placing these women's writings within the wider context of the politics of culture and discourses of power in their society.

Problematizing "The Woman," "Realizing" Women

The dominant discourse in Saudi Arabia has presented women as a generalized object of analysis and as a category—"the woman"—about which one may theorize. The notion of "the woman" sprang from the society's system of concealing women as real human beings and revealing them only as symbols. According to this notion, women exist as symbols at various levels: they exist for individual men in private relationships, and as symbols of honor or shame in public relations; they serve the state's political purposes in its attempt to achieve a balance of power; and they serve the religious apparatus in their response to civilizational challenge. Women writers, in writing about women's experiences, not only politicize women's lives but redefine women and transform their status from that of a "symbol" to that of a "real" human being. The idea is not only a revelation but also revolutionary.

From the outset women writers have resisted being confined to publication in the women's sections of newspapers and magazines because this has contributed to establishing women as a category of analysis. But this has also meant the risk of distancing themselves from the "feminine" altogether. The challenge for women writers has been to reconcile the need to represent the specific and diverse experiences of women while fostering a shared identification with other women's concerns, hopes, and aspirations.

In an attempt to deal with these contradictory elements, they write on women's experience, demonstrating a special sensitivity to what the "real experience" is. Readers' letters are a main source of inspiration in writing about the real lives of women with whom they are in touch. Thus, in their writings, they tend to select specific personal experiences and particular events in women's lives rather than those events that are merely representative of women's problems. These accounts of the real lives of women have resulted in generating a sense of sharing among women, but they could also succeed in presenting women as a nonhomogeneous group. These accounts are also an important source for illuminating the current situation of Saudi women whose lives have long been concealed.

In writing about women, women writers emphasize and even celebrate the qualities of nurturing, self-worth, mental strength, and loyalty to kin as part of being a woman. They emphasize that women are not "lacking" but rather that they possess necessary and indispensable qualities. In their use of women symbols, such as Balqees, Zarqa, and Sheherazade, they bring qualities of wisdom, unmatched visionary powers, and a remarkable memory and sense of womanhood. Sheherazade's mission was to change Shahrayar's tendency to generalize about women, that is, to believe that all women are untrustworthy based on the infidelity of one woman, or two. Sheherazade's main task, just like that of the writers', is to break down the category of "the woman, the infidel" in man's mind. Sheherazade teaches Shahrayar to "know" "the woman," and exacerbates for him a sense of loss when he generalizes about women. She also generates a sense of pride among women in simply being a woman whose experiences are certainly valued and consequential. But what is remarkable is that women's discourse has succeeded in creating conditions in which women can assert themselves as human subjects with a distinct experience but without this knowledge of themselves being used to oppress them further. The success of Saudi women writers lies in their ability to redefine women in such a way that they can no longer be perceived as belonging to a homogeneous category, one that can be easily manipulated for purposes of control.

Redefining women and politicizing women's lives has had serious implications in terms of limiting the exercise of power over women. While victimization literature allows the display of power, the publication of women's experiences has had the effect of limiting the dominant power by expressing the counter power of problematization.[1] By high-

lighting the diversity of women's experiences the writers have problema-
tized "the woman" as a category to the point where she becomes so
enigmatic that centers of power no longer know how to control her.
The assumptions of the inadequacy and deficiency of women that were
treated as indisputable truths are revealed to be just that—assumptions.
Many men are still dealing with the shocking idea of "realizing"
women, and are generally unsure of how to work out this transformation
of women from being regarded as symbols to being looked upon as real
people. Judging from men's response, which reveals a sense of discovery, fascination, puzzlement, and at times sympathy or even identification with the woman's experience, it seems that the long period of
treating women as a category by discourses of power has produced self-
deception rather than enlightenment.

Men as Women's Mates and Inmates: *Equality in Oppression*

Women's insistence on achieving the realization of women by escaping
the prison of symbolism is matched only by the challenge they take in
walking the fine line between difference and opposition in fostering
relations of alliance with men. Despite the various ways in which men
are portrayed and discussed in the selections presented here, one of the
striking characteristics of these women's writings, both in tone and
content, is the prevalence of conciliatory language and the lack of
antagonism or confrontation with men. In fictional as well as in nonfictional forms, and in their definition of issues as well as in their general
approach, men emerge—whether in the articles of Juhayer, Fatna, or
Sohaila, in the stories of Najwa, Sharifa, Khayriyya, or Ruqayya, in the
poems of Fowziyya or the plays of Rajaa—as indispensable parts of the
world that these writers aspire to create.

Arabian women writers not only do not see "the man" as the oppressor but they vindicate him. When men are portrayed as victimizing
women, they are usually portrayed as "a" man, not "the" man, and
forces outside are highlighted as the causes of his actions (i.e., societal
norms of honor and shame, arranged marriages, and so on). At times
these women use affectionate language toward men and remind them of
how they are needed in women's lives as husbands, fathers, and sons.
For these women, man, in the words of Juhayer, is an "unknown

continent," which establishes him as an object of discovery rather than one of antagonism. In fact, these women often encourage men to engage in a mutual discovery of the opposite sex—a discovery that has been hindered by the mazes and webs in which their social existences have been entangled.

Their conception of man establishes him not only as a needed mate but also as a victimized "inmate." The connection between contemporary man and contemporary woman springs from the fact that both were "betrayed" by forces of time and place. They unite not only in their struggle to combat the forces that oppress them as human beings but in their shared experiences of "labor," "birth," and "anger." This view of men as society's victims, similar to the victimization of women, generates a sense of "equality" between men and women. In a subtle way, this implies that men are not qualified to stand as models for women or to be imitated. This helps explain why the Western concept of equality between men and women holds little value for Arab women, and also explains why the notion of such equality has been met with ridicule and viewed as a "lie."[2] For these women, it is almost inconceivable to envy men.

Patriarchy Versus Patriarchal Discourse: The Traffic in Words about Women

Women writers' view of men as mates and inmates stands in stark contrast to the dominant discourse's antagonistic language about women. The men's dominant discourse on women reflects a tendency to assert woman's deficiency, and to shoulder her with the responsibility for social problems. The factors that contribute to this antagonism are related to political, religious, and popular discourses. The shift from a tribal society to a modern state has undermined the traditional individual male function of protector as a member of a tribe, not only vis-à-vis other male members but, more important, vis-à-vis women. Men's lack of power was exacerbated by the incorporation of women into the labor force, a move that not only established women's allegiance to the state but posed a challenge to men's function as provider.

Women's writings reveal that relations between the sexes are only partly a product of patriarchal rules. Women writers' tendency to locate forces of oppression outside the dyadic relations between men and women is a reflection of their social approach to societal problems. Patriarchy, in their view, is only one of the techniques used by the centers of power to control both men and women in the power game. Their writings suggest an important distinction that has to be made between patriarchy as a social fact and patriarchy as ideology used for the purpose of control. Scholars researching the Arabian Peninsula and Muslim women have contended that patriarchy is a salient feature of Arab societies, and have treated it as a concrete social fact.[3] This questionable characterization of the Arab social structure as patrilineal and patriarchal centers on the premise that men determine the organization of society.[4] As a result, women were and are depicted as isolated from men, as passive actors in the so-called public domain, as confined to their kin groups, and so on.[5]

Among the theoreticians of patriarchy, however,[6] Gayle Rubin (1975) has come closest to identifying the ideological function of patriarchy as distinctive from its use as an all-embracing explanatory social fact. She points out that patriarchy should be treated as a specific form of male dominance and its use should be confined to the Old Testament-type of pastoral nomads from which the term originated. Rubin contends that the power of males is not founded on their roles as fathers or patriarchs but rather on their "collective adult maleness" (Rubin 1975:168). In the context of the contemporary society of Arabia, like elsewhere in the world, while patriarchal practices, in which individual males assert their power over individual females, do exist, it is that "collective adult maleness" that constitutes a driving discursive force, reflecting the collective need to control society in and through women. Patriarchy—whether practiced on the collective or individual level—is mediated by the fact that it is men who control other men, but through women. The patriarchal discourse acquires its ideological force because it satisfies the need for power of religious leaders, the state, and individual men. On the one hand, where religious leaders perceive women to be the floodgate to Western influence, control of women also becomes useful to the state, if only because it ensures that the male half of the population is in charge of the female half. The religious ideology stipulates that "men are in charge of women," but men respond in diverse ways to this stipulation. Some men see this as a privilege; others, however, find it burdensome in that their powerlessness is

274 Conclusions and Implications

compounded by their responsibility for another being who is equally powerless. The patriarchal ideology may be sustained either because it serves some men's psychological need for power or because of the social incentives of the high status rewarded to those who acquire the skill of controlling women. For example, men's zeal to conceal women is usually justified as protection for women, but it can also be seen as a means by which a man protects his honor and through which he maintains his social prestige vis-à-vis other males.

In the patriarchal discourse, patriarchy need not be maintained in real interpersonal relations between men and women in order for it to be effective on the discursive level. For in this particular instance, men acquire social prestige and status not through "trafficking" in women but rather through trafficking in words about women.[7] This is in line with Ong's and Strathern's proposition that gender need not be the primary organizational factor in society but rather an idiom for other kinds of social differentiations, such as social prestige and status ranking (Ong 1987; Strathern 1981).

Realities of Segregation and Socialization: Fostering Women's Loyalty and Independence

My contention that patriarchy is maintained more on the level of discourse than on the level of dyadic relations between men and women is based both on Saudi women writers' tendency to speak amicably about men in general and my own observations of relatively young Saudi couples themselves. I found the relationships among the couples of my acquaintance to be extremely affectionate and I was indeed impressed by the extent to which the husband considered and yielded to his wife's desires. These observations, supported by evidence from women's writings, suggests that the more functions of control are invested in patriarchal discourse, the less patriarchy is realized on the level of personal relations between men and women, and the more it diminishes in importance and loses its power as a social fact. This proposition requires further research, however. Here, I focus on one type of relationship between men and women, namely, that between women and their fathers as depicted in women's writings, with my own supplementary observations when possible.

This exercise is intended both to throw more light on the ideological nature of the patriarchal discourse and to explain the absence of opposition to men in general in the writings of Saudi women. My emphasis is on three points. First, the realities of physical segregation have precluded competition between men and women and have thus minimized antagonism. In this situation the man becomes an unknown "continent" that women aspire to discover. The second point has to do with women's early socialization, in which men as fathers and as brothers are present in the girls' lives as sources of unconditional love and support. Third, women's loyalty to various cultural institutions can be explained in terms of this early socialization that later plays an essential role in binding these women not only to their fathers but also to their culture as a whole.

The reality of segregation, by virtue of its removal of men from the world of women as potential competitors, has also imbued women with the power of relative independence and self-assurance. Segregation has, in many vital ways, contributed to the development of women's personalities so as to emphasize the qualities of independence and interdependence. While women have constituted a world of their own, segregation has not prevented them from knowing what happens in the outside world nor has it prevented them from affecting the outside world in many crucial areas.[8] While competition between women can by no means be minimized given the existence of polygynous marriages, even within this institution women develop networks of support and of informational exchange.

Decades ago Clara Thompson, an American psychoanalyst, pointed out that in the context of a competitive society, women hate to be women because it is disadvantageous to be a woman. Not only does competition stimulate envy but women also have to be competitive and, in order to succeed, have to adopt men's attributes (Thompson 1971). This has not been the case in Saudi Arabia. Saudi women, writers as well as nonwriters, not only express their unwillingness to emulate maleness but also take pride in being women. In fact, in my ten years of observing Saudi women students in American universities living independently and away from their families, I have always been impressed by their strength, endurance, and self-assuredness, as well as their self-assertion. The relative ease with which they make the transition from one way of life to another that is markedly different, with its new sets of demands and expectations, is remarkable, not only in comparison with other Arab women who were socialized to more relaxed rules of segregation but also by American standards of self-reliance and independence. Sex segregation is precisely the training ground for women's empowerment.

Within the context of Saudi sex segregation, only male family members, such as fathers, brothers, and to some extent uncles on both sides, play a part in a girl's initial socialization. Men outside this circle are virtually unknown to the female. Even after marriage, women's only interaction with men, with the exception of her husband's family, remains within the same circle. Although boys are more desired, girls, once they arrive in the world, are treated with the utmost love and affection. Based on my observations of Saudi families both inside Saudi Arabia and abroad, the use of physical punishment for young girls, or even a harsh scolding, is found generally contemptible. In most cases the girls' demands are gladly met by their fathers, and their desires play an essential role in the planning of many family affairs, including travel. I have encountered various scenes in parks and markets of little girls holding tightly to their father's *thobes,* and of fathers spending time, energy, and money trying to please their endearing little "princesses."

Feeling loved and consequential, these girls grow up with self-esteem, self-assertiveness, and able to appreciate their desires and choices. Until recently, Makkan women were raised and prepared to succeed in their fathers' or brothers' vocational pursuits, especially that of *ṭiwafa* (making *hajj* arrangements). As *muṭawwifa,* the woman assumes responsibility for organizing the annual pilgrimage for groups of Muslim men and women coming from various parts of the world. Although male family members usually help, the task demands that the woman, in addition to knowing the religious rules, is highly competent in the management of travel, accommodation, food, and health care. Although women's participation in this institution has dwindled considerably during the last decade, scores of women throughout the country engage today in many other business ventures.

In spite of this, situations still exist in which young women are treated not only unkindly but even with outright cruelty and violence. Even in women's writing, fathers are often depicted as being cruel to their daughters. The daughter's relationship to the family is altered most significantly at puberty. Until she reaches puberty, a daughter's treatment as a child is subject to much parental love and affection. After puberty, however, treatment of a daughter must correspond to the cultural realities of honor and shame. The rules that govern the relationship of a daughter to her father become conditioned by the extent to which the daughter makes an effort to preserve family honor. It is as if, because the family has proven its love for the girl throughout her childhood years, she must now prove her love for the family by preserving its honor. In her adult years, the value of the woman as a symbol of honor emerges as the overarching principle. The victimization of women, which may reach such drastic measures as death in cases related to what is defined as honor crimes, can be partly understood as a response to a deep sense of betrayal and the "social death" a female inflicts on her family for generations to come if she breaks a cultural rule that stipulates that no one and nothing is above family honor.

Outside these parameters, women writers depict a relationship between fathers and daughters that is characterized by admiration and gratitude, if not awe. Whether in fiction or in their own book dedications, they show their deep attachment to their father and acknowledge their father's support.[9] This attachment, formed in the early years of a girl's socialization, may lie behind the women writers' general lack of radical critique of their culture, and their tendency to retain a degree of loyalty to it, whereby even when they attempt to change it, they still affirm its basic institutions and assumptions. It seems as if the love and affection girls receive early in their lives work to mitigate the outside constraints placed on them. This attachment to their fathers is later transferred to an attachment to the culture as a whole.

Questioning Social Institutions as a Form of Affirmation

This attachment to their culture is evident in the manner in which women approach social institutions in their society, especially those by which they are seen to be controlled. It seems only logical that when they vindicate men and accuse society, their target should be social institutions. As cultural critics, these Arabian women writers are, by definition, in a position to question the premises on which cultural institutions are based. However, they only question certain institutions, not others. In the case of those institutions that enjoy the support of the

political or religious structures, women writers have to move within a
compass that defines what they can say, how much they can say, and
the way in which it must be said. For example, their texts say little and
speak with caution on such issues as polygyny, class cleavages along
economic and tribal lines, disparity in the distribution of wealth and
the monopoly of wealth and power by a small group, the nonparticipa-
tory nature of the political system, the presence of Western oil experts
and oil companies in Arabia, and the direction and goal of Islamic
revivalism as related to the direction of the culture as a whole.

Tribalism is also rarely addressed directly in a way that highlights its
complex social, political, and economic components. At times it appears
in women's writings, mainly in fiction, as a hindrance to women's
pursuit of happiness in relation to the choice of marriage partners, not
as a problem of class distinction. By the same token, poverty may
appear in the background of some of their fiction but is portrayed as
something of the past. The issues of contemporary cultural obsession
with the accumulation of wealth or the existence of corruption, when
addressed, present the economic field as an arena that is equally open to
all, deemphasizing the monopoly of the few as something inherent in
the system itself.

Aside from these issues, these women writers are constantly engaged
in a critique of the social institutions by which women are controlled.
Regardless of their ideological orientation or degree of conservatism,
women's proposals for change are essentially made within the established social institutions, such as family, marriage, birth, and even
veiling and sex segregation. This loyalty naturally furnishes them with
the right and legitimacy to speak, but traditional institutions do in fact
form an important part of the world they paint for themselves.

In their endeavor, they direct their attention toward uncovering the
ideological presuppositions that underlie these institutions. The process
of change in their society has created a tension between form and
content, plaguing their existence with severe contradictions and incon-
gruities. The result is that certain forms have been preserved while their
content has been altered, or vice versa. This phenomenon, previously
referred to as the "collage" culture, occurs on various levels—from the
form of government and the political system, to religion, the economy,
the family, and marriage. These women's writings, while exacerbating
a sense of incoherence in their universe, advance a critique of social

institutions without denying the premises on which they are based. Rather, they generally accept these premises but focus their arguments on how conclusions drawn by the makers of dominant discourse to justify women's oppression are inadequately supported by these premises themselves. For example, the emphasis on preserving the institution of the family is so strong that they do not challenge this institution either in reality or in fiction. Severing family relations is never advocated. To be sure, neither *family (usra)* nor *motherhood (u'mouma)* is seen in their writing as negative words.[10] Even when family life is portrayed as infested with troubling conflicts, "the family" manages to escape persecution. Troubles in the family, as depicted in their fiction, are usually attributed to some other social institution to which blame is directed. For example, family conflicts are seen as resulting from the woman not "knowing" the man she was obliged to marry, and arranged incompatible marriage is seen as setting in motion a vicious chain of cause and effect from failed marriages that can last for generations.

Given this criticism of arranged incompatible marriage, one might think that it would naturally lead to a critique of the institutions of segregation and concealment, which prevent the woman from "knowing" the man. But these latter institutions are seldom explicitly treated, and writers never suggest their abolition—such ideas are either left at the implicit level or not suggested at all. As a result, it is never clear how a woman could get to "know" a man before marriage within a system of segregation and concealment. That writers provide no clues is testimony to how sensitive the issue is to religious leaders. The growing tendency for segregation and veiling to stand as symbols of distance from Western culture and its norms also charges the issue with much emotional import. But one should not ignore the fact that women writers possibly view segregation as a means of autonomy and empowerment, if only because it provides women, as a collective group, with a world of their own.

The institution of physical concealment in public, as manifested in veiling, is criticized even less than segregation. The *abaya* is not portrayed as a restriction on their freedom but rather as the key to women's accessibility to the public field. But other reasons account for why women have not severely criticized the institution of concealment. Judging by my own experience with veiling while in Saudi Arabia, I can attest to the sense of power and control a woman feels in having the advantage of being the seer, not the seen. Both men and women recognize this advantage of the *abaya,* and it has led women writers to frequently assert its existence in their texts, either to indicate a setting (i.e., that events are taking place in Saudi Arabia) or to symbolize oppression in relation to its black color, rather than to complain about its restrictive function. In many writings by women, the *abaya* emerges as being good in reality but bad in its symbolic meaning.

Civilizational Challenge and Global Discourses of Power

Edward Said's *Orientalism* (1978) has opened the door for inquiries in the domain of civilizational challenge and response in which "the other" (in his case the Muslim and Arab Orient) becomes integral to the structure of knowledge in the West. Said pinpoints the ideological function embedded in intercultural politics through his concept of "positional superiority."[11] Laura Nader (1989) extends Said's main argument that the Muslim world exists "for" the West and argues that, inversely, the West also exists "for" the Muslim world. Drawing on internal discourses of religious interpretations in Egypt and global discourses of modernization, Nader shows how images of women in other societies can be prejudicial to women in one's own society. Eastern constructions, she points out, are dependent on Western constructions for purposes of control, especially of women who are key figures in the construction and deconstruction of both civilizations.

Nader's model of explaining gender constructions as a result of interactions between two world civilizations acquires importance in the study of women in Arabia because the processes of resistance in which Arabian women writers are engaged are linked to the particular response of their culture to the West.[12] One characteristic of their writings is the tendency to be critical of the West and its ideals about women. These women either explicitly criticize the West or implicitly deemphasize its ideals. Whatever form their critique takes, a common thread in their writings is the general lack of recognition of the tenets of Western feminism and its ideals of equality and the liberation of women.

Their resistance to adopting Western ideals and their emphasis on differences from the West is naturally reassuring of these women's loyalty to religion and tradition. But resistance to Western ideals, while it may be viewed as symptomatic of constraints placed on women or as a tactic to ensure a degree of acceptability of their messages, is in fact a fundamental part of their thought. For their discourse is neither a reaction to Western discourse nor to the local discourses but rather an autonomous enterprise readily distinguishable from both. Far from being a blind negation of local or global discourses of power, as women they are faced with a fundamental difference in definition and conceptualizations of problems, as well as a difference in philosophical traditions and the specific cultural premises from which these traditions sprang.

In the Western definition of problems that face women in Saudi Arabia, veiling and segregation are seen as important indicators of their restricted existence. In fact, those who chronicle the emergence of feminism and women's resistance in the area usually mark it by those events in which women had engaged in a public defiance of veiling.[13] The "issue" of Muslim woman's veiling takes on such an importance for Westerners that Saudi women—even the most Westernized—are often puzzled by the outpouring of pity that comes to them from the West. (Westerners are perhaps equally puzzled by Arabian women's constant defense of the Islamic codes of modesty, including the veil). In fact, Muslim women see the emphasis on "un"-veiling women in Western culture as a reflection of seeing women as physical beings that must constantly be exhibited.

One possible reason for their puzzlement is perhaps the fact that, in the Arabian context, men are expected to observe the same codes of modesty as women, except perhaps for the covering of the face emphasized by the Wahhabis. Although the man has more freedom to slip into a Western costume in public, men still choose to wear the Arabian dress, which for men consists of a long *thobe,* an *'abaya,* and a headdress. These pieces cover the man—literally—from head to toe, and are basically no different than women's clothing except in color and design. Yet no Westerners, neither men nor women, make any conscious attempt to "unveil" the Arabian man!

Arabian women writers rarely define veiling as a problem or give it much recognition in their writings. But why, within Arabia itself, where women are already veiled and where veiling enjoys the support of religion and tradition and even of women themselves, has veiling become an issue—if not "the" issue—around which women are discussed by the religious discourse? Ironically, the Arabian internal discourse converges with the external Western discourse in viewing veiling as the defining characteristic of Muslim women. This is because the religious discourse takes cues from the West on what Islam is all about. That the West takes special interest in destroying the institution of veiling leads the religious discourse to emphasize it even further as a symbol of civilizational survival.

While for the West the Saudi woman is seen to be held captive by or in the name of Islam, for Saudi internal discourses she is seen as a prey to be swallowed by the West. The cultural concern about women as the "gate" of Westernization has led to cultural discourses on gender that derive their power from the imperatives of resistance to Western encroachment rather than from Islamic principles themselves. The power of this response is such that what came to be defined as Islamic is in relation to negative identification with Western ideals, rather than to its own ideals. Islam becomes restrictive of whatever the West permits and not necessarily of what Islam itself forbids. This has led to a definition of Islam that is contrived if only because it is idealized to fit new ideological needs.[14] Even what came to be defined as Islamic fundamentalism has more to do with the cultural crisis that resulted from Western domination than a revival of the fundamentals of Islam itself. For example, if in the West, women's education, work outside the home, or independence and autonomy are propagated as the ideal, then a "true" Islamic view of women would have to move away from such ideals even though the Qur'an not only condoned but also celebrated women who displayed such qualities.

The veil becomes such a charged issue because the West cheers for those women who abandon the veil. This is because, as Fanon points out, it gives the West a sense of victory over Islam. Because unveiling was considered a type of "conversion," a victory for the West, the resistance of the Muslims becomes centered around those elements by which the West defines "conversion." Here Fanon, with his humanistic depth and insight, teaches us an important lesson in the subtle ways in which Western dominant discourses of power shape the response of the dominated: "It was the colonialist's frenzy to unveil the Algerian woman, it was his gamble on winning the battle of the veil at whatever cost, that were to provoke the native's bristling resistance" (Fanon 1965:46–47).

The historical precedence set by the French has established the tone for a type of relationship between the dominant West and the Muslim world in which a strategy of targeting women has consistently been adopted. Women become the key to controlling the whole culture. Unveiling and mobilizing women outside the home were the means the French chose to accomplish their dominance over the Algerian people. Even more serious is the fact that the colonialists have also posited themselves as "defenders" of the Algerian woman. In so doing, the French set a mechanism in motion by which a type of relationship has emerged between Algerian men and Algerian women in which the definition of "the problem" for the man becomes nothing less than the Algerian woman herself, and vice versa.

Saudi women writers' unacceptance of Western propositions are linked to these historical facts. By rejecting the Western definition of their problem as veiling, they are not driven by blind loyalty to their culture but rather exhibit an acute awareness of the dynamics of relationships between their world and the world of "the other." They sabotage the attempts of Westerners to act as their "defenders" by simply being in charge of interpreting their own universe. They even go further and abort attempts to define the woman's problem as nothing less than the man himself, by taking a stand toward the man that is devoid of antagonism. And above all, they reject the idea that Islam itself is the agent behind women's oppression, and thus that Islam is an enemy of women. By going back to the texts, they uncover how cultural discourses that emphasize the need to control women derive their power from the imperatives of resistance to Western encroachment rather than from Islam itself.

Women, Religion, and Tradition: Crisis of Interpretation

It is the civilizational challenge that produces a crisis of religious interpretation within the culture itself. Women writers, in their attempt to liberate themselves from both global and local discourses of power, feel the need to first liberate Islam itself from shackles of cultural politics by speaking directly from and to the texts. This has posed a considerable challenge to the religious leaders not only because it breaks their monopoly on religious interpretation but, more important, because it exposes their attempt to reduce religion to its ideological use. By virtue of their knowledge, they are capable of dealing directly with the texts themselves, to elicit the Islamic principles as revealed in the

Book of the Qur'an. They shift the emphasis of the dominant discourse on women as "deficient," which the prophet was believed to have stipulated, to the Qur'anic conception that men and women are complementary to each other, a principle inseparable from justice. In their cry for justice, their emphasis on men and women being complementary to each other based on what each gender possesses rather than what each one lacks was supported by a reference to the Qur'an itself.[15] Authority is no longer invested solely in traditional "interpretations" of the text, since these interpretations more often than not are contaminated with cultural imperatives. Women have challenged the interpretations and legal opinions (*fatwas*) of religious leaders, both in a direct confrontational manner (such as in the case of Juhayer and Shaikh Tantawi) or indirectly through attempts at critiquing or reinterpreting certain concepts that bear on their life experiences.

But the task of religious interpretation has never been a simple rendition of "the fundamentals" of Islam, as revealed in the texts. Rather, it is made more complex by the imposition of the social on the religious, something that is not peculiar to the Wahhabi doctrine nor to Saudi Arabia. As discussed in chapter 4, women writers more or less consciously tend to struggle for their separation and expose how social factors tend to masquerade as religious ones in religious interpretations pertaining to women. In the Saudi society many traditional customs (*'adat*) are justified as religious stipulations (*'ibadāt*). This fusion of the religious concept of *ḥarām* (the religiously condemned act) with the social concept of *'ayb* (the culturally shameful act) is manifested in the *'ulama*'s interpretation of the concept of women as *'owra* and as deficient, of modesty codes, and of notions of honor and shame.

The Qur'an, in speaking of men's and women's creation, states: "We have perfected Our creation of the *insan* [humankind]" (95:4). Whether in the story of the creation or in the stories of more than twenty women mentioned in the Qur'an, women are not described as incomplete or deficient, nor are they spoken of as an abstract category or symbol. Men, as well as women, are spoken about as accountable agents in life with rights, duties, and roles, judged only according to the quality of their performance. Often through their own voice, women are represented as accountable participants in the creation of the history of humankind whether they are portrayed as wise, independent, and knowledgeable (the Queen of Sheba), as believers (the mother of Moses), as miracle carriers (Mary and Sarah [the wife of Abraham]), as desperate lovers (Rachel, in her story with Joseph), as disbelievers (the wives of Lot and Noah), as rebellious (the wife of the Farroah), and so on. In the story of the creation, Eve was presented as a historical personality who fell victim, just as Adam did, to Satan's seduction. According to the Qur'an, Eve was not created from Adam's rib but rather both Adam and Eve were created from "one soul." Her banishment from Eden was not because she was a seducer but rather because she was a participant. Eve was not entirely vindicated in the Qur'an either, precisely because she, as a full human being, bears the responsibility for her actions.

Against this Qur'anic background it becomes all the more remarkable for the women writers that woman is transformed in many religious interpretations to a physical being, who is "deficient," "incomplete,"[16] and who has a "natural" propensity for perversion. Moreover the religious discourse has transformed the woman in her totality into 'owra, which has to be concealed, with the result that restrictions on their mobility have been institutionalized and even religiously justified. But Islam has set modesty codes to be enforced equally on both men and women to allow for a type of interaction between men and women that is free of sexual implications. That is, the original Qur'anic intention in setting modesty standards appears to have been to secure a high degree of participation for Muslim women in social and public life and not to restrict them.[17] The religious leaders become the prime defenders of cultural values that are alien even to the condition of women in the first century of Islam—a period they supposedly see as ideal—a period in which women moved freely and constituted the social backbone during Islam's formative years.

The emphasis on complete concealment and immobility of women in the particular case of Saudi Arabia finds its roots in the Wahhabi doctrine, although the Wahhabis have in fact introduced measures that regained for women their right to inheritance, as well as to free choice in marriage.[18] A vigilant religious police called *mutawwi'* emerged to enforce public compliance—by both men and women—to Islamic prescriptions, such as prayers, fasting, and observing codes of modesty. But this vigilant religious police had the special task of enforcing modesty codes on women in particular. They considered veiling the face a required element of Islamic *hijab,* rather than a function of cultural customs.

The fusion of the *'ayb,* the shameful, as a socially unacceptable act with *ḥarām,* the religiously condemned act, has important and serious religious implications. The concept of shame is a social rather than a religious concept if only because it runs counter to the Qur'anic conception of accountability, which is woman's accountability to God—not to a man or a group of men. From its inception, one of the most challenging tasks Islam faced was to transfer the existing cultural emphasis on the accountability of one human being to other human beings, which constituted the core of the central concept of *'ayb* in pre-Islamic Arabia, to one in which all human beings become accountable to God. This fundamental transformation formed the basis of the social revolution Islam had inaugurated on the peninsula in the seventh century. Because of the fundamental value of the distinction between the social and the religious, the Qur'an continuously warns against confusing what is done to satisfy people with what satisfies God.[19] While requiring the individual to bring the social and the religious into congruity through encouraging good and forbidding evil, ultimately the social has to be subordinated to the religious, not vice versa. The presentation of these social concepts as religious, although false, has the function of imbuing them with considerable controlling power.

Women, History, and the Politics of Concealment and Revelation

Women writers, conscious of the controlling power of the "other" becoming an integral part of cultural construction of gender and of the definition of Islam itself, as well as the power of tradition, are also equally conscious of the controlling power of defining history. The crisis of interpretation in the culture has extended to the interpretation and definition of women's history, making it a subject of the ideological needs and imperatives of control by centers of power. The state, by virtue of its emphasis on integrating women in development programs, uses a comparison with the uneducated unemployed women of the near past. The religious leaders, on the other hand, bring to the forefront leading women of early periods of Islam, but they do so while stressing their incomparability with contemporary women and representing them as an idealized version as if they were a different species—a species with whom contemporary women can find no affinity.

It is this ideological function of control that history performs in contemporary Arabian society that leads women writers to balance the requirements of concealment and revelation of certain historical facts. Speaking directly to remote generations, they introduce reports of witnesses, and confront these reports with each other, even giving precedence to "witnesses in spite of themselves."[20] In constructing their own sense of the past, and in forming their own response to the civilizational conflict, they seem to be geared toward accumulating what Bourdieu (1984) once called "symbolic capital" in order to combat the monopoly over historical interpretation. The nature of the reading these women provide of their cultural and civilizational history, recent as well as that which stretches back for thousands of years, reflects a dialectical relationship that they establish between the past and the present. Women writers make statements on the decline of a civilization that was once known to have led the world, by bringing its traditional heroes, both male and female, to bear on the present. By so doing they advance a cultural critique of their contemporary society in which to examine the relationship between men and women as one manifestation of that decline, and even as one of its causes.

A style of presentation that uses civilizational history is, by definition, a form of affirmation of society's basic values, but at the same time it endows women writers' questioning of present society with legitimacy and wards off accusations of subversion. By recalling historical symbols (mainly but not exclusively women) these authors attempt to redeem their past while using it to transform the present. They use a number of key symbols as a means of remembering, recounting, and learning from that history, turning history to an effective means of empowerment and of gaining plausibility for serious messages. The key status of these symbols is indicated by their recurrence in the literary representations as feminine motifs, metaphors, images, and myths.[21] They are used in many different ways: some are historical symbols that are invested with meaning—either religious, cultural, or political—such as Balqees, the Queen of Sheba; Asma, the daughter of the second Caliph; Zarqa Al-Yamama, the Arabian woman legend whose power of vision was said to be unsurpassed; and Sheherazade, a fictional character who was the heroine of the well-known *One Thousand and One Nights.*

Sheherazade's inexhaustible memory, her use of words to save herself and other women, her wisdom, courage, sacrifice, wit, and imagination, and—more important—her strategy for resistance, are what endow her with special significance for women writers. Sheherazade, by telling her fascinating stories, has chosen a method of resistance through words—a persistent and systematic form of resistance that was aimed at "preserving blood," not shedding it. Unlike Balqees, Sheherazade was not willing to adopt Shahrayar's model of power but pursued her mission of resistance with her own qualities. She worked through long nights to change her destiny. As a result night, in the writings of these women, becomes not a time for romance but rather a time for the exercise of independence, self-confrontation, reflection on history, hard work, and building courage, in a word for making history.

These models are also not difficult to imitate. Except for Balqees, the Queen of Sheba, these models were mostly ordinary women who held no positions of formal power but changed history in a profound way without adopting men's model of power. Saudi women writers revive a whole tradition of women making their mark on history through their own qualities of vision, their ability to see what is beyond, through their memory, their nurturing, and their sacrifice, through the very qualities they possess as women. By redefining which figures should be remembered and revived, and reworking them into models for action, they break the historical silence over their history.

The silence on women's history and the alienation of women from their own heritage, which is promoted by the centers of power, has the serious consequences of depriving women from drawing confidence from their tradition and disrupting the flow of continuity that links contemporary women with their predecessors. Whether by ignoring or by idealizing women of the past to the point where they no longer serve as models for action, the result is that contemporary women demonstrate a minimal affinity with the accomplishment of women of the past. To diminish the affinity of contemporary women with their predecessors is bound to have serious consequences. Given the civilizational challenge of the West, and the belief that it can only win through women, it sets the stage for placing women of the present in a greater degree of affinity with their Western contemporaries rather than with their own history. This historical void gives legitimacy to the religious discourse's claim that contemporary women are influenced by the West, thus heightening the need to control women. Women writers' manipulation of historical symbols is used as a political strategy for resistance of this hegemony over time. This point should also be considered in understanding why

Arabian women writers felt the need to dissociate themselves from the West and to emphasize that they are not inspired by Western women in their critique of their own cultural practices.

The Feminism Question: The Arabian Answer— Bridging Discourses

Within a context in which Saudi women writers themselves question Western concepts of liberation and equality, there is an inherent difficulty in any attempt to impose Western labels, such as feminism, on their endeavor. What happens when the axioms of their resistance are based on different premises than the Western feminist advocacy of boundaries or separatism? Is there a way to think outside these predetermined categories? Any attempt to bridge the discourse of the Arabian women writers with that of Western feminism is faced with the problem of adequate language and adequate theory that are more capable of conceptualizing realities other than or "outside" the Western world than what exists today in the social sciences.[22] Although both Arabian and Western women aspire to outline a theory of liberation from the webs of discourses of power, the philosophical traditions and the cultural presuppositions in which the enterprise of Saudi women writers is rooted and the conceptual apparatus by which they are maintained are fundamentally different than those from which Western feminism sprang. In fact, they also differ from Arab feminism which is viewed by some of these writers (chapter 4) as uncritical in its adoption of the Western model, and even was made a subject of mockery as a form of imitation of the West rather than as a genuine movement.[23]

To begin with, feminism as a concept not only does not exist in Saudi women's writing but even as a word has no Arabic translation. The concept of female (the biological woman) exists in Arabic (*untha*), and as in English denotes the sex rather than the gender (the latter being *mar'aa*, or woman). The closest translation of the word *feminism* into Arabic would be *unthawiyya*, which defines the woman not as a social being but rather as a biological being.[24] This would constitute an ironic transformation of the idea of feminism itself, because in the West feminism is driven, at least in most of its versions, by the desire to emphasize the social aspect of the woman rather than the biological.[25] Ironically, the emphasis on the social in Western feminist thought was accompanied by a self-defeating tendency aimed at placing the feminine body at the basis of defining self and at the core of women's identity.[26]

Despite the different points of contention exhibited in Western feminist movements, they all share a general preoccupation with the psychological separateness and autonomy of women.[27] Chodorow points out that these tendencies are ingrained in Western culture's notions of individualism, selfhood, and separation. She posits a relationship between these notions and gender differentiation, pointing out that the notion of difference in the West is based on the notion of separation, because separation is seen as the core of a notion of self in Western culture (Chodorow 1985:11; see also 3–19). Even the notion of equality is related to the notion of self in Western culture, "where self is opposed to other, where society has to be protected from the encroachment of the individual" (Nelson and Olesen 1977:26).

One also has to take into account that Western feminism's assertion that women are different than men has arisen as a form of resistance to the concept of "lack," which, although manifested socially, is believed to be based on immutable female physical attributes. The philosophy of lack has mainly been engendered on the psychological level by Freud, and on the social level by Marx. As theoreticians of conflict par excellence, they both posited conflict—whether personal or societal—as perpetual, and engendered a notion of lack based on defining human relations in negative and oppositional terms: those who have and those who do not. Promoting a notion of difference based on the qualities that each human being possesses is not a matter of semantic difference but rather one that has far-reaching implications on all dimensions of human relations. The notion of lack promotes a cycle of perpetual feelings of inadequacy, and results in competition, hierarchy, individualism, and opposition (Thompson 1971).

The valuable insight Saudi writers bring us is that physical segregation from men has different consequences than psychological separation. This distinction affects the main concepts developed to study Middle Eastern women. The institution of sex segregation has led many scholars to equate the seclusion of women with their exclusion from society. This has led to the deployment of such concepts as "public" and "private" to explain the working dynamics of the society.[28] The dual concept of public/private was first developed as a universal dichotomy (Rosaldo and Lamphere 1974). However, it took a special hold in the studies of Muslim-Arab societies because of the convenience the segregation of sexes provided for its application (Nelson 1974). Taking the spatial segregation of sexes as a point of departure, the studies proceeded to clarify the various implications of the public/private concept on the power of women either as a function of their separation from men or in spite of it.[29]

Whether seen as oppositional or complementary, as conducive to more power for women or to a greater powerlessness, the dual concept of public/private was treated as a reality, just like patriarchy, not as an ideological construct or an instrument of control for dominant ideologies. In the Arabian context, while women's seclusion may have restricted their participation in certain domains of action deemed by Westerners as more "indicative" of "freedom and power" (i.e., being performed in the so-called public sphere which is not gender-segregated), it has not resulted in their exclusion from performing various types of ideological functions, especially through institutions that are in charge of the creation of culture and of institutionalizing consciousness such as literature. In fact, pervasive sex segregation has in almost no period in Arabic/Islamic history been a factor in excluding women from the production of various forms of thought—by definition a public sphere.

Transcending Gender: Reflection, Consciousness, and Action

The question of consciousness and consciousness-raising has been an important component of the Western notions of feminism and resistance (McWilliams 1974). The question of consciousness is problematic, not only because it is hard to measure but also because one should draw a distinction between reflection, consciousness, and action. Habermas points out that a general intensification of reflexivity does not necessarily mean an intensification of consciousness; rather, it may lead to increasing alienation (Habermas 1987). The intensification of the religious and historical discourses in Arabia that provides a contrived version of both is a good example of such an alienating process. Keohane and Gelpi make a useful distinction between three types of consciousness; feminine, female, and feminist. The feminine "involves consciousness of oneself as the object of attention of another; . . . the woman as defined by a male gaze"; the female centers on "the experience of women in giving and preserving life"; and the feminist consciousness develops as a consequence of women "reflect[ing] on women's experience, and on the asymmetries in power, opportunity, and situation" (1982:ix–x).

Arabian women writers exhibit a degree of all three types of consciousness by their awareness of the positions from which they speak, by their being the objects of others' scrutiny, and by the uses to which their words are put. In their naming and publication of women's private experiences, they emphasize the power of reflection as manifested in their use of stream of consciousness in their fiction, and their general use of words as a means of engendering consciousness. But within their enterprise, the tendency has been for theoretical as well as ideological, organizational, and cultural considerations to override or transcend the question of gender, with an inherent possibility of crippling the ability both to act and express consciousness as a group. In the absence of an embracing framework that brings them together as women writers, it is difficult, if not altogether impossible, for them to enact together any concerted effort. In fact only a small number of them are acquainted on a personal level, and mostly from attending gatherings in women's associations. This general lack of association has been the result of both personal and ideological differences, as well as the absence of any means to further any association (when suggested, the idea of a literary club for women was vehemently attacked by conservatives). But this absence of association may be a blessing in disguise, in that it maintains for them a status of relative independence and shields them from the hegemony of the dominant discourses of power. Absence of organization not only makes these women look or sound harmless but also, with some exceptions, may make their control and containment by centers of power difficult.

Beyond personal reasons and a lack of means, a concerted effort by these women is essentially undermined by the fact that in their enterprise ideology takes precedence over gender. Although they fall mostly in the middle of a continuum between right and left, some of the writers can be placed closer to either end.[30] Because various forces in society are competing for these women's services, many times women, despite their inclincations, are relegated to one group or another. Competition for their services, although they can use as a means of granting them more autonomy, and it occasionally does, often works to disparage their shared feeling of being a community of women writers. Saudi women writers are divided along ideological lines and can easily be set against one another (an example of which was discussed in chapter 4). Another example can be drawn from the battle of modernism versus traditionalism, in which some women were "positioned" to serve the ideological purposes of the contending groups who, more often than not, demonstrate little sensitivity to the plight of women.

If social and ideological reasons are not enough to divide these women, an even more compelling reason that undermines gender consciousness is theory. Women writers' view of gender within a social theory of change contributes to the weakening of women being unified as women. That they see women's issues not as separate but rather as a viable part of a larger discourse of power places them in a difficult dilemma. In order for these women to reach wider relations of power, they have to transcend and override gender. In fact, even when these women attempt to assert female qualities, they tend to highlight the notion of difference from each other as women in an attempt not to fall back on the notion of femaleness.

Theoretical Reflections on Dialectics of Protest and Affirmation

As can be seen, whatever their theoretical or ideological leanings are, women writers choose to use strategies of conciliation, appropriation, and compromise over clear-cut opposition to existing relations of power or to men as a category. This poses problems for conceptualizing their enterprise as a form of resistance. I contend here, however, that this strategy not only enables them to form a discourse of their own but, more important, enables them to gain access into the field of cultural politics in general, and hence to transform the entire cultural discourse in a most fundamental way.

Early attempts to explain the relationship of power and resistance, especially but not exclusively within feminist theories, have tended to focus on the clear-cut oppositional practices that are aimed at the destruction of power; these efforts have also assumed a concerted and conscious effort toward separation and autonomy.[31] More recently, feminist scholars have increasingly tended to give cognizance to the diverse ways in which power, as well as resistance, manifest themselves and shape women's lives although oppositional language has not entirely disappeared.[32]

Another tendency Abu-Lughod pointed out is "to romanticize resistance, to read all forms of resistance as signs of the ineffectiveness of systems of power" (Abu-Lughod 1989:42). A conceptualization of resistance based on neither opposition and separation nor on vulnerabilities of power structures is best illustrated by Foucault who sees the flow of power as multidirectional, that is, it can be exercised on everyone and by everyone.[33]

Foucault's "analytics of power" is also merited by its emphasis on the plurality of forms and even the contradictory functions of resistance, where it may reinforce and support power or may function as an adversary, undermining and exposing it, or even do both. In its functioning in these contradictory capacities, resistance need not be a "reaction or rebound . . . an underside that is in the end always passive, doomed to perpetual defeat" (Foucault 1978:95–96). Far from being a passive reaction to discourses of power, the Saudi women writers carve out a discourse of their own that is culturally and politically effective precisely because it is "formed right at the point where relations of power are exercised" (Gordon 1980:142).

Although some forms of resistance that Saudi women writers choose are based on supporting certain institutions and thus appear to be supportive of power, others are in reality undermining power. To be sure, the victimization literature of Saudi women writers (see chapter 4) is a recognition of power if only by allowing it to display itself through a system of discipline and punishment as manifested in the women's writers' tendency to sentence the resisting women characters to madness or death. But Saudi women writers tend to undermine power by the use of what may be called the "strategy of measured challenge and response." Given the nature of Saudi cultural concerns about women, measured challenge and response become an effective form of resistance because it takes into account two facts. First, resistance, if too organized and apparent, may spark alarm and lead to increasing oppression. It can also be incorporated into the structure of existing power as an agency through which power is displayed. Second, if resistance is too masked or hidden, it may be incorporated as a means by which the dominant discourse displays its tolerance for opposite views and may confuse this tolerance with participation.

The need of the structures of power to incorporate resistance as a means by which to hide their oppressive nature has been recognized by several scholars in the context of European cultures. Foucault has asserted throughout his works that power can only be effective when it is concealed and hidden. Bourdieu finds in this concealment of power the means by which dominant groups accumulate the "symbolic capital" necessary for domination (Bourdieu 1984). Williams points out that, in the context of nineteenth-century England, dominant structures were required to incorporate the working-class writings and the radical popular press in their strategies, and also found it advantageous to do so (Williams 1977:124). Habermas theorizes that this need of power structures for resistance to perform this function of concealing power leads centers of power to what he calls "the institutionalization of continuing reflection" (Habermas 1975:127–29).

This notion of "continuing reflection" is especially important because it captures the essence of power as being mainly double-edged. For while continuing reflection is institutionalized as proof of the extended scope of tolerance and to perpetuate the existing power relations, it also functions in a way that is antithetical to the intentions of the dominant power structures, carrying the seeds of its destruction. The double-edged nature of "continuing reflection" springs from the fact that it leads to an active interpretation of tradition and to the creation of "Hermeneutic consciousness." Hermeneutic consciousness, which involves interpretation of tradition, is an ironic process that has unpredictable consequences. For in the process, interpreting tradition becomes in itself destructive to its "naturelike character," although tradition itself is still retained at a reflective level (Habermas 1975:70).

By virtue of their participation in a symbolic discourse, the Saudi women writers play an important role in intensifying this hermeneutic consciousness. Their interpretation of religion and tradition is, by definition, an assertion of power over a text. The "naturelike character" of tradition, both sacred and secular, is challenged not only by continuing reflection on it but, more important, because women have redefined the traditional structure of authority in terms of who and what can or cannot be considered an authority. Their appeal to the authority of texts first and foremost has gained the status of "truth" for their claims, and lent force to their arguments. It enabled them to uncover the many fallacies embedded in the religious leaders' inversion of Islamic concepts to suit their needs of control and their confusion of the secular culture with the religious precepts. Women's persistent attempts to disentangle these concepts is revealing of the powerful impact of their confusion on women's lives.

Another important consequence of women's participation in hermeneutic consciousness is that it functions in a way that undermines the "suppression of generalizable interests," a strategy the centers of power use to shift social conflicts to the level of psychic problems, charging them to individuals as private matters (Habermas 1975:19, 129). Habermas speaks of this strategy in the context of a broader process of increasing privatization that accompanies modernity, which is found in other societies. But in the particular case of Saudi women writers' enterprise, it is manifested in the tendency of male commentators to push women's experiences back into the domain of the private. As discussed in chapter 5, women writers face the challenge of preventing their "published" matters from becoming "public" matters by means of a systematic discrediting of women's knowledge and an invalidation of their experiences by relegating them to the private. The imperatives of control have shifted the emphasis from "the woman as private" yet a subject of public discourse to a situation in which the products of women's minds, which are made public, are privatized with the objective of putting women back in "their place."

This drive to privatize women's products is further aided by a "language game," based on recognizing certain rules to determine the intelligibility and truth of the message, and the sincerity and legitimacy of the speaker (Habermas 1975:xvi, xvii). In the case of the Saudi women writers, when one of these rules (i.e., intelligibility of message, sincerity of speaker) becomes problematic or is called into question, truth claims are denied, discredited, and relegated to the private, often with accusations of subversion and even perversion. But these attempts at privatization are ultimately defeated because hermeneutic consciousness, by virtue of "stirring up cultural affairs that are taken for granted thus furthers the politicization of areas of life previously assigned to the private sphere" (Habermas 1975:72). Women writers have secured a high degree of politicization of women's lives by highlighting the personal experience of women, and by forging the affinity of the personal and the political. They have become agents of publication of the private, despite efforts to assign them as women and as writers to the private sphere.

When considering the question of consciousness and resistance, one has to take into account a society's self-regulated censorship, in which a version of Bentham's panopticon model of constant surveillance exists. Arabian women—and men—are in what Foucault calls "a state of conscious and permanent visibility that assures the automatic functioning of power" (Foucault 1979:201). The internalization of rules of culture present themselves in different degrees among these writers, but rather than implying an absence of consciousness, this internalization should be seen as a reflection of their being under surveillance. To ensure a safe passage for their message, these women writers seem to be in a constant state of decision making—and probably of compromise— regarding certain elements of storytelling. It is by virtue of this fact that they demonstrate a high degree of creativity in their enterprise, especially in maintaining the balance between social constraints on the spoken and their desire for their literature to be an element of resistance and protest—not only in relation to issues that pertain to women but to other serious issues as well, such as social classes.

Arabian Women Waging Peace

These women's contribution to the construction of their culture must be understood in relation to these and other forces in society that define the scope of institutional constraints on the woman writer as a woman first and as a writer second. Their attempt has not been geared toward showing the emperor without his clothes. Given the modesty codes governing both men and women, such an attempt would have literally and figuratively been met with disdain. Rather, these women show the emperor as being dressed like a clown, in tattered clothes made of ragged patches of old and new material, full of holes and inconsistencies. Their message has been that if the emperor is to be regarded as a true emperor, then he should dress like one.

Although some women writers may at times assume the values and even logic of the dominant discourses about them, they all seek, to different degrees, to undermine the legitimacy of the dominant discourse. The degree of autonomy and independence from that discourse should be assessed in the light of the dialectics of protest and affirmation and the delicate balance of challenge and response. The significance of this strategy lies in its effectiveness in preventing the complete integration of these women into the existing power structure and at the same time guarding against oppressive measures against them.

Their enterprise demonstrates a remarkable ability to carve out a discourse of their own that is part rather than apart, while at the same time resisting attempts at forcing their discourse to an oppositional stand, whether to local or global discourses of power. These women have chosen to wage peace rather than war, a process that is by far more demanding of self-restraint, of wisdom, and of self-discipline. For them, waging peace does not mean romanticizing harmony but rather providing the conditions for justice that in their society is by no means gender specific.

The literary discourse of the Saudi Arabian women should be understood as a "double struggle," an effort to free themselves from both local and global discourses of power, which made of them, as Muslim and Arab women, an object of speaking by others who have taken the tasks of writing, conceptualizing, and discovering the truth about them. In this study they have seized the enterprise of presenting themselves, of defining their problems and their aspirations. In doing so, the Saudi women writers have demonstrated remarkable awareness of the interconnectedness of local and global discourses of power that impact on women. The processes by which they counter the discourses of power are processes that, as Clifford points out, "inform the activity of a people not living alone, but *reckoning* itself among nations" (Clifford 1988: 338 [emphasis mine]).

This study, in its ethnographic, analytic, theoretical, and methodological aims, hopes to contribute to the wider contexts of anthropological scholarship by drawing attention to the valuable knowledge indigenous literature provides us in the study of complex, literate, or civilizational societies. "Anthropological work," Scheper-Hughes points out, "if it is to be in the nature of an ethical and a radical project, is one that is transformative of the self but not . . . transformative of the other. It demands a 'relationship with the other, who is reached *without showing itself touched*' " (Scheper-Hughes 1992:24). Presenting Saudi women writers in their own words is a way of minimizing the transformation of the "other," and an attempt to "reach" them without being "touched," especially by the other's marring—and in many cases dehumanizing—cultural and ideological baggages.[34]

As a case study of the role of Arab women intellectuals in generating consciousness about human conditions in their own society, I hope it inspires new ways of thinking both about Arab women and Arab societies and provides bases for comparative civilizations but especially comparative feminisms. For despite the specificity of their enterprise, Saudi women writers provide a model not only to women but also to other human beings who may be entangled, but should never be paralyzed by the web of discourses about them. Although their response to the forces that impinge on their lives is culturally and historically situated, their model of resistance is a model that is not far removed from Western feminist scholars' own aspirations. Michelle Rosaldo perceived the challenge for feminist theory in "provid[ing] new ways of linking the particulars of women's lives, activities, and goals to inequalities wherever they exist" (Rosaldo 1980:417). M. Strathern expressed the hope that feminist-inspired scholarship in anthropology would "change not just ways of writing about women or about women and men but would change ways of writing about culture and society (Strathern 1988:ix).

But the full theoretical implications of the Arabian model cannot be recognized without remembering an important methodological caveat put forward by Spivak: "The academic feminist must learn to learn from [the women we study], to speak to them, to suspect that their access to the political and sexual scene is not merely to be corrected by our [supposed] superior theory and enlightened compassion" (Spivak 1987:135).

Notes

Introduction: On Women and Words in Arabia— Discourses of Power

1. The word *'ulama* is the plural for *'alim,* which comes from the root word *'ilm* meaning knowledge. *'Ulama* may be used to refer to a group of people who are scholars in different branches of knowledge and use their knowledge to further the Muslims' understanding of their religion. I use the term "religious *'ulama"* interchangeably with 'ulama to refer to those whose primary knowledge is in theology and religious tradition. In the Saudi case, however, *'ulama* is a term that is traditionally reserved for those who have the religious-moral authority legitimizing the government. These are usually the religious judges officially headed by the mufti. But in a broader sense the term refers to the scores of religious office or nonoffice holders who are considered a part of the religious elite either by training in the various religious institutions, such as the Islamic universities, or by private tutoring in a teacher/disciple relationship. All these are considered the custodians of the religious tradition. Eickelman (1985) provides a social biography of a rural Moroccan judge, through which he examines Islamic education and the Islamic concept of knowledge, and he uses the terms "men of learning," "notables," and *'ulama* interchangeably with intellectuals, although the latter bears secular connotations in the Arabic language.

2. Al-Baadi 1982:119. The woman writer went even further in her challenge to men and entitled her piece "Geula and the Perfumed Letters," in reference to an Israeli woman who was the author of the measure for the annexation of East Jerusalem. The woman writer sniped at these men who think of their women in the fashion she described, while Israeli women further the occupation of Arab lands (142).

3. Ibid., 132. This piece, written by a female writer, appeared in the *'Ukaz* newspaper in 1978.

4. *Fatwas* are legal religious opinions given by the highest religious authority in the country (the Mufti, hence the derivation) to settle a dispute in a matter of great significance for religion.

5. Ibid., 133–34.

6. For this I am indebted to many Arabian female friends who were fellow students in the United States. But I owe the most to Dr. Hanan Atalla who, as an ardent reader of her country's newspapers and magazines and a Saudi writer herself, took the time and effort to make the literary and journalistic material available to me during the seven years between 1982 and 1989, during which time she was a graduate student in the United States. To her I should like to express my deepest gratitude.

7. Ethnography, by definition, requires an awareness of the larger whole in which the acquired data are embedded. As Alfred Kroeber has pointed out, it is not possible to attain complete control of the totality (of the larger whole) but a good ethnographer has to make that totality constantly relevant to his or her study (Kroeber 1963:136).

8. Anthropology through literature is receiving little treatment. The most recent anthropologically oriented study is Herbert Phillips (1987), in which he investigates the context in which a body of Thai literature was written, providing translated examples and exploring the social organization of the writers. Certainly the latest collection of essays from Pierre Bourdieu on art and literature will break ground in the field of cultural production (1993). Arebi (1983) experiments with indigenous literature to understand problems of the Libyan society in a specific historical period. Rockwell (1974) has accomplished an elaborate work on sociological interpretation of literature, and N. Schmidt (1965) provides an anthropological interpretation of the Nigerian novel. In relation to the Arab-speaking societies, little effort has been made to provide sociologically oriented analyses of Arabic literature (i.e., Accad 1978; Amyuni 1985; Mikhail 1979). Anthologies such as those collected by Jayyusi (1987, 1988, 1992) and Boullata (1978), as well as the numerous English translations of contemporary Arabic literature, especially Munif's *Cities of Salt* (1987) and Salih's *Season of Migration to the North* (1980), as well as those sparked by the winning of the Nobel Prize in literature by Naguib Mahfouz, the Egyptian novelist, provide valuable sources that are yet to be subjected to anthropological analysis.

9. In this respect F. Malti-Douglas's study of the contemporary Arab feminist writers (1991) exemplifies such an approach, in which she locates the writings of these women vertically in time and horizontally in space. M. Cooke's 1987 study of women writings on the Lebanese Civil War is a valuable contribution to the field. See also E. Accad's 1990 study of sexuality and war.

10. In Foucault's works (1970, 1972, 1978, 1979, 1980) a broad but

concise definition of discourse is difficult to come by. For the purpose of this study, this definition is meant to bring out the essence of the concept of discourse.

11. Anthropology's traditional commitment had been to the study of "simple" preliterate societies as a part of the division of labor between anthropology and sociology. Goody (1968; Goody and Watt 1963) points out that anthropologists who have worked with preliterate societies have tended to look upon writing as an "intrusive" element. Moreover, anthropologists, even when dealing with the difference between "simple" and "advanced" societies, have neglected to examine the implications of the very feature or variable by which they defined the difference—namely, the presence or absence of writing. This neglect is even more remarkable since, as Goody points out, the vast majority of the people of the world have lived, during the past two thousand years, in neither "simple" nor "advanced" societies but in cultures that have been on the margins of literacy and have been influenced by the circulation of the written word (Goody 1968). Studies that address these questions of literacy and its effects on literate societies are admittedly scarce. For excellent material on the role of literacy and the effect of transition from oral tradition to a literate tradition, see Ruth Finnegan (1988). See also Jack Goody (1986, 1987).

12. Works that deal with debates about the formation of cultural institutions rather than the structures of the institutions themselves that is discourse-centered studies are scarce. The most recent relevant study is John R. Bowen's *Muslims Through Discourse: Religion and Ritual in Gayo Society* (1993), in which he examines how men and women in Highland Sumatra in Indonesia debate ideas of what Islam is as pertaining to all areas of their lives. Fischer and Abedi's *Debating Muslims: Cultural Dialogues in Postmodernity and Tradition* (1990) explores the cultural dialogues among Muslims on an intracultural level, as well as on the level of intercultural or what they refer to as "cultural interreference," moving between Iran, Makkah, and Houston, Texas. Hisham Sharabi (1991) brings out an account of the Arab intellectuals' internal debates rarely found in other sources. Hijab's 1988 work, *Womanpower: The Arab Debate on Women at Work*, concern the internal debates in the various Arab countries, including Saudi Arabia, regarding women working outside the home. Liela Ahmed's recent book, *Women and Gender in Islam: Historical Roots of a Modern Debate* (1992), provides the link between past and present debates on gender in the Muslim world. Her chapter "Discourse of the Veil" and her conclusion are illuminating and rare pieces of honest scholarship.

13. J. G. A. Pocock (1971), as quoted in Giddens 1979:200.

14. A discourse for Foucault is not expressed in individual statements, but rather it is articulated in a group of statements: "to define a system of formation

in its specific individuality is therefore to characterize a discourse or a group of statements by the regularity of a practice" (Foucault 1972: 74).

15. Kroeber among early anthropologists may be credited for highlighting the creative aspect of culture through the concept of style in which creativity manifests itself (Kroeber 1963). In fact, although I see the concept of discourse as yielding to creativity, Foucault himself did not view discursive formation as a manifestation of creativity but rather as a consequence of the will to power. Lavie et al.'s recent collection *Creativity/Anthropology* (1992) is a welcome contribution to the exploration of this area.

16. See H. White 1976:25

17. A basic assumption of structuralism, for example, is that the informants, even if they are conscious of themselves and one another in everyday life, base their understanding on erroneous common sense that "science" is supposed to transcend. Informants who have come to understand the whole theoretical background of the explanation are seen by the structuralists as having a tendency toward rationalization, hence concealing the true models. The Marxists stipulate that because consciousness does not faithfully represent the social conditions of existence, we can never fully understand those conditions through the representation of a subjective consciousness. The subject's view, whether consciously or unconsciously, is quite likely to be a mystification of underlying social relations. Interpretive anthropology is supposedly based on "the Native's Point of View," as Geertz asserts in one of his articles (1976). But in the interpretive approach there is more of the researcher than of the native, and more exacerbation of difference. While interpretive anthropology has highlighted the epistemological basis of ethnographic interpretation, especially the way the fieldworker's personal encounters affect the primary data of anthropological research, it only has shifted the conventional contrast of us/ them to a form of me/them (see Marcus and Cushman 1982:48; Clifford and Marcus 1986).

18. Said 1978:291. In addition, Said contrasts Orientalists' lack of interest in indigenous literature with their ironic keen interest in the Arabic language, where they "heaped [exaggerated value] upon Arabic as a language [because this] permits the Orientalist to make the language equivalent to mind, society, history, and nature. For the Orientalist the language speaks the Arab Oriental, not vice versa" (321).

19. In the same vein, Giddens suggests that no such thing as an ideology exists. Rather, only ideological aspects of symbolic systems exist. The symbolic system is not readily identified as an ideology except by studying it as ideological (Giddens 1978:191–92).

20. In doing so, the Saudi women writers are perhaps no different than other women writers in the Arab world. Malti-Douglas speaks of the same

tendency in her study of feminist Arab women writers where she points out that they tie themselves to tradition while they pull away from it (Malti-Douglas 1991). See also F. Mernissi 1991, M. Fayyadh 1987, Hale 1986, and E. Accad and Ghurayyib 1985.

21. Dorothy Smith points out that this is an ideologically structured mode of action, similar to the use of mathematical symbolic forms in Western societies. The creation of concepts and categories becomes a means of institutionalizing social forms through which to govern. As ideologies become increasingly important with processes of social change, they gain importance not only as a mode of thinking, legitimizing, and sanctioning social order but also as an integral part of the organization of society itself (1975:354–55). In relation to the ideological use of words, especially of poetry, see Abu-Lughod's study of Awlad 'Ali (1986) and T. B. Joseph's article on Riffian Berber women (1980).

22. (Geertz 1983:109–11). Scholars are almost unanimous about this point. Laroui asserts that "no civilization has vested the guarantee of its logico-metaphysical truth in the structures of its language more than the Arab civilization has, or in such an unvarying and conscious manner" (Laroui 1976:5). Bishai points out that Arabic "has been and still is to the Arabs not only a vehicle of expression but also a religious symbol, a national identity, and an articulation of their achievements" (1973:66). Rosenthal emphasizes similar facts about writing, which became a highly refined craft in the Islamic tradition (1971:62).

23. Reflection on the history of the tribe, which took place in *majalis* (social gatherings) through the recounting of the *ayyam* (the past days) was most significant in the development of a historical consciousness in the Arab societies. Al-Tayob points out that as a form of historical recollection, the *majalis,* which tended to focus on the recounting of epic battles, "fostered a historical consciousness that valued the past only for the immediate present" (1988:221).

24. Although Levi-Strauss speaks of the "traffic in women," which is distinctly different from my focus on the "traffic in words," his likening of women to words is instructive: "Woman could never become just a sign and nothing more, since even in a man's world she is still a person, and since in so far as she is defined as a sign she must be recognized as a generator of signs . . . In contrast to words, which have wholly become signs, woman has remained at once a sign and a value" (1969:496).

25. In Islam itself, there is no apparent differentiation of public from private or at least it is not a salient feature of its principles. In fact, given the intertwining nature of politics and religion, no issue is considered to be intrinsically public or private, rather "privatization" is a complex process that

occurs in time and space and is bound by meaning and interests. During the history of Islam a push and pull has existed between "publication" and "privatization" as ideological interests demand. But the Qur'an itself elaborates on matters commonly seen as private, such as eating, dressing, marriage, birth, and even sexual rights for men and women, regulating them to the status of the public because of their consequence on the well-being of the *Umma* as a whole.

26. For an early history of Arab women's participation in writing and publishing, see Baron 1988, Cooke 1986, and Harlow 1989. See also Harvard University Library Notes, March 24, 1988.

27. Lichtenstadter presents noteworthy material on the role of women in pre-Islamic Arabia (Jahiliya). In her analysis in *Women in the Aiyam Al-Arab* (1935), she suggests that women played an important role that goes beyond family life. Women as matrons, wives, and daughters participated in wars as warriors, mediators, and spies. Women also, more often than not, have emerged as poetry singers for fighting men, providing various forms of exhortation. Abu-Shuqqah's (1990) study of "Liberation of Women in the Islamic Era" is one of the most comprehensive studies written in Arabic on the role of women as conceived by the Qur'an and the Sunnah. Abbott is credited with introducing Arab women as active participants in power struggles in the political domain in her *Two Queens of Baghdad* ([1946] 1986) and her *Aishah, Beloved of Mohammed* ([1942] 1985), and in her article "Women and the State in Early Islam" (1942). Abbott's analysis is also notable for her early attention to the class distinction she makes between free women and slave women.

28. Wajida Al-Atraqji's book on the literary women in the Abbasid period (1981) is a comprehensive source on literary women of the period. However, Malti-Douglas disagrees with what Al-Atraqji considers to be "women's literature," which for Malti-Douglas are only remarks of women quoted in works by men. This, according to Malti-Douglas, does not constitute socially sanctioned literary production (1991:5). But any assessment of "women's literature" has to take into consideration that, historically, Arabian women were not allowed to attend men's *majalis* because of pervasive sex segregation and other cultural norms related to honor and shame. This ban has minimized women's opportunity to participate in the institutionalized literary criticism that constitutes an important function of the *majalis*. See L. Al-Faruqi 1972; A. Marsot 1979; B. Stowasser in Freda Hussain 1984.

29. See the article "Eve: Islamic Image of Women" by Jane Smith and Yvonne Haddad in Al-Hibri 1982.

30. A thorough book that deals with the philosophical foundations of main Islamic principles in relation to gender is S. Murata's (1992) in which she provides an anthology of Islamic teachings on the nature of the relationships

between God and human beings. Consulting Muslim authorities, she focuses on gender symbolism and analyzes the divine realities with a view toward complementary principles that is analogous to the idea of Yin/Yang in the Chinese tradition.

31. See Abbott 1985.

32. Burckhardt 1831:268–69.

33. For excellent material on the process of transformation from tribe to state in its historical, economic, and cultural facets, see Said 1979, Piscatori 1983, Nibloc 1981, Helms 1981, Edens 1974, Altorki and Cole 1989, and Bahry 1982. A powerful depiction of these social transformations is to be found in the exiled Saudi writer A. Munif's novel, *Cities of Salt* (1987).

34. Even with all the evidence that point to the *'ulama*'s being increasingly stripped of their *institutional* basis of power, it is incorrect to assume, as Bligh did when he declared in an article written in 1985, that "today their [the *'ulama*'s] political power has literally evaporated" (1985:49). It is an astonishing statement given that the article was published six years after the revolt of the Haram and the Iranian Islamic revolution with its deep implications on the status of the *'ulama* everywhere in the Muslim world, yet no mention of either event was made in the article. Even though such facts would have disproved his thesis, even more important, the article was built on faulty assumptions that the decreasing number of Al al-Shaikh *'ulama* has caused a decline in the prestige of the *'alim* "*because* a commoner *'alim* does not have a noble origin" (48). The notion of "nobility," being alien to the Islamic religious parlance, is hardly the legitimate term for the context.

35. Thus, in the wake of the United States' decision in August 1990 to secure a military presence in Saudi Arabia and to prepare for the war with Iraq, while the whole world knew of the Saudi government's approval of the step, the state had to mobilize a number of key religious institutions, such as judicial councils in Makkah and Riyadh, to find and issue a *fatwa,* or "religious opinion," that would justify the alliance of "believers" with "nonbelievers" against other "believers." It took the government more than a week to announce that Americans were actually landing, during which time people were told that "friendly forces" had started to arrive.

36. While the 1988 summer Olympics were shown almost in their entirety, those activities that involved women were censored. Also, acting or doing commercials on television may be performed by foreign but not Saudi women.

37. This, however, needs to be qualified as more and more girls are increasingly dictating their wills on whom to marry. Parents often have to succumb to their daughters' or sons' desires out of fear of divorce or, worse yet, a moral scandal caused by elopement.

38. These contradictions in social life are sometimes justified by the state in terms of a peculiar interpretation of a central Islamic concept, *"al-ummatul-wasat,"* which roughly translates as "the middle people." As elaborated by Abul-Fadl, who translates it as "the median community," the concept in its Qur'anic meaning refers to a distinct community that forms a recognizable entity among other communities, and that is charged with implementing the just order. This order is based on values of *shoura* (taking counsel), *ijtihad* (systematic intellectual effort), and *ijmaa* (the consensus of the people). Its purpose is to support the good and counter evil. But above all, it has the responsibility and the mission to set the balance of history in favor of justice among nations. Thus justice becomes the core and the integrating power of social values (Abul-Fadl 1990:18).

39. For lively and interesting accounts on women's work in Saudi Arabia, see Al-Oteiby 1982 and Altorki 1992. On other parts of the Arab world, including Saudi Arabia, see Hijab 1988.

40. For an excellent account of the emergence of the "woman question" in different parts of the Muslim world and the role of state and Islam, see Deniz Kandiyoti's collection *Women, State and Islam* (1991).

41. These ideas are embedded in Ahmad Jamal's well-known lecture, Rif-qan Bil-Qawarir ("Be Kind to the [Brittle] Vases"), which was published in the local newspapers and, in more elaborate form, in his book *Makanoki Tuhmady* ("Stay Put in Your Place, Thank You" [1981]).

42. This was in reaction to the woman who ridiculed the concept of "lack" mentioned earlier (Al-Baadi 1982:133).

43. Ironically, books produced in the West also use the same metaphor of "opening gates" in connection with Muslim women who are involved in thinking about their situation or making any attempt to intellectualize their existence. Badran and Cooke's collection, *Opening the Gates,* is one example where Arab feminists speak out with the implication that they are in prison and need to free themselves. Just as in the internal discourse, these Western scholars emphasize that these "prison gates" do indeed open to the West!

44. See Sharabi 1991; Laroui 1976; Keddie 1979, 1990.

45. Warning that some may see Wahhabism as a substitute for "real" Islam, King Fahad was reported to have said, "If someone wants to insult this country, and its people, call them Wahhabis . . . no such a thing as Wahhabism exists in this country" (*Al-Yamama,* no. 1034 [1989]:15–19).

46. See Carroll 1976 regarding the issue of writing women's history in Western societies. In the Middle East, Keddie (1979) has pointed out that historical arguments are used in many Muslim societies in internal discourses to support claims of women's inferiority and to bolster practices of women's seclusion. According to Keddie, some groups (i.e., nationalists) think that

women were better off before other nations lowered their position. Others (i.e., the colonialists) use historical arguments to show that women's position was dreadful until they came to women's rescue. Keddie also observes that periods in which women exerted influence were generally regarded as periods of decline. In fact, such periods, designated as "Harem rule," became synonymous with decadence (Keddie 1979). See also Keddie 1990. Keddie and Baron 1992 is an excellent contribution. Ahmed's recent book, published in 1992, is a valuable addition in its enlightenment of the historical roots of current-day debates on gender in Islam.

47. Although it is not an uncommon experience for anthropologists to face difficulties entering the field, my experience would add another perspective on being an "Arab woman in the field." See Altorki and El-Solh 1988.

48. Some of my Saudi female friends were genuinely amused at my tendency to leave nothing unread in these newspapers and magazines, from the prices of vegetables and fruits to notices of births and deaths.

49. In relation to my use of first names for the Saudi women writers throughout the book, I am indebted to Professor Laura Nader and Professor Susan Ervin-Tripp of the University of California at Berkeley for drawing my attention to the issue of "naming" in Western culture. They have pointed out that in American society, women are addressed by their first names in public more so than men—even in cases where individuals are not acquainted. This suggests that the use of first names has become an issue of privatization and lack of respect. This contrasts with the Arab culture where using the first name among those of the same sex and same age is not considered a sign of disrespect but rather of personal recognition. Calling people by their last names is not a common practice in Arab societies, and seemed awkward when I attempted to do so. Therefore, I will take advantage of this cultural license and refer to these writers by their first names throughout. This allows me to escape the awkwardness of using their full names repeatedly; more important, I hope it will signify to these writers my sense of personal recognition and appreciation for them as individuals.

50. Whatever label one places on translations, it seems unlikely that anyone could reach the ideal translation defined by Wellwarth as "a completely transparent pane of glass through which people can see the original without being aware of anything interfering" (1981:140–46).

1. Women's Opportunities and the Social Organization of Writing

1. Historically, however, the Hijaz region, especially the cities of Makkah and Almadinah, preceded all other provinces as a center of intellectual activities

(exclusively male in the later Islamic periods) by virtue of its religious status. Local scholars published their works in Cairo before the Ottoman administration established the first publishing house in Makkah, where the newspaper *Al-Hijaz* was printed in 1883. In Najd, however, the first publishing house was not set up until 1953, with the establishment of Al-Yamama publishing house. For a background on the scholarly activities and the intellectual life in Makkah in the nineteenth century, see Hurgronje (1931). In his book, which originally appeared in 1889, the Orientalist Hurgronje provides one of the earliest ethnographies of the Muslims' holiest place through a firsthand experience in which he witnessed Makkah's intellectual life and interacted with its scholars for six months.

2. Najat Khayyat, *Makhadh Assamt* (The labor of silence), 1965.

3. Thurayya Gābel, *Al-Awzan El-Bakiya* (The weeping rhythms) (Beirut: Dar Al-Kitab, 1963).

4. See As-Sammadi 1981; 'Uthman 1982; Saleh 1983. For the early history of modern Arabic women's writings, see Cooke 1986 and Harlow 1989.

5. See Hashim 1981; Amin 1972; Raddawi 1984; As-Sasi 1986. For example, Raddawi mentions only two women. As-Sasi mentions eight women to whom he devotes 5 pages at the end of his book, which consists of 282 pages covering almost a hundred male writers over the last three generations.

6. See Al-Huqail 1983.

7. See Altorki 1986:19.

8. See Al-Baadi 1982 for an account of some of those debates.

9. The decree read: "Thanks be to Allah alone. We have decided to implement the desire of the *'ulama* (savants) of our great religion in the Kingdom to open schools that teach girls religious subjects such as the Qur'an, monotheism, jurisdiction, and other sciences that are harmonious with our religious beliefs, such as home management, the rearing of children, and others that, presently or at a later date, are not afraid to introduce change in our beliefs. These schools are to be remote from any influences that might affect the youngsters' manners, healthy beliefs, or traditions. We have ordered the formation of a commission made up of the chief *'ulama*, who are known for their protective jealousy of religion and their compassionate love for Muslim children, to organize these schools, establish their programs, and supervise their good behavior" (quoted in Al-Baadi 1982:97).

10. As a result, their opportunity to become deans and heads of departments is more pronounced than within the Western system. For example, within at least two Western societies, Canada and the United States, Dorothy Smith (1975) finds that not only do women have a major disadvantage in competing with men but that, while Western women participate widely in what she calls "domains of action," they are in fact excluded from participation in the production of various forms of thought. My data suggest that a correla-

tion between lack of work outside the home and a higher degree of participation in literary production obtains in at least one case. But one can also argue that, by the same token, restrictions of all kinds may also lead women to seek writing as a compensatory form of self-expression.

11. Ironically, while the physical segregation and immobility of women are maintained, writing is the only field in which the work of men and women is not "segregated," and in fact writing places men and women in a competitive relationship. In this field, women face realities of gender (qua women), share with men realities of literary production (qua writers), and even face a third reality as "women writers."

12. Videotapes are newcomers as an entertainment media and these are gaining ground and competing for women's time, especially among upper-class women.

13. In fact, the one woman writer known to be most productive, Sohaila Zain Al-Abedin, is not committed to any type of employment outside the home, and is also unmarried. This writer has published six books in addition to numerous articles and studies.

14. This phenomenon is probably not unique to Saudi Arabia but may be characteristic of societies that embody "great traditions." In the context of Thai literature, for example, Phillips establishes the same pattern of conflict between the "little" and the "great" tradition (see Phillips 1987).

15. See Ferguson 1959, 1971.

16. One example can be drawn from *Al-Yamama* magazine, which carries a weekly section of four to six pages of folk poetry. Almost all newspapers now feature sections of folk poetry. Regular programs featuring poetry are also aired on radio and national television which, on special occasions such as Janadiriyya festivals and National Day, may run for hours.

17. Geertz points out that Arabic becomes as much a symbol as a medium because the Qur'an contains "not reports about God by a prophet or his disciples but His direct speech" (Geertz 1983:110).

18. Marmura continues by pointing out that, as such, "No translation can adequately convey the magnificence and originality of its language, its rhythmic patterns, its assonances, its vivid imagery, the dramatic quality of its narratives, or the overall grandeur of its style" (Marmura 1976:62).

19. See Maurice Bucaille 1978.

20. See Al-Zaid 1981.

21. Al-Qarni's book (1988) is one example of the attacks led by various ardent conservative religious leaders on those who they see as injecting life into the folk tradition in an attempt to canonize it.

22. To appreciate the nature of the cleavage between the real and the ideal created by journalism, and to understand the dilemma of according status to contemporary literature, a word on creativity and its relation to literary cre-

ation is in order. In Arabic, creativity (*ib'da*) is frequently used interchangeably or in connection with creation (*khalq*). The latter use has been avoided historically because of its unacceptable religious connotations. However, through time, creativity itself came to acquire religious connotations by its association with *bid'a,* which means illegitimate innovation. The new meaning of the word *bid'a* as a religious concept has affected the meaning of creativity (*ib'da*) as a literary concept and, as a result, any literary innovation is regarded with suspicion or hostility by the religious *'ulama*.

23. Effective images are the backbone of the traditional Arab *qasidah*. Imru'al-Qays, a poet who lived in sixth-century Arabia, for example, is considered a classic writer, with his vivid description of "a horse charging through the wilderness, a desert storm, and the freshness of the dawn after the rain, when birds sing as if drunk with spiced wine" (see Bishai 1973:70). However, certain limitations on creativity and imagination are forced on contemporary poems. Works of imagination in the contemporary context have come to be subordinated to the rules of conduct in social life where images are considered to be good literature *if* they are socially acceptable.

24. However, individual attempts are made by a few university professors to use contemporary Arabian writings, mainly by males, in their curricula. The use of women's writings in universities and colleges has recently been on the rise to aide in the ideological battles. For example, one of Sohaila Zain Al-Abedin's books is used in the women's Shari'a College in Riyadh. Also, one of Rajaa 'Alim's plays has been taught in Letters College.

25. It is precisely this ideological function that is stressed in all discussions of the press's role "in development." The subject is often discussed in "literary" clubs, and such discussions are in themselves indicators of the fusion of journalism and creative writing. In a discussion of the topic by the chief editors of major newspapers, the main concern was posed in the form of a question "how to make *I'elam* (communication or information) complementary to *Ta'leem* (education). Both words however are derived from the word *Ilm* (knowledge). The priorities the editors set for the mass media include education, guidance, and information.

26. However, the Human Development Report of 1991 set the figures at a total of 58 percent, with 69 percent for males and 43 percent for females, as recorded in 1985 (128).

27. An example of borrowing from a private library involved Al-Attar's extensive home libraries that, with his wife's help, he made available to women. In their homes, both in Jeddah and Makkah, they maintained such libraries, and university women often telephoned them searching for books, and would frequently came to borrow them. I had the opportunity to speak to these women who spoke of the difficulties they encounter in borrowing books from public libraries.

28. According to one male writer, "I thought that the most difficult part of publishing a book was the government censorship, but I found out that the real problem is the high cost of printing. . . . Because there is no ministry of cultural affairs," the above writer concludes, "the book is not supported by any institution." The high cost of paper, he adds, compounds the situation even further. He points out that there is a 12 percent import tax on paper, whereas imported books are not taxed. This has resulted in higher prices for Saudi books and lower prices for imports, especially those from Egypt (Al-Ja'aithen 1987:5).

29. Hashim 1981:30; Almajalla 1989:44–45.

31. See Al-Saati 1987.

2. History of the Present and the Presence of History: Traffic in Symbols, Knowledge, and Experience

1. *Al-Yowm* 1988:17 (no. 5409, 8/19/1408 A.H.), my translation.

2. The author refers to the fact that even when women are allowed to attend the festival, they are confined to separate halls in which they can only see and hear by means of closed-circuit television.

3. These terms refer, respectively, to the traditional coffee pot, the brass water container, a milk container, a device for roasting (especially coffee), and a big wide basket that was used for carrying farm products such as dates and other fruits and vegetables. Some of these are still in use, such as *dallas;* others have become museum objects.

4. Cited in Saleh 1983, my translation.

5. *Shabbat* is the Hebrew name for the month of February, commonly used in the Arab East. The poem itself was written in February 1981.

6. The Maḍhloum neighborhood is one of the oldest quarters in Old Jeddah. In this neighborhood were many *rabats,* homes established for the needy and the old women through *waqf* (endowment). The name *Maḍhloum* means "the one who suffers injustice." The root word *ḍhalām* means both darkness and injustice.

7. Ṭofoul is the name of Fowziyya's first-born female child.

8. Abu-Khalid 1985, translated by Moneera Al-Ghadeer.

9. Ebgiag is a city in the eastern part of Arabia whose economy depends on the oil industry.

10. The poet points to the tel Zahter massacre of the Palestinians by the Israelis in the early 1980s.

11. She points to the 5 June 1967 Arab-Israeli War.

12. Yathrib is the old name for Al-Madinah, where the prophet Mohammed was born.

13. Al-Hassan and Al-Hussain, sons of Fatema and 'Ali, are grandchildren of the Prophet.

14. Translated by Moneera Al-Ghadeer.

15. Al-Qarni 1988:52–53, my translation.

16. A series of articles were written in *Al-haras Al-watani* magazine by Shaikh Abdul-Aziz Attowaijeri, the head of the council of the magazine, and Abdul-Aziz Al-Khowaiter, the Minister of Higher Education, in which they reflect on the days of their youth and compare them to those of their sons. These serve as examples of this tendency to romanticize the present.

17. The Arab people are known for training falcons. Many other women writers, especially Ruqayya, use the falcon as a favorite symbol of the Arab man. Falcons hunt only small game which they usually do not eat. This quality seems to signify hope of Arab women in the Arab man.

18. John Searle explains that reading allegorically is dependent on two conditions that are characteristics of all indirect speech acts. First, one has to decide that the speaker means something other than what the ordinary use of words would allow. Second, what that something is needs to be determined. Both can be resolved in the context of shared knowledge and mutual systems of inference between hearer and speaker. These include the speaker's attitude, intention, literary status and style of representation, the genre chosen, the content, and so forth. Context is also essential in facilitating understanding, especially in terms of discursive statements, location, and types of social practices (Searle 1979). (See also White 1987; Fletcher 1964). Taking these factors into consideration, Rajaa, Fowziyya, Ruqayya, and to some extent Sharifa (chapter 4) would be more likely to be read allegorically, or symbolically, than the rest. It is difficult, however, to assess the extent to which teaching literature in schools actually trains individuals for this mode of reading.

19. In regard to allegory, however, one has to keep in mind that although it is a valued form of signification (referred to in the Arabic literary tradition as *kinaya*), allegory has always been a challenging form in the Arabic literature. Dissident movements have always used it to express opposing political and ideological viewpoints and, as a result, allegory is linked to subversion.

20. Ash-Shabib 1987:35–45, my translation.

21. Ruqayya here not only alludes to the Qur'anic story of "The People of the Cave" but also adopts the narrative style of the Qur'an itself. While the invocation of their story is within the realm of the acceptable, it is not clear how the traditionalist reader would react, especially since it is used in a tone and within a context that may be interpreted as sarcastic. However, I have not encountered an explicit negative reaction to Ruqayya's style on the part of the religious leaders, except may be Al-Qarni's reference to her as modernist.

22. Ruqayya alludes here to the story of Jacob as it was narrated in the Qur'an.

23. Ash-Shabib 1984:36, my translation.

24. Ibn Al-Walid, who lived in the first century of Islam, was one of the greatest Muslim soldiers. He was nicknamed "the Sword of Allah" by the Prophet for his participation in many battles in Islam's formative years. He wished to die in battle but lived to die of old age.

25. A Lebanese leader.

26. *Adhan* is the call for prayers.

27. Balqees is the well-known Queen of Saba (biblical Sheba) of Yemen who is believed to have lived in the area of Ma'arb Dam about fifty miles from Sanaa (Yemen) at the time of King Solomon who ruled between 992 and 952 B.C. The queen of Sheba is believed to have had an affinity with Abyssinia and, along with her son, to have founded the Abyssinian dynasty. (The English translation of the meaning of the Holy Qur'an, 1096.)

28. This is an allusion to Yemen, which came to be referred to in Arab history as "The Happy Yemen" in reference to its natural beauty and abundant resources.

29. Ruqayya refers here to King Solomon, to whom some historical accounts assert Balqees was married.

30. Ash-Shabib 1984:75–83, my translation.

31. Asmaa, who was the daughter of Abu Baker the Second Caliph, and the sister of 'Aisha, the youngest wife of the Prophet, had, at an early age, taken the responsibility of keeping her father and the Prophet, in the early days of Islam, from being killed by their pursuers. In a most dangerous and hostile situation, she supplied them with food and water in their hiding place. When she became a mother later in life, her son 'Abdullah Ibn Azzubair was involved in a political struggle against the Umayyads, who were by far more powerful than he. Her son believed he was on the right path but recognized his own vulnerabilities. He knew he would be killed but worried that he would be mutilated and disgraced after his death. His mother told him, "Dear son, the sheep does not worry about being skinned after it is slaughtered." It has since become a saying.

32. The Arab Saudi Association of Culture and Arts is affiliated with the General Presidency of Youth and Sports. It is subsidized entirely by the government. Since the mid-1980s, the Association has published a variety of literary works for leading local writers, some of whom are women.

33. In a story called "Fear," published in *Al-Haras Al-Watani* magazine, the female protagonist tells the male: "A frightened man and a frightened woman, how could they meet?. . . . You are frightened . . . pursued in your home, in the street . . . you need a new kind of freedom, you need to

free yourself from this fear that inhabits you" (no. 82 [July 1989, Year 10], 118–19).

34. Ruqayya uses no word more often than *dream*. *Dream* is the title of one of her collections, of one of her stories, and even of her column in *Sayyidaty* magazine ("Short Dreams"). Ruqayya sees dreaming as functioning differently for men than for women. According to her, men should not dream before they "hold one thread of their reality," as a character says in one of her stories in the collection, *Dream*. On the other hand, women are capable of holding these threads of reality only through dreaming. Reality, in fact, lies in their dreaming. Women are represented as almost obsessed with seeing what is beyond their "reality," always needing to venture "outside" reality in order to have a grip on that reality. They seem always discontented with what they see, always seeking knowledge beyond what can be seen.

35. Sheherazade, as a symbol of storytelling, has held tremendous fascination for many writers, men as well as women, in the East as well as the West. Fedwa Malti-Douglas, in her inspiring analysis of Sheherazade, points out that Sheherazade's feminist qualities have been stripped away from her not only by male writers, such as Poe and Barth, but also by the Moroccan feminist Fatima Mernissi. By viewing Sheherazade as "an innocent young girl whom a fatal destiny led to Shahrayar's bed" and by describing her achievement as "the miraculous triumph of the innocent," Mernissi diminishes the strength of Sheherazade's personality and belittles her wisdom, cleverness, and mastery of the discourse (Malti-Douglas 1991:13).

36. Several centuries ago, Zarqa's legacy was described as follows: "Zarqa was a woman who lived prior to Islam in Al-Yamama [approximately in the area of Nejd]. Her eyesight was so powerful that she was able to see white hair in milk, and see horsemen three days' journey away. Zarqa was able to warn her people in advance every time armed groups attempted to attack them. As a result, no army could attack them without her people being prepared. One of those attackers had resorted to a trick in which he ordered his men to cut trees and hold them in front of themselves. When Zarqa looked, she said to her people: 'I see trees coming toward us.' Their answer to her was, 'You've become senile, your mind is growing fragile, and your eyesight is diminishing.' They would not believe her. But they were awakened one day by horsemen who attacked them, and Zarqa herself was killed in that invasion" (Ibn Abd Rabbah 1952:71).

37. 'Alim 1987b. I am greatly indebted to Moneera Al-Ghadeer for translating parts of this play.

38. Rajaa's ideas bear astonishing resemblance to Foucault's views reflected in his books and interviews (1988) on the role of the intellectual and the concept of liberation. Not having read Foucault thoroughly before I left for the field had its advantages in securing a degree of "purity" to my data, but it

resulted in a failure to recognize the resemblance at the time of the interview. I therefore missed the opportunity to ask her if she had ever read him.

39. This is by no means an exaggeration for in Arabic script the difference in letters most often is dependent, in addition to the shapes of letters, on the position and number of dots. See the Note on Transliteration in this book.

40. The tendency to break thought patterning is in fact embedded in the Sufi's tradition of Islamic mysticism. One example of the nature of the Sufi's teachings is a story told as a moral fable using a folk character called Mulla Nasrudin: "Mulla Nasrudin was walking along an alleyway one day when a man fell from a roof and landed on top of him. The other man was not hurt— but the Mulla was taken to the hospital. 'What teaching do you infer from this event, Master?' one of his disciples asked him. 'Avoid belief in inevitability, even if cause and effect seem inevitable! Shun theoretical questions like: "If a man falls off a roof, will his neck be broken?" He fell—but my neck is broken' " (see Bates and Rassam, 1983:71–72). The Sufis, who have historically played a vital political role, were considered "outside," or dissenters, *khawarej*. Sufism is considered heresy by the conservative religious discourse due to its advocacy of religious experience rather than dogma, and the multiplicity of interpretations of that experience, as well as of the Qur'an itself.

3. Victimization Literature: The Poetics of Justice and the Politics of Representation

1. *Ukaz* 1987 (no. 7587, April 6), my translation.

2. *Waqfa* is the most significant part of the pilgrimage to Makkah. It refers to "standing" on the Arafa's mountain the day before all Muslims celebrate the Eid of Sacrifice honoring Abraham, whom the Muslims call the "Father of the Prophets."

3. Ash-Shamlan 1989:23–29, my translation. I should note that my translation of Sharifa's "Secret and Death" was done without prior knowledge of Jayyusi's translation (1988). I should also note that Jayyusi's team of translators has done a superb job throughout the anthology.

4. Ash-Shamlan 1989:83–87, my translation.

5. As-Saggaf 1982:69–78, my translation.

6. The correct translation is "children of the dog," an interesting inversion of the insulting American expression "son of a bitch."

7. *Kadi* is an herb that has a distinct taste, which is distilled and used to flavor water in Arabia. A few drops are usually enough for approximately a gallon of water.

8. Hashim 1986:35–53, my translation.

9. This is an Arabic expression that designates decisiveness or putting an end to something. In Arabic, the dots determine the letter. Once letters are determined, meanings and intentions are supposedly determined as well.

10. The legendary love story between Qays the poet and Laila is believed to have taken place in the Arabian Peninsula during the seventh century A.D.

11. Most likely she is dead. This is a comment on the state of affairs in the society. The poverty of the village and lack of health care may have caused a high rate of mortality, especially among women who have to face health hazards similar to those faced by Zahra (i.e., thorns and prickles [palm-leaf spines]).

12. In fact, the Wahhabi movement has banned this kind of marriage and has gone so far as to nullify marriages that were not based on the woman's full consent (see Al-Baadi 1982).

13. Here, Sharifa is probably being careful to ensure publication of her story. Another story, in which the protagonist was a prostitute, was refused publication.

14. This is somehow reminiscent of Aristotle's key concept of "catharsis." In *The Poetics,* Aristotle uses "catharsis" to refer to the fact that "representations of suffering and death in drama paradoxically leave the audience feeling relieved rather than depressed. A tragic hero arouses in the viewer feelings of 'pity and fear,' pity, because the person is of great moral worth, and fear, because the viewers see themselves in the person of the hero" (see Abcarian and Klotz 1973:958).

15. The Arabic expression *hadha amrun dubbira belail* establishes, and means literally, that "works of subversion are planned or executed at night."

16. Najwa had a weekly column called "The Nights of Sheherazade" in *Ash-shrqul-Awsat,* a daily newspaper published by a Saudi publishing company in London. Rajaa 'Alim has also written a series of short articles called "Her Days," speculating on the kinds of events that might have occurred during the days of Sheherazade.

4. Redefining the Issues: The Politics of Re-vision and the Production of Difference

1. To date none of these writers is known to have published in any genre other than the essay. However, at the time of the interviews, Juhayer and Fatna indicated that they were both working on a novel.

2. *Al-Jazeera* 1989:7 (no. 6033, April 5).

3. *Al-Jazeera* 1982:7 (no. 3549, May 23).

4. *Al-Jazeera* 1984:7 (no. 4395, October 10).

5. However, the lack of expressed humor among other women writers (except in a limited way) does not mean a lack of appreciation of fun, either in the society as a whole or among these women themselves. Humor, especially among family members and friends, is applied widely. In public, humor is constrained by its cultural definition as a "private" matter to be practiced on a personal level. The same rule governs the expression of anger—whether for men or for women. The cultural distaste for women who display humor publically is rivaled only by the distaste for angry women—in that both carry connotations of laxity in moral standards.

6. "There Is No Woman in Our Home," *Al-Jazeera* 1983:12 (no. 3652, September 12).

7. This has to be understood in the context of the *'ulama*'s attempts to revive the practice on the ground that the sexual ratio in society is disturbed and that there are more women than men. Fear of spinsterhood leads women to accept the position of second wife. One of the most ardent proponents of this view is Shaikh Abdul-Aziz Al-musannad who put it in these terms: "Half a husband, one-third, or one-fourth of a husband is better than no husband" (*Iqra* [1988]:67, no. 663). For an examination of the discourse on polygyny and its implication on power relations in Saudi Arabia, see Arebi (forthcoming).

8. *Al-Jazeera* 1983:12 (no. 3652, September 12).

9. *Al-Jazeera* 1986 (n.d.)

10. This is an apparent allusion to an incident involving the Second Caliph Omar in the sixth century who, in a speech at the mosque, protested the demand for high-valued bridal gifts and gave the opinion that Islam considered it improper. Although Omar based his opinion on an essential characteristic of Islam, which is simplicity and moderation, he was found to be wrong by a woman who brought a verse from the Qur'an testifying that no limits should be set on what a woman asks for as a marriage gift from her prospective husband. See the Qur'an 4:20.

11. "Writing on Hot Tinfoil," Ash-Shadi, Hawamish Sahafiyya, *Al-Jazeera*, n.d.

12. *Ar-Riyadh* 1979:3 (no. 4308, 9/11/1399 A.H.).

13. The reference here is to a woman doctor who sent a letter to *Al-Yamama* magazine complaining of a lack of suitors and pointing to the inability of the Saudi man to accommodate women who have a profession or are highly educated. The letter sparked a series of exchanges about marriage to "overly" educated females. Letters poured in containing a mix of sentiments: support, pity, personal offers of marriage, along with an "I-told-you-so" kind of attitude. The response of the magazine's chief editor documents the dominant discourse about women: "The [woman] doctor wanted to draw attention to the

fact that a social situation exists that is in need of reevaluation. . . namely, the relation between education and marriage. . . . She should not be misunderstood as being regretful for her education . . . or for the services she renders to her country. What should be understood from her letter is that she wants other women to avoid the grave mistake she has committed [sic]. . . . When she did not try to put one foot here [in marriage] and the other there [in education] . . . that is, to marry while she was in school, before the "age of fourteen" passes, and the number of those who ask for her hand decreases. The female doctor wanted to stop all those who taught this generation something that they should never have learned: that marriage is in opposition to school . . . that having children precludes going to college, and that family is incompatible with notebooks, pencils, and homework (*Al-Yamama* 1988 [no. 1034]:8–9).

14. Ar-*Riyadh* 1979:3 (no. 4302, 9/4/1399 A.H.).

15. Ibid.

16. Shāker 1981:89–90.

17. Ibid., 124–25.

18. Ibid., 110–11.

19. Ibid., 108–9.

20. Shāker, unpublished manuscript.

21. Fatna is frequently criticized by conservative elements in the society, some of whom are women writers. For example, Sohaila Zain Al-Abedin has frequently voiced her criticism of Fatna and *Sayyedaty* magazine, of which she was chief editor, for printing photographs of Fatna, as well as other women, with less than fully covered hair.

22. Zain Al-Abedin, in press.

23. Here, Sohaila is pointing to Juhayer Al-Musa'ed.

24. May Ziada was a Lebanese writer who lived in Egypt at the turn of the century. Her salon in Cairo attracted the most prominent writers of the period, such as Jibran and Abbas Al-Accad.

25. Here, Sohaila is playing on the shared root word *adab* from which both the words *literature* and *politeness* are derived.

26. Zain Al-'Abedin, unpublished manuscript.

27. Zain Al-'Abedin 1985:69–71.

28. Ibid., 84–95.

29. Zain Al-'Abedin 1984b:5–6

30. Zain Al-'Abedin 1985:240.

31. This was part of a file prepared by the Jeddah-based *Ukaz* newspaper on "Women as an Issue and the Issue of Creativity," discussed over the period from April to September 1986. Indeed, the title escapes translation. In the original Arabic, it is *Al-Mar'a: Qadhiyya Wa-Ibdaa,* which literally means

"The Woman as an Issue and Creativity." While in Arabic the title is under-standable, in English it lacks coherence.

33. Zain Al-'Abedin 1984a:87–88.

34. This view rests on a statement attributed to the Prophet. Many Wah-habi *'ulama* believe that the authenticity of the *hadith* (statements made by the Prophet) is not to be questioned, despite verses in the Qur'an that run contrary to it. The interpretation of the *hadith* is usually sought in women's physiology and in searching the Qur'an for evidence. The reference is usually made to a verse that permits men to punish delinquent women (even by hitting them) and another that stipulates that the testimony of one man is equal to that of two women. "Should one woman forget, the other [will be in a position] to remind her" (Qur'an 2:282). Sohaila, as do many *'ulama,* invokes the hormonal changes in a woman's body during periods of menstruation, pregnancy, and childbirth in her explanations (as expounded especially in her book, *The Building of the Muslim Family* [Zain Al-'Abedin 1984b:26–28]). In another instance she points out, "The meaning of lack of mental capacity is related to a woman's natural tendency to let her emotions overwhelm her mind" (Zain Al-'Abedin 1987:43), rather than a lack of mental capacity per se.

5. *Literary Marginalization and the Privatization of the Public*

1. Quinn 1982:98.

2. According to Russ (1983), this is a phenomenon of wider universality. In her book *How to Suppress Women's Writing,* she explores the mechanisms by which women's writings in the Western world have been suppressed, a situa-tion that establishes the commonality of being a woman writer cross-culturally. Russ points out that within Western literature, "the absence of formal prohibi-tions against committing art does not preclude the presence of powerful informal ones" (1983:6).

3. Despite the fact that reviewing is done by regular readers who communi-cate their views to the newspapers or magazines, it would have been ideal for this study to also include responses of other regular readers who do not write their views. Measuring readers' response to a literary piece has always been a difficult and inexact task in literary studies, but in the context of Saudi Arabia, it is almost an impossibility. I had originally planned to give some account of the readers' response, but because of the inaccessibility of readers, the data were extremely inadequate. Extreme censorship and tight control exist within the educational institutions on discussion as well as distribution of material

outside the planned curricula. My request for permission to visit the University of Jeddah is still on the desks of the officials. Even questionnaires that I left with some of the university's literature professors, both men and women, were never returned. As a result, I confined this account to an exploration of the reviewer's response, rather than that of the reader.

4. This is despite the fact that critics such as 'Uthman Al-Ṣini have written on Rajaa 'Alim, Sharifa Ash-Shamlan, and Ruqayya Ash-Shabib; Al-Ghaḍh'thami has also written about Rajaa 'Alim and Moneera Al-Ghadeer. In their modernist approach, however, they tend to view the meaning of women's texts as being almost entirely separate from the writer's identity. This is in stark contrast to the tendency of the reviewers whose work is presented in this study to discuss women's writings entirely in terms of the author herself. Modernist critics do not seem to be interested in the writers themselves, whether men or women.

5. Regarding the place of the Jawari, see Goody 1982; Malti-Douglas 1992; Abbott 1946. In relation to women critics in the early years of Islam, a number of women were mentioned in literary sources as renowned critics. See Al-Abbassi 1984.

6. To be sure, the women who are known historically as distinguished in the fields of poetry are usually included under one condition: that their contribution meets the sociocultural criteria of what was defined as acceptable for women then, and what constitutes an ideal now. For example, there is not one literary history book that does not acknowledge Al-Khansa or Rabi'a Al-Adawiyya. The former, who lived in the seventh century A.D., was famed for poetry in which she eulogized her brother Sakhr and her sons whom she lost in battles. As such she has demonstrated, in form (eulogy) as well as in content (family), the qualities most admired in Arab women: namely, loyalty and devotion to family and kinship. Rabi'a is acknowledged as a woman who contributed to the subject of disinterested divine love in Arab poetry. As a mystic who lived in the eighth century A.D., she demonstrated qualities of devotion and deep commitment to God, also seen as the highest attributes of good women.

7. Abdullah Baj'bear, *Sayyedaty*, n.d.: 37, my translation.

8. *Al-Faisal* (122), n.d.: 47–49, my translation.

9. Khalid Al-Mahameed in *Al-Yowm*, n.d.: 10, my translation.

10. In fact, a series of discussions entitled "Woman: As an Issue and as an Issue of Creativity" was published in *'Ukaz* in 1986 and ran for three months.

11. See Showalter 1982.

12. Although women rarely report on political issues, women writers have in fact managed to gain space on the front pages, but only sporadically. In the

early 1980s, for example, Fatna Shāker was able to conduct an interview with Indira Ghandi, the late Indian Prime Minister. The interview not only was carried on the front pages and in the political sections but also sparked the idea of inviting her to visit the Arabian Peninsula, a proposal that she eventually carried out. Also, Amjad Ridha, who now holds the position of chief editor for Women's Affairs in *'Ukaz,* reported on Afghanistan in 1989, and her reports were carried on the front pages of the newspaper (personal communication, 1989).

13. The tendency to separate women's literature, interestingly enough, also exists in Western societies where sex segregation is not the norm. See Russ 1983.

14. This, in fact, extends beyond women's literature. An example of how imagination is subjected to rules of reality is clear in these comments in Al-Qarni's book, *Modernism in the Scale of Islam.* A poet says, "A blond black woman descended . . . wearing a fantastic garment of Horror." Al-Qarni, speaking to the reader, asks: "Have you ever seen a 'blond black woman or a garment of horror, and fantastic too, all at the same time!?' " He also cites a poet who wrote, "He paints cities made of black ice . . . and in a time in which the sun runs in the streets in terror." Here, speaking again to the reader, Al-Qarni asks: "Have you ever in your life seen black ice? Or heard of a sun that runs in the streets?" (Al-Qarni 1988:44–46). The "critic" was not able to see that "a blond black woman" refers to the deformation of the individual, of alienation, and of the lack of a sense of identity; further, it represents the West's (the blond's) encroachment on the black, as a symbol of Arabian identity. The "garment" is modernization, which is fantastic but carries a lot of horror. One can read similar messages in the "black ice" and the "sun that runs in terror," a symbol of light that is seen by centers of power as "the enemy."

15. Poets of pre-Islamic Arabia have in fact become legends on the basis of their accounts of their own unfulfilled love. Such poets include Jamil-Bothaina, Majnoon Laila, Antar-Abla, and others in the Islamic periods as well.

16. Al-Qarni 1988:135.

17. Ibid., 44.

18. Ibid., 53.

19. Ibid., 76.

20. Ibid., 78.

21. Ibid., 53.

22. In this the Arabian woman writer is no different perhaps than women in other parts of the world who are caught in a "Catch 22." "Good women" could not know that much. Women who know that much cannot be "good" or

324   5. *Literary Marginalization and the Privatization of the Public*

virtuous women (Russ 1983). A wealth of literature has been written by feminist literary critics indicating that these different types of critique to which Saudi women writers are subjected are in fact shared by women in other societies. See Benstock 1991; Todd 1980; Juhasz 1976; Christian 1980; de Lauretis 1986; Goulianos 1973; Bevilacqua 1983; Thiebaux 1982; Mahl and Koone 1977.

23. Shāker 1981:19.

24. Here I borrow Quinn's expression (1982).

6. Conclusions and Implications: Contexts of Resistance and the Dialectics of Protest and Affirmation

1. This phenomenon is reminiscent of a form of resistance that Foucault had recognized in the working of social sciences (Smart 1986:169–70).

2. Julie Peteet (1991) in her study of Palestinian women equates women's feeling of equality with men as equality in suffering and repression. Literature on feminism and nationalism also makes the same point, except that the sharing of feeling arises only at times of crisis such as colonialism. See Badran 1987, 1988; Philipp 1978.

3. Examples can be drawn from Knauss 1987; Joseph 1985; El Saadawi 1982; Altorki 1986; Kandiyoti 1988; and Sharabi 1988.

4. In fact, the opposite is believed to be true in some instances. To be sure, studies of Muslim women is redolent with contradictions and ambivalences. While on the one hand Muslim women come across in the literature as isolated strangers, alienated from society, on the other hand they are used as a vehicle for constructing an image of the whole culture from which they are seen as alienated (Arebi 1991). Also, while the Orientalists rendered them altogether "insignificant" within their own culture, the French colonial powers, for practical colonial purposes, had attributed absolute significance to women, building their policy on the assumption that the Algerian society has within it an element of matriarchy, which make women the key to conquering Algerian society. See also Graham-Brown 1988:17–18.

5. Jack Goody provides evidence from a variety of historical resources, periods, and locations to refute assumptions of "the large patriarchal family" and its accompanying domination of social life by men (Goody 1983:28). Goody locates the problem of the discrepancy of facts and images in the lack of criteria and in placing too much credence on vague analytic concepts of an all-embracing kind (Goody 1983:26). Said (1978) and Nelson (1974) point to a combination of Orientalism, functionalism, and feminism, as well as to the

maleness and foreignness of researchers as basic to the discrepancy between facts and images.

6. In his book *The Subjection of Women* (1988), John Stuart Mill advanced one of the earliest theses on patriarchy in terms of the notion of father domination. Kate Millett locates the family as the main patriarchal institution in her *Sexual Politics* (1971). Zillah R. Eisenstein (1979), Evelyn Reed (1975), and Gerda Lerner (1986) provide evolutionary perspectives on the development of patriarchal family through time and space.

7. This is fundamentally different than the prevalent notion of women themselves being an object of traffic, or a commodity exchanged among men in marriage (Levi-Strauss 1969; Van Baal 1975; Rubin 1975).

8. In addition to the pioneering work of Nelson 1978, this point has been illustrated in the context of different parts of the Arab world; examples include Altorki 1977, 1986, in the context of contemporary Saudi Arabia; Makhlouf 1979, in North Yemen; and Davis 1983, in a Moroccan Village.

9. Reflecting on her childhood, and on her relationship to her father one woman writer wrote: "Every time I close my eyes, a large screen lights up through which my life is shown. At the end, I discover that all I have kept in mind and treasured are those first and the sweetest years of my life . . . when joy used to come without an invitation card or appointment. Those short years when my father was to me the compass and the protective amulet. . . . . He gave me the love that no one will ever be able to replicate. I was for him the tender oak; if sadness loomed in my eyes, he would be horrified. His fatherhood was for me a green haven" (personal diary, 1989).

10. This is despite the fact that in Arabic the word *usra* is derived from the root word *asr* which means "captivity" or "bondage." Within a social structure that emphasizes a high degree of commitment and establishes obligations between members of a family and a number of families, the derivation of the word *family* is not entirely inappropriate.

11. Most scholarly works that emphasize the "interconnectedness" of human societies are cast in historical, political, economic, ecosystemic, or cultural terms. In the latter, "interconnectedness" is often studied as a phenomenon of diffusion, with little attention to the question of global distribution of power among nations. However, works such as those of Eric Wolf (1982) and June Nash (1979, 1989; Nash and Kelly 1983), in the tradition of Wallerstein (1974), address the question of "interconnections" between societies with special attention to power. For an excellent article on developing "comparative consciousness" while seeing connections, see Nader 1987 and Sen 1984.

The role played by women, real and imagined, has been critical to all types of encounters between the West and the Muslim Orient. Malek Alloula, in his analysis of the picture postcards of Algerian women produced and sent by the

French in Algeria, points out that the Oriental female inaccessibility behind the veil frustrated the colonialists to the point where possession of the indigenous woman came to serve as surrogate for and means to the political and military conquest of the Arab world. For a comprehensive account of the portrayal of women in photography and the different nature of encounters between Western travelers and anthropologists, both men and women, see Graham-Brown 1988.

12. Fatima Mernissi (1975) also argues the point of the woman's question being related to the civilizational challenge of the West.

13. See Badran 1991; Gendzier 1982; Ahmed 1982; El Saadawi 1982. Works that deal with the relationship of veiling to resistance of discourses of power in the contemporary Arab world, both local and global, are El-Guindi 1981; Abu-Lughod 1986; Fischer 1980; and Hoffman-Ladd 1987.

14. In his book *Islamic Fundamentalism and Modernity* (1988), William Montgomery Watt argues the point of idealization of early Islam among the fundamentalists. Watt is quite right in pointing out that one of the dangers inherent in this idealization is that "the community becomes so obsessed with re-creating something past that it fails to see and deal with the real challenges and problems of the present" (22). But Watt as an Orientalist was not able to free himself from two basic and erroneous assumptions that dominated the thinking of his predecessors. One is the underlying belief in the moral superiority of the West over the rest of the world, but especially over the Muslim world, and the imperative for others to follow the Western example if they are ever to "progress." The other is his failure to understand the full implications of the so-called unchanging nature of Islam. Abu Rabi', in his review of the book, points out that Watt does not take into consideration the "adaptive nature of the Shari'ah and the divergent opinions held by different Muslim scholars on matters relating to social and economic needs, historical change, and intellectual proclivities," nor does he take into account the exploitative nature of the relationship of the West to the Muslim World (Abu-Rabi' 1989).

15. See Murata 1992; Al-Faruqi 1972.

16. The notion of "lack" is linked to a saying of the Prophet: "Women are lacking in mind and religiosity." But the notion of lack is never mentioned in relation to people lacking in themselves; rather, lack was mentioned in the Qur'an only in relation to money and population. See Qur'an 2:155, 7:130.

17. Qur'an 33:59.

18. Al-Baadi 1982.

19. See especially the Qur'anic verses 9:13; 5:44; 33:37; 2:150; 5:3.

20. Ricoeur 1984:39.

21. One of the indicators that Sherry Ortner asserts about "key symbols" is their ability to arouse people positively or negatively. Ortner speaks also of the

cultural scenario some of these key symbols provide as "a species of generalizing symbols whose power lies in its ability to organize rather than represent experience. Its special capacity is that it formulates events as a process in terms of a goal and mode of action rather than as a general representative idea or cognitive model" (Ortner 1973:1338–39).

22. See Mohanty et al.'s excellent collection on Third World women and the politics of feminism (1991). Also, the works of such scholars as Spivak (1987) and Trinh (1986, 1989) make us optimistic that the social sciences have already begun the task of building awareness with theoretical implications and establishing vocabulary that is not centered on the West or that does not negate one society or the other but rather is characterized by a charitable attitude. Thus Spivak's Sudanese colleague who was held captive by "sexist" language, in her use of "female circumcision" rather than "clitoridectomy," was also "caught and held by Structural Functionalism, in a web of information retrieval inspired at best by 'what can I do for them' " (Spivak 1987:135). In her critique of French Feminism(s), she also states: "In spite of their occasional interest in touching the other of the West . . . their repeated question is obsessively self-centered: if we are not what official history and philosophy say we are, who then are we (not), how are we (not)" (137).

23. This is in itself an uncritical view of the feminist movements in the Arab world but is in tune with some scholars on the area, such as Sharabi who goes as far as asserting that "Arab criticism's main intellectual resources, including feminism, are all *Western* in origin" (1990:46). Although Sharabi's assertion should be examined with a caveat, the well-informed studies of feminist movements in the Arab world indicate a response to a specific cultural imperative dictated by time and space and the politics of culture rather than a blind imitation of Western models. See Cole 1981; Badran 1989; Ahmed 1989; Badran and Cooke 1990. See especially Lazreg 1990b who explicates gender politics in Algeria as it relates to religious paradigms.

24. In her excellent account of the historical development of the "woman question" in Egypt and the emergence of Egyptian feminism, Margot Badran (1991) uses *nisa'iyya* to signify feminism, rather than my use of *unthawiyya*. Admittedly awkward, it is a closer translation to feminism than *nisa'iyya* which signifies "womanness" rather than feminism (Badran 1991:231).

25. But Western feminism is itself a diverse phenomenon. As Marks and de Courtivron (1980) point out, while in the American context feminists have emphasized the "oppression" of women in terms of their sexual identity, and in conjunction have used the words *autonomy* and *power,* the French have emphasized *repression,* and have used such words as phallocentrism and jouissance, words that are themselves untranslatable into English. The French feminists, because of their emphasis on the deconstruction of culture and their

focus on the role of language in the inscription of the individual in culture, are accused by the Americans of being elitists. In turn, the French feminists accuse the American feminists of being held captive by the very linguistic and phenomenal categories they attempt to negate, and of being overly concerned with prescriptions for action (see Spivak 1987).

26. In both American and French feminist discourses, a woman's body and sexuality are placed at the center of a search for a female identity. MacKinnon asserts: "As work is to Marxism, sexuality is to feminism" (1982:2). The "essentialist" discourses on women explored by Fuss (1989) also follow the same lines. Sacks (1979) has also made an earlier critique of such tendencies in feminist anthropology in the 1970s. Within the French feminisms, the description of a woman's pleasure, using *jouissance* as a key word, becomes the central theme of analysis. In fact, within the French antifeminism, a woman's sexuality not only has remained at the center but is defined in individualistic rather than collective terms (see Marks and de Courtivron 1987).

27. See Eisenstein and Jardine 1985 for a critique of the concept of difference. Western women, seen as individuals rather than as part of a social group, have adopted a number of strategies to assert their difference from men, which ranges from denying or minimizing it and emphasizing culture or asserting that not only are women different than men but that they are also better than men. Men are also seen as "equally lacking." See Lazreg 1990a on the notions of feminism and difference.

28. This is despite the fact that Pastner (1978) points out the following: the division of women and men into separate spheres in the Victorian and post-Victorian period inhibited English writers who had a great impact on Middle Eastern anthropology, such as Burton, Daughty, and Dickson, from appreciating the interdependence of gender roles in the area.

29. The various implications of the existence of a private world of women are drawn in studies by Aswad 1978; Farrag 1971; Tapper 1978; Nelson 1974; Beck 1978; Dwyer 1977; Mernissi 1975, 1977; and Altorki 1977, 1986.

30. The nature of their thought should not be discerned in terms of traditionalist versus modernist, for such a polarization does not reflect the realities of their orientation. Their views can in fact be seen to fall along a continuum of conservatism and modernism. Traditionalism, prevalent among religious leaders, is of an unreflective and unselfconscious nature. The traditionalist, Carl Mannheim tells us, tends to see the ideas and styles of the past as sufficient guides to the present, while conservatism is conscious and reflective. Conservatism, however, tends to be a defense of the existing state of affairs in general and of the prevailing relations of power (Mannheim 1953:74–164).

31. See Rowbotham 1972 and Hartsock 1975. See also Marks and de Courtivron 1980. Works on feminism and feminist theory in France and the

United States are too numerous to list. For a comprehensive reference guide on this subject, see MacKinnon 1982.

32. Even when critiquing separatism within the tradition of French "anti-feminism," the notion of counter-community, as applied by Julia Kristeva (1982), for example, implies opposition. In fact, Diamond and Quinby (1988) remark that the American feminist's use of language of control "slips too readily into a language of domination" (195). For further exploration of Foucault's ideas and its bearing on the question of feminism, see Martin 1988; Lydon 1988 and Bartky 1988. See also Moi 1986; Bookman and Morgen (1988); and Martin 1987.

33. As Foucault put it, power "is not an institution, and not a structure; neither is it a certain strength with which we are endowed; it is the name one attributes to a complex strategical relationship in a particular society" (1978:93).

34. Many examples can be drawn from anthropological literature on Muslim Arab women. Sohier Morsey's "Zionist Ideology as Anthropology" (1983) is but one example of what one discovers when these writings are subjected to anthropological analysis themselves.

References

Abbott, Nabia. 1942. "Women and the State in Early Islam." *Journal of Near Eastern Studies* 1:106–26.

———. [1942] 1985. *Aishah, Beloved of Muhammad*. London: Al Saqi Books.

———. [1946] 1985. *Two Queens of Baghdad*. London: Al Saqi Books.

Abcarian, Richard, and M. Klotz, eds. 1973. *Literature: The Human Experience*. New York: St. Martin's.

Abu-Khalid, Fowziyya. 1973. *Halta Mata Yakhtatifonaka Lailalat Al-'Ors (Until When They Will Abduct You on Your Wedding Night)*. Beirut, Lebanon: Dar Aladab.

———. 1985. *Qira'a Sirriyya fi tarikh Assumt Al-'arabi (Secret Reading in the History of Arab Silence)*. Beirut, Lebanon: Dar Aladab.

Abu-Lughod, Lila. 1986. *Veiled Sentiments: Honor and Poetry in a Bedouin Society*. Berkeley: University of California Press.

———. 1990. "The Romance of Resistance: Tracing Transformations of Power Through Bedouin Women." *American Ethnologist* 17(1):41–55.

Abu-Rabi' Ibrahim. 1989. Book review. *American Journal of Islamic Social Sciences* 6(1):167–70.

Abu-Shuqqah, 'Abd Al-Halin, M. 1990. *Tahrir Al-mar'aa fi 'Asr Arrisala*. Dar Al-Qalam, Kuwait.

Abul-Fadl, Mona. 1990. "Contrasting Epistemics: Towhid, the Vocationist and Social Theory." *American Journal of Islamic Social Sciences* 7(1):15–38.

Accad, Evelyne. 1978. *Veil of Shame: The Role of Women in the Contemporary Fiction of North Africa and the Arab World*. Canada: Sherbrooke.

———. 1990. *Sexuality and War: Literary Masks of the Middle East*. New York: New York University Press.

Accad, E., and R. Ghurayyib. 1985. *Contemporary Arab Women Writers and Poets*. Beirut: Institute for Women's Studies in the Arab World.

Ahmed, Leila. 1982. "Feminism and the Feminist Movement in the Middle East: A Preliminary Exploration—Turkey, Egypt, Algeria, People's Democratic Republic of Yemen." *Women's Studies International Forum* 5(2): 153–68.

―――. 1989. "Feminism and Cross Cultural Inquiry: The Terms of Discourse in Islam." In Elizabeth Weed, ed., *Coming to Terms: Feminism, Theory, Politics*, pp. 143–51. New York: Routledge.

―――. 1992. *Women and Gender in Islam: Historical Roots of a Modern Debate.* New Haven: Yale University Press.

Al-'Abbassi, Abdullah. 1984. *Wajeez Annaqid 'Inda Al-'Arab.* Jeddah: Tihama.

Al-Atraqji, Wajida M. A. 1981. *Al-mar'aa fi Adab Al-'Ast Al-'Abbassi.* Baghdad: Dar Al-Rashid Lil nashr.

Al-Baadi, Hamad Muhammad. 1982. "Social Change, Education, and the Roles of Women in Arabia." Ph.D dissertation, Stanford University.

Al-Faruqi, Lamia. 1972. "Women's Rights and the Muslim Women." *Islam and the Modern Age* 3(2): 76–99.

―――. 1988. *Women, Muslim Society and Islam.* Indianapolis: American Trust Publications.

Al-Ghazali, Mohammed. 1989. *Assunna Anna-bawiyya Bayna Ahl Al-Figh Wa-ahl Al-Hadith.* Beirut, Lebanon: Dar Ash-Shuruq.

Al-Hazimi, Mansour. 1981. "Alqissa Al-Qasira Fil-adab As-Saudi Alhadith." *Alem Alkutub* 1(4):486–503.

Al-Hibri, Azizah, ed. 1982. *Women and Islam.* Oxford: Pergamon Press.

Al-Huqail, Abdul-Karim Hamad. 1983. *Min Adab Almar'a As-Saudiyya Al-mu'asara.* Ar-Riyadh, Saudi Arabia.

Al-Oteiby, Mohamed K. 1982. "The Participation of Women in the Labor Force of Saudi Arabia." Ph.D. dissertation, University of California, San Diego.

Al-Qarni, A'wadh Ben Mohammed. 1988. *Al-Hadatha Fi Mizan Al-Islam.* Cairo: Hajar.

Al-Sa'ati, Yahya. 1987. *An-Nasher fi Almamlaka Al-Arabiyya As-Saudiyya: Madkhil Li Dirasa.* Ar-Riyadh, Saudi Arabia: King Fahad Library.

Al-Tayob, Abdul Kader. 1988. "The Transformation of a Historical Tradition: From Khabar to Ta'rikh." *The American Journal of Islamic Social Sciences* 5(2).

Al-Yassini, Ayman. 1985. *Religion and State in the Kingdom of Saudi Arabia.* Boulder, Colo.: Westview Press.

Al-Zaid, Abdulla Mohamed. 1981. *Education in Saudi Arabia: A Model with Difference.* Translated by Omar Afifi. Jeddah, Saudi Arabia: Tihama.

'Alim, Rajaa. 1987a. *Almouto Al-Akhir Lil-Mumath'thal (The Final Death of the Actor).* Beirut, Lebanon: Dar al-Adab.

―――. 1987b. *Arba'alŞifr (4/Zero).* Jeddah, Saudi Arabia: Annadi Aththa-qafi Aladabi.

————. 1987c. *Thoqoub fi Adh-dhahr (Holes in the Back)*. Beirut, Lebanon: Dar al-Adab.

Alloula, Malek. 1986. *The Colonial Harem*. Translated by Myrna and Wlad Godzick. Manchester: Manchester University Press.

Altorki, Soraya. 1977. "Family Organization and Women's Power in Urban Saudi Arabian Society." *Journal of Anthropological Research* 33 (3):277–87.

————. 1986. *Women in Saudi Arabia: Ideology and Behavior among the Elite*. New York: Columbia University Press.

————. 1992. "Women, Development and Employment in Saudi Arabia: The Case of 'Unayzah." In J. Jabbra and N. Jabbra, eds., *Women and Development in the Middle East and North Africa,* pp. 96–110. Lieden, N.Y.: E. J. Brill.

Altorki, Soraya, and Donald Cole. 1989. *Arabian Oasis City: The Transformation of 'Unayza*. Austin: University of Texas Press.

Altorki, Soraya, and Camillia Fawzi El-Solh, eds. 1988. *Arab Women in the Field: Studying Your Own Society*. New York: Syracuse University Press.

Amin, Bakri Shaikh. 1972. *Alharaka Aladabiyya Fil-mamlaka Al-arabiyya As-saudiyya*. Beirut, Lebanon: Dar Sader.

Amyuni, Mona. 1985. "Images of Arab Women in Midaqq Alley, by Najuib Mahfouz, and Season of Migration to the North, by Tayeb Saleh." *International Journal of Middle Eastern Studies* 17:25–36.

Arebi, Saddeka. 1983. "An Experiment in Anthropology Through Literature: Problems of Libyan Society in the 1950s and 1960s Through Two Libyan Short Stories." Unpublished manuscript.

————. 1991. "Gender Anthropology in the Middle East: The Politics of Muslim Women's Misrepresentation." *American Journal of Islamic Social Sciences* 8(1):99–108.

————. Forthcoming. "When the past Borrows from the Present: Discourses of Historical Representations in Saudi Arabia." *American Journal of Islamic Social Sciences*.

As-Saggaf, Khayriyya. 1982. *Litobhira nahwa Al-Ab'ad (Sailing Toward the Dimensions)*. Ar-Riyadh, Saudi Arabia: Dar Al-Uloum.

As-Sammadi, Naseem. 1981. "Dirasa fi Adab Almar'a As-Saudiyya Al-Qasasi." *'Alim Alkutub* 1(4):512–27.

As-Sasi, Umar Att-Tayeb. 1986. *Almoujez fi Tarikh Al-adab Alarabi Assaudi*. Jeddah, Saudi Arabia: Tihama.

Ash-Shabib, Ruqayya. 1984. *Holm (A Dream)*. Ar-Riyadh, Saudi Arabia: Al-jam'iyya Al-Arabiyya As-saudiyya lith-thaqafa Wal-fonoun.

————. 1987. *Al Hozn Ar-ramadi (The Gray Sadness)*. Ar-Riyadh, Saudi Arabia: Al-jam'iyya Al-Arabiyya As-saudiyya lith-thaqafa Wal-fonoun.

Ash-Shamlan, Sharifa. 1989. *Muntahal Hudou' (Extremely Quiet)*. Ar-Riyadh,

Saudi Arabia: Nadi Al-Qissa Al-Saudi, Al-jam'iyya Al-Arabiyya As-sau-diyya lith-thaqafa Wal-fonoun.

Aswad, Barbara. 1978. "Women, Class, and Power: Example from the Hatay Turkey." In L. Beck and N. Keddie, eds., *Women in the Muslim World*, pp. 473–81. Cambridge, Mass.: Harvard University Press).

Baal, Jan van. 1975. *Reciprocity and the Position of Women*. Assen: Van Gorcum.

Badran, Margot. 1987. "Dual Liberations: Feminism and Nationalism in Egypt, 1870s–1920s." *Feminist Issues* (Fall).

———. 1988. "Dual Liberations: Feminism and Nationalism in Egypt, 1970s–1985." *Feminist Issues* (Spring).

———. 1989. "The Origins of Feminism in Egypt." In Jacqueline Zirkzee and Arina Angerman, eds., *Current Issues in Women's History*. London: Routledge.

———. 1991. "Competing Agenda: Feminism, Islam, and the State in Nineteenth- and Twentieth-Century Egypt." In Kandiyoti, *Women, Islam, and the Islam*, pp. 201–36.

Badran, Margot, and Miriam Cooke, eds. 1990. *Opening the Gates: A Century of Arab Feminist Writings*. London and Bloomington: Virago and Indiana University Press.

Bahry, Louay. 1982. "The New Saudi Women: Modernizing in an Islamic Framework." *Middle East Journal* 36(4):509.

Baron, Beth. 1988. "The Early Years of the Women's Arabic Press in Egypt." Ph.D. dissertation, University of California, Los Angeles.

Bartky, Sandra Lee. 1988. "Foucault, Femininity, and the Modernization of Patriarchal Power." In Irene Diamond and Lee Quinby, eds., *Feminism and Foucault: Reflections on Resistance*, pp. 61–86. Boston: Northeastern University Press.

Bates, Daniel, and Amal Rassam. 1983. *Peoples and Cultures of the Middle East*. Englewood Cliffs, N.J.: Prentice-Hall.

Beck, L. 1978. "Women among the Qashqai Nomadic Pastoralist in Iran." In L. Beck and N. Keddie, eds., *Women in the Muslim World*, pp. 351–73. Cambridge, Mass.: Harvard University Press.

Benstock, Shari. 1991. "Textualizing the Feminine: Over the Limits of Genre." *Oklahoma Project for Discourse and Theory* no. 7. Norman: University of Oklahoma Press.

Bevilacqua, Winifred Farrant, ed. 1983. *Fiction by American Women: Recent Views*. Port Washington, N.Y.: Associated Faculty Press, National University Publications.

Bishai, Wilson B. 1973. *Humanities in the Arabic-Islamic World*. Dubuque, Ia.: Brown.

Bligh, Alexander. 1985. "The Saudi Religious Elite (Ulama) as Participant in the Political System of the Kingdom." *International Journal of Middle East Studies* 17(1) (February):37–50.

Bloch, Maurice. 1977. "The Past and the Present." *Man* 12:278–92.

Bookman, Ann, and Sandra Morgen, eds. 1988. *Women and the Politics of Empowerment.* Philadelphia: Temple University Press.

Boullata, Kamal, ed. and trans. 1978. *Women of the Fertile Crescent: An Anthology of Modern Poetry by Arab Women.* Washington, D.C.: Three Continents Press.

Bourdieu, Pierre. 1984. *Distinctions: A Social Critique of the Judgment of Taste.* Translated by Richard Nice. Cambridge, Mass.: Harvard University Press.

———. 1993. *The Field of Cultural Production: Essays on Art and Literature.* Edited by R. Johnson. New York: Columbia University Press.

Bowen, John R. 1993. *Muslims through Discourse: Religion and Ritual in Gayo Society.* Princeton, N.J.: Princeton University Press.

Bucaille, Maurice. 1979. *The Bible, the Qur'an and Science: The Holy Scriptures Examined in the Light of Modern Knowledge.* Indianapolis: American Trust Publications.

Burckhardt, John Lewis. 1931. *Notes on the Bedouins and the Wahhabys.* London: Henry Coburn and Richard Bentley.

Carroll, Bernice A., ed. 1976. *Liberating Women's History: Theoretical and Critical Essays.* Urbana: University of Illinois Press.

Chodorow, Nancy. 1985. "Gender, Relation, and Difference in Psychoanalytic Perspective." In Eisenstein and Jardine, eds., *The Future of Difference,* pp. 3–19.

Christian, Barbara. 1980. *Black Women Novelists: The Development of a Tradition, 1892–1976.* Westport, Conn.: Greenwood Press.

Clifford, James. 1986. "Introduction: Partial Truths." In James Clifford and George Marcus, eds., *Writing Culture: The Poetics and Politics of Ethnography,* pp. 1–26. Berkeley: University of California Press.

———. 1988. *The Predicament of Culture: Twentieth-Century Ethnography, Literature, and Art.* Cambridge, Mass.: Harvard University Press.

Cole, Donald Powell. 1975. *Nomads of the Nomads: The Al Murrah Bedouin of the Empty Quarter.* Arlington Heights, Ill.: AHM Publishing.

Cole, Juan R. 1981. "Feminism, Class, and Islam in Turn-of-the-Century Egypt." *International Journal of Middle East Studies* 13(1981):384–407.

———, ed. 1992. *Comparing Muslim Societies: Knowledge and the State in a World Civilization.* Ann Arbor: University of Michigan Press.

Cooke, Miriam. 1986. "Telling Their Lives: A Hundred Years of Arab Women's Writings." *World Literature Today* 60 (Spring):212–16.

———. 1987. *War's Other Voices: Women Writers on the Lebanese Civil War.* Cambridge: Cambridge University Press.

Cunnison, Ian George. 1966. *Baggara Arabs: Power and the Lineage in a Sudanese Nomad Tribe.* Oxford: Clarendon Press.

Davis, Susan. 1983. *Patience and Power: Women's Lives in a Moroccan Village.* Cambridge, Mass.: Schenkman.

de Lauretis, Teresa, ed. 1986. *Feminist Studies, Critical Studies.* Bloomington: Indiana University Press.

Diamond, Irene, and Lee Quinby. 1988. "American Feminism and the Language of Control." In Irene Diamond and Lee Quinby, eds., *Feminism and Foucault: Reflections on Resistance,* pp. 123–206. Boston: Northeastern University Press.

Dwyer, D. 1977. "Bridging the Gap Between the Sexes in Moroccan Legal Practice." In A. Schlegel, ed., *Sexual Stratification: A Cross Cultural View,* pp. 41–61. New York: Columbia University Press.

Edens, David G. 1974. "The Anatomy of the Saudi Revolution." *International Journal of Middle East Studies* 5:50–64.

Edholm, E., et al. 1977. "Conceptualizing Women." *Critique of Anthropology* 3(9–10):101–30.

Eickelman, Dale. 1992. *Knowledge and Power in Morocco: The Education of a Twentieth Century Notable.* Princeton, N.J.: Princeton University Press.

Eisenstein, Hester, and Alice Jardine, eds. 1985. *The Future of Difference.* New Brunswick, N.J.: Rutgers University Press.

Eisenstein, Zillah R. 1979. "Some Notes on the Relations of Capitalist Patriarchy." In Zillah R. Eisenstein, ed., *Capitalist Patriarchy and the Case for Socialist Feminism.* New York: Monthly Review Press.

El-Guindi, Fadwa. 1981. "Veiling Infitah with Muslim Ethic: Egypt Contemporary Islamic Movement." *Social Problems* 28:465–83.

El Saadawi, Nawal. 1982. "Women and Islam." In Al-Hibri, ed. *Women and Islam.*

Fabian, Johannes. 1983. *Time and the Other: How Anthropology Makes Its Object.* New York: Columbia University Press.

Fanon, Frantz. 1965. *A Dying Colonialism.* Translated by Haakon Chevalier. New York: Grove Press.

Farrag, Amina. 1971. "Social Control among the Mzabite Women of Beni-Isquen." *Middle Eastern Studies* 3:317–27.

Fayyadh, Muna. 1987. *The Road to Feminism: Arab Women Writers.* East Lansing: Michigan State University Press.

Ferguson, Charles A. 1956. "Diglossia." *Word* 15:325–40.

Finnegan, Ruth H. 1988. *Literacy and Orality: Studies in the Technology of Communication.* Oxford: Blackwell.

Fischer, Michael. 1980. *Iran: From Religious Dispute to Revolution.* Cambridge, Mass.: Harvard University Press.

————. 1986. "Ethnicity and the Post-Modern Arts of Memory in the Modern World System." In James Clifford and George Marcus, eds., *Writing Culture: The Poetics and Politics of Ethnography*, pp. 124–233. Berkeley: University of California Press.

Fischer, Michael, and Mehdi Abedi. 1990. *Debating Muslims: Cultural Dialogues in Postmodernity and Tradition*. Madison: University of Wisconsin Press.

Fletcher, Angus. 1964. *Allegory: The Theory of a Symbolic Mode*. Ithaca, N.Y.: Cornell University Press.

Foucault, Michel. 1970. *The Order of Things: An Archaeology of the Human Sciences*. London: Tavistock.

————. 1972. *The Archaeology of Knowledge*. Translated by A. M. Sheridan Smith. New York: Pantheon.

————. 1978. *The History of Sexuality*. Translated by Robert Hurley. New York: Vintage.

————. 1979. *Discipline and Punish: The Birth of the Prison*. Translated by Alan Sheridan. New York: Vintage.

————. 1980. *Power/Knowledge: Selected Interviews and Other Writings: 1972–1977*. Edited by Colin Gordon. New York: Pantheon.

————. 1988. *Politics, Philosophy, Culture: Interviews and Other Writings, 1977–1984*. Edited by Lawrence Kritzman, translated by A. Sheridan et al. New York: Routledge.

Fuss, Diane. 1989. *Essentially Speaking: Feminism, Nature, and Difference*. New York: Routledge.

Gābel, Thurayya. 1963. *Al-Awzan El-Bakiya (Weeping Rhythms)*. Beirut: Dar Al-Kutub.

Geertz, Clifford. 1973. *The Interpretation of Cultures: Selected Essays*. New York: Basic Books.

————. 1976. "From the Native's Point of View: On the Nature of Anthropological Understanding." In Basso and Selby, eds., *Meaning in Anthropology*. Albuquerque: University of New Mexico Press.

————. 1983. "Art as a Cultural System." In Clifford Geertz, ed., *Local Knowledge: Further Essays in Interpretive Anthropology*, pp. 94–120. New York: Basic Books.

Gendzier, Irene. 1982. "Feminism East and West." *Gazelle Review* 10:41–55.

Ghoussoub, M. 1987. "Feminism or the Eternal Masculine in the Arab World." *New Left Review* 161 (January–February).

Giddens, Anthony. 1979. *Central Problems in Social Theory: Action, Structure, and Contradiction in Social Analysis*. Berkeley: University of California Press.

Goody, Jack, ed. 1968. *Literacy in Traditional Societies*. Cambridge: Cambridge University Press.

Goody, Jack. 1983. *The Development of the Family and Marriage in Europe.* Cambridge: Cambridge University Press.

———. 1986. *The Logic of Writing and the Organization of Society.* Cambridge: Cambridge University Press.

———. 1987. *The Interface Between the Written and the Oral.* Cambridge: Cambridge University Press.

Goody, Jack, and Ian Watt. 1963. "The Consequences of Literacy." *Comparative Studies in Society and History* 4:304–45.

Goulianos, Joan, ed. 1973. *By a Woman Writt: Literature from Six Centuries by and about Women.* Indianapolis: Bobbs-Merrill.

Graham-Brown, Sarah. 1988. *Images of Women: The Portrayal of Women in Photography of the Middle East 1860–1950.* New York: Columbia University Press.

Habermas, Jürgen. 1975. *Legitimation Crisis.* Translated by Thomas McCarthy. Boston: Beacon Press.

———. 1984. *The Theory of Communicative Action.* Vols 1 and 2. Translated by Thomas McCarthy. Boston: Beacon Press.

———. 1987. *The Philosophical Discourse of Modernity: Twelve Lectures.* Cambridge: Basil Blackwell.

———. 1989. *The Structural Transformation of the Public Sphere: An Inquiry into a Category of Bourgeois Society.* Cambridge, Mass.: MIT Press.

Hale, Sondra. 1986. "The Wing of the Patriarch: Sudanese Women and Revolutionary Parties." *MERIP Middle East Report* 16(1):25–30.

Harlow, Barbara. 1989. "The Middle East." In Marian Arkin and Barbara Shollar, eds., *Longman Anthology of World Literature by Women, 1875–1985,* pp. 1163–71. New York: Longman.

Hartsock, Nancy. 1975. "Fundamental Feminism: Process and Perspective." *Quest: A Feminist Quarterly* 2(2):67–80.

Hashim, Abdah Hashim. 1981. *Alittijahat Al-adadiyya Wal-Naweyya Lid-Dowriyyat As-Saudiyya.* Jeddah, Saudi Arabia: Tihama.

Hashim, Najwa. 1986. *Assafar fi Lail Al-Ahzan (Travel in the Night of Sadness).* Jeddah, Saudi Arabia: Addar Assaudia Linnasher Wattawzi.

Helms, Christine Moss. 1981. *The Cohesion of Saudi Arabia: Evolution of Political Identity.* London: Croom Helm.

Hijab, Nadia. 1988. *Womanpower: The Arab Debate on Women at Work.* New York: Cambridge University Press.

Hoffman-Ladd, Valerie. 1987. "Polemics on the Modesty and Segregation of Women in Contemporary Egypt." *International Journal of Middle East Studies* 12:23–50.

Holy Qur'an: English Translation of the Meanings and Commentary. 1985. Translated by Abdullah Yousef Ali. Revised and edited by Presidency of Islamic Research. Saudi Arabia: Muṣḥaf Al-Madinah An-Nabawiyyah.

Hurgronje, C. Snouck. [1889] 1931. *Mekka in the Later Part of the Nineteenth Century.* Translated by J. H. Monahan. Leiden: E. J. Brill.

Ibn 'Abd Rabbah, Abi 'Umar Aḥmad. 1952. *Al-Aqd El-Farid.* Vol. 3, 2d ed. Cairo: Mat'baat Attalif Wattarjuma Wannashir.

Jamal, Ahmad. [1974] 1981. *Makanoki Tuḥmady.* 4th ed. Jeddah, Saudi Arabia: Tihama.

Jayawardena, K. 1988. *Feminism and Nationalism in the Third World.* London: Zed Press.

Jayyusi, Salma Khadra. 1977. *Trends and Movements in Modern Arabic Poetry.* Leiden: Brill.

————. 1988. *The Literature of Modern Arabia: An Anthology.* London: Kegan Paul International in association with King Saud University, Riyadh.

————, ed. 1992. *Anthology of Modern Palestinian Literature.* New York: Columbia University Press.

Joseph, Suad. 1985. "Women, Family, and the State in the Middle East." Lecture given at the Center for Middle Eastern Studies, University of California, Berkeley, April 13.

Joseph, Terri B. 1980 "Poetry as a Strategy of Power: The Case of Riffian Berber Women." *Signs* 5:418–34.

Juhasz, Suzanne. 1976. *Naked and Fiery Forms: Modern American Poetry by Women: A New Tradition.* New York: Harper and Row.

Kah'hala, Umar Ridha. 1984. *Min A'alam Annisa fi Alamay Al-Arab Wal-Islam.* Beirut, Lebanon: Dar Alrisala.

Kandiyoti, Deniz. 1988. "Bargaining with Patriarchy." *Gender and Society* 2(3):274–90.

————, ed. 1991. *Women, Islam, and the State.* Philadelphia: Temple University Press.

Keddie, Nikki R. 1979. "Problems in the Study of Middle Eastern Women." *International Journal of Middle Eastern Studies* 10:225–40.

————. 1990. "The Past and Present of Women in the Muslim World" *Journal of World History* 1(1):77–108.

Keddie, Nikki R., and Beth Baron, eds. 1992. *Women in Middle Eastern History: Shifting Boundaries in Sex and Gender.* New Haven: Yale University Press.

Keohane, N., M. Rosaldo, and B. Gelpi, eds. 1982. *Feminist Theory: A Critique of Ideology.* Chicago: University of Chicago Press.

Khayyaṭ, Najat. 1965. *Makhala.dh Ala.ṣṣumt (The Labour of Silence).* Publisher unknown.

Knauss, Peter R. 1987. *The Persistence of Patriarchy: Class, Gender, and Ideology in Twentieth Century Algeria.* New York: Praeger.

Krestiva, Julia. 1982. "Women's Time." In Keohane, Rosaldo, and Gelpi, eds., *Feminist Theory,* pp. 31–54.

Kroeber, A. L. 1963. *An Anthropologist Looks at History.* Edited by Theodora Kroeber. Berkeley: University of California Press.

Laroui, Abd Allah. 1976. *The Crisis of the Arab Intellectual: Traditionalism or Historicism?* Berkeley: University of California Press.

Lavie, S., K. Narayan, and R. Rosaldo, eds. 1992. *Creativity/Anthropology.* New York: Cornell University Press.

Lazreg, Marnia. 1990a. "Feminism and Difference: The Perils of Writing as a Woman on Women in Algeria." In M. Hirsch and E. Fox Keller, eds., *Conflicts in Feminism,* pp. 326–48. New York: Routledge.

———. 1990b. "Gender and Politics in Algeria: Unraveling the Religious Paradigm." *Signs* 15 (Summer):755–80.

Lerner, Gerda. 1986. *The Creation of Patriarchy.* Oxford: Oxford University Press.

Lévi-Strauss, Claude. 1969. *The Elementary Structures of Kinship.* Translated by James Harle Bell and John Richard von Sturmer. Boston: Beacon Press.

Lichtenstadter, Ilse. 1935. *Women in the Aiyam al-Arab; A Study of Female Life During Warfare in Pre-Islamic Arabia.* London: Royal Asiatic Society of Great Britain and Ireland XIV.

Lipsky, George A. 1959. *Saudi Arabia: Its People, Its Society, Its Culture.* New Haven: HRAF Press.

Lydon, Mary. 1988. "Foucault and Feminism: A Romance of Many Dimensions." In Irene Diamond and Lee Quinby, eds., *Feminism and Foucault: Reflections on Resistance,* pp. 135–148. Boston: Northeastern University Press.

MacKinnon, Catherine. 1982. "Feminism, Marxism, Method, and the State in Feminist Theory: An Agenda for Theory." In Keohane, Rosaldo, and Gelpi, eds., *Feminist Theory.*

Macleod, Arlene. 1991. *Accommodating Protest: Working Women, the New Veiling, and Change in Cairo.* New York: Columbia University Press.

McWilliams, Nancy. 1974. "Contemporary Feminism, Consciousness Raising, and Changing Views of the Political." In Jane Jaquette, ed., *Women in Politics.* New York: Wiley.

Mahl, Mary R., and Helene Koone, eds. 1977. *The Female Spectator: English Women Writers Before 1800.* Bloomington: Indiana University Press.

Makhlouf, Carla. 1979. *Changing Veils: Women and Modernization in North Yemen.* London: Croom Helm.

Malti-Douglas, Fedwa. 1991. *Woman's Body, Woman's Word: Gender and Discourse in Arabo-Islamic Writing.* Princeton, N.J.: Princeton University Press.

Mannheim, Karl. 1953. "Conservative Thought." In Paul Kecskemeti, ed., *Essays in Sociology and Social Psychology,* pp. 74–164. New York: Oxford University Press.

Marcus, George. 1986. "Contemporary Problems of Ethnography in the Modern World System." In James Clifford and George Marcus, eds., *Writing Culture: The Poetics and Politics of Ethnography*, pp. 165–93. Berkeley: University of California Press.

Marcus, George, and D. Cushman. 1982. "Ethnographies as Texts." *Annual Review of Anthropology* 2:25–69.

Marks, Elaine, and Isabelle de Courtivron, eds. 1980. *New French Feminisms*. New York: Schocken.

Marmura, Ell. 1976. "Arabic Literature: A Living Heritage." In R. M. Savory, ed., *Introduction to Islamic Civilization*, pp. 61–70. Cambridge: Cambridge University Press.

Marsot, Afaf L. 1979. *Society and the Sexes in Medieval Islam*. Malinu: Undena.

Martin, Biddy. 1988. "Feminism, Criticism, and Foucault." In Irene Diamond and Lee Quinby, eds., *Feminism and Foucault: Reflections on Resistance*, pp. 3–20. Boston: Northeastern University Press.

Martin, Emily. 1987. *The Woman in the Body: A Cultural Analysis of Reproduction*. Boston: Beacon Press.

Meeker, Michael E. 1979. *Literature and Violence in North Arabia*. Cambridge: Cambridge University Press.

Mernissi, Fatima. 1975. *Beyond the Veil: Male/Female Dynamics in Modern Muslim Society*. Cambridge, Mass.: Schenkman.

———. 1977. "Women Saints and Sanctuaries." *Signs* 2(1):101–12.

———. 1991. *The Veil and the Male Elite: A Feminist Interpretation of Women's Rights in Islam*. Translated by Mary Jo Lakeland. Reading, Mass.: Addison-Wesley.

Mikhail, Mona. 1979. *Images of Arab Women: Fact and Fiction*. Washington, D.C.: Three Continents Press.

Mill, John Stuart. 1988. *The Subjection of Women*. Edited by Susan Moller Okin. Indianapolis: Hackett.

Millett, Kate. 1971. *Sexual Politics*. New York: Avon.

Mohanty, Chandra, et al., eds. 1991. *Third World Women and the Politics of Feminism*. Bloomington: Indiana University Press.

Moi, Toril. 1986. *Sexual/Textual Politics*. London: Methuen.

Moore, Henrietta L. 1988. *Feminism and Anthropology*. Minneapolis: University of Minnesota Press.

Morsey, Soheir. 1983. "Zionist Ideology as Anthropology: An Analysis of Joseph Ginat's Women in Muslim Rural Society." *Arab Studies Quarterly* 5:362–79.

Munif, Abdulrahman. 1987. *Cities of Salt*. Translated from the Arabic by Peter Theroux. New York: Vintage International.

Murata, Sachiko. 1992. *The Tao of Islam: A Sourcebook on Gender Relationships in Islamic Thought*. New York: State University of New York Press.

Nader, Laura. 1987. "The Subordination of Women in Comparative Perspective." *Urban Anthropology* 15(3–4).

———. 1989. "Orientalism, Occidentalism, and the Control of Women." *Cultural Dynamics* 2(3):323–55.

Nash, June. 1979. *We Eat the Mines and the Mines Eat Us: Dependency and Exploitation in Bolivian Tin Mines.* New York: Columbia University Press.

———. 1989. *From Tank Town to High Tech: The Clash of Community and Industrial Cycles.* New York: State University of New York Press.

Nash, June, and Maria Patricia Fernandez Kelly, eds. 1983. *Women, Men, and the International Division of Labor.* Albany: State University of New York Press.

Nehme, Michael. 1983. "Saudi Arabia: Political Implications of the Development Plans." Ph.D. dissertation, Rutgers University.

Nelson, Cynthia. 1974. "Public and Private Politics: Women in the Middle Eastern World." *American Ethnologist* 3:551–63.

Nelson, Cynthia, and Virginia Olesen. 1977. "Veil of Illusion: A Critique of the Concept of Equality in Western Thought." *Catalyst* 10–11:8–36.

Nibloc, Tim, ed. 1981. *State, Society and Economy in Saudi Arabia.* London: Croom Helm.

Ong, Aihwa. 1987. *Spirits of Resistance and Capitalist Discipline: Factory Women in Malaysia.* Albany: State University of New York Press.

Ortner, Sherry. 1973. "Key Symbols." *American Anthropologist* 75:1336–40.

Pastner, Carol. 1978. "English Men in Arabia: Encounters with Middle Eastern Women." *Signs* 4(2):309–23.

Philipp, Thomas. 1978. "Feminism and Nationalist Politics in Egypt." In L. Beck and N. Keddie, eds., *Women in the Muslim World,* pp. 277–94. Cambridge, Mass.: Harvard University Press.

Phillips, Herbert P. 1975. "The Culture of Siamese Intellectuals." In G. William Skinner and A. Thomas Kirsch, eds., *Change and Persistence in Thai Society,* pp. 324–57. Ithaca, N.Y.: Cornell University Press.

Phillips, Herbert P., in association Vinita Atmiyanandana. 1987. *Modern Thai Literature: With an Ethnographic Interpretation.* Honolulu: University of Hawaii Press.

Piscatori, James P. 1983. "Ideological Politics in Saudi Arabia." In James Piscatori, ed., *Islam in the Political Process.* Cambridge: Cambridge University Press.

Pocock, John G. A. 1971. *Politics, Language, and Time; Essays on Political Thought and History.* New York: Atheneum.

Quinn, Arthur. 1982. *Figures of Speech: Sixty Ways to Turn a Phrase.* Salt Lake City: G. M. Smith.

Rabinow, Paul, ed. 1984. *The Foucault Reader.* New York: Pantheon.

Raddawi, Mahmoud. 1984. *Dirasat Fil-qissa As-Saudiyya Wal-Khaleej Al-Arabi*. Ar-Riyadh, Saudi Arabia: Aljam'eyya Al-Arabiyya Lith-Thaqafa Walfunun.

Rassam, Amal. 1982. "Toward a Theoretical Framework for the Study of Women in the Arab World." *Cultures* 8(3):121–37.

Reed, Evelyn. 1975. *Woman's Evolution from Matriarchal Clan to Patriarchal Family*. New York: Pathfinder Press.

Ricoeur, Paul. 1984. *The Reality of the Historical Past*. Milwaukee, Wis.: Marquette University Press.

Riley, Denis. 1988. *Am I That Name? Feminism and the Category of "Women" in History*. Minneapolis: University of Minnesota Press.

Rockwell, J. 1974. *Fact in Fiction: The Use of Literature in the Systematic Study of Society*. London: Routledge and Kegan Paul.

Rosaldo, Michelle. 1980. "The Use and Abuse of Anthropology: Reflections on Feminism and Cross-Cultural Understanding." *Signs* 5(3):389–417.

Rosaldo, Michelle, and Louise Lamphere, eds. 1974. *Woman, Culture, and Society*. Stanford, Calif.: Stanford University Press.

Rosenthal, Franz. 1971. *Four Essays on Art and Literature in Islam*. Leiden: J. A. Brill.

Rowbotham, Shiela. 1972. *Women, Resistance, and Revolution: A History of Women and Revolution in the Modern World*. New York: Random House.

Rubin, Gayle. 1975. "The Traffic in Women: Notes on the 'Political Economy' of Sex." In Rayna Reiter, ed., *Toward an Anthropology of Women*, pp. 157–210. New York: Monthly Review Press.

Russ, Joanna. 1983. *How to Suppress Women's Writing*. Austin: University of Texas Press.

Sacks, Karen. 1979. *Sisters and Wives: The Past and Future of Sexual Equality*. Westport, Conn.: Greenwood Press.

Said, Abdul Rahman. 1979. "Saudi Arabia: The Transition from a Tribal Society to a Nation-State." Ph.D. dissertation, University of Missouri.

Said, Edward W. 1978. *Orientalism*. New York: Pantheon.

Saleh, Laila. 1983. *Adab Almar'a fi Aljazeera Wal-Khaleej Al-Arabi*. Kuwait: Alyaqaza Publishing House.

Salih, Tayeb. 1985. *Season of Migration to the North*. Translated from the Arabic by Denys Johnson-Davies. Washington, D.C.: Three Continents Press.

Sartain, E. M. 1975. *Jalal Al-din Al-Suyuti*. Cambridge: Cambridge University Press.

Saudi Arabia. 1990. Issued by the Royal Embassy of Saudi Arabia, 7(3).

Savory, R. M., ed. 1976. *Introduction to Islamic Civilization*. Cambridge: Cambridge University Press.

Scheper-Hughes, Nancy. 1992. *Death Without Weeping: The Violence of Everyday Life in Brazil*. Berkeley: University of California Press.

Schmidt, Nancy. 1965. "An Anthropological Analysis of Nigerian Fiction." Ph.D. dissertation, Northwestern University.

Searle, John. 1979. *Expression and Meaning: Studies in the Theory of Speech Acts*. Cambridge: Cambridge University Press.

Sen, Gita. 1984. "Subordination and Sexual Control: A Comparative View of the Control of Women." *Review of Radical Political Economics* 16(1):133–42.

Shāker, Fatna. 1981. *Nabt Al-Ard (The Earth's Plant)*. Jeddah, Saudi Arabia: Tihama.

Shalabi, Ahmad. 1954. *History of Muslim Education*. Beirut, Lebanon: Dar Al-Kash'shaf.

Shami, Setaney Khalid. 1990. *Women in Arab Society: Work Patterns and Gender Relations in Egypt*. Providence, R.I.: UNESCO.

Sharabi, Hisham. 1988. *Neo-Patriarchy: A Theory of Distorted Change in Arab Society*. New York: Oxford University Press.

———, ed. 1990. *Theory, Politics, and the Arab World: Critical Responses*. New York and London: Routledge.

Showalter, Elaine. 1985. *A Literature of Their Own: British Women Novelists from Brontë to Lessing*. Rev. ed. London: Virago.

Smart, Barry. 1986. "The Politics of Truth and the Problem of Hegemony." In David Couzens, ed., *Foucault: A Critical Reader*, pp. 157–74. New York: B. Blackwell.

Smith, Dorothy E. 1975. "An Analysis of Ideological Structures and How Women Are Excluded: Considerations for Academic Women." *Canadian Review of Sociology and Anthropology* 12(4):353–69.

Smith, Jane, and Yvonne Haddad. 1982. "Eve: Islamic Image of Woman." In A. Al-Hibri, ed., *Women in Islam*.

Spivak, Gayatri C. 1987. *In Other Worlds: Essays in Cultural Politics*. New York: Methuen.

Stowasser, B. F. 1987a. *The Islamic Impulse*. London: Croom Helm.

———. 1987b. "Liberated Equal or Protected Dependent? Contemporary Religious Paradigms on Women's Status in Islam." *Arab Studies Quarterly* 9(2):260–63.

Strathern, Marilyn. 1981. "Culture in a Netbag: The Manufacture of a Subdiscipline in Anthropology." *Man* 16:665–88.

———. 1988. *The Gender of the Gift*. Berkeley: University of California Press.

Tapper, N. 1978. "The Women's Subsociety among the Shahsevan Nomads of Iran." In L. Beck and N. Keddie, eds., *Women in the Muslim World*, pp. 374–98, Cambridge, Mass.: Harvard University Press.

Thiebaux, Marcelle. 1982. "Foucault's Fantasia for Feminists: The Woman

Reading." In Gabriela Mora and Karen S. Van Hooft, eds., *Theory and Practice of Feminist Literary Criticism,* pp. 45–61. Ypsilanti, Mich.: Bilingual Press.

Thompson, Clara. 1971. *On Women.* Edited by Maurice R.Green. New York: New American Library.

Todd, Janet, ed. 1980. *Gender and Literary Voice.* New York: Holmes and Meier.

Trinh, T. Minh-ha. 1986. "Difference: A Special Third World Women Issue." *Discourse* 8:11–37.

———. 1989. *Woman Native Other: Writing Postcoloniality and Feminism.* Bloomington: Indiana University Press.

Tritton, A. S. 1962. *Islam.* London: Hutchinson's University Library.

United Nations Development Program. 1991. *Human Development Report.* New York, Oxford: Oxford University Press.

'Uthman, Siba'i. 1982. *Qira'a Sari'a fi Sijill Al-Qissa As-Saudiyya.* Saudi Arabia: Abha.

Wallerstein, I. 1974. *The Modern World System.* New York: Academic Press.

Watt, William M. 1988. *Islamic Fundamentalism and Modernity.* New York: Routledge.

Wellwarth, George E. 1981. "Special Considerations in Drama Translation." In Marilyn Gaddis Rose, ed., *Translation Spectrum: Essays in Theory and Practice,* pp. 140–46. Albany: State University of New York Press.

White, Hayden. 1976. "The Fiction of Factual Representation." In Angus Fletcher, ed., *The Literature of Fact.* New York: Columbia University Press.

———. 1987. *The Content of the Form: Narrative Discourse and Historical Representation.* Baltimore: Johns Hopkins University Press.

Williams, Raymond. 1977. *Marxism and Literature.* Oxford: Oxford University Press.

Wolf, Eric R. 1982. *Europe and the People Without History.* Berkeley: University of California Press.

Zain Al-'Abedin, Sohaila. 1982. *Maseerat Almar'a Assaudia Ila Ayn?,* 3d ed. Jeddah, Saudi Arabia: Addar Assaudia Linnasher Wattawzi'.

———. 1984a. *Almar'a Baina Al Efrat Wattafreet.* Jeddah, Saudi Arabia: Addar Assaudia Linnasher Wattawzi'.

———. 1984b. *Binaa Al-Usra Al Muslima.* Jeddah, Saudi Arabia: Addar Assaudia Linnasher Wattawzi'.

———. 1985. *Min Umqul-Ruh, Wa Sulbul-Fikr.* Jeddah, Saudi Arabia: Addar Assaudia Linnasher Wattawzi'.

———. 1987. *Dowr A-mar'a Al-Muslima fi Wadh'ena Al-Rahen.* Jeddah, Saudi Arabia: Addar Assaudia Linnasher Wattawzi'.

———. 1989. "Almar'a Al-muslima Wal-Ibdaa'." Unpublished manuscript.

Newspapers, Magazines, and Newsletters

Al-Bilad (Jeddah)
Al-Jazeera (Ar-Riyadh)
Al-Haras Alwatani (Ar-Riyadh)
Al-Madinah (Jeddah)
Al-Yamama (Ar-Riyadh)
Al-Yowm (Addammam)
Al-Faisal (Ar-Riyadh)
Almajallah (London)
Almajallah Al-Arabiyya (Ar-Riyadh)
Annadwa (Makkah)
Ar-Riyadh (Ar-Riyadh)
Ash-Sharqul Awsat (London)
Iqra (Jeddah)
Saudi Arabia, issued by the Royal Embassy of Saudi Arabia
Sayyedaty (London)
'Ukaz (Jeddah)

Index

DATE DUE

APR 1 5 2008			

GAYLORD   PRINTED IN U.S.A.